PLUTARCH'S LIVES

stands among the first great books of world literature. It is read today both as history and for the brilliance of its style and reportorial skill.

Plutarch's scheme was to compare the lives of outstanding Greek figures with those of his own Roman compatriots, and his book placed Greek and Roman side by side. This selection from LIVES OF THE NOBLE GREEKS has been made as a companion volume to LIVES OF THE NOBLE ROMANS so that Plutarch's essential purpose could be perpetuated in this authoritative and inexpensive edition.

EDMUND FULLER teaches at Kent School. He is the author of three novels, *A Star Pointed North, Brothers Divided,* and *The Corridor,* and two books of critical essays, *Man in Modern Fiction* and *Books With Men Behind Them.* For Dell Laurel Editions Mr. Fuller has edited *Mark Twain: A Laurel Reader* and *Voltaire: A Laurel Reader.*

PLUTARCH

LIVES OF THE NOBLE GREEKS

A selection edited by

EDMUND FULLER

A Laurel Classic

Published by
DELL PUBLISHING CO., INC.
750 Third Avenue
New York 17, N.Y.

Laurel ® TM 674623, Dell Publishing Co., Inc.

Cover painting by Milton Glaser

First printing—December, 1959
Second printing—February, 1962
Third printing—May, 1963
Fourth printing—September, 1964
Fifth printing—April, 1966

Printed in U.S.A.

Contents

Editor's Note

No more terse or telling summation has been made of the merits of Plutarch—first of the world's great biographers and model in this art to all succeeding times—than that of the distinguished classical scholar, Moses Hadas.

It was after all Plutarch's main purpose in his *Lives* . . . to imbue his readers with Greek culture, which is embodied in Greek books; and if today a curious reader should ask for a single author who might communicate the fullest sense of the totality of classical culture, the answer would have to be Plutarch. . . . No author conveys a more complete sense of the political and intellectual climate of the Greco-Roman world. . . . He has indubitably had more European readers than any other pagan Greek and has been the greatest single channel for communicating to Europe a general sense of the men and manners of antiquity.

— *Ancilla to Classical Reading*

All the Roman plays of Shakespeare are drawn heavily from Plutarch. The great French essayist, Montaigne, was his disciple and emulator. His influence has permeated Western culture. In Emerson's words: "We cannot read Plutarch without a tingling of blood." This tingling arises from the recognition, in Plutarch, of those qualities of perception and evaluation from which arise man's noblest and worthiest actions and impulses. In those periodic times when, to many, the light of man's vision seems dimmed— and ours is such a time—Plutarch's affirmation, documented in his *Lives*, shines like a beacon.

In the opening paragraphs of the life of Timoleon, in this volume, he makes his own statement of purpose.

It was for the sake of others that I first commenced writing biographies; but I find myself proceeding and attaching myself to it for my own; the virtues of these great men serving me as a sort of looking-glass, in which I may see how to adjust and adorn my own life. Indeed, it can be compared to nothing but daily living and associating together; we receive, as it were, in our inquiry, and entertain each successive guest, view—

"Their stature and their qualities,"

and select from their actions all that is noblest and worthiest to know. . . . My method . . . is, by the study of history, and by the familiarity acquired in writing, to habituate my memory to receive and retain images of the best and worthiest characters. I am thus enabled to free myself from any ignoble, base, or vicious impressions, contracted from the contagion of ill company that I may be unavoidably engaged in; by the remedy of turning my thoughts in a happy and calm temper to view these noble examples.

Yet, as scrupulous historian and portraitist, he gives us his figures in the round, as men compounded both of good and evil, folly and wisdom.

The complete *Lives* is an enormous volume, in which notable Greeks and Romans are set in juxtaposition for purposes of comparison a scheme not perfectly preserved in the surviving text, as we have it. The present volume is a selection of nine of the *Lives of the Noble Greeks,* chosen with consideration both of the most important figures and the finest specimens of Plutarch's literary qualities. Of these nine, two are slightly abridged in merely peripheral matters, simply to make possible the inclusion of all.

In several of these, allusion is made to Roman figures whose careers are felt by Plutarch to be analogous and fruitful for comparative reading, as Romulus to Theseus, Caesar to Alexander, Cicero to Demosthenes. In every such instance, the life of the corresponding figure is to be found in the companion volume to this one *The Lives of the Noble Romans: A Selection.*

The nine lives included here give us the image of Greece from its mythic pre-history, through its height of political, artistic, and intellectual achievement, its dissolution and decline under its own tragic flaws, to its twilight under Macedonian domination. Thus these lives form a dramatic sequence, projecting for us the outlines of a story much larger than their actual compass. The central figures number great men of Sparta, Corinth, and Macedon, as well as those of Athens, yet it is the spell of glorious and faulty Athens that permeates all. Here the human spirit reached some kinds of heights, counterbalanced by depths, which, if matched, have seldom been excelled.

EDMUND FULLER

⚜
THESEUS

As geographers, Sosius, crowd into the edges of their
maps parts of the world which they do not know about,
adding notes in the margin to the effect, that beyond this
lies nothing but the sandy deserts full of wild beasts, un-
approachable bogs, Scythian ice, or a frozen sea, so in this
work of mine, in which I have compared the lives of the
greatest men with one another, after passing through those
periods which probable reasoning can reach to and real history find a footing in, I might very well say of those that
are farther off: "Beyond this there is nothing but prodigies
and fictions, the only inhabitants are the poets and inven-
tors of fables; there is no credit, or certainty any farther."
Yet, after publishing an account of Lycurgus the lawgiver
and Numa the king, I thought I might, not without reason,
ascend as high as to Romulus, being brought by my history
so near to his time. Considering therefore with myself—

"Whom shall I set so great a man to face?
Or whom oppose? Who's equal to the place?"

(as Aeschylus expresses it), I found none so fit as him that
peopled the beautiful and far-famed city of Athens, to be
set in opposition with the father of the invincible and renowned city of Rome. Let us hope that Fable may, in what
shall follow, so submit to the purifying processes of Reason
as to take the character of exact history. In any case, however, where it shall be found contumaciously slighting credi-
bility and refusing to be reduced to anything like probable
fact, we shall beg that we may meet with candid readers,

and such as will receive with indulgence the stories of antiquity.

Theseus seemed to me to resemble Romulus in many particulars. Both of them, born out of wedlock and of uncertain parentage, had the repute of being sprung from the gods.

"Both warriors; that by all the world's allowed."

Both of them united with strength of body an equal vigour of mind; and of the two most famous cities of the world, the one built Rome, and the other made Athens be inhabited. Both stand charged with the rape of women; neither of them could avoid domestic misfortunes nor jealousy at home; but towards the close of their lives are both of them said to have incurred great odium with their countrymen, if, that is, we may take the stories least like poetry as our guide to the truth.

The lineage of Theseus, by his father's side, ascends as high as to Erechtheus and the first inhabitants of Attica. By his mother's side he was descended of Pelops. For Pelops was the most powerful of all the kings of Peloponnesus, not so much by the greatness of his riches as the multitude of his children, having married many daughters to chief men, and put many sons in places of command in the towns round about him. One of whom named Pittheus, grandfather to Theseus, was governor of the small city of the Troezenians and had the repute of a man of the greatest knowledge and wisdom of his time; which then, it seems, consisted chiefly in grave maxims, such as the poet Hesiod got his great fame by, in his book of Works and Days. And, indeed, among these is one that they ascribe to Pittheus,—

"Unto a friend suffice
A stipulated price;"

which, also, Aristotle mentions. And Euripides, by calling Hippolytus "scholar of the holy Pittheus," shows the opinion that the world had of him.

Aegeus, being desirous of children, and consulting the oracle of Delphi, received the celebrated answer which forbade him the company of any woman before his return to Athens. But the oracle being so obscure as not to satisfy him that he was clearly forbid this, he went to Troezen, and communicated to Pittheus the voice of the god, which was in this manner,—

"Loose not the wine-skin foot, thou chief of men,
   Until to Athens thou art come again."

Pittheus, therefore, taking advantage from the obscurity of the oracle, prevailed upon him, it is uncertain whether by persuasion or deceit, to lie with his daughter Aethra. Aegeus afterwards, knowing her whom he had lain with to be Pittheus's daughter, and suspecting her to be with child by him, left a sword and a pair of shoes, hiding them under a great stone that had a hollow in it exactly fitting them; and went away making her only privy to it, and commanding her, if she brought forth a son who, when he came to man's estate, should be able to lift up the stone and take away what he had left there, she should send him way to him with those things with all secrecy, and with injunctions to him as much as possible to conceal his journey from every one; for he greatly feared the Pallantidae, who were continually mutinying against him, and despised him for his want of children, they themselves being fifty brothers, all sons of Pallas.

When Aethra was delivered of a son, some say that he was immediately named Theseus, from the tokens which his father had *put* under the stone; others that he had received his name afterwards at Athens, when Aegeus *acknowledged* him for his son. He was brought up under his grandfather Pittheus, and had a tutor and attendant set over him named Connidas, to whom the Athenians even to this time, the day before the feast that is dedicated to Theseus, sacrifice a ram, giving this honour to his memory upon much juster grounds than to Silanio and Parrhasius for making pictures and statues of Theseus. There being then a custom for the Grecian youth, upon their first coming to man's estate, to go to Delphi and offer first fruits of their hair to the god, Theseus also went thither, and a place there to this day is yet named Thesea, as it is said, from him. He clipped only the fore part of his head, as Homer says the Abantes did. And this sort of tonsure was from him named Theseus. The Abantes first used it, not in imitation of the Arabians, as some imagine, nor of the Mysians, but because they were a warlike people, and used to close fighting, and above all other nations accustomed to engage hand to hand; as Archilochus testifies in these verses:—

> "Slings shall not whirl, nor many arrows fly,
>   When on the plain the battle joins; but swords,
> Man against man, the deadly conflict try
>   As is the practice of Euboea's lords
> Skilled with the spear.—"

Therefore that they might not give their enemies a hold by their hair, they cut it in this manner. They write also that this was the reason why Alexander gave command to his captains that all the beards of the Macedonians should be shaved, as being the readiest hold for an enemy.

Aethra for some time concealed the true parentage of Theseus, and a report was given out by Pittheus that he was begotten by Neptune; for the Troezenians pay Neptune the highest veneration. He is their tutelar god; to him they offer all their first-fruits, and in his honour stamp their money with a trident.

Theseus displaying not only great strength of body, but equal bravery, and a quickness alike and force of understanding, his mother Aethra, conducting him to the stone, and informing him who was his true father, commanded him to take from thence the tokens that Aegeus had left, and sail to Athens. He without any difficulty set himself to the stone and lifted it up; but refused to take his journey by sea, though it was much the safer way, and though his mother and grandfather begged him to do so. For it was at that time very dangerous to go by land on the road to Athens, no part of it being free from robbers and murderers. That age produced a sort of men, in force of hand, and swiftness of foot, and strength of body, excelling the ordinary rate and wholly incapable of fatigue; making use, however, of these gifts of nature to no good or profitable purpose for mankind, but rejoicing and priding themselves in insolence, and taking the benefit of their superior strength in the exercise of inhumanity and cruelty, and in seizing, forcing, and committing all manner of outrages upon everything that fell into their hands; all respect for others, all justice, they thought, all equity and humanity, though naturally lauded by common people, either out of want of courage to commit injuries or fear to receive them, yet no way concerned those who were strong enough to win for themselves. Some of these, Hercules destroyed and cut off in his passage through these countries; but some escaping his notice while he was passing by, fled and hid themselves, or else were spared by him in contempt of their abject submission: and after that Hercules fell into misfortune, and, having slain Iphitus, retired to Lydia, and for a long time was there slave to Omphale, a punishment which he had imposed upon himself for the murder: then, indeed, Lydia enjoyed high peace and security, but in Greece and the countries about it the like villainies again revived and broke out, there being none to repress or chastise them. It was therefore a very hazardous journey to travel by land from Athens to Peloponnesus; and Pittheus, giving him an exact account of each of the robbers and villains, their strength, and the cruelty they used to all strangers, tried to persuade Theseus to go by sea. But he, it seems, had long since been secretly fired by the glory of Hercules, held him in the highest estimation, and was never more satisfied than in listening to any that gave an account of him; especially those that had seen him, or had been present at any action or saying of his. So that he was altogether in the same state of feeling as, in after ages, Themistocles was, when he said that he could not sleep for the trophy of Miltiades; entertaining such admiration for the

virtue of Hercules, that in the night his dreams were all of
that hero's actions, and in the day a continual emulation
stirred him up to perform the like. Besides, they were related, being born of cousins-german. For Aethra was daughter of Pittheus, and Alcmena of Lysidice; and Lysidice and
Pittheus were brother and sister, children of Hippodamia
and Pelops. He thought it therefore a dishonourable thing,
and not to be endured, that Hercules should go out everywhere, and purge both land and sea from wicked men, and
he himself should fly from the like adventures that actually
came in his way; disgracing his reputed father by a mean
flight by sea, and not showing his true one as good evidence
of the greatness of his birth by noble and worthy actions,
as by the token that he brought with him the shoes and the
sword.

With this mind and these thoughts, he set forward with
a design to do injury to nobody, but to repel and revenge
himself of all those that should offer any. And first of all,
in a set combat, he slew Periphetes, in the neighbourhood
of Epidaurus, who used a club for his arms, and from
thence had the name of Corynetes, or the club-bearer; who
seized upon him, and forbade him to go forward in his
journey. Being pleased with the club, he took it, and made
it his weapon, continuing to use it as Hercules did the lion's
skin, on whose shoulders that served to prove how huge a
beast he had killed; and to the same end Theseus carried
about him this club; overcome indeed by him, but now in
his hands, invincible.

Passing on further towards the Isthmus of Peloponnesus,
he slew Sinnis, often surnamed the Bender of Pines, after
the same manner in which he himself had destroyed many
others before. And this he did without having either practised or ever learnt the art of bending these trees, to show
that natural strength is above all art. This Sinnis had a
daughter of remarkable beauty and stature, called Peri-
gune, who, when her father was killed, fled, and was sought
after everywhere by Theseus; and coming into a place overgrown with brushwood, shrubs, and asparagus-thorn, there,
in a childlike innocent manner, prayed and begged them,

as if they understood her, to give her shelter, with vows
that if she escaped she would never cut them down nor
burn them. But Theseus calling upon her, and giving her
his promise that he would use her with respect, and offer
her no injury, she came forth, and in due time bore him a
son, named Melanippus; but afterwards was married to
Deioneus, the son of Eurytus, the Oechalian, Theseus himself giving her to him. Ioxus, the son of this Melanippus,
who was born to Theseus, accompanied Ornytus in the
colony that he carried with him into Caria, whence it is a
family usage amongst the people called Ioxids, both male
and female, never to burn either shrubs or asparagus-thorn,
but to respect and honour them.

The Crommyonian sow, which they called Phaea, was a
savage and formidable wild beast, by no means an enemy
to be despised. Theseus killed her, going out of his way on
purpose to meet and engage her, so that he might not seem
to perform all his great exploits out of mere necessity; being also of opinion that it was the part of a brave man to
chastise villainous and wicked men when attacked by them,
but to seek out and overcome the more noble wild beasts.
Others relate that Phaea was a woman, a robber full of
cruelty and lust, that lived in Crommyon, and had the
name of Sow given her from the foulness of her life and
manners, and afterwards was killed by Theseus. He slew
also Sciron, upon the borders of Megara, casting him down
from the rocks, being, as most report, a notorious robber
of all passengers, and, as others add, accustomed, out of
insolence and wantonness, to stretch forth his feet to strangers commanding them to wash them, and then while they
did it, with a kick to send them down the rock into the sea.
The writers of Megara, however, in contradiction to the received report, and, as Simonides expresses it, "fighting with
all antiquity," contend that Sciron was neither a robber
nor doer of violence, but a punisher of all such, and the
relative and friend of good and just men; for Aeacus, they
say, was ever esteemed a man of the greatest sanctity of all
the Greeks; and Cychreus, the Salaminian, was honoured
at Athens with divine worship; and the virtues of Peleus

and Telamon were not unknown to any one. Now Sciron was son-in-law to Cychreus, father-in-law to Aeacus, and grandfather to Peleus and Telamon, who were both of them sons of Endeis, the daughter of Sciron and Chariclo; it was not probable, therefore, that the best of men should make these alliances with one who was worst, giving and receiving mutually what was of greatest value and most dear to them. Theseus, by their account, did not slay Sciron in his first journey to Athens, but afterwards, when he took Eleusis, a city of the Megarians, having circumvented Diocles, the governor. Such are the contradictions in this story. In Eleusis he killed Cercyon, the Arcadian, in a wrestling match. And going on a little farther, in Erineus, he slew Damastes, otherwise called Procrustes, forcing his body to the size of his own bed, as he himself was used to do with all strangers; this he did in imitation of Hercules, who always returned upon his assailants the same sort of violence that they offered to him; sacrificed Busiris, killed Antaeus in wrestling, and Cycnus in single combat, and Termerus by breaking his skull in pieces (whence, they say, comes the proverb of "a Termerian mischief"), for it seems Termerus killed passengers that he met by running with his head against them. And so also Theseus proceeded in the punishment of evil men, who underwent the same violence from him which they had inflicted upon others, justly suffering after the manner of their own injustice.

As he went forward on his journey, and was come as far as the river Cephisus, some of the race of the Phytalidae met him and saluted him, and upon his desire to use the purifications, then in custom, they performed them with all the usual ceremonies, and, having offered propitiatory sacrifices to the gods, invited him and entertained him at their house, a kindness which, in all his journey hitherto, he had not met.

On the eighth day of Cronius, now called Hecatombaeon, he arrived at Athens, where he found the public affairs full of all confusion, and divided into parties and factions, Aegeus also, and his whole private family, labouring under the same distemper; for Medea, having fled from Corinth, and promised Aegeus to make him, by her art, capable of having children, was living with him. She first was aware of Theseus, whom as yet Aegeus did not know, and he being in years, full of jealousies and suspicions, and fearing everything by reason of the faction that was then in the city, she easily persuaded him to kill him by poison at a banquet, to which he was to be invited as a stranger. He, coming to the entertainment, thought it not fit to discover himself at once, but willing to give his father the occasion of first finding him out, the meat being on the table, he drew his sword as if he designed to cut with it; Aegeus, at once recognising the token, threw down the cup of poison, and, questioning his son, embraced him, and having gathered together all his citizens, owned him publicly before them, who, on their part, received him gladly for the fame of his greatness and bravery; and it is said, that when the cup fell, the poison was spilt there where now is the enclosed space in the Delphinium; for in that place stood Aegeus's house, and the figure of Mercury on the east side of the temple is called the Mercury of Aegeus's gate.

The sons of Pallas, who before were quiet upon expectation of recovering the kingdom after Aegeus's death, who was without issue, as soon as Theseus appeared and was acknowledged the successor, highly resenting that Aegeus first, an adopted son only of Pandion, and not at all related to the family of Erechtheus, should be holding the kingdom, and that after him, Theseus, a visitor and stranger, should be destined to succeed to it, broke out into open war. And dividing themselves into two companies, one part of them marched openly from Sphettus, with their father, against the city, the other, hiding themselves in the village of Gargettus, lay in ambush, with a design to set upon the enemy on both sides. They had with them a crier of the township of Agnus, named Leos, who discovered to Theseus all the designs of the Pallantidae. He immediately fell upon those that lay in ambuscade, and cut them all off; upon tidings of which Pallas and his company fled and were dispersed.

From hence they say is derived the custom among the

people of the township of Pallene to have no marriages or
any alliance with the people of Agnus, nor to suffer the
criers to pronounce in their proclamations the words used
in all other parts of the country, Acouëtë Leoi (Hear ye
people), hating the very sound of Leo, because of the
treason of Leos.

Theseus, longing to be in action, and desirous also to
make himself popular, left Athens to fight with the bull of
Marathon, which did no small mischief to the inhabitants
of Tetrapolis. And having overcome it, he brought it alive
in triumph through the city, and afterwards sacrificed it to
the Delphinian Apollo.

Not long after arrived the third time from Crete the col-
lectors of the tribute which the Athenians paid them upon
the following occasion. Androgeus having been treacher-
ously murdered in the confines of Attica, not only Minos,
his father, put the Athenians to extreme distress by a perpetual war, but the gods also laid waste their country; both
famine and pestilence lay heavy upon them, and even their
rivers were dried up. Being told by the oracle that, if they
appeased and reconciled Minos, the anger of the gods
would cease and they should enjoy rest from the miseries
they laboured under, they sent heralds, and with much
supplication were at last reconciled, entering into an agreement to send to Crete every nine years a tribute of seven
young men and as many virgins, as most writers agree in
stating; and the most poetical story adds, that the Minotaur
destroyed them, or that, wandering in the labyrinth, and
finding no possible means of getting out, they miserably
ended their lives there; and that this Minotaur was (as
Euripides hath it)—

"A mingled form where two strange shapes combined,
 And different natures, bull and man, were joined."

But Philochorus says that the Cretans will by no means
allow the truth of this, but say that the labyrinth was only
an ordinary prison, having no other bad quality but that it
secured the prisoners from escaping, and that Minos, hav-

ing instituted games in honour of Androgeus, gave, as a
reward to the victors, these youths, who in the meantime
were kept in the labyrinth; and that the first that overcame
in those games was one of the greatest power and command among them, named Taurus, a man of no merciful
or gentle disposition, who treated the Athenians that were
made his prize in a proud and cruel manner. Also Aristotle
himself, in the account that he gives of the form of government of the Bottiaeans, is manifestly of opinion that the
youths were not slain by Minos, but spent the remainder
of their days in slavery in Crete; that the Cretans, in former
times, to acquit themselves of an ancient vow which they
had made, were used to send an offering of the first-fruits
of their men to Delphi, and that some descendants of these
Athenian slaves were mingled with them and sent amongst
them, and, unable to get their living there, removed from
thence, first into Italy, and settled about Japygia; from
thence again, that they removed to Thrace, and were named
Bottiaeans; and that this is the reason why, in a certain
sacrifice, the Bottiaean girls sing a hymn beginning *Let
us go to Athens*. This may show us how dangerous it
is to incur the hostility of a city that is mistress of eloquence and song. For Minos was always ill spoken of,
and represented ever as a very wicked man, in the Athenian theatres; neither did Hesiod avail him by calling him
"the most royal Minos," nor Homer, who styles him *"Jupiter's familiar friend;"* the tragedians got the better, and
from the vantage ground of the stage showered down
obloquy upon him, as a man of cruelty and violence;
whereas, in fact, he appears to have been a king and a
law-giver, and Rhadamanthus, a judge under him, admin-
istering the statutes that he ordained.

Now, when the time of the third tribute was come, and
the fathers who had any young men for their sons were to
proceed by lot to the choice of those that were to be sent,
there arose fresh discontents and accusations against
Aegeus among the people, who were full of grief and indignation that he who was the cause of all their miseries
was the only person exempt from the punishment; adopt-

ing and settling his kingdom upon a bastard and foreign
son, he took no thought, they said, of their destitution and
loss, not of bastards, but lawful children. These things sensibly affected Theseus, who, thinking it but just not to disregard, but rather partake of, the sufferings of his fellow-
citizens, offered himself for one without any lot. All else
were struck with admiration for the nobleness and with
love for the goodness of the act; and Aegeus, after prayers
and entreaties, finding him inflexible and not to be persuaded, proceeded to the choosing of the rest by lot. Hellanicus, however, tells us that the Athenians did not send
the young men and virgins by lot, but that Minos himself
used to come and make his own choice, and pitched upon
Theseus before all others; according to the conditions
agreed upon between them, namely, that the Athenians
should furnish them with a ship and that the young men
that were to sail with him should carry no weapons of
war; but that if the Minotaur was destroyed, the tribute
should cease.

On the two former occasions of the payment of the
tribute, entertaining no hopes of safety or return, they sent
out the ship with a black sail, as to unavoidable destruction; but now, Theseus encouraging his father, and speaking greatly of himself, as confident that he should kill the
Minotaur, he gave the pilot another sail, which was white,
commanding him, as he returned, if Theseus were safe, to
make use of that; but if not, to sail with the black one,
and to hang out that sign of his misfortune. Simonides
says that the sail which Aegeus delivered to the pilot was
not white, but—

> "Scarlet, in the juicy bloom
> Of the living oak-tree steeped,"

and that this was to be the sign of their escape. Phereclus,
son of Amarsyas, according to Simonides, was pilot of the
ship. But Philochorus says Theseus had sent him by Scirus,
from Salamis, Nausithoüs to be his steersman, and Phaeax
his look-out-man in the prow, the Athenians having as yet

not applied themselves to navigation; and that Scirus did this because one of the young men, Menesthes, was his daughter's son; and this the chapels of Nausithoüs and Phaeax, built by Theseus near the temple of Scirus, confirm. He adds, also, that the feast named Cybernesia was in honour of them. The lot being cast, and Theseus having received out of the Prytaneüm those upon whom it fell, he went to the Delphinium, and made an offering for them to Apollo of his suppliant's badge, which was a bough of a consecrated olive tree, with white wool tied about it.

Having thus performed his devotion, he went to sea, the sixth day of Munychion, on which day even to this time the Athenians send their virgins to the same temple to make supplication to the gods. It is farther reported that he was commanded by the oracle of Delphi to make Venus his guide, and to invoke her as the companion and conductress of his voyage and that, as he was sacrificing a she goat to her by the sea-side, it was suddenly changed into a he, and for this cause that goddess had the name of Epitragia.

When he arrived at Crete, as most of the ancient historians as well as poets tell us, having a clue of thread given him by Ariadne, who had fallen in love with him, and being instructed by her how to use it so as to conduct him through the windings of the labyrinth, he escaped out of it and slew the Minotaur, and sailed back, taking along with him Ariadne and the young Athenian captives. Phercydes adds that he bored holes in the bottom of the Cretan ships to hinder their pursuit. Demon writes that Taurus, the chief captain of Minos, was slain by Theseus at the mouth of the port, in a naval combat as he was sailing out for Athens. But Philochorus gives us the story thus: That at the setting forth of the yearly games by King Minos, Taurus was expected to carry away the prize, as he had done before; and was much grudged the honour. His character and manners made his power hateful, and he was accused moreover of too near familiarity with Pasiphae, for which reason, when Theseus desired the combat, Minos readily complied. And as it was a custom in Crete that the women also should be admitted to the sight of these games, Ariadne, being present, was struck with admiration of the manly beauty of Theseus, and the vigour and address which he showed in the combat, overcoming all that encountered with him. Minos, too, being extremely pleased with him, especially because he had overthrown and disgraced Taurus, voluntarily gave up the young captives to Theseus, and remitted the tribute to the Athenians. Clidemus gives an account peculiar to himself, very ambitiously, and beginning a great way back: That it was a decree consented to by all Greece, that no vessel from any place, containing above five persons, should be permitted to sail, Jason only excepted, who was made captain of the great ship Argo, to sail about and scour the sea of pirates. But Daedalus having escaped from Crete, and flying by sea to Athens, Minos, contrary to this decree, pursued him with his ships of war, was forced by a storm upon Sicily, and there ended his life. After his decease, Deucalion, his son, desiring a quarrel with the Athenians, sent to them, demanding that they should deliver up Daedalus to him, threatening upon their refusal, to put to death all the young Athenians whom his father had received as hostages from the city. To this angry message Theseus returned a very gentle answer excusing himself that he could not deliver up Daedalus, who was nearly related to him, being his cousin-german, his mother being Merope, the daughter of Erechtheus. In the meanwhile he secretly prepared a navy, part of it at home near the village of Thymoetadae, a place of no resort, and far from any common roads, the other part by his grandfather Pittheus's means at Troezen, that so his design might be carried on with the greatest secrecy. As soon as ever his fleet was in readiness, he set sail, having with him Daedalus and other exiles from Crete for his guides; and none of the Cretans having any knowledge of his coming, but imagining when they saw his fleet that they were friends and vessels of their own, he soon made himself master of the port, and immediately making a descent,

reached Gnossus before any notice of his coming, and, in
a battle before the gates of the labyrinth, put Deucalion
and all his guards to the sword. The government by this
means falling to Ariadne, he made a league with her, and
received the captives of her, and ratified a perpetual friendship between the Athenians and the Cretans, whom he engaged under an oath never again to commence any war
with Athens.

There are yet many other traditions about these things,
and as many concerning Ariadne, all inconsistent with
each other. Some relate that she hung herself, being deserted
by Theseus. Others that she was carried away by his sailors
to the isle of Naxos, and married to Oenarus, priest of
Bacchus; and that Theseus left her because he fell in love
with another—

"For Aegle's love was burning in his breast;"

a verse which Hereas, the Megarian, says was formerly
in the poet Hesiod's works, but put out by Pisistratus, in
like manner as he added in Homer's Raising of the Dead, to
gratify the Athenians, the line—

"Theseus, Pirithous, mighty son of gods."

Others say Ariadne had sons also by Theseus, Oenopion
and Staphylus; and among these is the poet Ion of Chios,
who writes of his own native city—

"Which once Oenopion, son of Theseus built."

But the more famous of the legendary stories everybody
(as I may say) has in his mouth. In Paeon, however, the
Amathusian, there is a story given, differing from the rest.
For he writes that Theseus, being driven by a storm upon
the isle of Cyprus, and having aboard with him Ariadne,
big with child, and extremely discomposed with the rolling
of the sea, set her on shore, and left her there alone, to return himself and help the ship, when, on a sudden, a vio-

lent wind carried him again out to sea. That the women of the island received Ariadne very kindly, and did all they could to console and alleviate her distress at being left behind. That they counterfeited kind letters, and delivered them to her, as sent from Theseus, and, when she fell in labour, were diligent in performing to her every needful service; but that she died before she could be delivered, and was honourably interred. That soon after Theseus returned, and was greatly afflicted for her loss, and at his departure left a sum of money among the people of the island, ordering them to do sacrifice to Ariadne; and caused two little images to be made and dedicated to her, one of silver and the other of brass. Moreover, that on the second day of Gorpiaeus, which is sacred to Ariadne, they have this ceremony among their sacrifices, to have a youth lie down and with his voice and gesture represent the pains of a woman in travail; and that the Amathusians call the grove in which they show her tomb, the grove of Venus Ariadne.

Now Theseus, in his return from Crete, put in at Delos, and having sacrificed to the god of the island, dedicated to the temple the image of Venus which Ariadne had given him, and danced with the young Athenians a dance that, in memory of him, they say is still preserved among the inhabitants of Delos, consisting in certain measured turnings and returnings, imitative of the windings and twistings of the labyrinth. And this dance, as Dicaearchus writes, is called among the Delians the Crane. This he danced around the Ceratonian Altar, so called from its consisting of horns taken from the left side of the head. They say also that he instituted games in Delos, where he was the first that began the custom of giving a palm to the victors.

When they were come near the coast of Attica, so great was the joy for the happy success of their voyage, that neither Theseus himself nor the pilot remembered to hang out the sail which should have been the token of their safety to Aegeus, who, in despair at the sight, threw himself headlong from a rock, and perished in the sea. But Theseus being arrived at the port of Phalerum, paid there the sacri-

fices which he had vowed to the gods at his setting out to
sea, and sent a herald to the city to carry the news of his
safe return. At his entrance, the herald found the people
for the most part full of grief for the loss of their king;
others, as may well be believed, as full of joy for the tidings that he brought, and eager to welcome him and
crown him with garlands for his good news, which he indeed accepted of, but hung them upon his herald's staff;
and thus returning to the seaside before Theseus had finished his libation to the gods, he stayed apart for fear of
disturbing the holy rites; but, as soon as the libation was
ended, went up and related the king's death, upon the
hearing of which, with great lamentations and a confused
tumult of grief, they ran with all haste to the city. And
from hence, they say, it comes that at this day, in the feast
of Oschophoria, the herald is not crowned, but his staff,
and all who are present at the libation cry out *eleleu, iou,
iou,* the first of which confused sounds is commonly used
by men in haste, or at a triumph, the other is proper to
people in consternation or disorder of mind.

Theseus, after the funeral of his father, paid his vows
to Apollo the seventh day of Pyanepsion; for on that day
the youth that returned with him safe from Crete made
their entry into the city. They say, also, that the custom
of boiling pulse at this feast is derived from hence; because the young men that escaped put all that was left of
their provision together, and, boiling it in one common
pot, feasted themselves with it, and ate it all up together.
Hence, also, they carry in procession an olive branch
bound about with wool (such as they then made use of in
their supplications), which they call Eiresione, crowned
with all sorts of fruits, to signify that scarcity and barren-
ness was ceased, singing in their procession this song:—

"Eiresione bring figs, and Eiresione bring loaves;
  Bring us honey in pints, and oil to rub on our bodies,
  And a strong flagon of wine, for all to go mellow to bed
    on."

Although some hold opinion that this ceremony is retained in memory of the Heraclidae, who were thus entertained and brought up by the Athenians. But most are of
the opinion which we have given above.

The ship wherein Theseus and the youth of Athens returned had thirty oars, and was preserved by the Athenians down even to the time of Demetrius Phalereus, for
they took away the old planks as they decayed, putting in
new and stronger timber in their place, insomuch that this
ship became a standing example among the philosophers,
for the logical question of things that grow; one side holding that the ship remained the same, and the other contending that it was not the same.

The feast called Oschophoria, or the feast of boughs,
which to this day the Athenians celebrate, was then first
instituted by Theseus. For he took not with him the full
number of virgins which by lot were to be carried away,
but selected two youths of his acquaintance, of fair and
womanish faces, but of a manly and forward spirit, and
having, by frequent baths, and avoiding the heat and
scorching of the sun, with a constant use of all the oint-
ments and washes and dresses that serve to the adorning
of the head or smoothing the skin or improving the complexion, in a manner changed them from what they were
before, and having taught them farther to counterfeit the
very voice and carriage and gait of virgins so that there
could not be the least difference perceived, he, undiscovered by any, put them into the number of the Athenian
maids designed for Crete. At his return, he and these two
youths led up a solemn procession, in the same habit that
is now worn by those who carry the vine-branches. Those
branches they carry in honour of Bacchus and Ariadne,
for the sake of their story before related; or rather because
they happened to return in autumn, the time of gathering
the grapes. The women, whom they call Deipnopherae, or
supper-carriers, are taken into these ceremonies, and assist
at the sacrifice, in remembrance and imitation of the
mothers of the young men and virgins upon whom the lot

fell, for thus they ran about bringing bread and meat to
their children; and because the women then told their sons
and daughters many tales and stories, to comfort and encourage them under the danger they were going upon, it
has still continued a custom that at this feast old fables
and tales should be told. For these particularities we are
indebted to the history of Demon. There was then a place
chosen out, and a temple erected in it to Theseus, and
those families out of whom the tribute of the youth was
gathered were appointed to pay tax to the temple for sacrifices to him. And the house of the Phytalidae had the
overseeing of these sacrifices, Theseus doing them that
honour in recompense of their former hospitality.

Now, after the death of his father Aegeus, forming in
his mind a great and wonderful design, he gathered together all the inhabitants of Attica into one town, and
made them one people of one city, whereas before they
lived dispersed, and were not easy to assemble upon any
affair for the common interest. Nay, differences and even
wars often occurred between them, which he by his persuasions appeased, going from township to township, and
from tribe to tribe. And those of a more private and mean
condition readily embracing such good advice, to those of
greater power he promised a commonwealth without monarchy, a democracy, or people's government, in which he
should only be continued as their commander in war and
the protector of their laws, all things else being equally
distributed among them;—and by this means brought a
part of them over to his proposal. The rest, fearing his
power, which was already grown very formidable, and
knowing his courage and resolution, chose rather to be
persuaded than forced into a compliance. He then dissolved all the distinct state-houses, council halls, and magistracies, and built one common state-house and council
hall on the site of the present upper town, and gave the
name of Athens to the whole state, ordaining a common
feast and sacrifice, which he called Panathenaea, or the
sacrifice of all the united Athenians. He instituted also an-

other sacrifice called Metoecia, or Feast of Migration, which is yet celebrated on the sixteenth day of Hecatombaeon. Then, as he had promised, he laid down his regal power and proceeded to order a commonwealth, entering upon this great work not without advice from the gods. For having sent to consult the oracle of Delphi concerning the fortune of his new government and city, he received this answer:—

> "Son of the Pitthean maid,
>   To your town the terms and fates,
>   My father gives of many states.
>   Be not anxious nor afraid;
>   The bladder will not fail to swim
>   On the waves that compass him."

Which oracle, they say, one of the sibyls long after did in a manner repeat to the Athenians, in this verse:—

> "The bladder may be dipt, but not be drowned."

Farther yet designing to enlarge his city, he invited all strangers to come and enjoy equal privileges with the natives, and it is said that the common form, *Come hither, all ye people,* was the words that Theseus proclaimed when he thus set up a commonwealth, in a manner, for all nations. Yet he did not suffer his state, by the promiscuous multitude that flowed in, to be turned into confusion and be left without any order or degree, but was the first that divided the Commonwealth into three distinct ranks, the noblemen, the husbandmen, and artificers. To the nobility he committed the care of religion, the choice of magistrates, the teaching and dispensing of the laws, and interpretation and direction in all sacred matters; the whole city being, as it were, reduced to an exact equality, the nobles excelling the rest in honour, the husbandmen in profit, and the artificers in number. And that Theseus was the first, who, as Aristotle says, out of an inclination to popular government, parted with the regal power, Homer also seems to testify, in his catalogue of the ships, where he gives the name of *People* to the Athenians only.

He also coined money, and stamped it with the image of an ox, either in memory of the Marathonian bull, or of Taurus, whom he vanquished, or else to put his people in mind to follow husbandry; and from this coin came the expression so frequent among the Greeks, of a thing being worth ten or a hundred oxen. After this he joined Megara to Attica, and erected that famous pillar on the Isthmus, which bears an inscription of two lines, showing the bounds of the two countries that meet there. On the east side the inscription is,—

"Peloponnesus there, Ionia here."

and on the west side,—

"Peloponnesus here, Ionia there."

He also instituted the games, in emulation of Hercules, being ambitious that as the Greeks, by that hero's appointment, celebrated the Olympian games to the honour of Jupiter, so by his institution, they should celebrate the Isthmian to the honour of Neptune. For those that were there before observed, dedicated to Melicerta, were performed privately in the night, and had the form rather of a religious rite than of an open spectacle or public feast.

Concerning his voyage into the Euxine Sea, Philochorus and some others write that he made it with Hercules, offering him his service in the war against the Amazons, and had Antiope given him for the reward of his valour; but the greater number, of whom are Pherecydes, Hellanicus, and Herodorus, write that he made this voyage many years after Hercules, with a navy under his own command, and took the Amazon prisoner—the more probable story, for we do not read that any other, of all those that accompanied him in this action, took any Amazon prisoner. Bion adds, that, to take her, he had to use deceit and fly away;

for the Amazons, he says, being naturally lovers of men, were so far from avoiding Theseus when he touched upon their coasts, that they sent him presents to his ship; but he, having invited Antiope, who brought them, to come aboard, immediately set sail and carried her away.

This was the origin and cause of the Amazonian invasion of Attica, which would seem to have been no slight or womanish enterprise. For it is impossible that they should have placed their camp in the very city, and joined battle close by the Pnyx and the hill called Museum, unless, having first conquered the country around about, they had thus with impunity advanced to the city. That they made so long a journey by land, and passed the Cimmerian Bosphorus, when frozen, as Hellanicus writes, is difficult to be believed. That they encamped all but in the city is certain, and may be sufficiently confirmed by the names that the places hereabout yet retain, and the graves and monuments of those that fell in the battle. Both armies being in sight, there was a long pause and doubt on each side which should give the first onset; at last Theseus, having sacrificed to Fear, in obedience to the command of an oracle he had received, gave them battle; and this happened in the month of Boedromion, in which to this very day the Athenians celebrate the Feast Boedromia. Clidemus, desirous to be very circumstantial, writes that the left wing of the Amazons moved towards the place which is yet called Amazonium and the right towards the Pnyx, near Chrysa, that with this wing the Athenians, issuing from behind the Museum, engaged, and that the graves of those that were slain are to be seen in the street that leads to the gate called the Piraic, by the chapel of the hero Chalcodon; and that here the Athenians were routed, and gave way before the women, as far as to the temple of the Furies, but, fresh supplies coming in from the Palladium, Ardettus, and the Lyceum, they charged their right wing, and beat them back into their tents, in which action a great number of the Amazons were slain. At length, after four months, a peace was concluded between them by the mediation of Hippolyta (for so this historian calls the Amazon whom Theseus married, and not Antiope), though others write that she was slain with a dart by Molpadia, while fighting by Theseus's side, and that the pillar which stands by the temple of Olympian Earth was erected to her honour. Nor is it to be wondered at, that in events of such antiquity, history should be in disorder. For indeed we are also told that those of the Amazons that were wounded were privately sent away by Antiope to Chalcis, where many by her care recovered, but some that died were buried there in the place that is to this time called Amazonium. That this war, however, was ended by a treaty is evident, both from the name of the place adjoining to the temple of Theseus, called, from the solemn oath there taken, Horcomosium; and also from the ancient sacrifice which used to be celebrated to the Amazons the day before the Feast of Theseus.

This is as much as is worth telling concerning the Amazons. For the account which the author of the poem called the Theseid gives of this rising of the Amazons, how Antiope, to revenge herself upon Theseus for refusing her and marrying Phaedra, came down upon the city with her train of Amazons, whom Hercules slew, is manifestly nothing else but fable and invention. It is true, indeed, that Theseus married Phaedra, but that was after the death of Antiope, by whom he had a son called Hippolytus, or, as Pindar writes, Demophon. The calamities which befell Phaedra and this son, since none of the historians have contradicted the tragic poets that have written of them, we must suppose happened as represented uniformly by them.

There are also other traditions of the marriages of Theseus, neither honourable in their occasions nor fortunate in their events, which yet were never represented in the Greek plays. For he is said to have carried off Anaxo, a Troezenian, and having slain Sinnis and Cercyon, to have ravished their daughters; to have married Periboea, the mother of Ajax, and then Phereboea, and then Iope, the daughter of Iphicles. And further, he is accused of deserting Ariadne (as is before related), being in love with Aegle, the daughter of Panopeus, neither justly nor honourably; and lastly, of the rape of Helen, which filled all Attica with war and blood, and was in the end the occasion of his banishment and death, as will presently be related.

Herodorus is of opinion, that though there were many famous expeditions undertaken by the bravest men of his time, yet Theseus never joined in any of them, once only excepted, with the Lapithae, in their war against the Centaurs; but others say that he accompanied Jason to Colchis and Meleager to the slaying of the Calydonian boar, and that hence it came to be a proverb, *Not without Theseus;* that he himself, however, without aid of any one, performed many glorious exploits, and that from him began the saying, *He is a second Hercules.* He also joined Adrastus in recovering the bodies of those that were slain before Thebes, but not as Euripides in his tragedy says, by force of arms, but by persuasion and mutual agreement and composition, for so the greater part of the historians write; Philochorus adds further that this was the first treaty that ever was made for the recovering the bodies of the dead, but in the history of Hercules, it is shown that it was he who first gave leave to his enemies to carry off their slain. The burying-places of the most part are yet to be seen in the village called Eleutherae: those of the commanders, at Eleusis, where Theseus allotted them a place, to oblige Adrastus. The story of Euripides in his suppliants is disproved by Aeschylus in his Eleusinians, where Theseus himself relates the facts as here told.

The celebrated friendship between Theseus and Pirithoüs is said to have been thus begun; the fame of the strength and valour of Theseus being spread through Greece, Pirithoüs was desirous to make a trial and proof of it himself, and to this end seized a herd of oxen which belonged to Theseus, and was driving them away from Marathon, and, when the news was brought that Theseus pursued him in arms, he did not fly, but turned back and went to meet him. But as soon as they had viewed one another, each so admired the gracefulness and beauty, and was seized with such respect for the courage of the other, that they forgot all thoughts of fighting; and Pirithoüs, first stretching out his hand to Theseus, bade him be judge in this case himself, and promised to submit willingly to any penalty he should impose. But Theseus not only forgave him all, but entreated him to be his friend and brother in arms; and they ratified their friendship by oaths. After this Pirithoüs married Deidamia, and invited Theseus to the wedding, entreating him to come and see his country, and make acquaintance with the Lapithae; he had at the same time invited the Centaurs to the feast, who growing hot with wine and beginning to be insolent and wild, and offering violence to the women, the Lapithae took immediate revenge upon them, slaying many of them upon the place, and afterwards, having overcome them in battle, drove the whole race of them out of their country, Theseus all along taking their part and fighting on their side. But Herodorus gives a different relation of these things; that Theseus came not to the assistance of the Lapithae till the war was already begun; and that it was in this journey that he had his first sight of Hercules, having made it his business to find him out at Trachis, where he had chosen to rest himself after all his wanderings and his labours; and that this interview was honourably performed on each part, with extreme respect, and good-will, and admiration of each other. Yet it is more credible, as others write, that there were, before, frequent interviews between them, and that it was by the means of Theseus that Hercules was initiated at Eleusis, and purified before initiation, upon account of several rash actions of his former life.

Theseus was now fifty years old, as Hellanicus states, when he carried off Helen, who was yet too young to be married. Some writers, to take away this accusation of one of the greatest crimes laid to his charge, say, that he did not steal away Helen himself, but that Idas and Lynceus were the ravishers, who brought her to him, and committed her to his charge, and that, therefore, he refused to restore her at the demand of Castor and Pollux; or, indeed, they say her own father, Tyndarus, had sent her to be kept by him, for fear of Enarophorus, the son of Hippocoön, who would have carried her away by force when she was yet a child. But the most probable account, and that which has most witnesses on its side, is this: Theseus and Pirithoüs went both together to Sparta, and, having seized the young lady as she was dancing in the temple Diana Orthia, fled away with her. There were presently men sent in arms to pursue, but they followed no further than to Tegea; and Theseus and Pirithoüs, being now out of danger, having passed through Peloponnesus, made an agreement between themselves, that he to whom the lot should fall should have Helen to his wife, but should be obliged to assist in procuring another for his friend. The lot fell upon Theseus, who conveyed her to Aphidnae, not being yet marriageable, and delivered her to one of his allies, called Aphidnus, and, having sent his mother, Aethra, after to take care of her, desired him to keep them so secretly, that none might know where they were; which done, to return the same service to his friend Pirithoüs, he accompanied him in his journey to Epirus, in order to steal away the king of the Molossians' daughter. The king, his own name being Aidoneus, or Pluto, called his wife Proserpina, and his daughter Cora, and a great dog, which he kept, Cerberus, with whom he ordered all that came as suitors to his daughter to fight, and promised her to him that should overcome the beast. But having been informed that the design of Pirithoüs and his companion was not to court his daughter, but to force her away, he caused them both to be seized, and threw Pirithoüs to be torn in pieces by his dog, and put Theseus into prison, and kept him.

About this time, Menestheus, the son of Peteus, grandson of Orneus, and great-grandson of Erechtheus, the first man that is recorded to have affected popularity and ingratiated himself with the multitude, stirred up and exasperated the most eminent men of the city, who had long borne a secret grudge to Theseus, conceiving that he had robbed them of their several little kingdoms and lordships, and having pent them all up in one city, was using them as his subjects and slaves. He put also the meaner people into commotion, telling them, that, deluded with a mere

dream of liberty, though indeed they were deprived of
both that and of their proper homes and religious usages,
instead of many good and gracious kings of their own,
they had given themselves up to be lorded over by a new-
comer and a stranger. Whilst he was thus busied in infect-
ing the minds of the citizens, the war that Castor and Pollux brought against Athens came very opportunely to
further the sedition he had been promoting, and some say
that by his persuasions was wholly the cause of their in-
vading the city. At their first approach, they committed no
acts of hostility, but peaceably demanded their sister
Helen; but the Athenians returning answer that they neither had her there nor knew where she was disposed of,
they prepared to assault the city, when Academus, having,
by whatever means, found it out, disclosed to them that
she was secretly kept at Aphidnae. For which reason he
was both highly honoured during his life by Castor and
Pollux, and the Lacedaemonians, when often in aftertimes
they made incursions into Attica, and destroyed all the
country round about, spared the Academy for the sake of
Academus.

Aphidnae being won by Castor and Pollux, and the city
of Athens being in consternation, Menestheus persuaded
the people to open their gates, and receive them with all
manner of friendship, for they were, he told them, at enmity with none but Theseus, who had first injured them,
and were benefactors and saviours to all mankind beside.
And their behaviour gave credit to those promises; for,
having made themselves absolute masters of the place, they
demanded no more than to be initiated, since they were as
nearly related to the city as Hercules was, who had received
the same honour. This their desire they easily obtained,
and were adopted by Aphidnus, as Hercules had been by
Pylius. They were honoured also like gods, and were called
by a new name, Anaces, either from the *cessation* of the
war, or from the *care* they took that none should suffer
any injury, though there was so great an army within the
walls; for the phrase *anakos ekhein* is used of those who
look to or care for anything; kings for this reason, perhaps,

are called *anactes*. Others say, that from the appearance
of their star in the heavens, they were thus called, for in
the Attic dialect this name comes very near the words that
signify *above*.

Now Hercules, passing by the Molossians, was entertained in his way to Aidoneus the king, who, in conversation, accidentally spoke of the journey of Theseus and
Pirithoüs into his country, of what they had designed to do,
and what they were forced to suffer. Hercules was much
grieved for the inglorious death of the one and the miserable
condition of the other. As for Pirithoüs, he thought it useless to complain; but begged to have Theseus released for
his sake, and obtained that favour from the king. Theseus,
being thus set at liberty, returned to Athens, where his
friends were not wholly suppressed, and dedicated to Hercules all the sacred places which the city had set apart for
himself, changing their names from Thesea to Heraclea,
four only excepted, as Philochorus writes. And wishing immediately to resume the first place in the commonwealth,
and manage the state as before, he soon found himself involved in factions and troubles; those who long had hated
him had now added to their hatred contempt; and the minds
of the people were so generally corrupted, that, instead of
obeying commands with silence, they expected to be flattered into their duty. He had some thoughts to have reduced
them by force, but was overpowered by demagogues and
factions. And at last, despairing of any good success of his
affairs in Athens, he sent away his children privately to
Euboea, commending them to the care of Elephenor, the
son of Chalcodon; and he himself having solemnly cursed
the people of Athens in the village of Gargettus, in which
there yet remains the place called Araterion, or the place of
cursing, sailed to Scyros, where he had lands left him by his
father, and friendship, as he thought, with those of the
island. Lycomedes was then king of Scyros. Theseus, therefore, addressed himself to him and desired to have his lands
put into his possession, as designing to settle and to dwell
there, though others say that he came to beg his assistance
against the Athenians. But Lycomedes, either jealous of the

glory of so great a man, or to gratify Menestheus, having led him up to the highest cliff of the island, on pretence of showing him from thence the lands that he desired, threw him headlong down from the rock, and killed him. Others say he fell down of himself by a slip of his foot, as he was walking there, according to his custom, after supper. At that time there was no notice taken, nor were any concerned for his death, but Menestheus quietly possessed the kingdom of Athens. His sons were brought up in a private condition, and accompanied Elephenor to the Trojan war, but, after the decease of Menestheus in that expedition, returned to Athens, and recovered the government. But in succeeding ages, besides several other circumstances that moved the Athenians to honour Theseus as a demigod, in the battle which was fought at Marathon against the Medes, many of the soldiers believed they saw an apparition of Theseus in arms, rushing on at the head of them against the barbarians. And after the Median war, Phaedo being archon of Athens, the Athenians, consulting the oracle at Delphi, were commanded to gather together the bones of Theseus, and, laying them in some honourable place, keep them as sacred in the city. But it was very difficult to recover those relics, or so much as to find out the place where they lay, on account of the inhospitable and savage temper of the barbarous people that inhabited the island. Nevertheless, afterwards, when Cimon took the island and had a great ambition to find out the place where Theseus was buried, he, by chance, spied an eagle upon a rising ground pecking with her beak and tearing up the earth with her talons, when on the sudden it came into his mind, as it were by some divine inspiration, to dig there, and search for the bones of Theseus. There were found in that place a coffin of a man of more than ordinary size, and a brazen spear-head, and a sword lying by it, all which he took aboard his galley and brought with him to Athens. Upon which the Athenians, greatly delighted, went out to meet and receive the relics with splendid processions and sacrifices, as if it were Theseus himself returning alive to the city. He lies interred in the middle of the city, near the present gymnasium. His tomb is a sanctuary and refuge for slaves, and all those of mean condition that fly from the persecution of men in power, in memory that Theseus while he lived was an assister and protector of the distressed, and never refused the petitions of the afflicted that fled to him. The chief and most solemn sacrifice which they celebrate to him is kept on the eighth day of Pyanepsion, on which he returned with the Athenian young men from Crete. Besides which they sacrifice to him on the eighth day of every month, either because he returned from Troezen the eighth day of Hecatombaeon, as Diodorus the geographer writes, or else thinking that number to be proper to him, because he was reputed to be born of Neptune, because they sacrifice to Neptune on the eighth day of every month. The number eight being the first cube of an even number, and the double of the first square, seemed to be an emblem of the steadfast and immovable power of this god, who from thence has the names of Asphalius and Gaeiochus, that is, the establisher and stayer of the earth.

LYCURGUS

There is so much uncertainty in the accounts which historians have left us of Lycurgus, the lawgiver of Sparta, that scarcely anything is asserted by one of them which is not called into question or contradicted by the rest. Their sentiments are quite different as to the family he came of, the voyages he undertook, the place and manner of his death, but most of all when they speak of the laws he made and the commonwealth which he founded. They cannot, by any means, be brought to an agreement as to the very age in which he lived; for some of them say that he flourished in the time of Iphitus, and that they two jointly contrived the ordinance for the cessation of arms during the solemnity of the Olympic games. Of this opinion was Aristotle; and for confirmation of it, he alleges an inscription upon one of the copper quoits used in those sports, upon which the name of Lycurgus continued uneffaced to his time. But Eratosthenes and Apollodorus and other chronologers, computing the time by the successions of the Spartan kings, pretend to demonstrate that he was much more ancient than the institution of the Olympic games. Timaeus conjectures that there were two of this name, and in diverse time, but that the one of them being much more famous than the other, men gave to him the glory of the exploits of both; the elder of the two, according to him, was not long after Homer; and some are so particular as to say that he had seen him. But that he was of great antiquity may be gathered from a passage in Xenophon, where he makes him contemporary with the Heraclidae. By descent, indeed, the very last kings of Sparta were Heraclidae too; but he seems in that place to speak of the first and more immediate successors of Hercules. But not-withstanding this confusion and obscurity, we shall en-deavour to compose the history of his life, adhering to those statements which are least contradicted, and depending upon those authors who are most worthy of credit.

The poet Simonides will have it that Lycurgus was the son of Prytanis, and not of Eunomus; but in this opinion he is singular, for all the rest deduce the genealogy of them both as follows:—

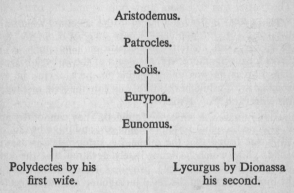

Aristodemus.

Patrocles.

Soüs.

Eurypon.

Eunomus.

Polydectes by his   Lycurgus by Dionassa
first wife.   his second.

Dieuchidas says he was the sixth from Patrocles and the eleventh from Hercules. Be this as it will, Soüs certainly was the most renowned of all his ancestors, under whose con-duct the Spartans made slaves of the Helots, and added to their dominions, by conquest, a good part of Arcadia. There goes a story of this king Soüs, that, being besieged by the Clitorians in a dry and stony place so that he could come at no water, he was at last constrained to agree with them upon these terms, that he would restore to them all his con-quests, provided that himself and all his men should drink of the nearest spring. After the usual oaths and ratifications, he called his soldiers together, and offered to him that would forbear drinking his kingdom for a reward; and when not a man of them was able to forbear, in short, when they had all drunk their fill, at last comes King Soüs himself to the spring, and, having sprinkled his face only, without swallowing one drop, marches off in the face of his enemies, refusing to yield up his conquests, because himself and all his men had not, according to the articles, drunk of their water.

Although he was justly had in admiration on this account, yet his family was not surnamed from him, but from his son Eurypon (of whom they were called Eurypontids); the reason of which was that Eurypon relaxed the rigour of the monarchy, seeking favour and popularity with the many. They, after this first step, grew bolder; and the succeeding kings partly incurred hatred with their people by trying to use force, or, for popularity's sake and through weakness, gave way; and anarchy and confusion long prevailed in Sparta, causing, moreover, the death of the father of Lycurgus. For as he was endeavouring to quell a riot, he was stabbed with a butcher's knife, and left the title of king to his eldest son, Polydectes.

He, too, dying soon after, the right of succession (as every one thought) rested in Lycurgus; and reign he did, until it was found that the queen, his sister-in-law, was with child; upon which he immediately declared that the kingdom belonged to her issue, provided it were male, and that he himself exercised the regal jurisdiction only as his guardian; the Spartan name for which office is *prodicus*. Soon after, an overture was made to him by the queen, that she would herself in some way destroy the infant, upon condition that he would marry her when he came to the crown. Abhorring the woman's wickedness, he nevertheless did not reject her proposal, but, making show of closing with her, despatched the messenger with thanks and expressions of joy, but dissuaded her earnestly from procuring herself to miscarry, which would impair her health, if not endanger her life; he himself, he said, would see to it, that the child, as soon as born, should be taken out of the way. By such artifices having drawn on the woman to the time of her lying-in, as soon as he heard that she was in labour, he sent persons to be by and observe all that passed, with orders that if it were a girl they should deliver it to the women, but if a boy, should bring it to him wheresoever he were, and whatsoever doing. It fell out that when he was at supper with the principal magistrates the queen was brought to bed of a boy, who was soon after presented to him as he was at the table; he, taking him into his arms, said to those about him, "Men of Sparta, here is a king born unto us"; this said, he laid him down in the king's place, and named him Charilaus, that is, the joy of the people; because that all were transported with joy and with wonder at his noble and just spirit. His reign had lasted only eight months, but he was honoured on other accounts by the citizens, and there were more who obeyed him because of his eminent virtues, than because he was regent to the king and had the royal power in his hands. Some, however, envied and sought to impede his growing influence while he was still young; chiefly the kindred and friends of the queen-mother, who pretended to have been dealt with injuriously. Her brother Leonidas, in a warm debate which fell out betwixt him and Lycurgus, went so far as to tell him to his face that he was well assured that ere long he should see him king; suggesting suspicions and preparing the way for an accusation of him, as though he had made away with his nephew, if the child should chance to fail, though by a natural death. Words of the like import were designedly cast abroad by the queen-mother and her adherents.

Troubled at this, and not knowing what it might come to, he thought it his wisest course to avoid their envy by a voluntary exile, and to travel from place to place until his nephew came to marriageable years, and, by having a son, had secured the succession; setting sail, therefore, with this resolution, he first arrived at Crete, where, having considered their several forms of government, and got an acquaintance with the principal men among them, some of their laws he very much approved of, and resolved to make use of them in his own country; a good part he rejected as useless. Among the persons there the most renowned for their learning and their wisdom in state matters was one Thales, whom Lycurgus, by importunities and assurances of friendship, persuaded to go over to Lacedaemon; where, though by his outward appearance and his own profession he seemed to be no other than a lyric poet, in reality he per-

formed the part of one of the ablest lawgivers in the world.
The very songs which he composed were exhortations to
obedience and concord, and the very measure and cadence
of the verse, conveying impressions of order and tranquillity, had so great an influence on the minds of the listeners,
that they were insensibly softened and civilised, insomuch
that they renounced their private feuds and animosities, and
were reunited in a common admiration of virtue. So that it
may truly be said that Thales prepared the way for the discipline introduced by Lycurgus.

From Crete he sailed to Asia, with design, as is said, to
examine the difference betwixt the manners and rules of
life of the Cretans, which were very sober and temperate,
and those of the Ionians, a people of sumptuous and delicate habits, and so to form a judgment; just as physicians do
by comparing healthy and diseased bodies. Here he had the
first sight of Homer's works, in the hands, we may suppose,
of the posterity of Creophylus; and, having observed that
the few loose expressions and actions of ill example which
are to be found in his poems were much outweighed by serious lessons of state and rules of morality, he set himself
eagerly to transcribe and digest them into order, as thinking
they would be of good use in his own country. They had,
indeed, already obtained some slight repute among the
Greeks, and scattered portions, as chance conveyed them,
were in the hands of individuals; but Lycurgus first made
them really known.

The Egyptians say that he took a voyage into Egypt, and
that, being much taken with their way of separating the soldiery from the rest of the nation, he transferred it from
them to Sparta, a removal from contact with those employed in low and mechanical occupations giving high re-
finement and beauty to the state. Some Greek writers also
record this. But as for his voyages into Spain, Africa and
the Indies, and his conferences there with the Gymnosophists, the whole relation, as far as I can find, rests on the
single credit of the Spartan Aristocrates, the son of Hipparchus.

Lycurgus was much missed at Sparta, and often sent for,

"for kings indeed we have," they said, "who wear the marks and assume the titles of royalty, but as for the qualities of their minds, they have nothing by which they are to be distinguished from their subjects;" adding, that in him alone was the true foundation of sovereignty to be seen, a nature made to rule, and a genius to gain obedience. Nor were the kings themselves averse to see him back, for they looked upon his presence as a bulwark against the insolence of the people.

Things being in this posture at his return, he applied himself, without loss of time, to a thorough reformation, and resolved to change the whole face of the commonwealth; for what could a few particular laws and a partial alteration avail? He must act as wise physicians do, in the case of one who labours under a complication of diseases, by force of medicines reduce and exhaust him, change his whole temperament, and then set him upon a totally new regimen of diet. Having thus projected things, away he goes to Delphi to consult Apollo there; which having done, and offered his sacrifice, he returned with that renowned oracle, in which he is called beloved of God, and rather God than man; that his prayers were heard, that his laws should be the best, and the commonwealth which observed them the most famous in the world. Encouraged by these things he set himself to bring over to his side the leading men of Sparta, exhorting them to give him a helping hand in his great undertaking; he broke it first to his particular friends, and then by degrees, gained others, and animated them all to put his design in execution. When things were ripe for action, he gave orders to thirty of the principal men of Sparta to be ready armed at the market-place by break of day, to the end that he might strike a terror into the opposite party. Hermippus hath set down the names of twenty of the most eminent of them; but the name of him whom Lycurgus most confided in, and who was of most use to him, both in making his laws and putting them in execution was Arthmiadas. Things growing to a tumult, King Charilaus, apprehending that it was a conspiracy against his person, took sanctuary in the temple of Minerva of the Brazen House; but, being soon after undeceived, and having taken an oath of them that they had no designs against him, he quitted his refuge, and himself also entered into the confederacy with them; of so gentle and flexible a disposition he was, to which Archelaus, his brother-king, alluded, when, hearing him extolled for his goodness, he said, "Who can say he is anything but good? he is so even to the bad."

Amongst the many changes and alterations which Lycurgus made, the first and of greatest importance was the establishment of the senate, which having a power equal to the king's in matters of great consequence, and, as Plato expresses it, allaying and qualifying the fiery genius of the royal office, gave steadiness and safety to the commonwealth. For the state, which before had no firm basis to stand upon, but leaned one while towards an absolute monarchy, when the kings had the upper hand, and another while towards a pure democracy, when the people had the better, found in this establishment of the senate a central weight, like ballast in a ship, which always kept things in a just equilibrium; the twenty-eight always adhering to the kings so far as to resist democracy, and on the other hand, supporting the people against the establishment of absolute monarchy. As for the determinate number of twenty-eight, Aristotle states, that it so fell out because two of the original associates, for want of courage, fell off from the enterprise; but Sphaerus assures us that there were but twenty-eight of the confederates at first; perhaps there is some mystery in the number, which consists of seven multiplied by four, and is the first of perfect numbers after six, being, as that is, equal to all its parts. For my part, I believe Lycurgus fixed upon the number of twenty-eight, that, the two kings being reckoned amongst them, they might be thirty in all. So eagerly set was he upon this establishment, that he took the trouble to obtain an oracle about it from Delphi, the Rhetra, which runs thus: "After that you have built a temple to Jupiter Hellanius, and to Minerva Hellania, and after that you have *phyle'd* the people into *phyles*, and *obe'd* them into *obes*, you shall establish a council of thirty elders, the leaders included, and shall, from time to

time, *apellazein* the people betwixt Babyca and Cnacion,
there propound and put to the vote. The commons have the
final voice and decision." By *phyles* and *obes* are meant the
divisions of the people; by the *leaders,* the two kings; *apellazein,* referring to the Pythian Apollo, signifies to assemble;
Babyca and Cnacion they now call Oenus; Aristotle says
Cnacion is a river, and Babyca a bridge. Betwixt this Babyca
and Cnacion, their assemblies were held, for they had no
council-house or building to meet in. Lycurgus was of opinion that ornaments were so far from advantaging them in
their counsels, that they were rather an hindrance, by diverting their attention from the business before them to statues
and pictures, and roofs curiously fretted, the usual embel-
lishments of such places amongst the other Greeks. The
people then being thus assembled in the open air, it was not
allowed to any one of their order to give his advice, but
only either to ratify or reject what should be propounded to
them by the king or senate. But because it fell out afterwards that the people, by adding or omitting words, dis-
torted and perverted the sense of propositions, Kings Poly-
dorus and Theopompus inserted into the Rhetra, or grand
covenant, the following clause: "That if the people decide
crookedly it should be lawful for the elders and leaders to
dissolve;" that is to say, refuse ratification, and dismiss
the people as depravers and perverters of their counsel. It
passed among the people, by their management, as being
equally authentic with the rest of the Rhetra, as appears by
these verses of Tyrtaeus,—

"These oracles they from Apollo heard,
   And brought from Pytho home the perfect word:
   The heaven-appointed kings, who love the land,
   Shall foremost in the nation's council stand;
   The elders next to them; the commons last;
   Let a straight *Rhetra* among all be passed."

Although Lycurgus had, in this manner, used all the
qualifications possible in the constitution of his commonwealth, yet those who succeeded him found the oligarchical

element still too strong and dominant, and to check its high temper and its violence, put, as Plato says, a bit in its mouth, which was the power of the ephori, established an hundred and thirty years after the death of Lycurgus. Elatus and his colleagues were the first who had this dignity conferred upon them in the reign of King Theopompus, who, when his queen upbraided him one day that he would leave the regal power to his children less than he had received it from his ancestors, said in answer, "No, greater; for it will last longer." For, indeed, their prerogative being thus reduced within reasonable bounds, the Spartan kings were at once freed from all further jealousies and consequent danger, and never experienced the calamities of their neighbours at Messene and Argos, who, by maintaining their prerogative too strictly, for want of yielding a little to the populace, lost it all.

Indeed, whosoever shall look at the sedition and misgovernment which befell these bordering nations to whom they were as near related in blood as situation, will find in them the best reason to admire the wisdom and foresight of Lycurgus. For these three states, in their first rise, were equal, or, if there were any odds, they lay on the side of the Messenians and Argives, who, in the first allotment, were thought to have been luckier than the Spartans; yet was their happiness of but small continuance, partly the tyrannical temper of their kings and partly the ungovernableness of the people quickly bringing upon them such disorders, and so complete an overthrow of all existing institutions, as clearly to show how truly divine a blessing the Spartans had had in that wise lawgiver who gave their government its happy balance and temper. But of this I shall say more in its due place.

After the creation of the thirty senators, his next task, and, indeed, the most hazardous he ever undertook, was the making a new division of their lands. For there was an extreme inequality amongst them, and their state was overloaded with a multitude of indigent and necessitous persons, while its whole wealth had centred upon a very few. To the end, therefore, that he might expel from the state arro-

gance and envy, luxury and crime, and those yet more inveterate diseases of want and superfluity, he obtained of
them to renounce their properties, and to consent to a new
division of the land, and that they should live all together
on an equal footing; merit to be their only road to eminence, and the disgrace of evil, and credit of worthy acts,
their one measure of difference between man and man.

Upon their consent to these proposals, proceeding at once
to put them into execution, he divided the country of Laconia in general into thirty thousand equal shares, and the
part attached to the city of Sparta into nine thousand; these
he distributed among the Spartans, as he did the others to
the country citizens. Some authors say that he made but six
thousand lots for the citizens of Sparta, and that King Poly-
dorus added three thousand more. Others say that Poly-
dorus doubled the number Lycurgus had made, which, according to them, was but four thousand five hundred. A
lot was so much as to yield, one year with another, about
seventy bushels of grain for the master of the family, and
twelve for his wife, with a suitable proportion of oil and
wine. And this he thought sufficient to keep their bodies in
good health and strength; superfluities they were better
without. It is reported, that, as he returned from a journey
shortly after the division of the lands, in harvest time, the
ground being newly reaped, seeing the stacks all standing
equal and alike, he smiled, and said to those about him,
"Methinks all Laconia looks like one family estate just divided among a number of brothers."

Not contented with this, he resolved to make a division of
their movables too, that there might be no odious distinction
or inequality left amongst them; but finding that it would be
very dangerous to go about it openly, he took another
course, and defeated their avarice by the following strategem: he commanded that all gold and silver coin should be
called in, and that only a sort of money made of iron should
be current, a great weight and quantity of which was very
little worth; so that to lay up twenty or thirty pounds there
was required a pretty large closet, and, to remove it, nothing
less than a yoke of oxen. With the diffusion of this money,

at once a number of vices were banished from Lacedaemon; for who would rob another of such a coin? Who would unjustly detain or take by force, or accept as a bribe, a thing which it was not easy to hide, nor a credit to have, nor indeed of any use to cut in pieces? For when it was just red hot, they quenched it in vinegar, and by that means spoilt it, and made it almost incapable of being worked.

In the next place, he declared an outlawry of all needless and superfluous arts; but here he might almost have spared his proclamation; for they of themselves would have gone after the gold and silver, the money which remained being not so proper payment for curious work; for, being of iron, it was scarcely portable, neither, if they should take the means to export it, would it pass amongst the other Greeks, who ridiculed it. So there was now no more means of purchasing foreign goods and small wares; merchants sent no shiploads into Laconian ports; no rhetoric-master, no itinerate fortune-teller, no harlot-monger, or gold or silversmith, engraver, or jeweller, set foot in a country which had no money; so that luxury, deprived little by little of that which fed and fomented it, wasted to nothing and died away of itself. For the rich had no advantage here over the poor, as their wealth and abundance had no road to come abroad by but were shut up at home doing nothing. And in this way they became excellent artists in common, necessary things; bedsteads, chairs, and tables, and such like staple utensils in a family, were admirably well made there; their cup, particularly, was very much in fashion, and eagerly bought up by soldiers, as Critias reports; for its colour was such as to prevent water, drunk upon necessity and disagreeable to look at, from being noticed; and the shape of it was such that the mud stuck to the sides, so that only the purer part came to the drinker's mouth. For this, also, they had to thank their lawgiver, who, by relieving the artisans of the trouble of making useless things, set them to show their skill in giving beauty to those of daily and indispensable use.

The third and most masterly stroke of this great lawgiver, by which he struck a yet more effectual blow against luxury and the desire of riches, was the ordinance he made, that they should all eat in common, of the same bread and same meat, and of kinds that were specified, and should not spend their lives at home, laid on costly couches at splendid tables, delivering themselves up into the hands of their tradesmen and cooks, to fatten them in corners, like greedy brutes, and to ruin not their minds only but their very bodies which, enfeebled by indulgence and excess, would stand in need of long sleep, warm bathing, freedom from work, and, in a word, of as much care and attendance as if they were continually sick. It was certainly an extraordinary thing to have brought about such a result as this, but a greater yet to have taken away from wealth, as Theophrastus observes, not merely the property of being coveted, but its very nature of being wealth. For the rich, being obliged to go to the same table with the poor, could not make use of or enjoy their abundance, nor so much as please their vanity by looking at or displaying it. So that the common proverb, that Plutus, the god of riches, is blind, was nowhere in all the world literally verified but in Sparta. There, indeed, he was not only blind, but like a picture, without either life or motion. Nor were they allowed to take food at home first, and then attend the public tables, for every one had an eye upon those who did not eat and drink like the rest, and reproached them with being dainty and effeminate.

This last ordinance in particular exasperated the wealthier men. They collected in a body against Lycurgus, and from ill words came to throwing stones, so that at length he was forced to run out of the market-place, and take to sanctuary to save his life; by good-hap he outran all, excepting one Alcander, a young man otherwise not ill accomplished, but hasty and violent, who came up so close to him, that when he turned to see who was so near him, he struck him upon the face with his stick, and put out one of his eyes. Lycurgus, so far from being daunted and discouraged by this accident, stopped short and showed his disfigured face and eye beat out to his countrymen; they, dismayed and ashamed at the sight, delivered Alcander into his hands to be punished, and escorted him home, with expressions of great concern for his ill-usage. Lycurgus, having thanked them for their care of his person, dismissed them all, excepting only Alcander; and, taking him with him into his house, neither did nor said anything severely to him, but, dismissing those whose place it was, bade Alcander to wait upon him at table. The young man, who was of an ingenuous temper, without murmuring did as he was commanded; and being thus admitted to live with Lycurgus, he had an opportunity to observe in him, besides his gentleness and calmness of temper, an extraordinary sobriety and an indefatigable industry, and so, from an enemy, became one of his most zealous admirers, and told his friends and relations that Lycurgus was not that morose and ill-natured man they had formerly taken him for, but the one mild and gentle character of the world. And thus did Lycurgus, for chastisement of his fault, make of a wild and passionate young man one of the discreetest citizens of Sparta.

In memory of this accident, Lycurgus built a temple to Minerva, surnamed Optilētis; *optilus* being the Doric of these parts for *ophthalmus*, the eye. Some authors, however, of whom Dioscorides is one (who wrote a treatise on the commonwealth of Sparta), say that he was wounded, indeed, but did not lose his eye with the blow; but that he built the temple in gratitude for the cure. Be this as it will, certain it is, that, after this misadventure, the Lacedaemonians made it a rule never to carry so much as a staff into their public assemblies.

But to return to their public repast;—these had several names in Greek; the Cretans called them *andria*, because the men only came to them. The Lacedaemonians called them *phiditia*, that is, by changing *l* into *d*, the same as *philitia*, love feasts, because that, by eating and drinking together, they had opportunity of making friends. Or perhaps from *phido*, parsimony, because they were so many schools of sobriety; or perhaps the first letter is an addition, and the word at first was *editia*, from *edode*, eating. They met by companies of fifteen, more or less, and each of them stood bound to bring in monthly a bushel of meal, eight gallons of wine, five pounds of cheese, two pounds and a half of figs, and some very small sum of money to buy flesh or fish with.

Besides this, when any of them made sacrifice to the gods, they always sent a dole to the common hall; and, likewise, when any of them had been a hunting, he sent thither a part of the venison he had killed; for these two occasions were the only excuses allowed for supping at home. The custom of eating together was observed strictly for a great while afterwards; insomuch that King Agis himself, after having vanquished the Athenians, sending for his commons at his return home, because he desired to eat privately with his queen, was refused them by the polemarchs; which refusal when he resented so much as to omit next day the sacrifice due for a war happily ended, they made him pay a fine.

They used to send their children to these tables as to schools of temperance; here they were instructed in state affairs by listening to experienced statesmen; here they learned to converse with pleasantry, to make jests without scurrility and take them without ill humour. In this point of good breeding, the Lacedaemonians excelled particularly, but if any man were uneasy under it, upon the least hint given, there was no more to be said to him. It was customary also for the eldest man in the company to say to each of them, as they came in, "Through this" (pointing to the door), "no words go out." When any one had a desire to be admitted into any of these little societies, he was to go through the following probation: each man in the company took a little ball of soft bread, which they were to throw into a deep basin, which a waiter carried round upon his head; those that liked the person to be chosen dropped their ball into the basin without altering its figure, and those who disliked him pressed it betwixt their fingers, and made it flat; and this signified as much as a negative voice. And if there were but one of these flattened pieces in the basin, the suitor was rejected, so desirous were they that all the members of the company should be agreeable to each other. The basin was called *caddichus,* and the rejected candidate had a name thence derived. Their most famous dish was the black broth, which was so much valued that the elderly men fed only upon that, leaving what flesh there was to the younger.

They say that a certain king of Pontus, having heard much of this black broth of theirs, sent for a Lacedaemonian cook on purpose to make him some, but had no sooner tasted it than he found it extremely bad, which the cook observing, told him, "Sir, to make this broth relish, you should have bathed yourself first in the river Eurotas."

After drinking moderately, every man went to his home without lights, for the use of them was, on all occasions, forbid to the end that they might accustom themselves to march boldly in the dark. Such was the common fashion of their meals.

Lycurgus would never reduce his laws into writing; nay there is a Rhetra expressly to forbid it. For he thought that the most material points, and such as most directly tended to the public welfare, being imprinted on the hearts of their youth by a good discipline, would be sure to remain, and would find a stronger security, than any compulsion would be, in the principles of action formed in them by their best lawgiver, education. And as for things of lesser importance, as pecuniary contracts, and such like, the forms of which have to be changed as occasion requires, he thought it the best way to prescribe no positive rule or inviolable usage in such cases, willing that their manner and form should be altered according to the circumstances of time, and determinations of men of sound judgment. Every end and object of law and enactment it was his design education should effect.

One, then, of the Rhetras was, that their laws should not be written; another is particularly levelled against luxury and expensiveness, for by it was ordained that the ceilings of their houses should only be wrought by the axe, and their gates and doors smoothed only by the saw. Epaminondas's famous dictum about his own table, that "Treason and a dinner like this do not keep company together," may be said to have been anticipated by Lycurgus. Luxury and a house of this kind could not well be companions. For a man might have a less than ordinary share of sense that would furnish such plain and common rooms with silver-footed couches and purple coverlets and gold and silver plate. Doubtless he had good reason to think that they would proportion their beds to their houses, and their coverlets to their beds, and the rest of their goods and furniture to these. It is reported that king Leotychides, the first of that name, was so little used to the sight of any other kind of work, that, being entertained at Corinth in a stately room, he was much surprised to see the timber and ceiling so finely carved and panelled, and asked his host whether the trees grew so in his country.

A third ordinance of Rhetra was, that they should not make war often, or long, with the same enemy, lest that they should train and instruct them in war, by habituating them to defend themselves. And this is what Agesilaus was much blamed for, a long time after; it being thought, that, by his continual incursions into Boeotia, he made the Thebans a match for the Lacedaemonians; and therefore Antalcidas, seeing him wounded one day, said to him, that he was very well paid for taking such pains to make the Thebans good soldiers, whether they would or no. These laws were called the Rhetras, to intimate that they were divine sanctions and revelations.

In order to the good education of their youth (which, as I said before, he thought the most important and noblest work of a lawgiver), he went so far back as to take into consideration their very conception and birth, by regulating their marriages. For Aristotle is wrong in saying, that, after he had tried all ways to reduce the women to more modesty and sobriety, he was at last forced to leave them as they were, because that in the absence of their husbands, who spent the best part of their lives in the wars, their wives, whom they were obliged to leave absolute mistresses at home, took great liberties and assumed the superiority; and were treated with overmuch respect and called by the title of lady or queen. The truth is, he took in their case, also, all the care that was possible; he ordered the maidens to exercise themselves with wrestling, running, throwing the quoit, and casting the dart, to the end that the fruit they conceived might, in strong and healthy bodies, take firmer root and find better growth, and withal that they,

with this greater vigour, might be the more able to undergo
the pains of child-bearing. And to the end he might take
away their overgreat tenderness and fear of exposure to the
air, and all acquired womanishness, he ordered that the
young women should go naked in the processions, as well
as the young men, and dance, too, in that condition, at certain solemn feasts, singing certain songs, whilst the young
men stood around, seeing and hearing them. On these occasions they now and then made, by jests, a befitting reflec-
tion upon those who had misbehaved themselves in the
wars; and again sang encomiums upon those who had done
any gallant action, and by these means inspired the younger
sort with an emulation of their glory. Those that were thus
commended went away proud, elated, and gratified with
their honour among the maidens; and those who were ral-
lied were as sensibly touched with it as if they had been
formally reprimanded; and so much the more, because the
kings and the elders, as well as the rest of the city, saw
and heard all that passed. Nor was there anything shameful in this nakedness of the young women; modesty attended
them, and all wantonness was excluded. It taught them simplicity and a care for good health, and gave them some
taste of higher feelings, admitted as they thus were to the
field of noble action and glory. Hence it was natural for
them to think and speak as Gorgo, for example, the wife
of Leonidas, is said to have done, when some foreign lady,
as it would seem, told her that the women of Lacedaemon
were the only women in the world who could rule men;
"With good reason," she said, "for we are the only women
who bring forth men."

These public processions of the maidens, and their appearing naked in their exercises and dancings, were incite-
ments to marriage, operating upon the young with the rigour and certainty, as Plato says, of love, if not of mathe-
matics. But besides all this, to promote it yet more effectu-
ally, those who continued bachelors were in a degree disfranchised by law; for they were excluded from the sight
of those public processions in which the young men and
maidens danced naked, and in winter-time, the officers

compelled them to march naked themselves round the
market-place, singing as they went a certain song to their
own disgrace, that they justly suffered this punishment for
disobeying the laws. Moreover, they were denied that respect and observance which the younger men paid their
elders; and no man, for example, found fault with what
was said to Dercyllidas, though so eminent a commander;
upon whose approach one day, a young man, instead of rising, retained his seat, remarking, "No child of yours will
make room for me."

In their marriages, the husband carried off his bride by
a sort of force; nor were their brides ever small and of tender years, but in their full bloom and ripeness. After this,
she who superintended the wedding comes and clips the hair
of the bride close round her head, dresses her up in man's
clothes, and leaves her upon a mattress in the dark; afterwards comes the bridegroom, in his everyday clothes, sober
and composed, as having supped at the common table, and,
entering privately into the room where the bride lies, unties
her virgin zone, and takes her to himself; and, after staying
some time together, he returns composedly to his own apartment, to sleep as usual with the other young men. And so
he continues to do, spending his days, and, indeed, his
nights, with them, visiting his bride in fear and shame, and
with circumspection, when he thought he should not be
observed; she, also, on her part, using her wit to help and
find favourable opportunities for their meeting, when company was out of the way. In this manner they lived a long
time, insomuch that they sometimes had children by their
wives before ever they saw their faces by daylight. Their
interviews, being thus difficult and rare, served not only
for continual exercise of their self-control, but brought
them together with their bodies healthy and vigorous, and
their affections fresh and lively, unsated and undulled by
easy access and long continuance with each other; while
their partings were always early enough to leave behind
unextinguished in each of them some remaining fire of
longing and mutual delight. After guarding marriage with
this modesty and reserve, he was equally careful to banish

empty and womanish jealousy. For this object, excluding all licentious disorders, he made it, nevertheless, honourable for men to give the use of their wives to those whom they should think fit, that so they might have children by them; ridiculing those in whose opinion such favours are so unfit for participation as to fight and shed blood and go to war about it. Lycurgus allowed a man who was advanced in years and had a young wife to recommend some virtuous and approved young man, that she might have a child by him, who might inherit the good qualities of the father, and be a son to himself. On the other side, an honest man who had love for a married woman upon account of her modesty and the well-favouredness of her children, might without formality, beg her company of her husband, that he might raise, as it were, from this plot of good ground, worthy and well-allied children for himself. And indeed, Lycurgus was of a persuasion that children were not so much the property of their parents as of the whole commonwealth, and, therefore, would not have his citizens begot by the first-comers, but by the best men that could be found; the laws of other nations seemed to him very absurd and inconsistent, where people would be so solicitous for their dogs and horses as to exert interest and to pay money to procure fine breeding, and yet kept their wives shut up, to be made mothers only by themselves, who might be foolish, infirm, or diseased; as if it were not apparent that children of a bad breed would prove their bad qualities first upon those who kept and were rearing them, and well-born children, in like manner, their good qualities. These regulations, founded on natural and social grounds, were certainly so far from that scandalous liberty which was afterwards charged upon their women, that they knew not what adultery meant. It is told, for instance, of Geradas, a very ancient Spartan, that, being asked by a stranger what punishment their law had appointed for adulterers, he answered, "There are no adulterers in our country." "But," replied the stranger, "suppose there were?" "Then," answered he, "the offender would have to give the plaintiff a bull with a neck so long as that he might drink from the top of Taygetus of the Eurotas river below it." The man, surprised at this, said, "Why, 'tis impossible to find such a bull." Geradas smilingly replied, " 'Tis as possible as to find an adulterer in Sparta." So much I had to say of their marriages.

Nor was it in the power of the father to dispose of the child as he thought fit; he was obliged to carry it before certain triers at a place called Lesche; these were some of the elders of the tribe to which the child belonged; their business it was carefully to view the infant, and, if they found it stout and well made, they gave order for its rearing, and allotted to it one of the nine thousand shares of land above mentioned for its maintenance, but, if they found it puny and ill-shaped, ordered it to be taken to what was called the Apothetae, a sort of chasm under Taygetus; as thinking it neither for the good of the child itself, nor for the public interest, that it should be brought up, if it did not, from the very outset, appear made to be healthy and vigorous. Upon the same account, the women did not bathe the new-born children with water, as is the custom in all other countries, but with wine, to prove the temper and complexion of their bodies; from a notion they had that epileptic and weakly children faint and waste away upon their being thus bathed, while, on the contrary, those of a strong and vigorous habit acquire firmness and get a temper by it, like steel. There was much care and art, too, used by the nurses; they had no swaddling bands; the children grew up free and unconstrained in limb and form, and not dainty and fanciful about their food; not afraid in the dark, or of being left alone; and without peevishness, or ill-humour, or crying. Upon this account Spartan nurses were often bought up, or hired by people of other countries; and it is recorded that she who suckled Alcibiades was a Spartan; who, however, if fortunate in his nurse, was not so in his preceptor; his guardian, Pericles, as Plato tells us, chose a servant for that office called Zopyrus, no better than any common slave.

Lycurgus was of another mind; he would not have masters bought out of the market for his young Spartans, nor such as should sell their pains; nor was it lawful, indeed, for the father himself to breed up the children after his own fancy; but as soon as they were seven years old they were to be enrolled in certain companies and classes, where they all lived under the same order and discipline, doing their exercises and taking their play together. Of these, he who showed the most conduct and courage was made captain; they had their eyes always upon him, obeyed his orders, and underwent patiently whatsoever punishment he inflicted; so that the whole course of their education was one continued exercise of a ready and perfect obedience. The old men, too, were spectators of their performances, and often raised quarrels and disputes among them, to have a good opportunity of finding out their different characters, and of seeing which would be valiant, which a coward, when they should come to more dangerous encounters. Reading and writing they gave them, just enough to serve their turn; their chief care was to make them good subjects, and to teach them to endure pain and conquer in battle. To this end, as they grew in years, their discipline was proportionately increased; their heads were close-clipped, they were accustomed to go barefoot, and for the most part to play naked.

After they were twelve years old, they were no longer allowed to wear any undergarments, they had one coat to serve them a year; their bodies were hard and dry, with but little acquaintance of baths and unguents; these human indulgences they were allowed only on some few particular days in the year. They lodged together in little bands upon beds made of the rushes which grew by the banks of the river Eurotas, which they were to break off with their hands without a knife; if it were winter, they mingled some thistle-down with their rushes, which it was thought had the property of giving warmth. By the time they were come to this age there was not any of the more hopeful boys who had not a lover to bear him company. The old men, too, had an eye upon them, coming often to the grounds to hear and see them contend either in wit or strength with one another, and this as seriously and with as much concern as if they were their fathers, their tutors, or their magistrates; so that there scarcely was any time or place without some one present to put them in mind of their duty, and punish them if they had neglected it.

Besides all this, there was always one of the best and honestest men in the city appointed to undertake the charge and governance of them; he again arranged them into their several bands, and set over each of them for their captain the most temperate and boldest of those they called Irens, who were usually twenty years old, two years out of the boys; and the oldest of the boys, again, were Mell-Irens, as much as to say, who would shortly be men. This young man, therefore, was their captain when they fought and their master at home, using them for the offices of his house; sending the eldest of them to fetch wood, and the weaker and less able to gather salads and herbs, and these they must either go without or steal; which they did by creeping into the gardens, or conveying themselves cunningly and closely into the eating-houses; if they were taken in the fact, they were whipped without mercy, for thieving so ill and awkwardly. They stole, too, all other meat they could lay their hands on, looking out and watching all opportunities, when people were asleep or more careless than usual. If they were caught, they were not only punished with whipping, but hunger, too, being reduced to their ordinary allowance, which was but very slender, and so contrived on purpose, that they might set about to help themselves, and be forced to exercise their energy and address. This was the principal design of their hard fare; there was another not inconsiderable, that they might grow taller; for the vital spirits, not being overburdened and oppressed by too great a quantity of nourishment, which necessarily discharges itself into thickness and breadth, do, by their natural lightness, rise; and the body, giving and yielding because it is pliant, grows in height. The same thing seems, also, to conduce to beauty of shape; a dry and lean habit is a better subject for nature's configuration, which the gross and over-fed are too heavy to submit to properly. Just as we find that women who take physic whilst they are with child, bear leaner and smaller but better-shaped and prettier children; the material they come of having been more pliable and easily moulded. The reason, however, I leave others to determine.

To return from whence we have digressed. So seriously did the Lacedaemonian children go about their stealing, that a youth, having stolen a young fox and hid it under his coat, suffered it to tear out his very bowels with its teeth and claws and died upon the place, rather than let it be seen. What is practised to this very day in Lacedaemon is enough to gain credit to this story, for I myself have seen several of the youths endure whipping to death at the foot of the altar of Diana surnamed Orthia.

The Iren, or under-master, used to stay a little with them after supper, and one of them he bade to sing a song, to another he put a question which required an advised and deliberate answer; for example, Who was the best man in the city? What he thought of such an action of such a man? They used them thus early to pass a right judgment upon persons and things, and to inform themselves of the abilities or defects of their countrymen. If they had not an answer ready to the question, Who was a good or who an ill-reputed citizen, they were looked upon as of a dull and careless disposition, and to have little or no sense of virtue and honour; besides this, they were to give a good reason for what they said, and in as few words and as comprehensive as might be; he that failed of this, or answered not to the purpose, had his thumb bit by the master. Sometimes the Iren did this in the presence of the old men and magistrates, that they might see whether he punished them justly and in due measure or not, and when he did amiss, they would not reprove him before the boys, but, when they were gone, he was called to an account and underwent correction, if he had run far into either of the extremes of indulgence or severity.

Their lovers and favourers, too, had a share in the young boy's honour or disgrace; and there goes a story that one of them was fined by the magistrate, because the lad whom he loved cried out effeminately as he was fighting. And though this sort of love was so approved among them, that the most virtuous matrons would make professions of it to young girls, yet rivalry did not exist, and if several men's fancies met in one person, it was rather the beginning of an intimate friendship, whilst they all jointly conspired to render the object of their affection as accomplished as possible.

They taught them, also, to speak with a natural and graceful raillery, and to comprehend much matter of thought in few words. For Lycurgus, who ordered, as we saw, that a great piece of money should be but of an inconsiderable value, on the contrary would allow no discourse to be current which did not contain in few words a great deal of useful and curious sense; children in Sparta, by a habit of long silence, came to give just and sententious answers; for, indeed, as loose and incontinent livers are seldom fathers of many children, so loose and incontinent talkers seldom originate many sensible words. King Agis, when some Athenian laughed at their short swords, and said that the jugglers on the stage swallowed them with ease, answered him, "We find them long enough to reach our enemies with;" and as their swords were short and sharp, so, it seems to me, were their sayings. They reach the point and arrest the attention of the hearers better than any. Lycurgus himself, seems to have been short and sententious, if we may trust the anecdotes of him; as appears by his answer to one who by all means would set up a democracy in Lacedaemon. "Begin, friend," said he, "and set it up in your family." Another asked him why he allowed of such mean and trivial sacrifices to the gods. He replied, "That we may always have something to offer to them." Being asked what sort of martial exercises or combats he approved of, he answered, "All sorts, except that in which you stretch out your hands." Similar answers, addressed to his countrymen by letter, are ascribed to him; as, being consulted how they might best oppose an invasion of their enemies, he returned this answer, "By continuing poor, and not coveting each man to be greater than his fellow." Being consulted again whether it were requisite to enclose the city with a wall, he sent them word, "The city is well fortified which hath a wall of men instead of brick." But whether these letters are counterfeit or not is not easy to determine.

Of their dislike to talkativeness, the following apophthegms are evidence. King Leonidas said to one who held discourse upon some useful matter, but not in due time and place, "Much to the purpose, Sir, elsewhere." King Charilaus, the nephew of Lycurgus, being asked why his uncle had made so few laws, answered, "Men of few words require but few laws." When one, blamed Hecataeus the sophist, because that, being invited to the public table, he had not spoken one word all supper-time, Archidamidas answered in his vindication, "He who knows how to speak, knows also when."

The sharp and yet not ungraceful retorts which I mentioned may be instanced as follows. Demaratus, being asked in a troublesome manner by an importunate fellow, Who was the best man in Lacedaemon? answered at last, "He, Sir, that is the least like you." Some, in company where Agis was, much extolled the Eleans for their just and honourable management of the Olympic games; "Indeed," said Agis, "they are highly to be commended if they can do justice one day in five years." Theopompus answered a stranger who talked much of his affection to the Lacedaemonians, and said that his countrymen called him Philolacon (a lover of the Lacedaemonians), that it had been more for his honour if they had called him Philopolites (a lover of his own countrymen). And Plistoanax, the son of Pausanias, when an orator of Athens said the Lacedaemonians had no learning, told him, "You say true, Sir; we alone of all the Greeks have learned none of your bad qualities." One asked Archidamidas what number there might be of the Spartans, he answered: "Enough, Sir, to keep out wicked men."

We may see their character, too, in their very jests. For they did not throw them out at random, but the very wit of them was grounded upon something or other worth thinking about. For instance, one, being asked to go hear a man who exactly counterfeited the voice of a nightingale, answered, "Sir, I have heard the nightingale itself." Another, having read the following inscription upon a tomb—

"Seeking to quench a cruel tyranny,
   They, at Selinus, did in battle die,"

said, it served them right; for instead of trying to quench the tyranny, they should have let it burn out. A lad, being offered some game-cocks that would die upon the spot, said that he cared not for cocks that would die, but for such that would live and kill others. Another, seeing people easing themselves on seats, said, "God forbid I should sit where I could not get up to salute my elders." In short, their answers were so sententious and pertinent, that one said well that intellectual much more truly than athletic exercise was the Spartan characteristic.

Nor was their instruction in music and verse less carefully attended to than their habits of grace and good-breeding in conversation. And their very songs had a life and spirit in them that inflamed and possessed men's minds with an enthusiasm and ardour for action; the style of them was plain and without affectation; the subject always serious and moral; most usually, it was in praise of such men as had died in defence of their country, or in derision of those that had been cowards; the former they declared happy and glorified; the life of the latter they described as most miserable and abject. There were also vaunts of what they would do, and boasts of what they had done, varying with the various ages, as, for example, they had three choirs in their solemn festivals, the first of the old men, the second of the young men, and the last of the children; the old men began thus:—

"We once were young, and brave, and strong;"

the young men answered them singing:—

"And we're so now, come on and try;"

the children came last and said:—

"But we'll be strongest by and by."

Indeed, if we will take the pains to consider their com-
positions, some of which were still extant in our days,
and the airs on the flute to which they marched when going
to battle, we shall find that Terpander and Pindar had
reason to say that musing and valour were allied. The first
says of Lacedaemon—

"The spear and song in her do meet,
    And Justice walks about her street;"

And Pindar—

"Councils of wise elders here,
    And the young men's conquering spear,
    And dance, and song, and joy appear;"

both describing the Spartans as no less musical than warlike; in the words of one of their own poets—

"With the iron stern and sharp,
    Comes the playing on the harp."

For, indeed, before they engaged in battle, the king first
did sacrifice to the Muses, in all likelihood to put them in
mind of the manner of their education, and of the judgment that would be passed upon their actions, and thereby
to animate them to the performance of exploits that should
deserve a record. At such times, too, the Lacedaemonians
abated a little the severity of their manners in favour of
their young men, suffering them to curl and adorn their
hair, and to have costly arms and fine clothes; and were
well pleased to see them, like proud horses, neighing and
pressing to the course. And, therefore, as soon as they
came to be well-grown, they took a great deal of care of
their hair, to have it parted and trimmed, especially against

a day of battle, pursuant to a saying recorded of their law-giver, that a large head of hair added beauty to a good face, and terror to an ugly one.

When they were in the field, their exercises were generally more moderate, their fare not so hard, nor so strict a hand held over them by their officers, so that they were the only people in the world to whom war gave repose. When their army was drawn up in battle array, and the enemy near, the king sacrificed a goat, commanded the soldiers to set their garlands upon their heads, and the pipers to play the tune of the hymn to Castor, and himself began the paean of advance. It was at once a magnificent and a terrible sight to see them march on to the tune of their flutes, without any disorder in their ranks, any discomposure in their minds, or change in their countenances, calmly and cheerfully moving with the music to the deadly fight. Men, in this temper, were not likely to be possessed with fear or any transport of fury, but with the deliberate valour of hope and assurance, as if some divinity were attending and conducting them. The king had always about his person some one who had been crowned in the Olympic games; and upon this account a Lacedaemonian is said to have refused a considerable present, which was offered to him upon condition that he would not come into the lists; and when he had with much to-do thrown his antagonist, some of the spectators saying to him, "And now, Sir Lacedaemonian, what are you the better for your victory?" he answered, smiling, "I shall fight next the king." After they had routed an enemy, they pursued him till they were well assured of the victory, and then they sounded a retreat, thinking it base and unworthy of a Grecian people to cut men in pieces, who had given up and abandoned all resistance. This manner of dealing with their enemies did not only show magnanimity, but was politic too; for, knowing that they killed only those who made resistance, and gave quarter to the rest, men generally thought it their best way to consult their safety by flight.

Hippius the sophist says that Lycurgus himself was a great soldier and an experienced commander. Philostephanus attributes to him the first division of the cavalry into troops of fifties in a square body; but Demetrius the Phalerian says quite the contrary, and that he made all his laws in a continued peace. And, indeed, the Olympic holy truce, or cessation of arms, that was procured by his means and management, inclines me to think him a kind-natured man, and one that loved quietness and peace. Notwithstanding all this Hermippus tells us that he had no hand in the ordinance, that Iphitus made it, and Lycurgus came only as a spectator, and that by mere accident too. Being there, he heard as it were a man's voice behind him, blaming and wondering at him that he did not encourage his countrymen to resort to the assembly, and, turning about and seeing no man, concluded that it was a voice from heaven, and upon this immediately went to Iphitus and assisted him in ordering the ceremonies of that feast, which, by his means, were better established, and with more repute than before.

To return to the Lacedaemonians. Their discipline continued still after they were full-grown men. No one was allowed to live after his own fancy; but the city was a sort of camp, in which every man had his share of provisions and business set out, and looked upon himself as not so much born to serve his own ends as the interest of his country. Therefore if they were commanded nothing else, they went to see the boys perform their exercises, to teach them something useful or to learn it themselves of those who knew better. And indeed one of the greatest and highest blessings Lycurgus procured his people was the abundance of leisure which proceeded from his forbidding to them the exercise of any mean and mechanical trade. Of the money-making that depends on troublesome going about and seeing people and doing business, they had no need at all in a state where wealth obtained no honour or respect. The Helots tilled their ground for them, and paid them yearly in kind the appointed quantity, without any trouble of theirs. To this purpose there goes a story of a Lacedaemonian who, happening to be at Athens when the courts were sitting, was told of a citizen that had been fined for living an

idle life, and was being escorted home in much distress of
mind by his condoling friends; the Lacedaemonian was
much surprised at it and desired his friend to show him
the man who was condemned for living like a freeman.
So much beneath them did they esteem the frivolous devotion of time and attention to the mechanical arts and to
money-making.

It need not be said that upon the prohibition of gold and
silver, all lawsuits immediately ceased, for there was now
neither avarice nor poverty amongst them, but equality,
where every one's wants were supplied, and independence,
because those wants were so small. All their time, except
when they were in the field, was taken up by the choral
dances and the festivals, in hunting, and in attendance on
the exercise-grounds and the places of public conversation. Those who were under thirty years of age were not
allowed to go into the market-place, but had the necessaries of their family supplied by the care of their relations
and lovers; nor was it for the credit of elderly men to be
seen too often in the market-place; it was esteemed more
suitable for them to frequent the exercise-grounds and
places of conversation, where they spent their leisure ra-
tionally in conversation, not on money-making and market-
prices, but for the most part in passing judgment on some
action worth considering; extolling the good, and censur-
ing those who were otherwise, and that in a light and
sportive manner, conveying, without too much gravity, lessons of advice and improvement. Nor was Lycurgus himself unduly austere; it was he who dedicated, says Sosibius,
the little statue of Laughter. Mirth, introduced seasonably
at their suppers and places of common entertainment, was
to serve as a sort of sweetmeat to accompany their strict
and hard life. To conclude, he bred up his citizens in such
a way that they neither would nor could live by themselves;
they were to make themselves one with the public good,
and, clustering like bees around their commander, be by
their zeal and public spirit carried all but out of themselves,
and devoted wholly to their country. What their sentiments
were will better appear by a few of their sayings. Paedare-

tus, not being admitted into the list of the three hundred, returned home with a joyful face, well pleased to find that there were in Sparta three hundred better men than himself. And Polycratidas, being sent with some others ambassador to the lieutenants of the king of Persia, being asked by them whether they came in a private or in a public character, answered, "In a public, if we succeed; if not, in a private character." Argileonis, asking some who came from Amphipolis if her son Brasidas died courageously and as became a Spartan, on their beginning to praise him to a high degree, and saying there was not such another left in Sparta, answered, "Do not say so; Brasidas was a good and brave man, but there are in Sparta many better than he."

The senate, as I said before, consisted of those who were Lycurgus's chief aiders and assistants in his plans. The vacancies he ordered to be supplied out of the best and most deserving men past sixty years old, and we need not wonder if there was much striving for it; for what more glorious competition could there be amongst men, than one in which it was not contested who was swiftest among the swift or strongest of the strong, but who of many wise and good was wisest and best, and fittest to be intrusted for ever after, as the reward of his merits, with the supreme authority of the commonwealth, and with power over the lives, franchises, and highest interests of all his countrymen? The manner of their election was as follows: The people being called together, some selected persons were locked up in a room near the place of election, so contrived that they could neither see nor be seen, but could only hear the noise of the assembly without; for they decided this, as most other affairs of moment, by the shouts of the people. This done, the competitors were not brought in and presented all together, but one after another by lot, and passed in order through the assembly without speaking a word. Those who were locked up had writing-tables with them, in which they recorded and marked each shout by its loudness, without knowing in favour of which candidate each of them was made, but merely that they came first, second, third, and so forth. He who was found to have the most and loudest acclamations was declared senator duly elected. Upon this he had a garland set upon his head, and went in procession to all the temples to give thanks to the gods; a great number of young men followed him with applauses, and women, also, singing verses in his honour, and extolling the virtue and happiness of his life. As he went round the city in this manner, each of his relations and friends set a table before him, saying "The city honours you with this banquet;" but he, instead of accepting, passed round to the common table where he formerly used to eat, and was served as before, excepting that now he had a second allowance, which he took and put by. By the time supper was ended, the women who were of kin to him had come about the door; and he, beckoning to her whom he most esteemed, presented to her the portion he had saved, saying, that it had been a mark of esteem to him, and was so now to her; upon which she was triumphantly waited upon home by the women.

Touching burials, Lycurgus made very wise regulations; for, first of all, to cut off all superstition, he allowed them to bury their dead within the city, and even round about their temples, to the end that their youth might be accustomed to such spectacles, and not be afraid to see a dead body, or imagine that to touch a corpse or to tread upon a grave would defile a man. In the next place, he commanded them to put nothing into the ground with them, except, if they pleased, a few olive leaves, and the scarlet cloth that they were wrapped in. He would not suffer the names to be inscribed, except only of men who fell in the wars, or women who died in a sacred office. The time, too, appointed for mourning, was very short, eleven days; on the twelfth, they were to do sacrifice to Ceres, and leave it off; so that we may see, that as he cut off all superfluity, so in things necessary there was nothing so small and trivial which did not express some homage of virtue or scorn of vice. He filled Lacedaemon all through with proofs and examples of good conduct; with the constant sight of which from their youth up the people would hardly fail to be gradually formed and advanced in virtue.

And this was the reason why he forbade them to travel abroad, and go about acquainting themselves with foreign rules of morality, the habits of ill-educated people, and different views of government. Withal he banished from Lacedaemon all strangers who would not give a very good reason for their coming thither; not because he was afraid lest they should inform themselves of and imitate his manner of government (as Thucydides says), or learn anything to their good; but rather lest they should introduce something contrary to good manners. With strange people, strange words must be admitted; these novelties produce novelties in thought; and on these follow views and feelings whose discordant character destroys the harmony of the state. He was as careful to save his city from the infection of foreign bad habits, as men usually are to prevent the introduction of a pestilence.

Hitherto I, for my part, see no sign of injustice or want of equity in the laws of Lycurgus, though some who admit them to be well contrived to make good soldiers, pronounce them defective in point of justice. The Cryptia, perhaps (if it were one of Lycurgus's ordinances, as Aristotle says it was), gave both him and Plato, too, this opinion alike of the lawgiver and his government. By this ordinance, the magistrates despatched privately some of the ablest of the young men into the country, from time to time, armed only with their daggers, and taking a little necessary provision with them; in the daytime, they hid themselves in out-of-the-way places, and there lay close, but in the night issued out into the highways, and killed all the Helots they could light upon; sometimes they set upon them by day, as they were at work in the fields, and murdered them. As, also, Thucydides, in his history of the Peloponnesian war, tells us, that a good number of them, after being singled out for their bravery by the Spartans, garlanded, as enfranchised persons, and led about to all the temples in token of honours, shortly after disappeared all of a sudden, being about the number of two thousand; and no man either then or since could give an account how they came by their deaths. And Aristotle, in particular, adds, that the ephori, so soon as

they were entered into their office, used to declare war
against them, that they might be massacred without a
breach of religion. It is confessed, on all hands, that the
Spartans dealt with them very hardly; for it was a common thing to force them to drink to excess, and to lead
them in that condition into their public halls, that the children might see what a sight a drunken man is; they made
them to dance low dances, and sing ridiculous songs, forbidding them expressly to meddle with any of a better kind.
And accordingly, when the Thebans made their invasion
into Laconia, and took a great number of the Helots, they
could by no means persuade them to sing the verses of
Terpander, Alcman, or Spendon, "For," said they, "the masters do not like it." So that it was truly observed by one,
that in Sparta he who was free was most so, and he that
was a slave there, the greatest slave in the world. For my
part, I am of opinion that these outrages and cruelties
began to be exercised in Sparta at a later time, especially
after the great earthquake, when the Helots made a general
insurrection, and, joining with the Messenians, laid the
country waste, and brought the greatest danger upon the
city. For I cannot persuade myself to ascribe to Lycurgus
so wicked and barbarous a course, judging of him from the
gentleness of his disposition and justice upon all other
occasions; to which the oracle also testified.

When he perceived that his more important institutions
had taken root in the minds of his countrymen, that custom had rendered them familiar and easy, that his commonwealth was now grown up and able to go alone, then,
as Plato somewhere tells us, the Maker of the world, when
first he saw it existing and beginning its motion, felt joy,
even so Lycurgus, viewing with joy and satisfaction the
greatness and beauty of his political structure, now fairly
at work and in motion, conceived the thought to make it
immortal too, and, as far as human forecast could reach,
to deliver it down unchangeable to posterity. He called an
extraordinary assembly of all the people, and told them
that he now thought everything reasonably well established,
both for the happiness and the virtue of the state; but that

there was one thing still behind, of the greatest importance, which he thought not fit to impart until he had consulted the oracle; in the meantime, his desire was that they would observe the laws without any the least alteration until his return, and then he would do as the god should direct him. They all consented readily, and bade him hasten his journey; but, before he departed, he administered an oath to the two kings, the senate, and the whole commons, to abide by and maintain the established form of polity until Lycurgus should be come back. This done, he set out for Delphi, and, having sacrificed to Apollo, asked him whether the laws he had established were good, and sufficient for a people's happiness and virtue. The oracle answered that the laws were excellent, and that the people, while it observed them, should live in the height of renown. Lycurgus took the oracle in writing, and sent it over to Sparta; and, having sacrificed the second time to Apollo, and taken leave of his friends and his son, he resolved that the Spartans should not be released from the oath they had taken, and that he would, of his own act, close his life where he was. He was now about that age in which life was still tolerable, and yet might be quitted without regret. Everything, moreover, about him was in a sufficiently prosperous condition. He therefore made an end of himself by a total abstinence from food, thinking it a statesman's duty to make his very death, if possible, an act of service to the state, and even in the end of his life to give some example of virtue and effect some useful purpose. He would, on the one hand, crown and consummate his own happiness by a death suitable to so honourable a life, and on the other hand, would secure to his countrymen the enjoyment of the advantages he had spent his life in obtaining for them, since they had solemnly sworn the maintenance of his institutions until his return. Nor was he deceived in his expectations, for the city of Lacedaemon continued the chief city of all Greece for the space of five hundred years, in strict observance of Lycurgus's laws; in all which time there was no manner of alteration made, during the reign of fourteen kings down to the time of Agis, the son of Archidamus. For the new creation of the ephori, though thought to be in favour of the people, was so far from diminishing, that it very much heightened, the aristocratical character of the government.

In the time of Agis, gold and silver first flowed into Sparta, and with them all those mischiefs which attend the immoderate desire of riches. Lysander promoted this disorder; for by bringing in rich spoils from the wars, although himself incorrupt, he yet by this means filled his country with avarice and luxury, and subverted the laws and ordinances of Lycurgus; so long as which were in force, the aspect presented by Sparta was rather that of a rule of life followed by one wise and temperate man, than of the political government of a nation. And as the poets feign of Hercules, that, with his lion's skin and his club, he went over the world, punishing lawless and cruel tyrants, so may it be said of the Lacedaemonians, that, with a common staff and a coarse coat, they gained the willing and joyful obedience of Greece, through whose whole extent they suppressed unjust usurpations and despotisms, arbitrated in war, and composed civil dissensions; and this often without so much as taking down one buckler, but barely by sending some one single deputy to whose direction all at once submitted, like bees swarming and taking their places around their prince. Such a fund of order and equity, enough and to spare for others, existed in their state.

And therefore I cannot but wonder at those who say that the Spartans were good subjects, but bad governors, and for proof of it allege a saying of King Theopompus, who when one said that Sparta held up so long because their kings could command so well, replied, "Nay, rather because the people know so well how to obey." For people do not obey, unless rulers know how to command; obedience is a lesson taught by commanders. A true leader himself creates the obedience of his own followers; as it is the last attainment in the art of riding to make a horse gentle and tractable, so is it of the science of government, to inspire men with a willingness to obey. The Lacedaemonians inspired men not with a mere willingness, but with an ab-

solute desire to be their subjects. For they did not send petitions to them for ships or money, or a supply of armed
men, but only for a Spartan commander; and, having obtained one, used him with honour and reverence; so the
Sicilians behaved to Gylippus, the Chalcidians to Brasidas,
and all the Greeks in Asia to Lysander, Callicratidas, and
Agesilaus; they styled them the composers and chasteners
of each people or prince they were sent to, and had their
eyes always fixed upon the city of Sparta itself, as the perfect model of good manners and wise government. The
rest seemed as scholars, they the masters of Greece; and
to this Stratonicus pleasantly alluded, when in jest he pretended to make a law that the Athenians should conduct
religious processions and the mysteries, the Eleans should
preside at the Olympic games, and, if either did amiss, the
Lacedaemonians be beaten. Antisthenes, too, one of the
scholars of Socrates, said, in earnest, of the Thebans, when
they were elated by their victory at Leuctra, that they
looked like school-boys who had beaten their master.

However, it was not the design of Lycurgus that his city
should govern a great many others; he thought rather that
the happiness of a state, as a private man, consisted chiefly
in the exercise of virtue, and in the concord of the inhabitants; his aim, therefore, in all his arrangements, was to
make and keep them free-minded, self-dependent, and temperate. And therefore all those who have written well on
politics, as Plato, Diogenes and Zeno, have taken Lycurgus
for their model, leaving behind them, however, mere projects and words; whereas Lycurgus was the author, not in
writing but in reality, of a government which none else
could so much as copy; and while men in general have
treated the individual philosophic character as unattain-
able, he, by the example of a complete philosophic state,
raised himself high above all other lawgivers of Greece. And
so Aristotle says they did him less honour at Lacedaemon
after his death than he deserved, although he has a temple
there, and they offer sacrifices yearly to him as to a god.

It is reported that when his bones were brought home to
Sparta his tomb was struck with lightning, an accident

which befell no eminent person but himself and Euripides, who was buried at Arethusa in Macedonia; and it may serve that poet's admirers as a testimony in his favour, that he had in this the same fate with that holy man and favourite of the gods. Some say Lycurgus died in Cirrha. Apollothemis says, after he had come to Elis; Timaeus and Aristoxenus, that he ended his life in Crete; Aristoxenus adds that his tomb is shown by the Cretans in the district of Pergamus, near the strangers' road. He left an only son, Antiorus, on whose death without issue his family became extinct. But his relations and friends kept up an annual commemoration of him down to a long time after; and the days of the meeting were called Lycurgides. Aristocrates, the son of Hipparchus, says that he died in Crete, and that his Cretan friends, in accordance with his own request, when they had burned his body, scattered the ashes into the sea; for fear lest, if his relics should be transported to Lacedaemon, the people might pretend to be released from their oaths, and make innovations in the government. Thus much may suffice for the life and actions of Lycurgus.

✤

SOLON

Didymus, the grammarian, in his answer to Asclepiades concerning Solon's Tables of Law, mentions a passage of one Philocles, who states that Solon's father's name was Euphorion, contrary to the opinion of all others who have written concerning him; for they generally agree that he was the son of Execestides, a man of moderate wealth and power in the city, but of a most noble stock, being descended from Codrus; his mother, as Heraclides Ponticus affirms, was cousin to Pisistratus's mother, and the two at first were great friends, partly because they were akin, and partly because of Pisistratus's noble qualities and beauty. And they say Solon loved him; and that is the reason, I suppose, that when afterwards they differed about the government, their enmity never produced any hot and violent passion, they remembered their old kindnesses, and retained—

"Still in its embers living the strong fire"

of their love and dear affection. For that Solon was not proof against beauty, nor of courage to stand up to passion and meet it—

"Hand to hand as in the ring,"

we may conjecture by his poems, and one of his laws, in which there are practices forbidden to slaves, which he would appear, therefore, to recommend to freemen. Pisistratus, it is stated, was similarly attached to one Charmus;

he it was who dedicated the figure of Love in the Academy, where the runners in the sacred torch race light their torches. Solon, as Hermippus writes, when his father had ruined his estate in doing benefits and kindnesses to other men, though he had friends enough that were willing to contribute to his relief, yet was ashamed to be beholden to others, since he was descended from a family who were accustomed to do kindnesses rather than receive them; and therefore applied himself to merchandise in his youth; though others assure us that he travelled rather to get learning and experience than to make money. It is certain that he was a lover of knowledge, for when he was old he would say, that he—

"Each day grew older, and learnt something new;"

and yet no admirer of riches, esteeming as equally wealthy the man—

"Who hath both gold and silver in his hand,
  Horses and mules, and acres of wheat-land,
  And him whose all is decent food to eat,
  Clothes to his back and shoes upon his feet,
  And a young wife and child, since so 'twill be,
  And no more years than will with that agree;"

and in another place—

"Wealth I would have, but wealth by wrong procure
  I would not; justice, e'en if slow, is sure."

And it is perfectly possible for a good man and a statesman, without being solicitous for superfluities, to show some concern for competent necessaries. In his time, as Hesiod says,—"Work was a shame to none," nor was distinction made with respect to trade, but merchandise was a noble calling, which brought home the good things which the barbarous nations enjoyed, was the occasion of friendship with their kings, and a great source of experience. Some merchants have built great cities, as Protis, the founder of Massilia, to whom the Gauls, near the Rhone, were much attached. Some report also, that Thales and Hippocrates the mathematician traded; and that Plato defrayed the charges of his travels by selling oil in Egypt. Solon's softness and profuseness, his popular rather than philosophical tone about pleasure in his poems, have been ascribed to his trading life; for, having suffered a thousand dangers, it was natural they should be recompensed with some gratifications and enjoyments; but that he accounted himself rather poor than rich is evident from the lines—

> "Some wicked men are rich, some good are poor,
>   We will not change our virtue for their store:
> Virtue's a thing that none can take away;
>   But money changes owners all the day."

At first he used his poetry only in trifles, not for any serious purpose, but simply to pass away his idle hours; but afterwards he introduced moral sentences and state matters, which he did, not to record them merely as an historian, but to justify his own actions, and sometimes to correct, chastise, and stir up the Athenians to noble performances. Some report that he designed to put his laws into heroic verse, and that they began thus:—

> "We humbly beg a blessing on our laws
>   From mighty Jove, and honour, and applause."

In philosophy, as most of the wise men then, he chiefly esteemed the political part of morals; in physics, he was very plain and antiquated, as appears by this:—

> "It is the clouds that make the snow and hail,
>   And thunder comes from lightning without fail;
> The sea is stormy when the winds have blown,
>   But it deals fairly when 'tis left alone."

And, indeed, it is probable that at that time Thales alone
had raised philosophy above mere practice into speculation;
and the rest of the wise men were so called from prudence
in political concerns. It is said, that they had an interview
at Delphi, and another at Corinth, by the procurement of
Periander, who made a meeting for them, and a supper.
But their reputation was chiefly raised by sending the tripod
to them all, by their modest refusal, and complaisant yielding to one another. For, as the story goes, some of the
Coans fishing with a net, some strangers, Milesians, bought
the draught at a venture; the net brought up a golden tripod, which, they say, Helen, at her return from Troy,
upon the remembrance of an old prophecy, threw in there.
Now, the strangers at first contesting with the fishers about
the tripod, and the cities espousing the quarrel so far as to
engage themselves in a war, Apollo decided the controversy by commanding to present it to the wisest man; and
first it was sent to Miletus to Thales, the Coans freely presenting him with that for which they fought against the
whole body of the Milesians; but Thales declaring Bias the
wiser person, it was sent to him; from him to another; and
so, going round them all, it came to Thales a second time;
and, at last, being carried from Miletus to Thebes, was
there dedicated to Apollo Ismenius. Theophrastus writes
that it was first presented to Bias at Priene; and next to
Thales at Miletus, and so through all it returned to Bias,
and was afterwards sent to Delphi. This is the general
report, only some, instead of a tripod, say this present was
a cup sent by Croesus; others, a piece of plate that one
Bathycles had left. It is stated, that Anacharsis and Solon,
and Solon and Thales, were familiarly acquainted and some
have delivered parts of their discourse; for, they say, Anacharsis, coming to Athens, knocked at Solon's door, and
told him, that he, being a stranger, was come to be his guest,
and contract a friendship with him; and Solon replying, "It
is better to make friends at home," Anacharsis replied,
"Then you that are at home make friendship with me."
Solon, somewhat surprised at the readiness of the repartee,
received him kindly, and kept him some time with him,

being already engaged in public business and the compilation of his laws; which, when Anacharsis understood, he laughed at him for imagining the dishonesty and covetousness of his countrymen could be restrained by written laws, which were like spiders' webs, and would catch, it is true, the weak and poor, but easily be broken by the mighty and rich. To this Solon rejoined that men keep their promises when neither side can get anything by the breaking of them; and he would so fit his laws to the citizens, that all should understand it was more eligible to be just than to break the laws. But the event rather agreed with the conjecture of Anacharsis than Solon's hope. Anacharsis, being once at the Assembly, expressed his wonder at the fact that in Greece wise men spoke and fools decided.

Solon went, they say, to Thales, at Miletus, and wondered that Thales took no care to get him a wife and children. To this, Thales made no answer for the present; but a few days after procured a stranger to pretend that he had left Athens ten days ago; and Solon inquiring what news there, the man, according to his instructions, replied, "None but a young man's funeral, which the whole city attended; for he was the son, they said, of an honourable man, the most virtuous of the citizens, who was not then at home, but had been travelling a long time." Solon replied, "What a miserable man is he! But what was his name?" "I have heard it," says the man, "but have now forgotten it, only there was a great talk of his wisdom and his justice." Thus Solon was drawn on by every answer, and his fears heightened, till at last, being extremely concerned, he mentioned his own name, and asked the stranger if that young man was called Solon's son; and the stranger assenting, he began to beat his head, and to do and say all that is usual with men in transports of grief. But Thales took his hand, and, with a smile, said, "These things, Solon, keep me from marriage and rearing children, which are too great for even your constancy to support; however, be not concerned at the report, for it is a fiction." This Hermippus relates, from Pataecus, who boasted that he had Aesop's soul.

However, it is irrational and poor-spirited not to seek conveniences for fear of losing them, for upon the same account we should not allow ourselves to like wealth, glory, or wisdom, since we may fear to be deprived of all these; nay, even virtue itself, than which there is no greater nor more desirable possession, is often suspended by sickness or drugs. Now Thales, though unmarried, could not be free from solicitude unless he likewise felt no care for his friends, his kinsman, or his country; yet we are told he adopted Cybisthus, his sister's son. For the soul, having a principle of kindness in itself, and being born to love, as well as perceive, think, or remember, inclines and fixes upon some stranger, when a man has none of his own to embrace. And alien or illegitimate objects insinuate themselves into his affections, as into some estate that lacks lawful heirs; and with affection come anxiety and care; insomuch that you may see men that use the strongest language against the marriage-bed and the fruit of it, when some servant's or concubine's child is sick or dies, almost killed with grief, and abjectly lamenting. Some have given way to shameful and desperate sorrow at the loss of a dog or horse; others have borne the death of virtuous children without any extravagant or unbecoming grief, have passed the rest of their lives like men, and according to the principles of reason. It is not affection, it is weakness that brings men, unarmed against fortune by reason, into these endless pains and terrors; and they indeed have not even the present enjoyment of what they dote upon, the possibility of the future loss causing them continual pangs, tremors, and distresses. We must not provide against the loss of wealth by poverty, or of friends by refusing all acquaintance, or of children by having none, but by morality and reason. But of this too much.

Now, when the Athenians were tired with a tedious and difficult war that they conducted against the Megarians for the island Salamis, and made a law that it should be death for any man, by writing or speaking to assert that the city ought to endeavour to recover it, Solon, vexed at the disgrace, and perceiving thousands of the youth wished for

somebody to begin, but did not dare to stir first for fear
of the law, counterfeited a distraction, and by his own
family it was spread about the city that he was mad. He
then secretly composed some elegiac verses, and getting
them by heart, that it might seem extempore, ran out into
the market-place with a cap upon his head, and, the people gathering about him, got upon the herald's stand, and
sang that elegy which begins thus:—

> "I am a herald come from Salamis the fair,
>   My news from thence my verses shall declare."

The poem is called Salamis; it contains an hundred verses
very elegantly written; when it had been sung, his friends
commended it, and especially Pisistratus exhorted the citizens to obey his directions; insomuch that they recalled the
law, and renewed the war under Solon's conduct. The popular tale is, that with Pisistratus he sailed to Colias, and,
finding the women, according to the custom of the country
there, sacrificing to Ceres, he sent a trusty friend to Salamis,
who should pretend himself a renegade, and advise them,
if they desired to seize the chief Athenian women, to come
with him at once to Colias; the Megarians presently sent
off men in the vessel with him; and Solon, seeing it put off
from the island, commanded the women to be gone, and
some beardless youths, dressed in their clothes, their shoes
and caps, and privately armed with daggers, to dance and
play near the shore till the enemies had landed and the vessel was in their power. Things being thus ordered, the
Megarians were lured with the appearance, and, coming
to the shore, jumped out, eager who should first seize a
prize, so that not one of them escaped; and the Athenians
set sail for the island and took it.

Others say that it was not taken this way, but that he
first received this oracle from Delphi:—

> "Those heroes that in fair Asopia rest,
>   All buried with their faces to the west,
>   Go and appease with offerings of the best;"

and that Solon, sailing by night to the island, sacrificed to the heroes Periphemus and Cychreus, and then taking five hundred Athenian volunteers (a law having passed that those that took the island should be highest in the government), with a number of fisher-boats and one thirty-oared ship, anchored in a bay of Salamis that looks towards Nisaea; and the Megarians that were then in the island, hearing only an uncertain report, hurried to their arms, and sent a ship to reconnoitre the enemies. This ship Solon took, and, securing the Megarians, manned it with Athenians, and gave them orders to sail to the island with as much privacy as possible; meantime he, with the other soldiers, marched against the Megarians by land, and whilst they were fighting, those from the ship took the city. And this narrative is confirmed by the following solemnity, that was afterwards observed: An Athenian ship used to sail silently at first to the island, then, with noise and a great shout, one leapt out armed, and with a loud cry ran to the promontory Sciradium to meet those that approached upon the land. And just by there stands a temple which Solon dedicated to Mars. For he beat the Megarians, and as many as were not killed in the battle he sent away upon conditions.

The Megarians, however, still contending, and both sides having received considerable losses, they chose the Spartans for arbitrators. Now, many affirm that Homer's authority did Solon a considerable kindness, and that, introducing a line into the Catalogue of Ships, when the matter was to be determined, he read the passage as follows:—

> "Twelve ships from Salamis stout Ajax brought,
> And ranked his men where the Athenians fought."

The Athenians, however, call this but an idle story, and report that Solon made it appear to the judges, that Philaeus and Eurysaces, the sons of Ajax, being made citizens of Athens, gave them the island, and that one of them dwelt at Brauron in Attica, the other at Melite; and they have a township of Philaidae, to which Pisistratus belonged, deriving its name from this Philaeus. Solon took a farther argument against the Megarians from the dead bodies, which, he said, were not buried after their fashion, but according to the Athenian; for the Megarians turn the corpse to the east, the Athenians to the west. But Hereas the Megarian denies this, and affirms that they likewise turn the body to the west, and also that the Athenians have a separate tomb for everybody, but the Megarians put two or three into one. However, some of Apollo's oracles, where he calls Salamis Ionian, made much for Solon. This matter was determined by five Spartans, Critolaidas, Amompharetus, Hypsechidas, Anaxilas, and Cleomenes.

For this, Solon grew famed and powerful; but his advice in favour of defending the oracle at Delphi, to give aid, and not to suffer the Cirrhaeans to profane it, but to maintain the honour of the god, got him most repute among the Greeks; for upon his persuasion the Amphictyons undertook the war, as amongst others, Aristotle affirms, in his enumeration of the victors at the Pythian games, where he makes Solon the author of this counsel. Solon, however, was not general in that expedition, as Hermippus states, out of Evanthes the Samian; for Aeschines the orator says no such thing, and, in the Delphian register, Alcmaeon, not Solon, is named as commander of the Athenians.

Now the Cylonian pollution had a long while disturbed the commonwealth, ever since the time when Megacles the archon persuaded the conspirators with Cylon that took sanctuary in Minerva's temple to come down and stand to a fair trial. And they, tying a thread to the image, and holding one end of it, went down to the tribunal; but when they came to the temple of the Furies, the thread broke of its own accord, upon which, as if the goddess had refused them protection, they were seized by Megacles and the other magistrates; as many as were without the temples were stoned, these that fled for sanctuary were butchered at the altar, and only those escaped who made supplication to the wives of the magistrates. But they from that time were considered under pollution, and regarded with hatred. The remainder of the faction of Cylon grew strong again, and had continual quarrels with the family of Megacles; and now the quarrel being at its height, and the people divided, Solon, being in reputation, interposed with the chiefest of the Athenians, and by entreaty and admonition persuaded the polluted to submit to a trial and the decision of three hundred noble citizens. And Myron of Phlya being their accuser, they were found guilty, and as many as were then alive were banished, and the bodies of the dead were dug up, and scattered beyond the confines of the country. In the midst of these distractions, the Megarians falling upon them, they lost Nisaea and Salamis again; besides, the city was disturbed with superstitious fears and strange appearances, and the priests declared that the sacrifices intimated some villainies and pollutions that were to be expiated. Upon this, they sent for Epimenides the Phaestian from Crete, who is counted the seventh wise man by those that will not admit Periander into the number. He seems to have been thought a favourite of heaven, possessed of knowledge in all the supernatural and ritual parts of religion; and, therefore, the men of his age called him a new Curies, and son of a nymph named Balte. When he came to Athens, and grew acquainted with Solon, he served him in many instances, and prepared the way for his legislation. He made them moderate in their forms of worship, and abated their mourning by ordering some sacrifices presently after the funeral, and taking off those severe and barbarous ceremonies which the women usually practised; but the greatest benefit was his purifying and sanctifying the city, by certain propitiatory and expiatory lustrations, and foundations of sacred buildings, by that means making them more submissive to justice, and more inclined to harmony. It is reported that, looking upon Munychia, and considering a long while, he said to those that stood by, "How blind is man in future things! for did the Athenians foresee what mischief this would do their city, they would even eat it with their own teeth to be rid of it." A similar anticipation is ascribed to Thales; they say he commanded his friends to bury him in an obscure and contemned quarter of the territory of Miletus, saying that it should some day be the market-place of the Milesians. Epimenides, being much honoured, and receiving from the city rich offers of large gifts and privileges, requested but one branch of the sacred olive, and, on that being granted, returned.

The Athenians, now the Cylonian sedition was over and the polluted gone into banishment, fell into their old quarrels about the government, there being as many different parties as there were diversities in the country. The Hill quarter favoured democracy, the Plain, oligarchy, and those that lived by the Seaside stood for a mixed sort of government, and so hindered either of the other parties from prevailing. And the disparity of fortune between the rich and the poor, at that time, also reached its height; so that the city seemed to be in a truly dangerous condition, and no other means for freeing it from disturbances and settling it to be possible but a despotic power. All the people were indebted to the rich; and either they tilled their land for their creditors, paying them a sixth part of the increase, and were, therefore, called Hectemorii and Thetes, or else they engaged their body for the debt, and might be seized, and either sent into slavery at home, or sold to strangers; some (for no law forbade it) were forced to sell their children, or fly their country to avoid the cruelty of their creditors; but the most part and the bravest of them began to combine together and encourage one another to stand to it, to choose a leader, to liberate the condemned debtors, divide the land, and change the government.

Then the wisest of the Athenians, perceiving Solon was of all men the only one not implicated in the troubles, that he had not joined in the exactions of the rich, and was not involved in the necessities of the poor, pressed him to succour the commonwealth and compose the differences. Though Phanias the Lesbian affirms, that Solon, to save his country, put a trick upon both parties, and privately promised the poor a division of the lands, and the rich security for their debts. Solon, however, himself says, that it was reluctantly at first that he engaged in state affairs, being afraid of the pride of one party and the greediness of the other; he was chosen archon, however, after Philom-

brotus, and empowered to be an arbitrator and lawgiver;
the rich consenting because he was wealthy, the poor because he was honest. There was a saying of his current before the election, that when things are *even* there never can
be war, and this pleased both parties, the wealthy and the
poor; the one conceiving him to mean, when all have
their fair proportion; the others, when all are absolutely
equal. Thus, there being great hopes on both sides, the
chief men pressed Solon to take the government into his
own hands, and, when he was once settled, manage the
business freely and according to his pleasure; and many
of the commons, perceiving it would be a difficult change
to be effected by law and reason, were willing to have one
wise and just man set over the affairs; and some say that
Solon had this oracle from Apollo—

> "Take the mid-seat, and be the vessel's guide;
>   Many in Athens are upon your side."

But chiefly his familiar friends chid him for disaffecting
monarchy only because of the name, as if the virtue of the
ruler could not make it a lawful form; Euboea had made
this experiment when it chose Tynnondas, and Mitylene,
which had made Pittacus its prince; yet this could not
shake Solon's resolution; but, as they say, he replied to his
friends, that it was true a tyranny was a very fair spot,
but it had no way down from it; and in a copy of verses to
Phocus he writes—

> "that I spared my land,
> And withheld from usurpation and from violence my hand,
> And forbore to fix a stain and a disgrace on my good name,
> I regret not; I believe that it will be my chiefest fame."

From which it is manifest that he was a man of great reputation before he gave his laws. The several mocks that were
put upon him for refusing the power, he records in these
words:—

"Solon surely was a dreamer, and a man of simple mind;
When the gods would give him fortune, he of his own will
    declined;
When the net was full of fishes, over-heavy thinking it,
He declined to haul it up, through want of heart and
    want of wit.
Had but I that chance of riches and of kingship, for one
    day,
I would give my skin for flaying, and my house to die
    away."

Thus he makes the many and the low people speak of him. Yet, though he refused the government, he was not too mild in the affair; he did not show himself mean and submissive to the powerful, nor make his laws to pleasure those that chose him. For where it was well before, he applied no remedy, nor altered anything, for fear lest—

"Overthrowing altogether and disordering the state,"

he should be too weak to new-model and recompose it to a tolerable condition; but what he thought he could effect by persuasion upon the pliable, and by force upon the stubborn, this he did, as he himself says—

"With force and justice working both in one."

And, therefore, when he was afterwards asked if he had left the Athenians the best laws that could be given, he replied, "The best they could receive." The way which, the moderns say, the Athenians have of softening the badness of a thing, by ingeniously giving it some pretty and innocent appellation, calling harlots, for example, mistresses, tributes customs, a garrison a guard, and the jail the chamber, seem originally to have been Solon's contrivance, who called cancelling debts Seisacthea, a relief, or disencumbrance. For the first thing which he settled was, that what debts remained should be forgiven, and no man, for the future, should engage the body of his debtor for security.

Though some, as Androtion, affirm that the debts were not cancelled, but the interest only lessened, which sufficiently pleased the people; so that they named this benefit the Seisacthea, together with the enlarging their measures, and raising the value of their money; for he made a pound, which before passed for seventy-three drachmas, go for a hundred; so that, though the number of pieces in the payment was equal, the value was less; which proved a considerable benefit to those that were to discharge great debts, and no loss to the creditors. But most agree that it was the taking off the debts that was called Seisacthea, which is confirmed by some places in his poem, where he takes honour to himself, that—

"The mortgage-stones that covered her, by me
    Removed,—the land that was a slave is free:"

that some who had been seized for their debts he had brought back from other countries, where—

"—so far their lot to roam,
    They had forgot the language of their home;"

and some he had set at liberty—

"Who here in shameful servitude were held."

While he was designing this, a most vexatious thing happened; for when he had resolved to take off the debts, and was considering the proper form and fit beginning for it, he told some of his friends, Conon, Clinias, and Hipponicus, in whom he had a great deal of confidence, that he would not meddle with the lands, but only free the people from their debts; upon which they, using their advantage, made haste and borrowed some considerable sums of money, and purchased some large farms; and when the law was enacted, they kept the possessions, and would not return the money; which brought Solon into great suspicion and dislike, as if he himself had not been abused, but was con-

cerned in the contrivance. But he presently stopped this
suspicion, by releasing his debtors of five talents (for he
had lent so much), according to the law; others, as Poly-
zelus the Rhodian, say fifteen; his friends, however, were
ever afterward called Chreocopidae, repudiators.

In this he pleased neither party, for the rich were angry
for their money, and the poor that the land was not divided, and, as Lycurgus ordered in his commonwealth, all
men reduced to equality. He, it is true, being the eleventh
from Hercules, and having reigned many years in Lacedaemon, had got a great reputation and friends and power,
which he could use in modelling his state; and applying
force more than persuasion, insomuch that he lost his eye
in the scuffle, was able to employ the most effectual means
for the safety and harmony of a state, by not permitting any
to be poor or rich in his commonwealth. Solon could not
rise to that in his polity, being but a citizen of the middle
classes; yet he acted fully up to the height of his power,
having nothing but the good-will and good opinion of his
citizens to rely on; and that he offended the most part, who
looked for another result, he declares in the words—

"Formerly they boasted of me vainly; with averted eyes
  Now they look askance upon me; friends no more, but
      enemies."

And yet had any other man, he says, received the same
power—

  "He would not have forborne, nor let alone,
    But made the fattest of the milk his own."

Soon, however, becoming sensible of the good that was
done, they laid by their grudges, made a public sacrifice,
calling it Seisacthea, and chose Solon to new-model and
make laws for the commonwealth, giving him the entire
power over everything, their magistracies, their assemblies,
courts, and councils; that he should appoint the number,
times of meeting, and what estate they must have that

could be capable of these, and dissolve or continue any of the present constitutions, according to his pleasure.

First, then, he repealed all Draco's laws, except those concerning homicide, because they were too severe, and the punishment too great; for death was appointed for almost all offences, insomuch that those that were convicted of idleness were to die, and those that stole a cabbage or an apple to suffer even as villains that committed sacrilege or murder. So that Demades, in after time, was thought to have said very happily, that Draco's laws were written not with ink but blood; and he himself, being once asked why he made death the punishment of most offences, replied, "Small ones deserve that, and I have no higher for the greater crimes."

Next, Solon, being willing to continue the magistracies in the hands of the rich men, and yet receive the people into the other part of the government, took an account of the citizens' estates, and those that were worth five hundred measures of fruit, dry and liquid, he placed in the first rank, calling them Pentacosiomedimni; those that could keep an horse, or were worth three hundred measures, were named Hippada Teluntes, and made the second class; the Zeugitae, that had two hundred measures, were in the third; and all the others were called Thetes, who were not admitted to any office, but could come to the assembly, and act as jurors; which at first seemed nothing, but afterwards was found an enormous privilege, as almost every matter of dispute came before them in this latter capacity. Even in the cases which he assigned to the archon's cognisance, he allowed an appeal to the courts. Besides, it is said that he was obscure and ambiguous in the wording of his laws, on purpose to increase the honour of his courts; for since their differences could not be adjusted by the letter, they would have to bring all their causes to the judges, who thus were in a manner masters of the laws. Of this equalisation he himself makes mention in this manner:—

"Such power I gave the people as might do,
Abridged not what they had, nor lavished new,

Those that were great in wealth and high in place
My counsel likewise kept from all disgrace.
Before them both I held my shield of might,
And let not either touch the other's right."

And for the greater security of the weak commons, he
gave general liberty of indicting for an act of injury; if any
one was beaten, maimed, or suffered any violence, any
man that would and was able might prosecute the wrong-
doer; intending by this to accustom the citizens, like members of the same body, to resent and be sensible of one another's injuries. And there is a saying of his agreeable to
his law, for, being asked what city was best modelled,
"That," said he, "where those that are not injured try and
punish the unjust as much as those that are."

When he had constituted the Areopagus of those who
had been yearly archons, of which he himself was a member
therefore, observing that the people, now free from their
debts, were unsettled and imperious, he formed another
council of four hundred, a hundred out of each of the
four tribes, which was to inspect all matters before they
were propounded to the people, and to take care that
nothing but what had been first examined should be
brought before the general assembly. The upper council,
or Areopagus, he made inspectors and keepers of the laws,
conceiving that the commonwealth, held by these two councils, like anchors, would be less liable to be tossed by tumults, and the people be more quiet. Such is the general
statement, that Solon instituted the Areopagus; which seems
to be confirmed, because Draco makes no mention of the
Areopagites, but in all causes of blood refers to the Ephetae;
yet Solon's thirteenth table contains the eighth law set down
in these very words: "Whoever before Solon's archonship
were disfranchised, let them be restored, except those that,
being condemned by the Areopagus, Ephetae, or in the
Prytaneum by the kings, for homicide, murder, or designs
against the government, were in banishment when this law
was made;" and these words seem to show that the Areopagus existed before Solon's laws, for who could be con-

demned by that council before his time, if he was the first that instituted the court? unless, which is probable, there is some ellipsis, or want of precision in the language, and it should run thus:—"Those that are convicted of such offences as belong to the cognisance of the Areopagites, Ephetae, or the Prytanes, when this law was made," shall remain still in disgrace, whilst others are restored; of this the reader must judge.

Amongst his other laws, one is very peculiar and surprising, which disfranchises all who stand neuter in a sedition; for it seems he would not have any one remain insensible and regardless of the public good, and securing his private affairs, glory that he has no feeling of the distempers of his country; but at once join with the good party and those that have the right upon their side, assist and venture with them, rather than keep out of harm's way and watch who would get the better. It seems an absurd and foolish law which permits an heiress, if her lawful husband fail her, to take his nearest kinsman; yet some say this law was well contrived against those who, conscious of their own unfitness, yet, for the sake of the portion, would match with heiresses, and make use of law to put a violence upon nature; for now, since she can quit him for whom she pleases, they would either abstain from such marriages, or continue them with disgrace, and suffer for their covetousness and designed affront; it is well done, moreover, to confine her to her husband's nearest kinsman, that the children may be of the same family. Agreeable to this is the law that the bride and bridegroom shall be shut into a chamber, and eat a quince together; and that the husband of an heiress shall consort with her thrice a month; for though there be no children, yet it is an honour and due affection which an husband ought to pay to a virtuous, chaste wife; it takes off all petty differences, and will not permit their little quarrels to proceed to a rupture.

In all other marriages he forbade dowries to be given; the wife was to have three suits of clothes, a little inconsiderable household stuff, and that was all; for he would not have marriages contracted for gain or an estate, but for pure love, kind affection, and birth of children. When the mother of Dionysius desired him to marry her to one of his citizens, "Indeed," said he, "by my tyranny I have broken my country's laws, but cannot put a violence upon those of nature by an unseasonable marriage." Such disorder is never to be suffered in a commonwealth, nor such unseasonable and unloving and unperforming marriages, which attain no due end or fruit; any provident governor or lawgiver might say to an old man that takes a young wife what is said to Philoctetes in the tragedy—

"Truly, in a fit state thou to marry!"

and if he find a young man, with a rich and elderly wife, growing fat in his place, like the partridges, remove him to a young woman of proper age. And of this enough.

Another commendable law of Solon's is that which forbids men to speak evil of the dead; for it is pious to think the deceased sacred, and just, not to meddle with those that are gone, and politic, to prevent the perpetuity of discord. He likewise forbade them to speak evil of the living in the temples, the courts of justice, the public offices, or at the games, or else to pay three drachmas to the person, and two to the public. For never to be able to control passion shows a weak nature and ill-breeding; and always to moderate it is very hard, and to some impossible. And laws must look to possibilities, if the maker designs to punish few in order to their amendment, and not many to no purpose.

He is likewise much commended for his law concerning wills; for before him none could be made, but all the wealth and estate of the deceased belonged to his family; but he by permitting them, if they had no children, to bestow it on whom they pleased, showed that he esteemed friendship a stronger tie than kindred, and affection than necessity; and made every man's estate truly his own. Yet he allowed not all sorts of legacies, but those only which were not extorted by the frenzy of a disease, charms, imprisonment, force, or the persuasions of a wife; with good reason thinking that being seduced into wrong was as bad as being forced, and that between deceit and necessity, flattery and compulsion, there was little difference, since both may equally suspend the exercise of reason.

He regulated the walks, feasts, and mourning of the women, and took away everything that was either unbecoming or immodest; when they walked abroad, no more than three articles of dress were allowed them; an obol's worth of meat and drink; and no basket above a cubit high; and at night they were not to go about unless in a chariot with a torch before them. Mourners tearing themselves to raise pity, and set wailings, and at one man's funeral to lament for another, he forbade. To offer an ox at the grave was not permitted, nor to bury above three pieces of dress with the body, or visit the tombs of any besides their own family, unless at the very funeral; most of which are likewise forbidden by our laws, but this is further added in ours, that those that are convicted of extravagance in their mournings are to be punished as soft and effeminate by the censors of women.

Observing the city to be filled with persons that flocked from all parts into Attica for security of living, and that most of the country was barren and unfruitful, and that traders at sea import nothing to those that could give them nothing in exchange, he turned his citizens to trade, and made a law that no son be obliged to relieve a father who had not bred him up to any calling. It is true, Lycurgus, having a city free from all strangers, and land, according to Euripides—

"Large for large hosts, for twice their number much,"

and, above all, an abundance of labourers about Sparta, who should not be left idle, but be kept down with continual toil and work, did well to take off his citizens from laborious and mechanical occupations, and keep them to their arms, and teach them only the art of war. But Solon, fitting his laws to the state of things, and not making things to suit his laws, and finding the ground scarce rich enough to main-

tain the husbandmen, and altogether incapable of feeding
an unoccupied and leisured multitude, brought trades into
credit, and ordered the Areopagites to examine how every
man got his living, and chastise the idle. But that law was
yet more rigid which, as Heraclides Ponticus delivers, declared the sons of unmarried mothers not obliged to relieve their fathers; for he that avoids the honourable form
of union shows that he does not take a woman for children,
but for pleasure, and thus gets his just reward, and has
taken away from himself every title to upbraid his children,
to whom he has made their very birth a scandal and reproach.

Solon's laws in general about women are his strangest;
for he permitted any one to kill an adulterer that found
him in the act; but if any one forced a free woman, a hundred drachmas was the fine; if he enticed her, twenty; except those that sell themselves openly, that is, harlots, who
go openly to those that hire them. He made it unlawful
to sell a daughter or a sister, unless, being yet unmarried,
she was found wanton. Now it is irrational to punish the
same crime sometimes very severely and without remorse,
and sometimes very lightly, and as it were in sport, with a
trivial fine; unless there being little money then in Athens,
scarcity made those mulcts the more grievous punishment.
In the valuation for sacrifices, a sheep and a bushel were
both estimated at a drachma; the victor in the Isthmian
games was to have for reward an hundred drachmas; the
conqueror in the Olympian, five hundred; he that brought a
wolf, five drachmas; for a whelp, one; the former sum, as
Demetrius the Phalerian asserts, was the value of an ox,
the latter, of a sheep. The prices which Solon, in his sixteenth table, sets on choice victims, were naturally far
greater; yet they, too, are very low in comparison of the
present. The Athenians were, from the beginning, great
enemies to wolves, their fields being better for pasture than
corn. Some affirm their tribes did not take their names from
the sons of Ion, but from the different sorts of occupation
that they followed; the soldiers were called Hoplitae, the

craftsmen Ergades, and, of the remaining two, the farmers Gedeontes, and the shepherds and graziers Aegicores.

Since the country has but few rivers, lakes, or large springs, and many used wells which they had dug, there was a law made, that, where there was a public well within a *hippicon*, that is, four furlongs, all should draw at that; but when it was farther off, they should try and procure a well of their own; and if they had dug ten fathoms deep and could find no water, they had liberty to fetch a pitcherful of four gallons and a half in a day from their neighbours'; for he thought it prudent to make provision against want, but not to supply laziness. He showed skill in his orders about planting, for any one that would plant another tree was not to set it within five feet of his neighbour's field; but if a fig or an olive not within nine; for their roots spread farther, nor can they be planted near all sorts of trees without damage, for they draw away the nourishment, and in some cases are noxious by their effluvia. He that would dig a pit or a ditch was to dig it at the distance of its own depth from his neighbour's ground; and he that would raise stocks of bees was not to place them within three hundred feet of those which another had already raised.

He permitted only oil to be exported, and those that exported any other fruit, the archon was solemnly to curse, or else pay an hundred drachmas himself; and this law was written in his first table, and, therefore, let none think it incredible, as some affirm, that the exportation of figs was once unlawful, and the informer against the delinquents called a sycophant. He made a law, also, concerning hurts and injuries from beasts, in which he commands the master of any dog that bit a man to deliver him up with a log about his neck, four and a half feet long; a happy device for men's security. The law concerning naturalising strangers is of doubtful character; he permitted only those to be made free of Athens who were in perpetual exile from their own country, or came with their whole family to trade there; this he did, not to discourage strangers, but rather

to invite them to a permanent participation in the privileges of the government; and, besides, he thought those
would prove the more faithful citizens who had been
forced from their own country, or voluntarily forsook it.
The law of public entertainment (*parasitein* is his name for
it) is also peculiarly Solon's; for if any man came often, or
if he that was invited refused, they were punished, for he
concluded that one was greedy, the other a contemner of the
state.

All his laws he established for an hundred years, and
wrote them on wooden tables or rollers, named axones,
which might be turned round in oblong cases; some of their
relics were in my time still to be seen in the Prytaneum,
or common hall at Athens. These, as Aristotle states, were
called cyrbes, and there is a passage of Cratinus the comedian—

"By Solon, and by Draco, if you please,
Whose Cyrbes make the fires that parch our peas."

But some say those are properly cyrbes, which contain laws
concerning sacrifices and the rites of religion, and all the
others axones. The council all jointly swore to confirm
the laws, and every one of the Thesmothetae vowed for
himself at the stone in the market-place, that if he broke
any of the statutes, he would dedicate a golden statue, as
big as himself, at Delphi.

Observing the irregularity of the months, and that the
moon does not always rise and set with the sun, but often
in the same day overtakes and gets before him, he ordered
the day should be named the Old and New, attributing
that part of it which was before the conjunction to the old
moon, and the rest to the new, he being the first, it seems,
that understood that verse of Homer—

"The end and the beginning of the month,"—

and the following day he called the new moon. After the
twentieth he did not count by addition, but, like the moon

itself in its wane, by subtraction; thus up to the thirtieth.

Now when these laws were enacted, and some came to Solon every day, to commend or disparise them, and to advise, if possible, to leave out or put in something, and many criticised and desired him to explain, and tell the meaning of such and such a passage, he, knowing that to do it was useless, and not to do it would get him ill-will, and desirous to bring himself out of all straits, and to escape all displeasure and exceptions, it being a hard thing, as he himself says—

"In great affairs to satisfy all sides,"

as an excuse for travelling, bought a trading vessel, and, having leave for ten years' absence, departed, hoping that by that time his laws would have become familiar.

His first voyage was for Egypt, and he lived, as he himself says—

"Near Nilus' mouth, by fair Canopus' shore,"

and spent some time in study with Psenophis of Heliopolis, and Sonchis the Saite, the most learned of all the priests; from whom, as Plato says, getting knowledge of the Atlantic story, he put it into a poem, and proposed to bring it to the knowledge of the Greeks. From thence he sailed to Cyprus, where he was made much of by Philocyprus, one of the kings there, who had a small city built by Demophon, Theseus's son, near the river Clarius, in a strong situation, but incommodious and uneasy of access. Solon persuaded him, since there lay a fair plain below, to remove, and build there a pleasanter and more spacious city. And he stayed himself, and assisted in gathering inhabitants, and in fitting it both for defence and convenience of living; insomuch that many flocked to Philocyprus, and the other kings imitated the design; and, therefore, to honour Solon, he called the city Soli, which was formerly named Aepea. And Solon himself, in his Elegies, addressing Philocyprus, mentions this foundation in these words:—

"Long may you live, and fill the Solian throne,
Succeeded still by children of your own;
And from your happy island while I sail,
Let Cyprus send for me a favouring gale;
May she advance, and bless your new command,
Prosper your town, and send me safe to land."

That Solon should discourse with Croesus, some think
not agreeable with chronology; but I cannot reject so famous and well-attested a narrative, and, what is more, so
agreeable to Solon's temper, and so worthy his wisdom and
greatness of mind, because, forsooth, it does not agree
with some chronological canons, which thousands have endeavoured to regulate, and yet, to this day, could never
bring their differing opinions to any agreement. They say,
therefore, that Solon, coming to Croesus at his request, was
in the same condition as an inland man when first he goes
to see the sea; for as he fancies every river he meets with
to be the ocean, so Solon, as he passed through the court,
and saw a great many nobles richly dressed, and proudly attended with a multitude of guards and footboys, thought
every one had been the king, till he was brought to Croesus,
who was decked with every possible rarity and curiosity, in
ornaments of jewels, purple, and gold, that could make a
grand and gorgeous spectacle of him. Now when Solon
came before him, and seemed not at all surprised, nor gave
Croesus those compliments he expected, but showed himself
to all discerning eyes to be a man that despised the gaudi-
ness and petty ostentation of it, he commanded them to
open all his treasure houses, and carry him to see his sumptuous furniture and luxuries, though he did not wish it;
Solon could judge of him well enough by the first sight of
him; and, when he returned from viewing all, Croesus asked
him if ever he had known a happier man than he. And
when Solon answered that he had known one Tellus, a
fellow-citizen of his own, and told him that this Tellus had
been an honest man, had had good children, a competent
estate, and died bravely in battle for his country, Croesus
took him for an ill-bred fellow and a fool, for not measur-

ing happiness by the abundance of gold and silver, and preferring the life and death of a private and mean man before so much power and empire. He asked him, however, again, if, besides Tellus, he knew any other man more happy. And Solon replying, Yes, Cleobis and Biton, who were loving brothers, and extremely dutiful sons to their mother, and, when the oxen delayed her, harnessed themselves to the waggon, and drew her to Juno's temple, her neighbours all calling her happy, and she herself rejoicing; then, after sacrificing and feasting, they went to rest, and never rose again, but died in the midst of their honour a painless and tranquil death. "What," said Croesus, angrily, "and dost not thou reckon us amongst the happy men at all?" Solon, unwilling either to flatter or exasperate him more, replied, "The gods, O king, have given the Greeks all other gifts in moderate degree; and so our wisdom, too, is a cheerful and a homely, not a noble and kingly wisdom; and this, observing the numerous misfortunes that attend all conditions, forbids us to grow insolent upon our present enjoyments, or to admire any man's happiness that may yet, in course of time, suffer change. For the uncertain future has yet to come, with every possible variety of fortune; and him only to whom the divinity has continued happiness unto the end we call happy; to salute as happy one that is still in the midst of life and hazard, we think as little safe and conclusive as to crown and proclaim as victorious the wrestler that is yet in the ring." After this, he was dismissed, having given Croesus some pain, but no instruction.

Aesop, who wrote the fables, being then at Sardis upon Croesus's invitation, and very much esteemed, was concerned that Solon was so ill received, and gave him this advice: "Solon, let your converse with kings be either short or seasonable." "Nay, rather," replied Solon, "either short or reasonable." So at this time Croesus despised Solon; but when he was overcome by Cyrus, had lost his city, was taken alive, condemned to be burnt, and laid bound upon the pile before all the Persians and Cyrus himself, he cried out as loud as possibly he could three times, "O Solon!" and Cyrus being surprised, and sending some to inquire what man or god this Solon was, who alone he invoked in this extremity, Croesus told him the whole story, saying, "He was one of the wise men of Greece, whom I sent for, not to be instructed, or to learn anything that I wanted, but that he should see and be a witness of my happiness; the loss of which was, it seems, to be a greater evil than the enjoyment was a good; for when I had them they were goods only in opinion, but now the loss of them has brought upon me intolerable and real evils. And he, conjecturing from what then was, this that now is, bade look to the end of my life, and not rely and grow proud upon uncertainties." When this was told Cyrus, who was a wiser man than Croesus, and saw in the present example Solon's maxim confirmed, he not only freed Croesus from punishment, but honoured him as long as he lived; and Solon had the glory, by the same saying, to save one king and instruct another.

When Solon was gone, the citizens began to quarrel; Lycurgus headed the Plain; Megacles, the son of Alcmaeon, those to the Seaside; and Pisistratus the Hill-party, in which were the poorest people, the Thetes, and greatest enemies to the rich; insomuch that, though the city still used the new laws, yet all looked for and desired a change of government, hoping severally that the change would be better for them, and put them above the contrary faction. Affairs standing thus, Solon returned, and was reverenced by all, and honoured; but his old age would not permit him to be as active, and to speak in public, as formerly; yet, by privately conferring with the heads of the factions, he endeavoured to compose the differences, Pisistratus appearing the most tractable; for he was extremely smooth and engaging in his language, a great friend to the poor, and moderate in his resentments; and what nature had not given him, he had the skill to imitate; so that he was trusted more than the others, being accounted a prudent and orderly man, one that loved equality, and would be an enemy to any that moved against the present settlement. Thus he deceived the majority of people; but Solon quickly discovered his character, and found out his design before any one else; yet did not hate him upon this, but endeavoured to humble him, and bring him off from his ambition, and often told him and others, that if any one could banish the passion for pre-eminence from his mind, and cure him of his desire of absolute power, none would make a more virtuous man or a more excellent citizen. Thespis, at this time, beginning to act tragedies, and the thing, because it was new, taking very much with the multitude, though it was not yet made a matter of competition, Solon, being by nature fond of hearing and learning something new, and now, in his old age, living idly, and enjoying himself, indeed, with music and with wine, went to see Thespis himself, as the ancient custom was, act: and after the play was done, he addressed him, and asked him if he was not ashamed to tell so many lies before such a number of people; and Thespis replying that it was no harm to say or do so in play, Solon vehemently struck his staff against the ground: "Ah," said he, "if we honour and commend such play as this, we shall find it some day in our business."

Now when Pisistratus, having wounded himself, was brought into the market-place in a chariot, and stirred up the people, as if he had been thus treated by his opponents because of his political conduct, and a great many were enraged and cried out, Solon, coming close to him, said, "This, O son of Hippocrates, is a bad copy of Homer's Ulysses; you do, to trick your countrymen, what he did to deceive his enemies." After this, the people were eager to protect Pisistratus, and met in an assembly where one Ariston making a motion that they should allow Pisistratus fifty clubmen for a guard to his person, Solon opposed it, and said much to the same purport as what he has left us in his poems—

"You dote upon his words and taking phrase;"

and again—

"True, you are singly each a crafty soul,
But all together make one empty fool."

But observing the poor men bent to gratify Pisistratus, and tumultuous, and the rich fearful and getting out of harm's way, he departed, saying he was wiser than some and stouter than others; wiser than those that did not understand the design, stouter than those that, though they understood it, were afraid to oppose the tyranny. Now, the people, having passed the law, were not nice with Pisistratus about the number of his clubmen, but took no notice of it, though he enlisted and kept as many as he would, until he seized the Acropolis. When that was done, and the city in an uproar, Megacles, with all his family, at once fled; but Solon, though he was now very old, and had none to back him, yet came into the market-place and made a speech to the citizens, partly blaming their inadvertency and meanness of spirit, and in part urging and exhorting them not thus tamely to lose their liberty; and likewise then spoke that memorable saying, that, before, it was an easier task to stop the rising tyranny, but now the great and more glorious action to destroy it, when it was begun already, and had gathered strength. But all being afraid to side with him, he returned home, and, taking his arms, he brought them out and laid them in the porch before his door, with these words: "I have done my part to maintain my country and my laws," and then he busied himself no more. His friends advising him to fly, he refused, but wrote poems, and thus reproached the Athenians in them:—

"If now you suffer, do not blame the Powers,
For they are good, and all the fault was ours,
All the strongholds you put into his hands,
And now his slaves must do what he commands."

And many telling him that the tyrant would take his life for this, and asking what he trusted to, that he ventured to speak so boldly, he replied, "To my old age." But Pisistratus, having got the command, so extremely courted Solon, so honoured him, obliged him, and sent to see him, that Solon gave him his advice, and approved many of his actions; for he retained most of Solon's laws, observed them himself, and compelled his friends to obey. And he himself, though already absolute ruler, being accused of murder before the Areopagus, came quietly to clear himself; but his accuser did not appear. And he added other laws, one of which is that the maimed in the wars should be maintained at the public charge; this Heraclides Ponticus records, and that Pisistratus followed Solon's example in this, who had decreed it in the case of one Thersippus, that was maimed; and Theophrastus asserts that it was Pisistratus, not Solon, that made that law against laziness, which was the reason that the country was more productive, and the city tranquiller.

Now Solon, having begun the great work in verse, the history or fable of the Atlantic Island, which he had learned from the wise men in Sais, and thought convenient for the Athenians to know, abandoned it; not, as Plato says, by reason of want of time, but because of his age, and being discouraged at the greatness of the task; for that he had leisure enough, such verses testify, as—

"Each day grow older, and learn something new;"

and again—

"But now the Powers, of Beauty, Song, and Wine,
    Which are most men's delights, are also mine."

Plato, willing to improve the story of the Atlantic Island, as if it were a fair estate that wanted an heir and came with some title to him, formed, indeed, stately entrances, noble enclosures, large courts, such as never yet introduced any story, fable, or poetic fiction; but, beginning it late, ended his life before his work; and the reader's regret for the unfinished part is the greater, as the satisfaction he takes in that which is complete is extraordinary. For as the city of Athens left only the temple of Jupiter Olympius unfinished, so Plato, amongst all his excellent works, left this only piece about the Atlantic Island imperfect. Solon lived after Pisistratus seized the government, as Heraclides Ponticus asserts, a long time; but Phanias the Eresian says not two full years; for Pisistratus began his tyranny when Comias was archon, and Phanias says Solon died under Hegestratus, who succeeded Comias. The story that his ashes were scattered about the island Salamis is too strange to be easily believed, or be thought anything but a mere fable; and yet it is given, amongst other good authors, by Aristotle, the philosopher.

THEMISTOCLES

The birth of Themistocles was somewhat too obscure to do him honour. His father, Neocles, was not of the distinguished people of Athens, but of the township Phrearrhi, and of the tribe Leontis; and by his mother's side, as it is reported, he was base-born—

> "I am not of the noble Grecian race,
> I'm poor Abrotonon, and born in Thrace;
> Let the Greek women scorn me, if they please,
> I was the mother of Themistocles."

Yet Phanias writes that the mother of Themistocles was not of Thrace, but of Caria, and that her name was not Abrotonon, but Euterpe; and Neanthes adds farther that she was of Halicarnassus in Caria. And, as illegitimate children, including those that were of half-blood or had but one parent an Athenian, had to attend at the Cynosarges (a wrestling-place outside the gates, dedicated to Hercules, who was also of half-blood amongst the gods, having had a mortal woman for his mother), Themistocles persuaded several of the young men of high birth to accompany him to anoint and exercise themselves together at Cynosarges; an ingenious device for destroying the distinction between the noble and the base-born, and between those of the whole and those of the half-blood of Athens. However, it is certain that he was related to the house of Lycomedae; for Simonides records that he rebuilt the chapel of Phlya, belonging to that family, and beautified it with pictures and other ornaments, after it had been burnt by the Persians.

It is confessed by all that from his youth he was of a vehement and impetuous nature, of a quick apprehension, and a strong and aspiring bent for action and great affairs. The holidays and intervals in his studies he did not spend in play or idleness, as other children, but would be always inventing or arranging some oration or declamation to himself, the subject of which was generally the excusing or accusing his companions, so that his master would often say to him, "You, my boy, will be nothing small, but great one way or other, for good or else for bad." He received reluctantly and carelessly instructions given him to improve his manners and behaviour, or to teach him any pleasing or graceful accomplishment, but whatever was said to improve him in sagacity, or in management of affairs, he would give attention to, beyond one of his years, from confidence in his natural capacities for such things. And thus afterwards, when in company where people engaged themselves in what are commonly thought the liberal and elegant amusements, he was obliged to defend himself against the observations of those who considered themselves highly accomplished, by the somewhat arrogant retort, that he certainly could not make use of any stringed instrument, could only, were a small and obscure city put into his hands, make it great and glorious. Notwithstanding this, Stesimbrotus says that Themistocles was a hearer of Anaxagoras, and that he studied natural philosophy under Melissus, contrary to chronology; Melissus commanded the Samians in the siege by Pericles, who was much Themistocles's junior; and with Pericles, also, Anaxagoras was intimate. They, therefore, might rather be credited who report, that Themistocles was an admirer of Mnesiphilus the Phrearrhian, who was neither rhetorician nor natural philosopher, but a professor of that which was then called wisdom, consisting in a sort of political shrewdness and practical sagacity, which had begun and continued, almost like a sect of philosophy, from Solon: but those who came afterwards, and mixed it with pleadings and legal artifices, and transformed the practical part of it into a mere art of speaking and an exercise of words, were generally called sophists. Themistocles resorted to Mnesiphilus when he had already embarked in politics.

In the first essays of his youth he was not regular nor happily balanced: he allowed himself to follow mere natural character, which, without the control of reason and instruction, is apt to hurry, upon either side, into sudden and violent courses and very often to break away and determine upon the worst; as he afterwards owned himself, saying, that the wildest colts make the best horses, if they only get properly trained and broken in. But those who upon this fasten stories of their own invention, as of his being disowned by his father, and that his mother died for grief of her son's ill-fame, certainly calumniate him; and there are others who relate, on the contrary, how that to deter him from public business, and to let him see how the vulgar behave themselves towards their leaders when they have at last no farther use of them, his father showed him the old galleys as they lay forsaken and cast about upon the sea-shore.

Yet it is evident that his mind was early imbued with the keenest interest in public affairs, and the most passionate ambition for distinction. Eager from the first to obtain the highest place, he unhesitatingly accepted the hatred of the most powerful and influential leaders in the city, but more especially of Aristides, the son of Lysimachus, who always opposed him. And yet all this great enmity between them arose, it appears, from a very boyish occasion, both being attached to the beautiful Stesilaus of Ceos, as Ariston the philosopher tells us; ever after which they took opposite sides, and were rivals in politics. Not but that the incompatibility of their lives and manners may seem to have increased the difference, for Aristides was of a mild nature, and of a nobler sort of character, and, in public matters, acting always with a view, not to glory or popularity, but to the best interest of the state consistently with safety and honesty, he was often forced to oppose Themistocles, and interfere against the increase of his influence, seeing him stirring up the people to all kinds of enterprises, and introducing various innovations. For it is said that Themistocles

was so transported with the thoughts of glory and so inflamed with the passion for great actions, that, though he
was still young when the battle of Marathon was fought
against the Persians, upon the skilful conduct of the general,
Miltiades, being everywhere talked about, he was observed
to be thoughtful and reserved, alone by himself; he passed
the nights without sleep, and avoided all his usual places of
recreation, and to those who wondered at the change, and
inquired the reason of it, he gave the answer, that "the
trophy of Miltiades would not let him sleep." And when
others were of opinion that the battle of Marathon would
be an end to the war, Themistocles thought that it was but
the beginning for far greater conflicts, and for these, to the
benefit of all Greece, he kept himself in continual readiness,
and his city also in proper training, foreseeing from far before what would happen.

And, first of all, the Athenians being accustomed to divide amongst themselves the revenue proceeding from the
silver mines at Laurium, he was the only man that durst propose to the people that this distribution should cease, and
that with the money ships should be built to make war
against the Aeginetans, who were the most flourishing people in all Greece, and by the number of their ships held the
sovereignty of the sea; and Themistocles thus was more
easily able to persuade them, avoiding all mention of danger
from Darius or the Persians, who were at a great distance,
and their coming very uncertain, and at that time not much
to be feared; but by a seasonable employment of the emulation and anger felt by the Athenians against the Aeginetans,
he induced them to preparation. So that with this money an
hundred ships were built, with which they afterwards fought
against Xerxes. And henceforward, little by little, turning
and drawing the city down towards the sea, in the belief
that, whereas by land they were not a fit match for their
next neighbours, with their ships they might be able to repel
the Persians and command Greece, thus, as Plato says, from
steady soldiers he turned them into mariners and seamen
tossed about the sea, and gave occasion for the reproach
against him, that he took away from the Athenians the spear

and the shield, and bound them to the bench and the oar.
These measures he carried in the assembly, against the opposition, as Stesimbrotus relates, of Miltiades; and whether or
no he hereby injured the purity and true balance of government may be a question for philosophers, but that the deliverance of Greece came at that time from the sea, and that
these galleys restored Athens again after it was destroyed,
were others wanting, Xerxes himself would be sufficient evidence, who, though his land-forces were still entire, after his
defeat at sea, fled away, and thought himself no longer able
to encounter the Greeks; and, as it seems to me, left Mardonius behind him, not out of any hopes he could have to
bring them into subjection, but to hinder them from pursuing him.

Themistocles is said to have been eager in the acquisition
of riches, according to some, that he might be the more liberal; for loving to sacrifice often, and to be splendid in his
entertainment of strangers, he required a plentiful revenue;
yet he is accused by others of having been parsimonious
and sordid to that degree that he would sell provisions which
were sent to him as a present. He desired Diphilides, who
was a breeder of horses, to give him a colt, and when he refused it, threatened that in a short time he would turn his
house into a wooden horse, intimating that he would stir up
dispute and litigation between him and some of his relations.

He went beyond all men in the passion for distinction.
When he was still young and unknown in the world, he entreated Episcles of Hermione, who had a good hand at the
lute and was much sought after by the Athenians, to come
and practise at home with him, being ambitious of having
people inquire after his house and frequent his company.
When he came to the Olympic games, and was so splendid
in his equipage and entertainments, in his rich tents and
furniture, that he strove to outdo Cimon, he displeased the
Greeks, who thought that such magnificence might be allowed in one who was a young man and of a great family,
but was a great piece of insolence in one as yet undistinguished, and without title or means for making any such
display. In a dramatic contest, the play he paid for won the

prize, which was then a matter that excited much emulation; he put up a tablet in record of it, with the inscription: "Themistocles of Phrearrhi was at the charge of it; Phryni-chus made it; Adimantus was archon." He was well liked by the common people, would salute every particular citizen by his own name, and always show himself a just judge in questions of business between private men; he said to Si-monides, the poet of Ceos, who desired something of him, when he was commander of the army, that was not reason-able, "Simonides, you would be no good poet if you wrote false measure, nor should I be a good magistrate if for favour I made false law." And at another time, laughing at Simonides, he said, that he was a man of little judgment to speak against the Corinthians, who were inhabitants of a great city, and to have his own picture drawn so often, hav-ing so ill-looking a face.

Gradually growing to be great, and winning the favour of the people, he at last gained the day with his faction over that of Aristides, and procured his banishment by ostra-cism.* When the king of Persia was now advancing against

* From "Aristides": Of all his virtues, the common people were most affected with his justice, because of its continual and com-mon use; and thus, although of mean fortune and ordinary birth, he possessed himself of the most kingly and divine appellation of Just: which kings, however, and tyrants have never sought after; but have taken delight to be surnamed besiegers of cities, thunderers, conquerors, or eagles again, and hawks; affecting, it seems, the reputation which proceeds from power and violence, rather than that of virtue. Although the divinity, to whom they desire to compare and assimilate themselves, excels, it is supposed, in three things, immortality, power, and virtue; of which three the noblest and divinest is virtue. For the elements and vacuum have an everlasting existence; earthquakes, thunders, storms, and torrents have great power; but in justice and equity nothing par-ticipates except by means of reason and the knowledge of that which is divine. And thus, taking the three varieties of feeling commonly entertained towards the diety, the sense of his happi-ness, fear, and honour of him, people would seem to think him blest and happy for his exemption from death and corruption, to fear and dread him for his power and dominion, but to love, honour, and adore him for his justice. Yet though thus disposed, they covet that immortality which our nature is not capable of, and that power the greatest part of which is at the disposal of

Greece, and the Athenians were in consultation who should be general, and many withdrew themselves of their own accord, being terrified with the greatness of the danger, there was one Epicydes, a popular speaker, son to Euphemides a

---

fortune; but give virtue, the only divine good really in our reach, the last place, most unwisely; since justice makes the life of such as are in prosperity, power, and authority the life of a god, and injustice turns it to that of a beast.

Aristides, therefore, had at first the fortune to be beloved for this surname, but at length envied. Especially when Themistocles spread a rumor amongst the people that, by determining and judging all matters privately, he had destroyed the courts of judicature, and was secretly making way for a monarchy in his own person, without the assistance of guards. Moreover the spirit of the people, now grown high, and confident with their late victory, naturally entertained feelings of dislike to all of more than common fame and reputation. Coming together, therefore, from all parts into the city, they banished Aristides by the ostracism, giving their jealousy of his reputation the name of fear of tyranny. For ostracism was not the punishment of any criminal act, but was speciously said to be the mere depression and humiliation of excessive greatness and power; and was in fact a gentle relief and mitigation of envious feeling, which was thus allowed to vent itself in inflicting no intolerable injury, only a ten years' banishment. . . .

. . . It was performed, to be short, in this manner. Every one taking an *ostracon*, a sherd, that is, or piece of earthenware, wrote upon it the citizen's name he would have banished, and carried it to a certain part of the market-place surrounded with wooden rails. First, the magistrates numbered all the sherds in gross (for if there were less than six thousand, the ostracism was imperfect); then, laying every name by itself, they pronounced him whose name was written by the larger number banished for ten years, with the enjoyment of his estate. As, therefore, they were writing the names on the sherds, it is reported that an illiterate clownish fellow, giving Aristides his sherd, supposing him a common citizen, begged him to write Aristides upon it; and he being surprised and asking if Aristides had ever done him any injury, "None at all," said he, "neither know I the man; but I am tired of hearing him everywhere called the Just." Aristides, hearing this, is said to have made no reply, but returned the sherd with his own name inscribed. At his departure from the city, lifting up his hands to heaven, he made a prayer (the reverse, it would seem of that of Achilles), that the Athenians might never have any occasion which should constrain them to remember Aristides.

man of an elegant tongue, but of a faint heart, and a slave to riches, who was desirous of the command, and was looked upon to be in a fair way to carry it by the number of votes; but Themistocles, fearing that, if the command should fall into such hands, all would be lost, bought off Epicydes and his pretensions, it is said, for a sum of money.

When the king of Persia sent messengers into Greece, with an interpreter, to demand earth and water, as an acknowledgment of subjection, Themistocles, by the consent of the people, seized upon the interpreter, and put him to death, for presuming to publish the barbarian orders and decrees in the Greek language; this is one of the actions he is commended for, as also for what he did to Arthmius of Zelea, who brought gold from the king of Persia to corrupt the Greeks, and was, by an order from Themistocles, degraded and disfranchised, he and his children and his posterity; but that which most of all redounded to his credit was, that he put an end to all the civil wars of Greece, composed their differences, and persuaded them to lay aside all enmity during the war with the Persians: and in this great work, Chileus the Arcadian was, it is said, of great assistance to him.

Having taken upon himself the command of the Athenian forces, he immediately endeavoured to persuade the citizens to leave the city, and to embark upon their galleys, and meet with the Persians at a great distance from Greece; but many being against this, he led a large force, together with the Lacedaemonians, into Tempe, that in this pass they might maintain the safety of Thessaly, which had not as yet declared for the king; but when they returned without performing anything, and it was known that not only the Thessalians, but all as far as Boeotia, was going over to Xerxes, then the Athenians more willingly hearkened to the advice of Themistocles to fight by sea, and sent him with a fleet to guard the straits of Artemisium.

When the contingents met here, the Greeks would have the Lacedaemonians to command, and Eurybiades to be their admiral; but the Athenians, who surpassed all the rest together in number of vessels, would not submit to come after any other, till Themistocles, perceiving the danger of the contest, yielded his own command to Eurybiades, and got the Athenians to submit, extenuating the loss by persuading them, that if in this war they behaved themselves like men, he would answer for it after that, that the Greeks, of their own will, would submit to their command. And by this moderation of his, it is evident that he was the chief means of the deliverance of Greece, and gained the Athenians the glory of alike surpassing their enemies in valour, and their confederates in wisdom.

As soon as the Persian armada arrived at Aphetae, Eurybiades was astonished to see such a vast number of vessels before him, and being informed that two hundred more were sailing around behind the island of Sciathus, he immediately determined to retire farther into Greece, and to sail back into some part of Peloponnesus, where their land army and their fleet might join, for he looked upon the Persian forces to be altogether unassailable by sea. But the Euboeans, fearing that the Greeks would forsake them, and leave them to the mercy of the enemy, sent Pelagon to confer privately with Themistocles, taking with him a good sum of money, which, as Herodotus reports, he accepted and gave to Eurybiades. In this affair none of his own countrymen opposed him so much as Architeles, captain of the sacred galley, who, having no money to supply his seamen, was eager to go home; but Themistocles so incensed the Athenians against them, that they set upon him and left him not so much as his supper, at which Architeles was much surprised, and took it very ill; but Themistocles immediately sent him in a chest a service of provisions, and at the bottom of it a talent of silver, desiring him to sup to-night, and to-morrow provide for his seamen; if not, he would report it among the Athenians that he had received money from the enemy. So Phanias the Lesbian tells the story.

Though the fights between the Greeks and Persians in the straits of Euboea were not so important as to make any final decision of the war, yet the experience which the Greeks obtained in them was of great advantage; for thus, by actual trial and in real danger, they found out that nei-

ther number of ships, nor riches and ornaments, nor boasting shouts, nor barbarous songs of victory, were any way
terrible to men that knew how to fight, and were resolved
to come hand to hand with their enemies; these things they
were to despise and to come up close and grapple with their
foes.

But when news came from Thermopylae to Artemisium
informing them that king Leonidas was slain, and that
Xerxes had made himself master of all the passages by land,
they returned back to the interior of Greece, the Athenians
having the command of the rear, the place of honour and
danger, and much elated by what had been done.

As Themistocles sailed along the coasts, he took notice
of the harbours and fit places for the enemy's ships to come
to land at, and engraved large letters in such stones as he
found there by chance, as also in others which he set up on
purpose near to the landing-places, or where they were to
water; in which inscriptions he called upon the Ionians to
forsake the Medes, if it were possible, and to come over to
the Greeks, who were their proper founders and fathers, and
were now hazarding all for their liberties; but, if this could
not be done, at any rate to impede and disturb the Persians
in all engagements. He hoped that these writings would prevail with the Ionians to revolt, or raise some trouble by
making their fidelity doubtful to the Persians.

Now, though Xerxes had already passed through Doris
and invaded the country of Phocis, and was burning and destroying the cities of the Phocians, yet the Greeks sent them
no relief; and, though the Athenians earnestly desired them
to meet the Persians in Boeotia, before they could come
into Attica, as they themselves had come forward by sea at
Artemisium, they gave no ear to their requests, being wholly
intent upon Peloponnesus, and resolved to gather all their
forces together within the Isthmus, and to build a wall from
sea to sea in that narrow neck of land; so that the Athenians
were enraged to see themselves betrayed, and at the same
time afflicted and dejected at their own destitution. For to
fight alone against such a numerous army was to no purpose, and the only expedient now left them was to leave

their city and cling to their ships; which the people were very unwilling to submit to, imagining that it would signify little now to gain a victory, and not understanding how there could be deliverance any longer after they had once forsaken the temples of their gods and exposed the tombs and monuments of their ancestors to the fury of their enemies.

Themistocles, being at a loss, and not able to draw the people over to his opinion by any human reason, set his machines to work, as in a theatre, and employed prodigies and oracles. The serpent of Minerva, kept in the inner part of her temple, disappeared; the priest gave it out to the people that the offerings which were set for it were found untouched, and declared, by the suggestion of Themistocles, that the goddess had left the city, and taken her flight before them towards the sea. And he often urged them with the oracle which bade them trust to walls of wood, showing them that walls of wood could signify nothing else but ships; and that the island of Salamis was termed in it, not miserable or unhappy, but had the epithet of divine, for that it should one day be associated with a great good fortune of the Greeks. At length his opinion prevailed, and he obtained a decree that the city should be committed to the protection of Minerva, "Queen of Athens;" that they who were of age to bear arms should embark, and that each should see to sending away his children, women, and slaves where he could. This decree being confirmed, most of the Athenians removed their parents, wives, and children to Troezen, where they were received with eager good-will by the Troezenians, who passed a vote that they should be maintained at the public charge, by a daily payment of two obols to every one, and leave be given to the children to gather fruit where they pleased, and schoolmasters paid to instruct them. This vote was proposed by Nicagoras.

There was no public treasure at that time in Athens; but the council of Areopagus, as Aristotle says, distributed to every one that served eight drachmas, which was a great help to the manning of the fleet; but Clidemus ascribes this also to the art of Themistocles. When the Athenians were

on their way down to the haven of Piraeus, the shield with
the head of Medusa was missing; and he, under the pretext
of searching for it, ransacked all places, and found among
their goods considerable sums of money concealed, which
he applied to the public use; and with this the soldiers and
seamen were well provided for their voyage.

When the whole city of Athens were going on board, it
afforded a spectacle worthy alike of pity and admiration, to
see them thus send away their fathers and children before
them, and, unmoved with their cries and tears, passed over
into the island. But that which stirred compassion most of
all was, that many old men, by reason of their great age,
were left behind; and even the tame domestic animals could
not be seen without some pity, running about the town and
howling, as desirous to be carried along with their masters
that had kept them; among which it is reported that Xanthippus, the father of Pericles, had a dog that would not
endure to stay behind, but leaped into the sea, and swam
along by the galley's side till he came to the island of Salamis, where he fainted away and died, and that spot in the
island, which is still called the Dog's Grave, is said to be his.

Among the great actions of Themistocles at this crisis, the
recall of Aristides was not the least, for, before the war, he
had been ostracised by the party which Themistocles
headed, and was in banishment; but now, perceiving that
the people regretted his absence, and were fearful that he
might go over to the Persians to revenge himself, and
thereby ruin the affairs of Greece, Themistocles proposed a
decree that those who were banished for a time might return
again, to give assistance by word and deed to the cause of
Greece with the rest of their fellow-citizens.

Eurybiades, by reason of the greatness of Sparta, was
admiral of the Greek fleet, but yet was faint-hearted in time
of danger, and willing to weigh anchor and set sail for the
isthmus of Corinth, near which the land army lay encamped; which Themistocles resisted; and this was the occasion of the well-known words, when Eurybiades, to check
his impatience, told him that at the Olympic games they
that start up before the rest are lashed; "And they," replied

Themistocles, "that are left behind are not crowned." Again, Eurybiades lifting up his staff as if he were going to strike, Themistocles said, "Strike if you will, but hear"; Eurybiades, wondering much at his moderation, desired him to speak, and Themistocles now brought him to a better understanding. And when one who stood by him told him that it did not become those who had neither city nor house to lose, to persuade others to relinquish their habitations and forsake their countries, Themistocles gave this reply: "We have indeed left our houses and our walls, base fellow, not thinking it fit to become slaves for the sake of things that have no life nor soul; and yet our city is the greatest of all Greece, consisting of two hundred galleys, which are here to defend you, if you please; but if you run away and betray us, as you did once before, the Greeks shall soon hear news of the Athenians possessing as fair a country, and as large and free a city, as that they have lost." These expressions of Themistocles made Eurybiades suspect that if he retreated the Athenians would fall off from him. When one of Eretria began to oppose him, he said, "Have you anything to say of war, that are like an inkfish? you have a sword, but no heart." Some say that while Themistocles was thus speaking upon the deck, an owl was seen flying to the right hand of the fleet, which came and sat upon the top of the mast; and this happy omen so far disposed the Greeks to follow his advice, that they presently prepared to fight. Yet, when the enemy's fleet was arrived at the haven of Phalerum, upon the coast of Attica, and with a number of their ships concealed all the shore, and when they saw the king himself in person come down with his land army to the seaside, with all his forces united, then the good counsel of Themistocles was soon forgotten, and the Peloponnesians cast their eyes again towards the isthmus, and took it very ill if any one spoke against their returning home; and, resolving to depart that night, the pilots had orders what course to steer.

Themistocles, in great distress that the Greeks should retire, and lose the advantage of the narrow seas and strait passage, and slip home every one to his own city, considered with himself, and contrived that stratagem that was carried

out by Sicinnus. This Sicinnus was a Persian captive, but
a great lover of Themistocles, and the attendant of his
children. Upon this occasion, he sent him privately to
Xerxes, commanding him to tell the king that Themistocles,
the admiral of the Athenians, having espoused his interest,
wished to be the first to inform him that the Greeks
were ready to make their escape, and that he counselled him
to hinder their flight, to set upon them while they were in
this confusion and at a distance from their land army, and
hereby destroy all their forces by sea. Xerxes was very joyful at this message, and received it as from one who wished
him all that was good, and immediately issued instructions
to the commanders of his ships, that they should instantly
set out with two hundred galleys to encompass all the
islands, and enclose all the straits and passages, that none of
the Greeks might escape, and that they should afterwards
follow with the rest of their fleet at leisure. This being done,
Aristides, the son of Lysimachus, was the first man that perceived it, and went to the tent of Themistocles, not out of
any friendship, for he had been formerly banished by his
means, as has been related, but to inform him how they
were encompassed by their enemies. Themistocles, knowing
the generosity of Aristides, and much struck by his visit at
that time, imparted to him all that he had transacted by
Sicinnus, and entreated him that, as he would be more readily believed among the Greeks, he would make use of his
credit to help induce them to stay and fight their enemies in
the narrow seas. Aristides applauded Themistocles, and
went to the other commanders and captains of the galleys,
and encouraged them to engage; yet they did not perfectly
assent to him, till a galley of Tenos, which deserted from
the Persians, of which Panaetius was commander, came in,
while they were still doubting, and confirmed the news that
all the straits and passages were beset; and then their rage
and fury, as well as their necessity, provoked them all to
fight.

As soon as it was day Xerxes placed himself high up, to
view his fleet, and how it was set in order. Phanodemus
says, he sat upon a promontory above the temple of Her-

cules, where the coast of Attica is separated from the island by a narrow channel; but Acestodorus writes, that it was in the confines of Megara, upon those hills which are called the Horns, where he sat in a chair of gold, with many secretaries about him to write down all that was done in the fight.

When Themistocles was about to sacrifice, close to the admiral's galley, there were three prisoners brought to him, fine looking men, and richly dressed in ornamented clothing and gold, said to be the children of Artayctes and Sandauce, sister to Xerxes. As soon as the prophet Euphrantides saw them, and observed that at the same time the fire blazed out from the offerings with a more than ordinary flame, and a man sneezed on the right, which was an intimation of a fortunate event, he took Themistocles by the hand, and bade him consecrate the three young men for sacrifice, and offer them up with prayers for victory to Bacchus the Devourer; so should the Greeks not only save themselves, but also obtain victory. Themistocles was much disturbed at this strange and terrible prophecy, but the common people, who in any difficult crisis and great exigency ever look for relief rather to strange and extravagant than to reasonable means, calling upon Bacchus with one voice, led the captives to the altar, and compelled the execution of the sacrifice as the prophet had commanded. This is reported by Phanias the Lesbian, a philosopher well read in history.

The number of the enemy's ships the poet Aeschylus gives in his tragedy called the Persians, as on his certain knowledge, in the following words:—

> "Xerxes, I know, did into battle lead
>   One thousand ships; of more than usual speed
>   Seven and two hundred. So it is agreed."

The Athenians had a hundred and eighty; in every ship eighteen men fought upon the deck, four of whom were archers and the rest men at arms.

As Themistocles had fixed upon the most advantageous place, so, with no less sagacity, he chose the best time of fighting; for he would not run the prows of his galleys against the Persians, nor begin the fight till the time of day was come, when there regularly blows in a fresh breeze from the open sea, and brings in with it a strong swell into the channel; which was no inconvenience to the Greek ships, which were low-built, and little above the water, but did much to hurt the Persians, which had high sterns and lofty decks, and were heavy and cumbrous in their movements, as it presented them broadside to the quick charges of the Greeks, who kept their eyes upon the motions of Themistocles, as their best example, and more particularly because, opposed to his ship, Ariamenes, admiral to Xerxes, a brave man and by far the best and worthiest of the king's brothers, was seen throwing darts and shooting arrows from his huge galley, as from the walls of a castle. Aminias the Decelean and Sosicles the Pedian, who sailed in the same vessel, upon the ships meeting stem to stem, and transfixing each the other with their brazen prows, so that they were fastened together, when Ariamenes attempted to board theirs, ran at him with their pikes, and thrust him into the sea; his body, as it floated amongst other shipwrecks, was known to Artemisia, and carried to Xerxes.

It is reported that, in the middle of the fight, a great flame rose into the air above the city of Eleusis, and that sounds and voices were heard through all the Thriasian plain, as far as the sea, sounding like a number of men accompanying and escorting the mystic Iacchus, and that a mist seemed to form and rise from the place from whence the sounds came, and, passing forward, fell upon the galleys. Others believed that they saw apparitions, in the shape of armed men, reaching out their hands from the island of Aegina before the Grecian galleys; and supposed they were the Aeacidae, whom they had invoked to their aid before the battle. The first man that took a ship was Lycomedes the Athenian, captain of the galley, who cut down its ensign, and dedicated it to Apollo the Laurel-crowned. And as the Persians fought in a narrow arm of the sea, and could bring but part of their fleet to fight, and fell foul of one another, the Greeks thus equalled them in strength, and fought with them till the evening forced them back, and obtained, as says Simonides, that noble and famous victory, than which neither amongst the Greeks nor barbarians was ever known more glorious exploit on the seas; by the joint valour, indeed, and zeal of all who fought, but by the wisdom and sagacity of Themistocles.

After this sea-fight, Xerxes, enraged at his ill-fortune, attempted, by casting great heaps of earth and stones into the sea, to stop up the channel and make a dam, upon which he might lead his land-forces over into the island of Salamis.

Themistocles, being desirous to try the opinion of Aristides, told him that he proposed to set sail for the Hellespont, to break the bridge of ships, so as to shut up, he said, Asia a prisoner within Europe; but Aristides, disliking the design, said: "We have hitherto fought with an enemy who has regarded little else but his pleasure and luxury; but if we shut him up within Greece, and drive him to necessity, he that is master of such great forces will no longer sit quietly with an umbrella of gold over his head, looking upon the fight for his pleasure; but in such a strait will attempt all things; he will be resolute, and appear himself in person upon all occasions, he will soon correct his errors, and supply what he has formerly omitted through remissness, and will be better advised in all things. Therefore, it is noways our interest, Themistocles," he said, "to take away the bridge that is already made, but rather to build another, if it were possible, that he might make his retreat with the more expedition." To which Themistocles answered: "If this be requisite, we must immediately use all diligence, art, and industry, to rid ourselves of him as soon as may be;" and to this purpose he found out among the captives one of the King of Persia's eunuchs, named Arnaces, whom he sent to the king, to inform him that the Greeks, being now victorious by sea, had decreed to sail to the Hellespont, where the boats were fastened together, and destroy the bridge; but that Themistocles, being concerned for the king, revealed this to him, that he might hasten towards the Asiatic seas, and pass over into his own dominions; and in the meantime would cause delays and hinder the confederates from pursuing him. Xerxes no

sooner heard this, but, being very much terrified, he proceeded to retreat out of Greece with all speed. The prudence
of Themistocles and Aristides in this was afterwards more
fully understood at the battle of Plataea, where Mardonius,
with a very small fraction of the forces of Xerxes, put the
Greeks in danger of losing all.

Herodotus writes, that of all the cities of Greece, Aegina
was held to have performed the best service in the war;
while all single men yielded to Themistocles, though, out of
envy, unwillingly; and when they returned to the entrance
of Peloponnesus, where the several commanders delivered
their suffrages at the altar, to determine who was most
worthy, every one gave the first vote for himself and the
second for Themistocles. The Lacedaemonians carried him
with them to Sparta, where, giving the rewards of valour
to Eurybiades, and of wisdom and conduct to Themistocles,
they crowned him with olive, presented him with the best
chariot in the city, and sent three hundred young men to
accompany him to the confines of their country. And at the
next Olympic games, when Themistocles entered the course,
the spectators took no further notice of those who were contesting the prizes, but spent the whole day in looking upon
him, showing him to the strangers, admiring him, and applauding him by clapping their hands, and other expressions
of joy, so that he himself, much gratified, confessed to his
friends that he then reaped the fruit of all his labours for
the Greeks.

He was, indeed, by nature, a great lover of honour, as is
evident from the anecdotes recorded of him. When chosen
admiral by the Athenians, he would not quite conclude any
single matter of business, either public or private, but deferred all till the day they were to set sail, that, by despatching a great quantity of business all at once, and having to
meet a great variety of people, he might make an appearance of greatness and power. Viewing the dead bodies cast
up by the sea, he perceived bracelets and necklaces of gold
about them, yet passed on, only showing them to a friend
that followed him, saying, "Take you these things, for you
are not Themistocles." He said to Antiphates, a handsome

young man, who had formerly avoided, but now in his glory
courted him, "Time, young man, has taught us both a lesson." He said that the Athenians did not honour him or admire him, but made, as it were, a sort of plane-tree of him;
sheltered themselves under him in bad weather, and as soon
as it was fine, plucked his leaves and cut his branches. When
the Seriphian told him that he had not obtained this honour
by himself, but by the greatness of the city, he replied, "You
speak truth; I should never have been famous if I had been
of Seriphus; nor you, had you been of Athens." When another of the generals, who thought he had performed considerable service for the Athenians, boastingly compared his
actions with those of Themistocles, he told him that once
upon a time the Day after the Festival found fault with the
Festival: "On you there is nothing but hurry and trouble
and preparation, but, when I come, everybody sits down
quietly and enjoys himself;" which the Festival admitted
was true, but "if I had not come first, you would not have
come at all." "Even so," he said, "if Themistocles had not
come before, where had you been now?" Laughing at his
own son, who got his mother, and, by his mother's means,
his father, also, to indulge him, he told him that he had the
most power of any one in Greece: "For the Athenians command the rest of Greece, I command the Athenians, your
mother commands me, and you command your mother."
Loving to be singular in all things, when he had land to sell,
he ordered the crier to give notice that there were good
neighbours near it. Of two who made love to his daughter,
he preferred the man of worth to the one who was rich, saying he desired a man without riches, rather than riches without a man. Such was the character of his sayings.

After these things, he began to rebuild and fortify the city
of Athens, bribing, as Theopompus reports, the Lacedaemonian ephors not to be against it, but, as most relate it,
overreaching and deceiving them. For, under the pretext of
an embassy, he went to Sparta, whereupon the Lacedaemonians charging him with rebuilding the walls, and Poli-
archus coming on purpose from Aegina to denounce it, he
denied the fact, bidding them to send people to Athens to

see whether it were so or no; by which delay he got time for
the building of the wall, and also placed these ambassadors
in the hands of his countrymen as hostages for him; and
so, when the Lacedaemonians knew the truth, they did him
no hurt, but, suppressing all display of their anger for the
present, sent him away.

Next he proceeded to establish the harbour of Piraeus,
observing the great natural advantages of the locality, and
desirous to unite the whole city with the sea, and to reverse,
in a manner, the policy of ancient Athenian kings, who,
endeavouring to withdraw their subjects from the sea, and
to accustom them to live, not by sailing about, but by planting and tilling the earth, spread the story of the dispute between Minerva and Neptune for the sovereignty of Athens,
in which Minerva, by producing to the judges an olive-tree,
was declared to have won; whereas Themistocles did not
only knead up, as Aristophanes says, the port and the city
into one, but made the city absolutely the dependent and the
adjunct of the port, and the land of the sea, which increased
the power and confidence of the people against the nobility;
the authority coming into the hands of sailors and boat-
swains and pilots. Thus it was one of the orders of the thirty
tyrants, that the hustings in the assembly, which had faced
towards the sea, should be turned round towards the land;
implying their opinion that the empire by sea had been the
origin of the democracy, and that the farming population
were not so much opposed to oligarchy.

Themistocles, however, formed yet higher designs with a
view to naval supremacy. For, after the departure of Xerxes,
when the Grecian fleet was arrived at Pagasae, where they
wintered, Themistocles, in a public oration to the people of
Athens, told them that he had a design to perform something that would tend greatly to their interests and safety,
but was of such a nature that it could not be made generally
public. The Athenians ordered him to impart it to Aristides
only; and, if he approved of it, to put it in practise. And
when Themistocles had discovered to him that his design
was to burn the Grecian fleet in the haven of Pagasae, Aristides coming out to the people, gave this report of the

stratagem contrived by Themistocles, that no proposal could be more politic, or more dishonourable; on which the Athenians commanded Themistocles to think no further of it.

He was also burdensome to the confederates, sailing about the islands and collecting money from them. Herodotus says, that, requiring money of those of the island of Andros, he told them that he had brought with him two goddesses, Persuasion and Force; and they answered him that they had also two great goddesses, which prohibited them from giving him any money, Poverty and Impossibility.

When the citizens of Athens began to listen willingly to those who traduced and reproached him, he was forced, with somewhat obnoxious frequency, to put them in mind of the great services he had performed, and ask those who were offended with him whether they were weary with receiving benefits often from the same person, so rendering himself more odious. And he yet provoked the people by building a temple to Diana with the epithet of Aristobule, or Diana of Best Counsel; intimating thereby, that he had given the best counsel, not only to the Athenians, but to all Greece. He built this temple near his own house, in the district called Melite, where now the public officers carry out the bodies of such as are executed, and throw the halters and clothes of those that are strangled or otherwise put to death. There is to this day a small figure of Themistocles in the temple of Diana of Best Counsel, which represents him to be a person not only of a noble mind, but also of a most heroic aspect. At length the Athenians banished him, making use of the ostracism to humble his eminence and authority, as they ordinarily did with all whom they thought too powerful, or, by their greatness, disproportionable to the equality thought requisite in a popular government. For the ostracism was instituted, not so much to punish the offender, as to mitigate and pacify the violence of the envious, who delighted to humble eminent men, and who, by fixing this disgrace upon them, might vent some part of their rancour.

Themistocles being banished from Athens, while he stayed at Argos the detection of Pausanias happened, which gave such advantage to his enemies, that Leobotes of Agra-ule, son of Alcmaeon, indicted him of treason, the Spartans supporting him in the accusation.

When Pausanias went about this treasonable design, he concealed it at first from Themistocles, though he were his intimate friend; but when he saw him expelled out of the commonwealth, and how impatiently he took his banish-ment, he ventured to communicate it to him, and desired his assistance, showing him the king of Persia's letters, and ex-asperating him against the Greeks, as a villainous, ungrate-ful people. However, Themistocles immediately rejected the proposals of Pausanias, and wholly refused to be a party in the enterprise, though he never revealed his communica-tions, nor disclosed the conspiracy to any man, either hoping that Pausanias would desist from his intentions, or expecting that so inconsiderate an attempt after such chimerical ob-jects would be discovered by other means.

After that Pausanias was put to death, letters and writings being found concerning this matter, which rendered Themis-tocles suspected, the Lacedaemonians were clamorous against him, and his enemies among the Athenians accused him; when, being absent from Athens, he made his defence by letters, especially against the points that had been previ-ously alleged against him. In answer to the malicious detrac-tions of his enemies, he merely wrote to the citizens, urging that he who was always ambitious to govern, and not of a character or a disposition to serve, would never sell himself and his country into slavery to a barbarous and hostile na-tion.

Notwithstanding this, the people, being persuaded by his accusers, sent officers to take him and bring him away to be tried before a council of the Greeks, but, having timely no-tice of it, he passed over into the island of Corcyra, where the state was under obligations to him; for, being chosen as arbitrator in a difference between them and the Corinthians, he decided the controversy by ordering the Corinthians to pay down twenty talents, and declaring the town and island of Leucas a joint colony from both cities. From thence he fled into Epirus, and, the Athenians and Lacedaemonians still pursuing him, he threw himself upon chances of safety that seemed all but desperate. For he fled for refuge to Admetus, king of the Molossians, who had formerly made some request to the Athenians, when Themistocles was in the height of his authority, and had been disdainfully used and insulted by him, and had let it appear plain enough, that, could he lay hold of him, he would take his revenge. Yet in this misfortune, Themistocles, fearing the recent hatred of his neighbours and fellow-citizens more than the old displeasure of the king, put himself at his mercy and became an humble suppliant to Admetus, after a peculiar manner different from the custom of other countries. For taking the king's son, who was then a child, in his arms, he laid himself down at his hearth, this being the most sacred and only manner of supplication among the Molossians, which was not to be refused. And some say that his wife, Phthia, intimated to Themistocles this way of petitioning, and placed her young son with him before the hearth; others, that king Admetus, that he might be under a religious obligation not to deliver him up to his pursuers, prepared and enacted with him a sort of stage-play to this effect. At this time Epicrates of Acharnae privately conveyed his wife and children out of Athens, and sent them hither, for which afterwards Cimon condemned him and put him to death; as Stesimbrotus reports, and yet somehow, either forgetting this himself, or making Themistocles to be little mindful of it, says presently that he sailed into Sicily, and desired in marriage the daughter of Hiero, tyrant of Syracuse, promising to bring the Greeks under his power; and, on Hiero refusing him, departed thence into Asia; but this is not probable.

A great part of his estate was privately conveyed away by his friends, and sent after him by sea into Asia; besides which, there was discovered and confiscated to the value of fourscore talents, as Theophrastus writes; Theopompus says an hundred; though Themistocles was never worth three talents before he was concerned in public affairs.

When he arrived at Cyme, and understood that all along the coast there were many laid wait for him, and particularly Ergoteles and Pythodorus (for the game was worth the hunting for such as were thankful to make money by any means, the king of Persia having offered by public proclamation two hundred talents to him that should take him), he fled to Aegae, a small city of the Aeolians, where no one knew him but only his host Nicogenes, who was the richest man in Aeolia, and well known to the great men of Inner Asia. While Themistocles lay hid for some days in his house, one night, after a sacrifice and supper insuing, Olbius, the attendant upon Nicogenes's children, fell into a sort of frenzy and fit of inspiration, and cried out in verse—

"Night shall speak, and night instruct thee,
  By the voice of night conduct thee."

After this, Themistocles, going to bed, dreamed that he saw a snake coil itself up upon his belly, and so creep to his neck; then, as soon as it touched his face, it turned into an eagle, which spread its wings over him, and took him up and flew away with him a great distance; then there appeared a herald's golden wand, and upon this at last it set him down securely, after infinite terror and disturbance.

His departure was effected by Nicogenes by the following artifice: The barbarous nations, and amongst them the Persians especially, are extremely jealous, severe, and suspicious about their women, not only their wives, but also their bought slaves and concubines, whom they keep so strictly that no one ever sees them abroad; they spend their lives shut up within doors, and, when they take a journey, are carried in close tents, curtained in on all sides, and set upon a wagon. Such a travelling carriage being prepared for Themistocles, they hid him in it, and carried him on his journey, and told those whom they met or spoke with upon the road that they were conveying a young Greek woman out of Ionia to a nobleman at court.

Thucydides and Charon of Lampsacus say that Xerxes was dead, and that Themistocles had an interview with his son; but Ephorus, Dinon, Clitarchus, Heraclides, and many others, write that he came to Xerxes. The chronological tables better agree with the account of Thucydides, and yet neither can their statements be said to be quite set at rest.

When Themistocles was come to the critical point, he applied himself first to Artabanus, commander of a thousand men, telling him that he was a Greek, and desired to speak with the king about important affairs concerning which the king was extremely solicitous. Artabanus answered him: "O stranger, the laws of men are different, and one thing is honourable to one man, and to others another; but it is honourable for all to honour and observe their own laws. It is the habit of the Greeks, we are told, to honour, above all things, liberty and equality; but amongst our many excellent laws, we account this the most excellent, to honour the king, and to worship him, as the image of the great preserver of the universe; if, then, you shall consent to our laws, and fall down before the king and worship him, you may both see him and speak to him; but if your mind be otherwise, you must make use of others to intercede for you, for it is not the national custom here for the king to give audience to any one that doth not fall down before him." Themistocles, hearing this, replied: "Artabanus, I, that come hither to increase the power and glory of the king, will not only submit myself to his laws, since so it hath pleased the god who exalteth the Persian empire to this greatness, but will also cause many more to be worshippers and adorers of the king. Let not this, therefore, be an impediment why I should not communicate to the king what I have to impart." Artabanus asking him, "Who must we tell him that you are? for your words signify you to be no ordinary person." Themistocles answered, "No man, O Artabanus, must be informed of this before the king himself." Thus Phanias relates; to which Eratosthenes, in his treatise on Riches, adds, that it was by the means of a woman of Eretria, who was kept by Artabanus, that he obtained this audience and interview with him.

When he was introduced to the king, and had paid his reverence to him, he stood silent, till the king commanding the interpreter to ask him who he was, he replied, "O king, I am Themistocles the Athenian, driven into banishment by the Greeks. The evils that I have done to the Persians are numerous; but my benefits to them yet greater, in withholding the Greeks from pursuit, so soon as the deliverance of my own country allowed me to show kindness also to you. I come with a mind suited to my present calamities; prepared alike for favours and for anger; to welcome your gracious reconciliation, and to deprecate your wrath. Take my own countrymen for witnesses of the services I have done for Persia, and make use of this occasion to show the world your virtue, rather than to satisfy your indignation. If you save me, you will save your suppliant; if otherwise, will destroy an enemy of the Greeks." He talked also of divine admonitions, such as the vision which he saw at Nicogenes's house, and the direction given him by the oracle of Dodona, where Jupiter commanded him to go to him that had a name like his, by which he understood that he was sent from Jupiter to him, seeing that they both were great, and had the name of kings.

The king heard him attentively, and, though he admired his temper and courage, gave him no answer at that time; but, when he was with his intimate friends, rejoiced in his great good fortune, and esteemed himself very happy in this, and prayed to his god Arimanius, that all his enemies might be ever of the same mind with the Greeks, to abuse and expel the bravest men amongst them. Then he sacrificed to the gods, and presently fell to drinking, and was so well pleased, that in the night, in the middle of his sleep, he cried out for joy three times, "I have Themistocles the Athenian."

In the morning, calling together the chiefs of his court, he had Themistocles brought before him, who expected no good of it, when he saw, for example, the guards fiercely set against him as soon as they learnt his name, and giving him ill language. As he came forward towards the king, who was seated, the rest keeping silence, passing by Roxanes, a commander of a thousand men, he heard him, with a slight groan, say, without stirring out of his place, "You subtle Greek serpent, the king's good genius hath brought thee thither." Yet, when he came into the presence, and again fell down, the king saluted him, and spake to him kindly, telling him he was now indebted to him two hundred talents; for it was just and reasonable that he should receive the reward which was proposed to whosoever should bring Themistocles; and promising much more, and encouraging him, he commanded him to speak freely what he would concerning the affairs of Greece. Themistocles replied, that a man's discourse was like to a rich Persian carpet, the beautiful figures and patterns of which can only be shown by spreading and extending it out; when it is contracted and folded up, they are obscure and lost; and, therefore, he desired time. The king being pleased with the comparison, and bidding him take what time he would, he desired a year; in which time, having learnt the Persian language sufficiently, he spoke with the king by himself without the help of an interpreter, it being supposed that he discoursed only about the affairs of Greece; but there happening, at the same time, great alterations at court, and removals of the king's favourites, he drew upon himself the envy of the great people, who imagined that he had taken the boldness to speak concerning them. For the favours shown to other strangers were nothing in comparison with the honours conferred on him; the king invited him to partake of his own pastimes and recreations both at home and abroad, carrying him with him a-hunting, and made him his intimate so far that he permitted him to see the queen-mother, and converse frequently with her. By the king's command, he also was made acquainted with the Magian learning.

When Demaratus the Lacedaemonian, being ordered by the king to ask whatsoever he pleased, that it should immediately be granted him, desired that he might make his public entrance, and be carried in state through the city of Sardis, with the tiara set in the royal manner upon his head, Mithropaustes, cousin to the king, touched him on the head, and told him that he had no brains for the royal tiara to cover, and if Jupiter should give him his lightning and thunder, he would not any the more be Jupiter for that; the king also repulsed him with anger, resolving never to be reconciled to him, but to be inexorable to all supplications on his behalf. Yet Themistocles pacified him, and prevailed with him to forgive him. And it is reported that the succeeding kings, in whose reigns there was a greater communication between the Greeks and Persians, when they invited any considerable Greek into their service, to encourage him, would write, and promise him that he should be as great with them as Themistocles had been. They relate, also, how Themistocles, when he was in great prosperity, and courted by many, seeing himself splendidly served at his table, turned to his children and said, "Children, we had been un-done if we had not been undone." Most writers say that he had three cities given him, Magnesia, Myus, and Lamp-sacus, to maintain him in bread, meat, and wine. Neanthes of Cyzicus, and Phanias, add two more, the city of Palae-scepsis, to provide him with clothes, and Percote, with bed-ding and furniture for his house.

As he was going down towards the sea-coast to take measures against Greece, a Persian whose name was Epixyes, governor of the upper Phrygia, laid wait to kill him, having for that purpose provided a long time before a number of Pisidians, who were to set upon him when he should stop to rest at a city that is called Lion's-head. But Themistocles, sleeping in the middle of the day, saw the Mother of the gods appear to him in a dream and say unto him, "Themistocles, keep back from the Lion's-head, for fear you fall into the lion's jaws; for this advice I expect that your daughter Mnesiptolema should be my servant." The-mistocles was much astonished, and when he had made his vows to the goddess, left the broad road, and, making a circuit, went another way, changing his intended station to avoid that place, and at night took up his rest in the fields. But one of the sumpter-horses, which carried the furniture for his tent, having fallen that day into the river, his servants spread out the tapestry, which was wet, and hung it up to dry; in the meantime the Pisidians made towards them with their swords drawn, and, not discerning exactly by the moon what it was that was stretched out, thought it to be the tent of Themistocles, and that they should find him resting himself within it; but when they came near, and lifted up the hangings, those who watched there fell upon them and took them. Themistocles, having escaped this great danger, in admiration of the goodness of the goddess that appeared to him, built, in memory of it, a temple in the city of Magnesia, which is dedicated to Dindymene, Mother of the gods, in which he consecrated and devoted his daughter Mnesiptolema to her service.

When he came to Sardis, he visited the temples of the gods, and observing, at his leisure, their buildings, ornaments, and the number of their offerings, he saw in the temple of the Mother of the gods the statue of a virgin in brass, two cubits high, called the water-bringer. Themistocles had caused this to be made and set up when he was surveyor of the waters at Athens, out of the fines of those whom he detected in drawing off and diverting the public water by pipes for their private use; and whether he had some regret to see this image in captivity, or was desirous to let the Athenians see in what great credit and authority he was with the king, he entered into a treaty with the governor to persuade him to send this statue back to Athens, which so enraged the Persian officer, that he told him he would write the king word of it. Themistocles, being affrighted hereat, got access to his wives and concubines, by presents of money to whom he appeased the fury of the governor; and afterwards behaved with more reserve and circumspection, fearing the envy of the Persians, and did not, as Theopompus writes, continue to travel about Asia, but lived quietly in his own house in Magnesia, where for a long time he passed his days in great security, being courted by all, and enjoying rich presents, and honoured equally with the greatest persons in the Persian empire; the king, at that time, not minding his concerns with Greece, being taken up with the affairs of inner Asia.

But when Egypt revolted, being assisted by the Athenians, and the Greek galleys roved about as far as Cyprus and Cilicia, and Cimon had made himself master of the seas, the king turned his thoughts thither, and, bending his mind chiefly to resist the Greeks, and to check the growth of their power against him, began to raise forces, and send out commanders, and to despatch messengers to Themistocles at Magnesia, to put him in mind of his promise, and to summon him to act against the Greeks. Yet this did not increase his hatred nor exasperate him against the Athenians, neither was he in any way elevated with the thoughts of the honour and powerful command he was to have in this war; but judging, perhaps, that the object would not be attained, the Greeks having at that time, beside other great commanders, Cimon, in particular, who was gaining wonderful military successes; but chiefly being ashamed to sully the glory of his former great actions, and of his many victories and trophies, he determined to put a conclusion to his life, agreeable to its previous course. He sacrificed to the gods, and invited his friends; and, having entertained them and shaken hands with them, drank bull's blood, as is the usual story; as others state, a poison producing instant death; and ended his days in the city of Magnesia, having lived sixty-five years, most of which he had spent in politics and in wars, in government and command. The king being informed of the cause and manner of his death, admired him more than ever, and continued to show kindness to his friends and relations.

The Magnesians possess a splendid sepulchre of Themistocles, placed in the middle of their market-place. Various honours also and privileges were granted to the kindred of Themistocles at Magnesia, which were observed down to our times, and were enjoyed by another Themistocles of Athens, with whom I had an intimate acquaintance and friendship in the house of Ammonius the philosopher.

✤

PERICLES

Caesar once, seeing some wealthy strangers at Rome, carrying up and down with them in their arms and bosoms young puppy-dogs and monkeys, embracing and making much of them, took occasion not unnaturally to ask whether the women in their country were not used to bear children; by that prince-like reprimand gravely reflecting upon persons who spend and lavish upon brute beasts that affection and kindness which nature has implanted in us to be bestowed on those of our own kind. With like reason may we blame those who misuse that love of inquiry and observation which nature has implanted in our souls, by expending it on objects unworthy of the attention either of their eyes or their ears, while they disregard such as are excellent in themselves, and would do them good.

The mere outward sense, being passive in responding to the impression of the objects that come in its way and strike upon it, perhaps cannot help entertaining and taking notice of everything that addresses it, be it what it will, useful or unuseful; but, in the exercise of his mental perception, every man, if he chooses, has a natural power to turn himself upon all occasions, and to change and shift with the greatest ease to what he shall himself judge desirable. So that it becomes a man's duty to pursue and make after the best and choicest of everything, that he may not only employ his contemplation, but may also be improved by it. For as that colour is more suitable to the eye whose freshness and pleasantness stimulates and strengthens the sight, so a man ought to apply his intellectual perception to such objects as, with the sense of delight, are apt to call it forth, and allure it to its own proper good and advantage.

Such objects we find in the acts of virtue, which also produce in the minds of mere readers about them an emulation and eagerness that may lead them on to imitation. In other things there does not immediately follow upon the admiration and liking of the thing done any strong desire of doing the like. Nay, many times, on the very contrary, when we are pleased with the work, we slight and set little by the workman or artist himself, as, for instance, in perfumes and purple dyes, we are taken with the things themselves well enough, but do not think dyers and perfumers otherwise than low and sordid people. It was not said amiss by Antisthenes, when people told him that one Ismenias was an excellent piper. "It may be so," said he, "but he is but a wretched human being, otherwise he would not have been an excellent piper." And King Philip, to the same purpose, told his son Alexander, who once at a merry-meeting played a piece of music charmingly and skilfully, "Are you not ashamed, son, to play so well?" For it is enough for a king or prince to find leisure sometimes to hear others sing, and he does the muses quite honour enough when he pleases to be but present, while others engage in such exercises and trials of skill.

He who busies himself in mean occupations produces, in the very pains he takes about things of little or no use, an evidence against himself of his negligence and indisposition to what is really good. Nor did any generous and ingenuous young man, at the sight of the statue of Jupiter at Pisa, ever desire to be a Phidias, or on seeing that of Juno at Argos, long to be a Polycletus, or feel induced by his pleasure in their poems to wish to be an Anacreon or Philetas or Archilochus. For it does not necessarily follow, that, if a piece of work please for its gracefulness, therefore he that wrought it deserves our admiration. Whence it is that neither do such things really profit or advantage the beholders, upon the sight of which no zeal arises for the imitation of them, nor any impulse or inclination, which may prompt any desire or endeavour of doing the like. But

virtue, by the bare statement of its actions, can so affect
men's minds as to create at once both admiration of the
things done and desire to imitate the doers of them. The
goods of fortune we would possess and would enjoy; those
of virtue we long to practise and exercise: we are content
to receive the former from others, the latter we wish others to experience from us. Moral good is a practical stimu-
lus; it is no sooner seen, than it inspires an impulse to practice, and influences the mind and character not by a mere
imitation which we look at, but by the statement of the fact
creates a moral purpose which we form.

And so we have thought fit to spend our time and pains
in writing of the lives of famous persons; and have composed this tenth book upon that subject, containing the life
of Pericles, and that of Fabius Maximus, who carried on
the war against Hannibal, men alike, as in their other virtues and good parts, so especially in their mind and up-
right temper and demeanour, and in that capacity to bear
the cross-grained humours of their fellow-citizens and colleagues in office, which made them both most useful and
serviceable to the interests of their countries. Whether we
take a right aim at our intended purpose, it is left to the
reader to judge by what he shall here find.

Pericles was of the tribe Acamantis, and the township
Cholargus, of the noblest birth both on his father's and
mother's side. Xanthippus, his father, who defeated the
King of Persia's generals in the battle of Mycale, took to
wife Agariste, the grandchild of Clisthenes, who drove out
the sons of Pisistratus, and nobly put an end to their tyrannical usurpation, and, moreover, made a body of laws,
and settled a model of government admirably tempered
and suited for the harmony and safety of the people.

His mother, being near her time, fancied in a dream that
she was brought to bed of a lion, and a few days after was
delivered of Pericles, in other respects perfectly formed,
only his head was somewhat longish and out of proportion.
For which reason almost all the images and statues that
were made of him have the head covered with a helmet, the
workmen apparently being willing not to expose him. The

poets of Athens called him *Schinocephalos,* or squill-head,
from *schinos,* a squill, or sea-onion. One of the comic poets,
Cratinus, in the Chirons, tells us that—

"Old Chronos once took queen Sedition to wife:
  Which two brought to life
  That tyrant far-famed,
Whom the gods the supreme skull-compeller have named;

and, in the Nemesis, addresses him—

    "Come, Jove, thou *head* of Gods."

And a second, Teleclides, says, that now, in embarrassment
with political difficulties, he sits in the city—

    "Fainting underneath the load
      Of his own head: and now abroad
      From his huge gallery of a pate
      Sends forth trouble to the state."

And a third, Eupolis, in the comedy called the Demi, in a
series of questions about each of the demagogues, whom
he makes in the play to come up from hell, upon Pericles
being named last, exclaims—

    "And here by way of summary, now we've done,
    Behold, in brief, the heads of all in one."

The master that taught him music, most authors are
agreed, was Damon (whose name, they say, ought to be
pronounced with the first syllable short). Though Aristotle tells us that he was thoroughly practised in all accomplishments of this kind by Pythoclides. Damon, it is not unlikely, being a sophist, out of policy sheltered himself under
the profession of music to conceal from people in general
his skill in other things, and under this pretence attended
Pericles, the young athlete of politics, so to say, as his
training-master in these exercises. Damon's lyre, however,

did not prove altogether a successful blind; he was banished the country by ostracism for ten years, as a dangerous intermeddler and a favourer of arbitrary power, and, by this means, gave the stage occasion to play upon him. As, for instance, Plato, the comic poet, introduces a character who questions him—

"Tell me if you please,
Since you're the Chiron who taught Pericles."

Pericles, also, was a hearer of Zeno, the Eleatic, who treated of natural philosophy in the same manner as Parmenides did, but had also perfected himself in an art of his own for refuting and silencing opponents in argument; as Timon of Phlius describes it—

"Also the two-edged tongue of mighty Zeno, who,
Say what one would, could argue it untrue."

But he that saw most of Pericles, and furnished him most especially with a weight and grandeur of sense, superior to all arts of popularity, and in general gave him his elevation and sublimity of purpose and of character, was Anaxagoras of Clazomenae; whom the men of those times called by the name of Nous, that is, mind, or intelligence, whether in admiration of the great and extraordinary gift he had displayed for the science of nature, or because that he was the first of the philosophers who did not refer the first ordering of the world to fortune or chance, nor to necessity or compulsion, but to a pure, unadulterated intelligence, which in all other existing mixed and compound things acts as a principle of discrimination, and of combination of like with like.

For this man, Pericles entertained an extraordinary esteem and admiration, and filling himself with this lofty and, as they call it, up-in-the-air sort of thought, derived hence not merely, as was natural, elevation of purpose and dignity of language, raised far above the base and dishonest buffooneries of mob eloquence, but, besides this, a composure of countenance, and a serenity and calmness in all his movements, which no occurrence whilst he was speaking could disturb, a sustained and even tone of voice, and various other advantages of a similar kind, which produced the greatest effect on his hearers. Once, after being reviled and ill-spoken of all day long in his own hearing by some vile and abandoned fellow in the open market-place, where he was engaged in the despatch of some urgent affair, he continued his business in perfect silence, and in the evening returned home composedly, the man still dogging him at the heels, and pelting him all the way with abuse and foul language; and stepping into his house, it being by this time dark, he ordered one of his servants to take a light, and to go along with the man and see him safe home. Ion, it is true, the dramatic poet, says that Pericles's manner in company was somewhat over-assuming and pompous; and that into his high-bearing there entered a good deal of slightingness and scorn of others; he reserves his commendation for Cimon's ease and pliancy and natural grace in society. Ion, however, who must needs make virtue, like a show of tragedies, include some comic scenes, we shall not altogether rely upon; Zeno used to bid those who called Pericles's gravity the affectation of a charlatan, to go and affect the like themselves; inasmuch as this mere counterfeiting might in time insensibly instil into them a real love and knowledge of those noble qualities.

Nor were these the only advantages which Pericles derived from Anaxagoras's acquaintance; he seems also to have become, by his instructions, superior to that superstition with which an ignorant wonder at appearances, for example, in the heavens, possesses the minds of people unacquainted with their causes, eager for the supernatural, and excitable through an inexperience which the knowledge of natural causes removes, replacing wild and timid superstition by the good hope and assurance of an intelligent piety.

There is a story, that once Pericles had brought to him from a country farm of his a ram's head with one horn, and that Lampon, the diviner, upon seeing the horn grow

strong and solid out of the midst of the forehead, gave it
as his judgment, that, there being at that time two potent
factions, parties, or interests in the city, the one of Thucydides and the other of Pericles, the government would
come about to that one of them in whose ground or estate
this token or indication of fate had shown itself. But that
Anaxagoras, cleaving the skull in sunder, showed to the bystanders that the brain had not filled up its natural place,
but being oblong, like an egg, had collected from all parts of
the vessel which contained it in a point to that place from
whence the root of the horn took its rise. And that, for that
time, Anaxagoras was much admired for his explanation
by those that were present; and Lampon no less a little
while after, when Thucydides was overpowered, and the
whole affairs of the state and government came into the
hands of Pericles.

And yet, in my opinion, it is no absurdity to say that they
were both in the right, both natural philosopher and diviner, one justly detecting the cause of this event, by which
it was produced, the other the end for which it was designed. For it was the business of the one to find out and
give an account of what it was made, and in what manner
and by what means it grew as it did; and of the other to
foretell to what end and purpose it was so made, and what
it might mean or portend. Those who say that to find out
the cause of a prodigy is in effect to destroy its supposed
signification as such, do not take notice, that, at the same
time, together with divine prodigies, they also do away with
signs and signals of human art and concert, as, for instance,
the clashings of quoits, fire-beacons, and the shadows of
sun-dials, every one of which has its cause, and by that
cause and contrivance is a sign of something else. But these
are subjects, perhaps, that would better befit another place.

Pericles, while yet but a young man, stood in considerable apprehension of the people, as he was thought in face
and figure to be very like the tyrant Pisistratus, and those
of great age remarked upon the sweetness of his voice, and
his volubility and rapidity in speaking, and were struck
with amazement at the resemblance. Reflecting, too, that

he had a considerable estate, and was descended of a noble family, and had friends of great influence, he was fearful all this might bring him to be banished as a dangerous person, and for this reason meddled not at all with state affairs, but in military service showed himself of a brave and intrepid nature. But when Aristides was now dead, and Themistocles driven out, and Cimon was for the most part kept abroad by the expeditions he made in parts out of Greece, Pericles, seeing things in this posture, now advanced and took his side, not with the rich and few, but with the many and poor, contrary to his natural bent, which was far from democratical; but, most likely fearing he might fall under suspicion of aiming at arbitrary power, and seeing Cimon on the side of the aristocracy, and much beloved by the better and more distinguished people, he joined the party of the people, with a view at once both to secure himself and procure means against Cimon.

He immediately entered, also, on quite a new course of life and management of his time. For he was never seen to walk in any street but that which led to the market-place and council-hall, and he avoided invitations of friends to supper, and all friendly visiting and intercourse whatever; in all the time he had to do with the public, which was not a little, he was never known to have gone to any of his friends to a supper, except that once when his near kinsman Euryptolemus married, he remained present till the ceremony of the drink-offering, and then immediately rose from table and went his way. For these friendly meetings are very quick to defeat any assumed superiority, and in intimate familiarity an exterior of gravity is hard to maintain. Real excellence, indeed, is most recognised when most openly looked into; and in really good men, nothing which meets the eyes of external observers so truly deserves their admiration, as their daily common life does that of their nearer friends. Pericles, however, to avoid any feeling of commonness, or any satiety on the part of the people, presented himself at intervals only, not speaking to every business, nor at all times coming into the assembly, but, as Critolaus says, reserving himself, like the Salaminian

galley, for great occasions, while matters of lesser importance were despatched by friends or other speakers under
his direction. And of this number we are told Ephialtes
made one, who broke the power of the council of Areopagus, giving the people, according to Plato's expression,
so copious and so strong a draught of liberty, that growing
wild and unruly, like an unmanageable horse, it, as the
comic poets say—

> "——got beyond all keeping in,
> Champing at Euboea, and among the islands leaping in."

The style of speaking most consonant to his form of life
and the dignity of his views he found, so to say, in the
tones of that instrument with which Anaxagoras had furnished him; of his teaching he continually availed himself, and deepened the colours of rhetoric with the dye of
natural science. For having, in addition to his great natural
genius, attained, by the study of nature, to use the words
of the divine Plato, this height of intelligence, and this universal consummating power, and drawing hence whatever
might be of advantage to him in the art of speaking, he
showed himself far superior to all others. Upon which
account, they say, he had his nickname given him, though
some are of opinion he was named the Olympian from the
public buildings with which he adorned the city; and others
again, from his great power in public affairs, whether of war
or peace. Nor is it unlikely that the confluence of many
attributes may have conferred it on him. However, the comedies represented at the time, which, both in good earnest
and in merriment, let fly many hard words at him, plainly
show that he got that appellation especially from his speaking; they speak of his "thundering and lightning" when he
harangued the people, and of his wielding a dreadful thunderbolt in his tongue.

A saying also of Thucydides, the son of Melesias, stands
on record, spoken by him by way of pleasantry upon Pericles's dexterity. Thucydides was one of the noble and distinguished citizens, and had been his greatest opponent; and,

when Archidamus, the King of the Lacedaemonians, asked him whether he or Pericles were the better wrestler, he made this answer: "When I," said he, "have thrown him and given him a fair fall, by persisting that he had no fall, he gets the better of me, and makes the bystanders, in spite of their own eyes, believe him." The truth, however, is, that Pericles himself was very careful what and how he was to speak, insomuch that, whenever he went up to the hustings, he prayed the gods that no one word might unawares slip from him unsuitable to the matter and the occasion.

He has left nothing in writing behind him, except some decrees; and there are but very few of his sayings recorded; one, for example, is, that he said Aegina must, like a gathering in a man's eye, be removed from Piraeus; and another, that he said he saw already war moving on its way towards them out of Peloponnesus. Again, when on a time Sophocles, who was his fellow-commissioner in the generalship, was going on board with him, and praised the beauty of a youth they met with in the way to the ship, "Sophocles," said he, "a general ought not only to have clean hands but also clean eyes." And Stesimbrotus tells us that, in his encomium on those who fell in battle at Samos, he said they were become immortal, as the gods were. "For," said he, "we do not see them themselves, but only by the honours we pay them, and by the benefits they do us, attribute to them immortality; and the like attributes belong also to those that die in the service of their country."

Since Thucydides describes the rule of Pericles as an aristocratical government, that went by the name of a democracy, but was, indeed, the supremacy of a single great man, while many others say, on the contrary, that by him the common people were first encouraged and led on to such evils as appropriations of subject territory, allowances for attending theatres, payments for performing public duties, and by these bad habits were, under the influence of his public measures, changed from a sober, thrifty people, that maintained themselves by their own labours, to lovers of expense, intemperance, and licence, let us examine the cause of this change by the actual matters of fact.

At the first, as has been said, when he set himself against Cimon's great authority, he did caress the people. Finding himself come short of his competitor in wealth and money, by which advantages the other was enabled to take care of the poor, inviting every day some one or other of the citizens that was in want to supper, and bestowing clothes on the aged people, and breaking down the hedges and enclosures of his grounds, that all that would might freely gather what fruit they pleased, Pericles, thus outdone in popular arts, by the advice of one Damonides of Oea, as Aristotle states, turned to the distribution of the public moneys; and in a short time having bought the people over, what with moneys allowed for shows and for service on juries, and what with other forms of pay and largess, he made use of them against the council of Areopagus of which he himself was no member, as having never been appointed by lot either chief archon, or lawgiver, or king, or captain. For from of old these offices were conferred on persons by lot, and they who had acquitted themselves duly in the discharge of them were advanced to the court of Areopagus. And so Pericles, having secured his power in interest with the populace, directed the exertions of his party against this council with such success, that most of these causes and matters which had been used to be tried there were, by the agency of Ephialtes, removed from its cognisance; Cimon, also, was banished by ostracism as a favourer of the Lacedaemonians and a hater of the people, though in wealth and noble birth he was among the first, and had won several most glorious victories over the barbarians, and had filled the city with money and spoils of war; as is recorded in the history of his life. So vast an authority had Pericles obtained among the people.

The ostracism was limited by law to ten years; but the Lacedaemonians in the meantime, entering with a great army into the territory of Tanagra, and the Athenians going out against them, Cimon, coming from his banishment before his time was out, put himself in arms and array with those of his fellow-citizens that were of his own tribe, and desired by his deeds to wipe off the suspicion of his favour-

ing the Lacedaemonians, by venturing his own person along
with his countrymen. But Pericles's friends, gathering in a
body, forced him to retire as a banished man. For which
cause also Pericles seems to have exerted himself more in
that than in any battle, and to have been conspicuous
above all for his exposure of himself to danger. All Cimon's
friends, also, to a man, fell together side by side, whom Pericles had accused with him of taking part with the Lacedaemonians. Defeated in this battle on their own frontiers, and
expecting a new and perilous attack with return of spring,
the Athenians now felt regret and sorrow for the loss of
Cimon, and repentance for their expulsion of him. Pericles, being sensible of their feelings, did not hesitate or
delay to gratify it, and himself made the motion for recalling him home. He, upon his return, concluded a peace
betwixt the two cities; for the Lacedaemonians entertained
as kindly feelings towards him as they did the reverse towards Pericles and the other popular leaders.

Yet some there are who say that Pericles did not propose
the order for Cimon's return till some private articles of
agreement had been made between them, and this by means
of Elpinice, Cimon's sister; that Cimon, namely, should go
out to sea with a fleet of two hundred ships, and be com-
mander-in-chief abroad, with a design to reduce the King of
Persia's territories, and that Pericles should have the power
at home.

This Elpinice, it was thought, had before this time procured some favour for her brother Cimon at Pericles's
hands, and induced him to be more remiss and gentle in
urging the charge when Cimon was tried for his life; for
Pericles was one of the committee appointed by the commons to plead against him. And when Elpinice came and
besought him in her brother's behalf, he answered, with a
smile, "O Elpinice, you are too old a woman to undertake
such business as this." But, when he appeared to impeach
him, he stood up but once to speak, merely to acquit himself of his commission, and went out of court, having done
Cimon the least prejudice of any of his accusers.

How, then, can one believe Idomeneus, who charges

Pericles as if he had by treachery procured the murder of Ephialtes, the popular statesman, one who was his friend, and of his own party in all his political course, out of jealousy, forsooth, and envy of his great reputation? This historian, it seems, having raked up these stories, I know not whence, has befouled with them a man who, perchance, was not altogether free from fault or blame, but yet had a noble spirit, and a soul that was bent on honour; and where such qualities are, there can no such cruel and brutal passion find harbour or gain admittance. As to Ephialtes, the truth of the story, as Aristotle has told it, is this: that having made himself formidable to the oligarchical party, by being an uncompromising asserter of the people's rights in calling to account and prosecuting those who any way wronged them, his enemies, lying in wait for him, by the means of Aristodicus the Tanagraean, privately despatched him.

Cimon, while he was admiral, ended his days in the Isle of Cyprus. And the aristocratical party, seeing that Pericles was already before this grown to be the greatest and foremost man of all the city, but nevertheless wishing there should be somebody set up against him, to blunt and turn the edge of his power, that it might not altogether prove a monarchy, put forward Thucydides of Alopece, a discreet person, and a near kinsman of Cimon's, to conduct the opposition against him; who, indeed, though less skilled in warlike affairs than Cimon was, yet was better versed in speaking and political business and keeping close guard in the city, and, engaging with Pericles on the hustings, in a short time brought the government to an equality of parties. For he would not suffer those who were called the honest and good (persons of worth and distinction) to be scattered up and down and mix themselves and be lost among the populace, as formerly, diminishing and obscuring their superiority amongst the masses; but taking them apart by themselves and uniting them in one body, by their combined weight he was able, as it were upon the balance, to make a counterpoise to the other party.

For, indeed, there was from the beginning a sort of concealed split, or seam, as it might be in a piece of iron, marking the different popular and aristocratical tendencies; but the open rivalry and contention of these two opponents made the gash deep, and severed the city into the two parties of the people and the few. And so Pericles, at that time, more than at any other, let loose the reins to the people, and made his policy subservient to their pleasure, contriving continually to have some great public show or solemnity, some banquet, or some procession or other in the town to please them, coaxing his countrymen like children with such delights and pleasures as were not, however, unedifying. Besides that every year he sent out threescore galleys, on board of which there were numbers of the citizens, who were in pay eight months, learning at the same time and practising the art of seamanship.

He sent, moreover, a thousand of them into the Chersonese as planters, to share the land among them by lot, and five hundred more into the isle of Naxos, and half that number to Andros, a thousand into Thrace to dwell among the Bisaltae, and others into Italy, when the city Sybaris, which now was called Thurii, was to be repeopled. And this he did to ease and discharge the city of an idle, and, by reason of their idleness, a busy meddling crowd of people; and at the same time to meet the necessities and restore the fortunes of the poor townsmen, and to intimidate, also, and check their allies from attempting any change, by posting such garrisons, as it were, in the midst of them.

That which gave most pleasure and ornament to the city of Athens, and the greatest admiration and even astonishment to all strangers, and that which now is Greece's only evidence that the power she boasts of and her ancient wealth are no romance or idle story, was his construction of the public and sacred buildings. Yet this was that of all his actions in the government which his enemies most looked askance upon and cavilled at in the popular assemblies, crying out how that the commonwealth of Athens had lost its reputation and was ill-spoken of abroad for removing the common treasure of the Greeks from the Isle of Delos into their own custody; and how that their fairest excuse for so doing, namely, that they took it away for fear the barbarians should seize it, and on purpose to secure it in a safe place, this Pericles had made unavailable, and how that "Greece cannot but resent it as an insufferable affront, and consider herself to be tyrannised over openly, when she sees the treasure, which was contributed by her upon a necessity for the war, wantonly lavished out by us upon our city, to gild her all over, and to adorn and set her forth, as it were some vain woman, hung round with precious stones and figures and temples, which cost a world of money."

Pericles, on the other hand, informed the people, that they were in no way obliged to give any account of those moneys to their allies, so long as they maintained their defence, and kept off the barbarians from attacking them; while in the meantime they did not so much as supply one horse or man or ship, but only found money for the service; "which money," said he, "is not theirs that give it, but theirs that receive it, if so be they perform the conditions upon which they receive it." And that it was good reason, that, now the city was sufficiently provided and stored with all things necessary for the war, they should convert the overplus of its wealth to such undertakings as would hereafter, when completed, give them eternal honour, and, for the present, while in process, freely supply all the inhabitants with plenty. With their variety of workmanship and of occasions for service, which summon all arts and trades and require all hands to be employed about them, they do actually put the whole city, in a manner, into state-pay; while at the same time she is both beautiful and maintained by herself. For as those who are of age and strength for war are provided for and maintained in the armaments abroad by their pay out of the public stock, so, it being his desire and design that the undisciplined mechanic multitude that stayed at home should not go without their share of public salaries, and yet should not have them given them for sitting still and doing nothing, to that end he thought fit to bring in among them, with the approbation of the people, these vast projects of buildings and designs of work, that would be of some continuance before they were finished, and would give employment to numerous arts, so that the part of the people that stayed at home might, no less than those that were at sea or in garrisons or on expeditions, have a fair and just occasion of receiving the benefit and having their share of the public moneys.

The materials were stone, brass, ivory, gold, ebony, cypresswood; and the arts or trades that wrought and fashioned them were smiths and carpenters, moulders, founders and braziers, stone-cutters, dyers, goldsmiths, ivory-workers, painters, embroiderers, turners; those again that conveyed them to the town for use, merchants and mariners and ship-masters by sea, and by land, cartwrights, cattle-breeders, waggoners, rope-makers, flax-workers, shoemakers and leather-dressers, road-makers, miners. And every trade in the same nature, as a captain in an army has his particular company of soldiers under him, had its own hired company of journeymen and labourers belonging to it banded together as in array, to be as it were the instrument and body for the performance of the service. Thus, to say all in a word, the occasions and services of these public works distributed plenty through every age and condition.

As then grew the works up, no less stately in size than exquisite in form, the workmen striving to outvie the material and the design with the beauty of their workmanship, yet the most wonderful thing of all was the rapidity of their execution.

Undertakings, any one of which singly might have required, they thought, for their completion, several successions and ages of men, were every one of them accomplished in the height and prime of one man's political service. Although they say, too, that Zeuxis once, having heard Agatharchus the painter boast of despatching his work with speed and ease, replied, "I take a long time." For ease and speed in doing a thing do not give the work lasting solidity or exactness of beauty; the expenditure of time allowed to a man's pains beforehand for the production of a thing is repaid by way of interest with a vital force for the preservation when once produced. For which reason Pericles's works are especially admired, as having been made quickly, to last long. For every particular piece of his work was immediately, even at that time, for its beauty and elegance, antique; and yet in its vigour and freshness looks to this day as if it were just executed. There is a sort of bloom of newness upon those works of his, preserving them from the touch of time, as if they had some perennial spirit and undying vitality mingled in the composition of them.

Phidias had the oversight of all the works, and was surveyor-general, though upon the various portions other great masters and workmen were employed. For Callicrates and Ictinus built the Parthenon; the chapel at Eleusis, where the mysteries were celebrated, was begun by Coroebus, who erected the pillars that stand upon the floor or pavement, and joined them to the architraves; and after his death Metagenes of Xypete added the frieze and the upper line of columns; Xenocles of Cholargus roofed or arched the lantern on top of the temple of Castor and Pollux; and the long wall, which Socrates says he himself heard Pericles propose to the people was undertaken by Callicrates. This work Cratinus ridicules, as long in finishing—

"'Tis long since Pericles, if words would do it,
    Talked up the wall; yet adds not one mite to it."

The Odeum, or music-room, which in its interior was full of seats and ranges of pillars, and outside had its roof made to slope and descend from one single point at the top, was constructed, we are told, in imitation of the King of Persia's Pavilion; this likewise by Pericles's order; which Cratinus again, in his comedy called the Thracian Women, made an occasion of raillery—

"So, we see here,
    Jupiter Long-pate Pericles appear,
    Since ostracism time, he's laid aside his head,
    And wears the new Odeum in its stead."

Pericles, also eager for distinction, then first obtained the decree for a contest in musical skill to be held yearly at the Panathenaea, and he himself, being chosen judge, arranged the order and method in which the competitors should sing and play on the flute and on the harp. And both at that time, and at other times also, they sat in this music-room to see and hear all such trials of skill.

The propylaea, or entrances to the Acropolis, were finished in five years' time, Mnesicles being the principal architect. A strange accident happened in the course of building, which showed that the goddess was not averse to the work, but was aiding and co-operating to bring it to perfection. One of the artificers, the quickest and the handiest workman among them all, with a slip of his foot fell down from a great height, and lay in a miserable condition, the physicians having no hope of his recovery. When Pericles was in distress about this, Minerva appeared to him at night in a dream, and ordered a course of treatment, which he applied, and in a short time and with great ease cured the man. And upon this occasion it was that he set up a brass statue of Minerva, surnamed Health, in the citadel near the altar, which they say was there before. But it was Phidias who wrought the goddess's image in gold, and he has his name inscribed on the pedestal as the workman of it; and indeed the whole work in a manner was under his charge, and he had, as we have said already, the oversight over all the artists and workmen, through Pericles's friendship for him; and this, indeed, made him much envied, and his patron shamefully slandered with stories, as if Phidias were in the habit of receiving, for Pericles's use, freeborn women that came to see the works. The comic writers of the town, when they had got hold of this story, made much of it, and bespattered him with all the ribaldry they could invent, charging him falsely with the wife of Menippus, one who was his friend and served as lieutenant under him in the wars; and with the birds kept by Pyrilampes, an acquaintance of Pericles, who, they pretended, used to give presents of peacocks to Pericles's female friends. And how can one wonder at any number of strange assertions from men whose whole lives were devoted to mockery, and who were ready at any time to sacrifice the reputation of their superiors to vulgar envy and spite, as to some evil genius, when even Stesimbrotus the Thracian has dared to lay to the charge of Pericles a monstrous and fabulous piece of criminality with his son's wife? So very difficult a matter is it to trace and find out the truth of anything by history, when, on the one hand, those who afterwards write it find long periods of time intercepting their view, and, on the other hand, the contemporary records of any actions and lives, partly through envy and ill-will, partly through favour and flattery, pervert and distort truth.

When the orators, who sided with Thucydides and his party, were at one time crying out, as their custom was, against Pericles, as one who squandered away the public money, and made havoc of the state revenues, he rose in the open assembly and put the question to the people, whether they thought that he had laid out much; and they saying, "Too much, a great deal," "Then," said he, "since it is so, let the cost not go to your account, but to mine; and let the inscription upon the buildings stand in my name." When they heard him say thus, whether it were out of a surprise to see the greatness of his spirit or out of emulation of the glory of the works, they cried aloud, bidding him to spend on, and lay out what he thought fit from the public purse, and to spare no cost, till all were finished.

At length, coming to a final contest with Thucydides which of the two should ostracise the other out of the country, and having gone through this peril, he threw his antagonist out, and broke up the confederacy that had been organised against him. So that now all schism and division being at an end, and the city brought to evenness and unity, he got all Athens and all affairs that pertained to the Athenians into his own hands, their tributes, their armies, and their galleys, the islands, the sea, and their wide-extended power, partly over other Greeks and partly over barbarians, and all that empire, which they possessed, founded and fortified upon subject nations and royal friendships and alliances.

After this he was no longer the same man he had been before, nor as tame and gentle and familiar as formerly with the populace, so as readily to yield to their pleasures and to comply with the desires of the multitude, as a steersman shifts with the winds. Quitting that loose, remiss, and, in some cases, licentious court of the popular will, he turned those soft and flowery modulations to the austerity of aristocratical and regal rule; and employing this uprightly and undeviatingly for the country's best interests, he was able generally to lead the people along, with their own wills and consents, by persuading and showing them what was to be done; and sometimes, too, urging and pressing them forward extremely against their will, he made them, whether they would or no, yield submission to what was for their advantage. In which, to say the truth, he did but like a skilful physician, who, in a complicated and chronic disease, as he sees occasion, at one while allows his patient the moderate use of such things as please him, at another while gives him keen pains and drug to work the cure. For there arising and growing up, as was natural, all manner of distempered feelings among a people which had so vast a command and dominion, he alone, as a great master, knowing how to handle and deal fitly with each one of them, and, in an especial manner, making that use of hopes and fears, as his two chief rudders, with the one to check the career of their confidence at any time, with the other to raise them up and cheer them when under any discouragement, plainly showed by this, that rhetoric, or the art of speaking, is, in Plato's language, the government of the souls of men, and that her chief business is to address the affections and passions, which are as it were the strings and keys to the soul, and require a skilful and careful touch to be played on as they should be. The source of this predominance was not barely his power of language, but, as Thucydides assures us, the reputation of his life, and the confidence felt in his character; his manifest freedom from every kind of corruption, and superiority to all considerations of money. Notwithstanding he had made the city of Athens, which was great of itself, as great and rich as can be imagined, and though he were himself in power and interest more than equal to many kings and absolute rulers, who some of them also bequeathed by will their power to their children, he, for his part, did not make the patrimony his father left him greater than it was by one drachma.

Thucydides, indeed, gives a plain statement of the greatness of his power; and the comic poets, in their spiteful manner, more than hint at it, styling his companions and friends the new Pisistratidae, and calling on him to abjure any intention of usurpation, as one whose eminence was too great to be any longer proportionable to and compatible with a democracy or popular government. And Teleclides says the Athenians had surrendered up to him—

"The tribute of the cities, and with them, the cities too, to
      do with them as he pleases, and undo;
  To build up, if he likes, stone walls around a town; and
      again, if so he likes, to pull them down:
  Their treaties and alliances, power, empire, peace, and
      war, their wealth and their success forever more."

Nor was all this the luck of some happy occasion; nor was it the mere bloom and grace of a policy that flourished for a season; but having for forty years together maintained the first place among statesmen such as Ephialtes and Leocrates and Myronides and Cimon and Tolmides and Thucydides were, after the defeat and banishment of Thucydides, for no less than fifteen years longer, in the exercise of one continuous unintermitted command in the office, to which he was annually re-elected, of General, he preserved his integrity unspotted; though otherwise he was not altogether idle or careless in looking after his pecuniary advantage; his paternal estate, which of right belonged to him, he so ordered that it might neither through negligence be wasted or lessened, nor yet, being so full of business as he was, cost him any great trouble or time with taking care of it; and put it into such a way of management as he thought to be the most easy for himself, and the most exact. All his yearly products and profits he sold together in a lump, and supplied his household needs afterwards by buying everything that he or his family wanted out of the market. Upon which account, his children, when they grew to age, were not well pleased with his management, and the women that lived with him were treated with little cost, and complained of his way of housekeeping, where everything was ordered and set down from day to day, and reduced to the greatest exactness; since there was not there, as is usual in a great family and a plentiful estate, anything to spare, or over and above; but all that went out or came in, all disbursements and all receipts, proceeded as it were by number and measure. His manager in all this was a single servant, Evangelus by name, a man either naturally gifted or instructed by Pericles so as to excel every one in this art of domestic economy.

All this, in truth, was very little in harmony with Anaxagoras's wisdom; if, indeed, it be true that he, by a kind of divine impulse and greatness of spirit, voluntarily quitted his house, and left his land to lie fallow and to be grazed by sheep like a common. But the life of a contemplative philosopher and that of an active statesman are, I presume, not the same thing; for the one merely employs, upon great and good objects of thought, an intelligence that requires no aid of instruments nor supply of any external materials; whereas the other, who tempers and applies his virtue to human uses, may have occasion for affluence, not as a matter of necessity, but as a noble thing; which was Pericles's case, who relieved numerous poor citizens.

However, there is a story that Anaxagoras himself, while Pericles was taken up with public affairs, lay neglected, and that, now being grown old, he wrapped himself up with a resolution to die for want of food; which being by chance brought to Pericles's ear, he was horror-struck, and instantly ran thither, and used all the arguments and entreaties he could to him, lamenting not so much Anaxagoras's condition as his own, should he lose such a counsellor as he had found him to be; and that, upon this, Anaxagoras unfolded his robe, and showing himself, made answer: "Pericles," said he, "even those who have occasion for a lamp supply it with oil."

The Lacedaemonians beginning to show themselves troubled at the growth of the Athenian power, Pericles, on the other hand, to elevate the people's spirit yet more, and to raise them to the thought of great actions, proposed a decree, to summon all the Greeks in what part soever, whether of Europe or Asia, every city, little as well as great, to send their deputies to Athens to a general assembly, or convention, there to consult and advise concerning the Greek temples which the barbarians had burnt down, and the sacrifices which were due from them upon vows they had made to their gods for the safety of Greece when they fought against the barbarians; and also concerning the navigation of the sea, that they might henceforward pass to and fro and trade securely and be at peace among themselves.

Upon this errand there were twenty men, of such as were above fifty years of age, sent by commission; five to summon the Ionians and Dorians in Asia, and the islanders as far as Lesbos and Rhodes; five to visit all the places in the Hellespont and Thrace, up to Byzantium; and other five besides these to go to Boeotia and Phocis and Peloponnesus, and from hence to pass through the Locrians over to the neighbouring continent as far as Acarnania and Ambracia; and the rest to take their course through Euboea to the Oetaeans and the Malian Gulf, and to the Achaeans of Phthiotis and the Thessalians; all of them to treat with the people as they passed, and persuade them to come and take their part in the debates for settling the peace and jointly regulating the affairs of Greece.

Nothing was effected, nor did the cities meet by their deputies, as was desired; the Lacedaemonians, as it is said, crossing the design underhand, and the attempt being disappointed and baffled first in Peloponnesus. I thought fit, however, to introduce the mention of it, to show the spirit of the man and the greatness of his thoughts.

In his military conduct, he gained a great reputation

for wariness; he would not by his good-will engage in any
fight which had much uncertainty or hazard; he did not
envy the glory of generals whose rash adventures fortune
favoured with brilliant success, however they were admired
by others; nor did he think them worthy his imitation, but
always used to say to his citizens that, so far as lay in his
power, they should continue immortal, and live for ever.
Seeing Tolmides, the son of Tolmaeus, upon the confidence
of his former successes, and flushed with the honour his
military actions had procured him, making preparations to
attack the Boeotians in their own country when there was
no likely opportunity, and that he had prevailed with the
bravest and most enterprising of the youth to enlist themselves as volunteers in the service, who besides his other
force made up a thousand, he endeavoured to withhold
him and to advise him from it in the public assembly, telling him in a memorable saying of his, which still goes
about, that, if he would not take Pericles's advice, yet he
would not do amiss to wait and be ruled by time, the wisest
counsellor of all. This saying, at that time, was but slightly
commended; but within a few days after, when news was
brought that Tolmides himself had been defeated and slain
in battle near Coronea, and that many brave citizens had
fallen with him, it gained him great repute as well as good-
will among the people, for wisdom and for love of his countrymen.

But of all his expeditions, that to the Chersonese gave
most satisfaction and pleasure, having proved the safety
of the Greeks who inhabited there. For not only by carrying along with him a thousand fresh citizens of Athens he
gave new strength and vigour to the cities, but also by
belting the neck of land, which joins the peninsula to the
continent, with bulwarks and forts from sea to sea, he put
a stop to the inroads of the Thracians, who lay all about
the Chersonese, and closed the door against a continual
and grievous war, with which that country had been long
harassed, lying exposed to the encroachments and influx
of barbarous neighbours, and groaning under the evils of a
predatory population both upon and within its borders.

Nor was he less admired and talked of abroad for his sailing around the Peloponnesus, having set out from Pegae, or The Fountains, the port of Megara, with a hundred galleys. For he not only laid waste the sea-coast, as Tolmides had done before, but also, advancing far up into the mainland with the soldiers he had on board, by the terror of his appearance drove many within their walls; and at Nemea, with main force, routed and raised a trophy over the Sicyonians, who stood their ground and joined battle with him. And having taken on board a supply of soldiers into the galleys out of Achaia, then in league with Athens, he crossed with the fleet to the opposite continent, and, sailing along by the mouth of the river Achelous, overran Acarnania and shut up the Oeniadae within their city walls, and having ravaged and wasted their country, weighed anchor for home with the double advantage of having shown himself formidable to his enemies, and at the same time safe and energetic to his fellow-citizens; for there was not so much as any chance miscarriage that happened, the whole voyage through, to those who were under his charge.

Entering also the Euxine Sea with a large and finely equipped fleet, he obtained for the Greek cities any new arrangements they wanted, and entered into friendly relations with them; and to the barbarous nations, and kings and chiefs round about them, displayed the greatness of the power of the Athenians, their perfect ability and confidence to sail wherever they had a mind, and to bring the whole sea under their control. He left the Sinopians thirteen ships of war, with soldiers under the command of Lamachus, to assist them against Timesileus the tyrant; and when he and his accomplices had been thrown out, obtained a decree that six hundred of the Athenians that were willing should sail to Sinope and plant themselves there with the Sinopians, sharing among them the houses and land which the tyrant and his party had previously held.

But in other things he did not comply with the giddy impulses of the citizens, nor quit his own resolutions to follow their fancies, when, carried away with the thought of their strength and great success, they were eager to interfere again in Egypt, and to disturb the King of Persia's maritime dominions. Nay, there were a good many who were, even then, possessed with that unblest and inauspicious passion for Sicily, which afterward the orators of Alcibiades's party blew up into a flame. There were some also who dreamt of Tuscany and Carthage, and not without plausible reason in their present large dominion and prosperous course of their affairs.

But Pericles curbed this passion for foreign conquest, and unsparingly pruned and cut down their ever busy fancies for a multitude of undertakings; and directed their power for the most part to securing and consolidating what they had already got, supposing it would be quite enough for them to do, if they could keep the Lacedaemonians in check; to whom he entertained all along a sense of opposition; which, as upon many other occasions, so he particularly showed by what he did in the time of the holy war. The Lacedaemonians, having gone with an army to Delphi, restored Apollo's temple, which the Phocians had got into their possession, to the Delphians; immediately after their departure, Pericles, with another army, came and restored the Phocians. And the Lacedaemonians, having engraven the record of their privilege of consulting the oracle before others, which the Delphians gave them, upon the forehead of the brazen wolf which stands there, he, also, having received from the Phocians the like privilege for the Athenians, had it cut upon the same wolf of brass on his right side.

That he did well and wisely in thus restraining the exertions of the Athenians within the compass of Greece, the events themselves that happened afterward bore sufficient witness. For, in the first place, the Euboeans revolted, against whom he passed over with forces; and then, immediately after, news came that the Megarians were turned their enemies; and a hostile army was upon the borders of Attica, under the conduct of Plistoanax, King of the Lacedaemonians. Wherefore Pericles came with his army back again in all haste out of Euboea, to meet the war which threatened at home; and did not venture to engage a numerous and brave army eager for battle; but perceiving that Plistoanax was a very young man, and governed himself mostly by the counsel and advice of Cleandrides, whom the ephors had sent with him, by reason of his youth, to be a kind of guardian and assistant to him, he privately made trial of this man's integrity, and, in a short time, having corrupted him with money, prevailed with him to withdraw the Peloponnesians out of Attica. When the army had retired and dispersed into their several states, the Lacedaemonians in anger fined their king in so large a sum of money, that, unable to pay it, he quitted Lacedaemon; while Cleandrides fled, and had sentence of death passed upon him in his absence. This was the father of Gylippus, who overpowered the Athenians in Sicily. And it seems that this covetousness was an hereditary disease transmitted from father to son; for Gylippus also afterwards was caught in foul practices, and expelled from Sparta for it.

When Pericles, in giving up his accounts of this expedition, stated a disbursement of ten talents, as laid out upon fit occasion, the people, without any question, nor troubling themselves to investigate the mystery, freely allowed of it. And some historians, in which number is Theophrastus the philosopher, have given it as a truth that Pericles every year used to send privately the sum of ten talents to Sparta, with which he complimented those in office, to keep off the war; not to purchase peace neither, but time, that he might prepare at leisure, and be the better able to carry on war hereafter.

Immediately after this, turning his forces against the revolters, and passing over into the island of Euboea with fifty sail of ships and five thousand men in arms, he reduced their cities, and drove out the citizens of the Chalcidians, called Hippobotae, horse-feeders, the chief persons for wealth and reputation among them; and removing all the Histiaeans out of the country, brought in a plantation of Athenians in their room; making them his one example of severity, because they had captured an Attic ship and killed all on board.

After this, having made a truce between the Athenians and Lacedaemonians for thirty years, he ordered, by public decree, the expedition against the isle of Samos, on the ground, that, when they were bid to leave off their war with the Milesians they had not complied. And as these measures against the Samians are thought to have been taken to please Aspasia, this may be a fit point for inquiry about the woman, what art or charming faculty she had that enabled her to captivate, as she did, the greatest statesmen, and to give the philosophers occasion to speak so much about her, and that, too, not to her disparagement. That she was a Milesian by birth, the daughter of Axiochus, is a thing acknowledged. And they say it was in emulation of Thargelia, a courtesan of the old Ionian times, that she made her addresses to men of great power. Thargelia was a great beauty, extremely charming, and at the same time sagacious; she had numerous suitors among the Greeks, and brought all who had to do with her over to the Persian interest, and by their means, being men of the greatest power and station, sowed the seeds of the Median faction up and down in several cities. Aspasia, some say, was courted and caressed by Pericles upon account of her knowledge and skill in politics. Socrates himself would sometimes go to visit her, and some of his acquaintance with him; and those who frequented her company would carry their wives with them to listen to her. Her occupation was anything but creditable, her house being a home for young courtesans. Aeschines tells us, also, that Lysicles, a sheep-dealer, a man of low birth and character, by keeping Aspasia company after Pericles's death, came to be a chief man in Athens. And in Plato's Menexenus, though we do not take the introduction as quite serious, still thus much seems to be historical, that she had the repute of being resorted to by many of the Athenians for instruction in the art of speaking. Pericles's inclination for her seems, however, to have rather proceeded from the passion of love. He had a wife that was near of kin to him, who had been

married first to Hipponicus, by whom she had Callias, surnamed the Rich; and also she brought Pericles, while she
lived with him, two sons, Xanthippus and Paralus. Afterwards, when they did not well agree, nor like to live together, he parted with her, with her own consent, to another man, and himself took Aspasia, and loved her with
wonderful affection; every day, both as he went out and as
he came in from the market-place, he saluted and kissed
her.

In the comedies she goes by the nicknames of the new
Omphale and Deianira, and again is styled Juno. Cratinus,
in downright terms, calls her a harlot.

> "To find him a Juno the goddess of lust
>   Bore that harlot past shame,
>   Aspasia by name."

It should seem also that he had a son by her; Eupolis, in
his Demi, introduced Pericles asking after his safety, and
Myronides replying—

> "My son?" "He lives: a man he had been long,
>   But that the harlot-mother did him wrong."

Aspasia, they say, became so celebrated and renowned, that
Cyrus, also who made war against Artaxerxes for the Persian monarchy, gave her whom he loved the best of all his
concubines the name of Aspasia, who before that was
called Milto. She was a Phocaean by birth, the daughter of
one Hermotimus, and, when Cyrus fell in battle, was carried to the king, and had great influence at court. These
things coming into my memory as I am writing this story,
it would be unnatural for me to omit them.

Pericles, however, was particularly charged with having
proposed to the assembly the war against the Samians, from
favour to the Milesians, upon the entreaty of Aspasia. For
the two states were at war for the possession of Priene; and
the Samians, getting the better, refused to lay down their
arms and to have the controversy betwixt them decided by

arbitration before the Athenians. Pericles, therefore, fitting out a fleet, went and broke up the oligarchical government at Samos, and taking fifty of the principal men of the town as hostages, and as many of their children, sent them to the isle of Lemnos, there to be kept, though he had offers, as some relate, of a talent apiece for himself from each one of the hostages, and of many other presents from those who were anxious not to have a democracy. Moreover, Pisuthnes the Persian, one of the king's lieutenants, bearing some good-will to the Samians, sent him ten thousand pieces of gold to excuse the city. Pericles, however, would receive none of all this; but after he had taken that course with the Samians which he thought fit, and set up a democracy among them, sailed back to Athens.

But they, however, immediately revolted, Pisuthnes having privily got away their hostages for them, and provided them with means for the war. Whereupon Pericles came out with a fleet a second time against them, and found them not idle nor slinking away, but manfully resolved to try for the dominion of the sea. The issue was, that after a sharp sea-fight about the island called Tragia, Pericles obtained a decisive victory, having with forty-four ships routed seventy of the enemy's, twenty of which were carrying soldiers.

Together with his victory and pursuit, having made himself master of the port, he laid siege to the Samians, and blocked them up, who yet, one way or another, still ventured to make sallies, and fight under the city walls. But after that another greater fleet from Athens was arrived, and that the Samians were now shut up with a close leaguer on every side, Pericles, taking with him sixty galleys, sailed out into the main sea, with the intention, as most authors give the account, to meet a squadron of Phoenician ships that were coming for the Samians' relief, and to fight them at as great distance as could be from the island; but, as Stesimbrotus says, with a design of putting over to Cyprus, which does not seem to be probable. But, whichever of the two was his intention, it seems to have been a miscalculation. For on his departure, Melissus, the son of Ithagenes, a philosopher, being at that time the general in Samos, despising either the small number of the ships that were left or the inexperience of the commanders, prevailed with the citizens to attack the Athenians. And the Samians having won the battle, and taken several of the men prisoners, and disabled several of the ships, were masters of the sea, and brought into port all necessaries they wanted for the war, which they had not before. Aristotle says, too, that Pericles had been once before this worsted by this Melissus in a sea-fight.

The Samians, that they might requite an affront which had before been put upon them, branded the Athenians, whom they took prisoners, in their foreheads, with the figure of an owl. For so the Athenians had marked them before with a Samaena, which is a sort of ship, low and flat in the prow, so as to look snub-nosed, but wide and large and well-spread in the hold, by which it both carries a large cargo and sails well. And it was so called, because the first of that kind was seen at Samos, having been built by order of Polycrates the tyrant. These brands upon the Samians' foreheads, they say, are the allusion in the passage of Aristophanes, where he says—

"For, oh, the Samians are a lettered people."

Pericles, as soon as news was brought him of the disaster that had befallen his army, made all the haste he could to come in to their relief, and having defeated Melissus, who bore up against him, and put the enemy to flight, he immediately proceeded to hem them in with a wall, resolving to master them and take the town, rather with some cost and time than with the wounds and hazards of his citizens. But as it was a hard matter to keep back the Athenians, who were vexed at the delay, and were eagerly bent to fight, he divided the whole multitude into eight parts, and arranged by lot that that part which had the white bean should have leave to feast and take their ease while the other seven were fighting. And this is the reason, they say, that people, when at any time they have been merry, and enjoyed themselves, called it white day, in allusion to this white bean.

Ephorus the historian tells us besides, that Pericles made use of engines of battery in this siege, being much taken with the curiousness of the invention, with the aid and presence of Artemon himself, the engineer, who, being lame, used to be carried about in a litter, where the works required his attendance, and for that reason was called Periphoretus. But Heraclides Ponticus disproves this out of Anacreon's poems, where mention is made of this Artemon Periphoretus several ages before the Samian war, or any of these occurrences. And he says that Artemon, being a man who loved his ease, and had a great apprehension of danger, for the most part kept close within doors, having two of his servants to hold a brazen shield over his head, that nothing might fall upon him from above; and if he were at any time forced upon necessity to go abroad, that he was carried about in a little hanging bed, close to the very ground, and that for this reason he was called Periphoretus.

In the ninth month, the Samians surrendering themselves and delivering up the town, Pericles pulled down their walls, and seized their shipping, and set a fine of a large sum of money upon them, part of which they paid down at once, and they agreed to bring in the rest by a certain time, and gave hostages for security. Duris the Samian makes a tragical drama out of these events, charging the Athenians and Pericles with a great deal of cruelty, which neither Thucydides, nor Ephorus, nor Aristotle have given any relation of, and probably with little regard to truth; how, for example, he brought the captains and soldiers of the galleys into the market-place at Miletus, and there having bound them fast to boards for ten days, then, when they were already all but half dead, gave order to have them killed by beating out their brains with clubs, and their dead bodies to be flung out into the open streets and fields, unburied. Duris, however, who, even where he has no private feeling concerned, is not wont to keep his narratives within the limits of truth, is the more likely

upon this occasion to have exaggerated the calamities which
befell his country, to create odium against the Athenians.
Pericles, however, after the reduction of Samos, returning
back to Athens, took care that those who died in the war
should be honourably buried, and made a funeral harangue,
as the custom is, in their commendation at their graves, for
which he gained great admiration. As he came down from
the stage on which he spoke, the rest of the women came
and complimented him, taking him by the hand, and crown-
ing him with garlands and ribbons, like a victorious athlete
in the games; but Elpinice, coming near to him, said,
"These are brave deeds, Pericles, that you have done, and
such as deserve our chaplets; who have lost us many a
worthy citizen, not in a war with Phoenicians or Medes,
like my brother Cimon, but for the overthrow of an allied
and kindred city." As Elpinice spoke these words, he, smiling quietly, as it is said, returned her answer with this
verse:—

"Old women should not seek to be perfumed."

Ion says of him, that upon this exploit of his, conquering
the Samians, he indulged very high and proud thoughts
of himself: whereas Agamemnon was ten years taking a
barbarous city, he had in nine months' time vanquished
and taken the greatest and most powerful of the Ionians.
And indeed it was not without reason that he assumed this
glory to himself, for, in real truth, there was much uncertainty and great hazard in this great war, if so be, as
Thucydides tells us, the Samian state were within a very
little of wresting the whole power and dominion of the sea
out of the Athenians' hands.

After this was over, the Peloponnesian war beginning to
break out in full tide, he advised the people to send help
to the Corcyraeans, who were attacked by the Corinthians,
and to secure to themselves an island possessed of great
naval resources, since the Peloponnesians were already all
but in actual hostilities against them. The people readily
consenting to the motion, and voting an aid and succour

for them, he despatched Lacedaemonius, Cimon's son, having only ten ships with him, as it were out of a design to affront him; for there was a great kindness and friendship betwixt Cimon's family and the Lacedaemonians; so, in order that Lacedaemonius might lie the more open to a charge, or suspicion at least, of favouring the Lacedaemonians and playing false, if he performed no considerable exploit in this service, he allowed him a small number of ships, and sent him out against his will; and indeed he made it somewhat his business to hinder Cimon's sons from rising in the state, professing that by their very names they were not to be looked upon as native and true Athenians, but foreigners and strangers, one being called Lacedaemonius, another Thessalus, and the third Eleus; and they were all three of them, it was thought, born of an Arcadian woman. Being, however, ill spoken of on account of these ten galleys, as having afforded but a small supply to the people that were in need, and yet given a great advantage to those who might complain of the act of intervention, Pericles sent out a larger force afterwards to Corcyra, which arrived after the fight was over. And when now the Corinthians, angry and indignant with the Athenians, accused them publicly at Lacedaemon, the Megarians joined with them, complaining that they were, contrary to common right and the articles of peace sworn to among the Greeks, kept out and driven away from every market and from all ports under the control of the Athenians. The Aeginetans, also, professing to be ill-used and treated with violence, made supplications in private to the Lacedaemonians for redress, though not daring openly to call the Athenians in question. In the meantime, also, the city Potidaea, under the dominion of the Athenians, but a colony formerly of the Corinthians, had revolted, and was beset with a formal siege, and was a further occasion of precipitating the war.

Yet notwithstanding all this, there being embassies sent to Athens, and Archidamus, the King of the Lacedaemonians, endeavouring to bring the greater part of the com-

plaints and matters in dispute to a fair determination, and
to pacify and allay the heats of the allies, it is very likely
that the war would not upon any other grounds of quarrel
have fallen upon the Athenians, could they have been prevailed with to repeal the ordinance against the Megarians,
and to be reconciled to them. Upon which account, since
Pericles was the man who mainly opposed it, and stirred up
the people's passions to persist in their contention with the
Megarians, he was regarded as the sole cause of the war.

They say, moreover, that ambassadors went, by order,
from Lacedaemon to Athens about this very business, and
that when Pericles was urging a certain law which made it
illegal to take down or withdraw the tablet of the decree,
one of the ambassadors, Polyalces by name, said, "Well, do
not take it down then, but *turn* it; there is no law, I suppose which forbids that;" which, though prettily said, did
not move Pericles from his resolution. There may have
been, in all likelihood, something of a secret grudge and
private animosity which he had against the Megarians.
Yet, upon a public and open charge against them, that
they had appropriated part of the sacred land on the frontier, he proposed a decree that a herald should be sent to
them, and the same also to the Lacedaemonians, with an accusation of the Megarians; an order which certainly shows
equitable and friendly proceeding enough. And after that
the herald who was sent, by name Anthemocritus, died, and
it was believed that the Megarians had contrived his death,
then Charinus proposed a decree against them, that there
should be an irreconcilable and implacable enmity thence-
forward betwixt the two commonwealths; and that if any
one of the Megarians should but set his foot in Attica, he
should be put to death; and that the commanders, when
they take the usual oath, should, over and above that, swear
that they will twice every year make an inroad into the
Megarian country; and that Anthemocritus should be buried near the Thracian Gates, which are now called the
Dipylon, or Double Gate.

On the other hand, the Megarians, utterly denying and

disowning the murder of Anthemocritus, throw the whole matter upon Aspasia and Pericles, availing themselves of the famous verses in the Acharnians—

"To Megara some of our madcaps ran,
   And stole Simaetha thence, their courtesan.
Which exploit the Megarians to outdo,
   Came to Aspasia's house, and took off two."

The true occasion of the quarrel is not so easy to find out. But of inducing the refusal to annul the decree, all alike charge Pericles. Some say he met the request with a positive refusal, out of high spirit and a view of the state's best interest, accounting that the demand made in those embassies was designed for a trial of their compliance, and that a concession would be taken for a confession of weakness as if they durst not do otherwise; while other some there are who say that it was rather out of arrogance and a wilful spirit of contention, to show his own strength, that he took occasion to slight the Lacedaemonians. The worst motive of all, which is confirmed by most witnesses, is to the following effect: Phidias the Moulder had, as has before been said, undertaken to make the statue of Minerva. Now he, being admitted to friendship with Pericles, and a great favourite of his, had many enemies upon this account, who envied and maligned him; who also, to make trial in a case of his, what kind of judges the commons would prove, should there be occasion to bring Pericles himself before them, having tampered with Menon, one who had been a workman with Phidias, stationed him in the market-place, with a petition desiring public security upon his discovery and impeachment of Phidias. The people admitting the man to tell his story, and the prosecution proceeding in the assembly, there was nothing of theft or cheat proved against him; for Phidias, from the very beginning, by the advice of Pericles, had so wrought and wrapt the gold that was used in the work about the statue, that they might take it all off, and make out the just weight of it, which Pericles at that time bade the accuser do. But the reputation of his works was what brought envy upon Phidias, especially that where he represents the fight of the Amazons upon the goddess's shield, he had introduced a likeness of himself as a bald old man holding up a great stone with both hands, and had put in a very fine representation of Pericles fighting with an Amazon. And the position of the hand which holds out the spear in front of the face, was ingeniously contrived to conceal in some degree the likeness, which meantime showed itself on either side.

Phidias then was carried away to prison, and there died of a disease; but, as some say, of poison, administered by the enemies of Pericles, to raise a slander, or a suspicion at least, as though he had procured it. The informer Menon, upon Glycon's proposal, the people made free from payment of taxes and customs, and ordered the generals to take care that nobody should do him any hurt. About the same time, Aspasia was indicted of impiety, upon the complaint of Hermippus the comedian, who also laid further to her charge that she received into her house freeborn women for the uses of Pericles. And Diopithes proposed a decree, that public accusations should be laid against persons who neglected religion, or taught new doctrines about things above, directing suspicion, by means of Anaxagoras, against Pericles himself. The people receiving and admitting these accusations and complaints, at length, by this means, they came to enact a decree, at the motion of Dracontides, that Pericles should bring in the accounts of the moneys he had expended, and lodge them with the Prytanes; and that the judges, carrying their suffrage from the altar in the Acropolis, should examine and determine the business in the city. This last clause Hagnon took out of the decree, and moved that the causes should be tried before fifteen hundred jurors, whether they should be styled prosecutions for robbery, or bribery, or any kind of malversation. Aspasia, Pericles begged off, shedding, as Aeschines says, many tears at the trial, and personally entreating the jurors. But fearing how it might go with Anaxagoras, he sent him out of the city. And finding that in Phidias's case he had miscarried with the people, being afraid of impeachment, he kindled the war, which hitherto had lingered and smothered, and blew it up into a flame; hoping, by that means, to disperse and scatter these complaints and charges, and to allay their jealousy; the city usually throwing herself upon him alone, and trusting to his sole conduct, upon the urgency of great affairs and public dangers, by reason of his authority and the sway he bore.

These are given out to have been the reasons which induced Pericles not to suffer the people of Athens to yield to the proposals of the Lacedaemonians; but their truth is uncertain.

The Lacedaemonians, for their part, feeling sure that if they could once remove him, they might be at what terms they pleased with the Athenians, sent them word that they should expel the "Pollution" with which Pericles on the mother's side was tainted, as Thucydides tells us. But the issue proved quite contrary to what those who sent the message expected; instead of bringing Pericles under suspicion and reproach, they raised him into yet greater credit and esteem with the citizens, as a man whom their enemies most hated and feared. In the same way, also, before Archidamus, who was at the head of the Peloponnesians, made his invasion into Attica, he told the Athenians beforehand, that if Archidamus, while he laid waste the rest of the country, should forbear and spare his estate, either on the ground of friendship or right of hospitality that was betwixt them, or on purpose to give his enemies an occasion of traducing him; that then he did freely bestow upon the state all his land and the buildings upon it for the public use. The Lacedaemonians, therefore, and their allies, with a great army, invaded the Athenian territories, under the conduct of King Archidamus, and laying waste the country, marched on as far as Acharnae, and there pitched their camp, presuming that the Athenians would never endure that, but would come out and fight them for their country's and their honour's sake. But Pericles looked upon it as dangerous to engage in battle, to the risk of the city itself, against sixty thousand men-at-arms of Peloponnesians and Boeotians; for so many they were in number that made the inroad at first;

and he endeavoured to appease those who were desirous to fight, and were grieved and discontented to see how things went, and gave them good words, saying, that "trees, when they are lopped and cut, grow up again in a short time, but men, being once lost, cannot easily be recovered." He did not convene the people into an assembly, for fear lest they should force him to act against his judgment; but, like a skilful steersman or pilot of a ship, who, when a sudden squall comes on, out at sea, makes all his arrangements, sees that all is tight and fast, and then follows the dictates of his skill, and minds the business of the ship, taking no notice of the tears and entreaties of the sea-sick and fearful passengers, so he, having shut up the city gates, and placed guards at all posts for security, followed his own reason and judgment, little regarding those that cried out against him and were angry at his management, although there were a great many of his friends that urged him with requests, and many of his enemies threatened and accused him for doing as he did, and many made songs and lampoons upon him, which were sung about the town to his disgrace, reproaching him with the cowardly exercise of his office of general, and the tame abandonment of everything to the enemy's hands.

Cleon, also, already was among his assailants, making use of the feeling against him as a step to the leadership of the people, as appears in the anapaestic verses of Hermippus—

> "Satyr-king, instead of swords,
> Will you always handle words?
> Very brave indeed we find them,
> But a Teles lurks behind them.

> "Yet to gnash your teeth you're seen,
> When the little dagger keen,
> Whetted every day anew,
> Of sharp Cleon touches you."

Pericles, however, was not at all moved by any attacks, but took all patiently, and submitted in silence to the disgrace they threw upon him and the ill-will they bore him;

and, sending out a fleet of a hundred galleys to Peloponnesus, he did not go along with it in person, but stayed behind, that he might watch at home and keep the city under his own control, till the Peloponnesians broke up their camp and were gone. Yet to soothe the common people, jaded and distressed with the war, he relieved them with distributions of public moneys, and ordained new divisions of subject land. For having turned out all the people of Aegina, he parted the island among the Athenians according to lot. Some comfort, also, and ease in their miseries, they might receive from what their enemies endured. For the fleet, sailing round the Peloponnese, ravaged a great deal of the country, and pillaged and plundered the towns and smaller cities; and by land he himself entered with an army the Megarian country, and made havoc of it all. Whence it is clear that the Peloponnesians, though they did the Athenians much mischief by land, yet suffering as much themselves from them by sea, would not have protracted the war to such a length, but would quickly have given it over, as Pericles at first foretold they would, had not some divine power crossed human purposes.

In the first place, the pestilential disease, or plague, seized upon the city, and ate up all the flower and prime of their youth and strength. Upon occasion of which, the people, distempered and afflicted in their souls, as well as in their bodies, were utterly enraged like madmen against Pericles, and, like patients grown delirious, sought to lay violent hands on their physician, or, as it were, their father. They had been possessed, by his enemies, with the belief that the occasion of the plague was the crowding of the country people together into the town, forced as they were now, in the heat of the summer-weather, to dwell many of them together even as they could, in small tenements and stifling hovels, and to be tied to a lazy course of life within doors, whereas before they lived in a pure, open, and free air. The cause and author of all this, said they, is he who on account of the war has poured a multitude of people in upon us within the walls, and uses all these men that he has here upon no employ or service, but keeps them pent up like cattle, to be overrun with infection from one another, affording them neither shift of quarters nor any refreshment.

With the design to remedy these evils, and do the enemy some inconvenience, Pericles got a hundred and fifty galleys ready, and having embarked many tried soldiers, both foot and horse, was about to sail out, giving great hope to his citizens, and no less alarm to his enemies, upon the sight of so great a force. And now the vessels having their complement of men, and Pericles being gone aboard his own galley, it happened that the sun was eclipsed, and it grew dark on a sudden, to the affright of all, for this was looked upon as extremely ominous. Pericles, therefore, perceiving the steersman seized with fear and at a loss what to do, took his cloak and held it up before the man's face, and screening him with it so that he could not see, asked him whether he imagined there was any great hurt, or the sign of any great hurt in this, and he answering No, "Why," said he, "and what does that differ from this, only that what has caused that darkness there, is something greater than a cloak?" This is a story which philosophers tell their scholars. Pericles, however, after putting out to sea, seems not to have done any other exploit befitting such preparations, and when he had laid siege to the holy city Epidaurus, which gave him some hope of surrender, miscarried in his design by reason of the sickness. For it not only seized upon the Athenians, but upon all others, too, that held any sort of communication with the army. Finding after this the Athenians ill-affected and highly displeased with him, he tried and endeavoured what he could to appease and re-encourage them. But he could not pacify or allay their anger, nor persuade or prevail with them any way, till they freely passed their votes upon him, resumed their power, took away his command from him, and fined him in a sum of money; which by their account that say least, was fifteen talents, while they who reckon most, name fifty. The name prefixed to the accusation was Cleon, as Idomeneus tells us; Simmias, according to Theophrastus; and Heraclides Ponticus gives it as Lacratidas.

After this, public troubles were soon to leave him unmolested; the people, so to say, discharged their passion in their stroke, and lost their stings in the wound. But his domestic concerns were in an unhappy condition, many of his friends and acquaintance having died in the plague time, and those of his family having long since been in disorder and in a kind of mutiny against him. For the eldest of his lawfully begotten sons, Xanthippus by name, being naturally prodigal, and marrying a young and expensive wife, the daughter of Tisander, son of Epilycus, was highly offended at his father's economy in making him but a scanty allowance, by little and little at a time. He sent, therefore, to a friend one day and borrowed some money of him in his father Pericles's name, pretending it was by his order. The man coming afterward to demand the debt, Pericles was so far from yielding to pay it, that he entered an action against him. Upon which the young man, Xanthippus, thought himself so ill-used and disobliged that he openly reviled his father; telling first, by way of ridicule, stories about his conversations at home, and the discourses he had with the sophists and scholars that came to his house. As, for instance, how one who was a practiser of the five games of skill, having with a dart or javelin unawares against his will struck and killed Epitimus the Pharsalian, his father spent a whole day with Protagoras in a serious dispute, whether the javelin, or the man that threw it, or the masters of the games who appointed these sports, were, according to the strictest and best reason, to be accounted the cause of this mischance. Besides this, Stesimbrotus tells us that it was Xanthippus who spread abroad among the people the infamous story concerning his own wife; and in general that this difference of the young man's with his father, and the breach betwixt them, continued never to be healed or made up till his death. For Xanthippus died in the plague time of the sickness. At which time Pericles also lost his sister, and the greatest part of his relations and friends, and those who had been most useful and serviceable to him in managing the affairs of state. However, he did not shrink or give in upon these occasions, nor betray or lower his high spirit and the greatness of his mind under all his misfortunes; he was not even so much as seen to weep or to mourn, or even attend the burial of any of his friends or relations, till at last he lost his only remaining legitimate son. Subdued by this blow, and yet striving still, as far as he could, to maintain his principle, and to preserve and keep up the greatness of his soul, when he came, however, to perform the ceremony of putting a garland of flowers upon the head of the corpse, he was vanquished by his passion at the sight, so that he burst into exclamations, and shed copious tears, having never done any such thing in his life before.

The city having made trial of other generals for the conduct of war, and orators for business of state, when they found there was no one who was of weight enough for such a charge, or of authority sufficient to be trusted with so great a command, regretted the loss of him, and invited him again to address and advise them, and to reassume the office of general. He, however, lay at home in dejection and mourning; but was persuaded by Alcibiades and others of his friends to come abroad and show himself to the people; who having, upon his appearance, made their acknowledgments, and apologised for their untowardly treatment of him, he undertook the public affairs once more; and, being chosen general, requested that the statute concerning baseborn children, which he himself had formerly caused to be made, might be suspended; that so the name and race of his family might not, for absolute want of a lawful heir to succeed, be wholly lost and extinguished. The case of the statute was thus: Pericles, when long ago at the height of his power in the state, having then, as has been said, children lawfully begotten, proposed a law that those only should be reputed true citizens of Athens who were born of such parents as were both Athenians. After this, the King of Egypt having sent to the people, by way of present, forty thousand bushels of wheat, which were to be shared out among the citizens, a great many actions and suits about legitimacy occurred, by virtue of that edict; cases which, till that time, had not been known nor taken notice of; and several persons suffered by false accusations. There were little less than five thousand who were convicted and sold for slaves; those who, enduring the test, remained in the government and passed muster for true Athenians were found upon the poll to be fourteen thousand and forty persons in number.

It looked strange, that a law, which had been carried so far against so many people, should be cancelled again by the same man that made it; yet the present calamity and distress which Pericles laboured under in his family broke through all objections, and prevailed with the Athenians to pity him, as one whose losses and misfortunes had sufficiently punished his former arrogance and haughtiness. His sufferings deserved, they thought, their pity, and even indignation, and his request was such as became a man to ask and men to grant; they gave him permission to enroll his son in the register of his fraternity, giving him his own name. This son afterward, after having defeated the Peloponnesians at Arginusae, was, with his fellow-generals, put to death by the people.

About the time when his son was enrolled, it should seem the plague seized Pericles, not with sharp and violent fits, as it did others that had it, but with a dull and lingering distemper, attended with various changes and alterations, leisurely, by little and little, wasting the strength of his body, and undermining the noble faculties of his soul. So that Theophrastus, in his Morals, when discussing whether men's characters change with their circumstances, and their moral habits, disturbed by the ailings of their bodies, start aside from the rules of virtue, has left it upon record, that Pericles, when he was sick, showed one of his friends that came to visit him an amulet or charm that the women had hung about his neck; as much as to say, that he was very sick indeed when he would admit of such a foolery as that was.

When he was now near his end, the best of the citizens and those of his friends who were left alive, sitting about him, were speaking of the greatness of his merit, and his power, and reckoning up his famous actions and the number of his victories; for there were no less than nine trophies, which, as their chief commander and conqueror of their enemies, he had set up for the honour of the city. They talked thus together among themselves, as though he were unable to understand or mind what they said, but had now lost his consciousness. He had listened, however, all the while, and attended to all, and speaking out among them, said that he wondered they should commend and take notice of things which were as much owing to fortune as to anything else, and had happened to many other commanders, and, at the same time, should not speak or make mention of that which was the most excellent and greatest thing of all. "For," said he, "no Athenian, through my means, ever wore mourning."

He was indeed a character deserving our high admiration not only for his equitable and mild temper, which all along in the many affairs of his life, and the great animosities which he incurred, he constantly maintained; but also for the high spirit and feeling which made him regard it the noblest of all his honours that, in the exercise of such immense power, he never had gratified his envy or his passion, nor ever had treated any enemy as irreconcilably opposed to him. And to me it appears that this one thing gives that otherwise childish and arrogant title a fitting and becoming significance; so dispassionate a temper, a life so pure and unblemished, in the height of power and place, might well be called Olympian, in accordance with our conceptions of the divine beings, to whom, as the natural authors of all good and of nothing evil, we ascribe the rule and government of the world. Not as the poets represent, who, while confounding us with their ignorant fancies, are themselves confuted by their own poems and fictions, and call the place, indeed, where they say the gods make their abode, a secure and quiet seat, free from all hazards and commotions, untroubled with winds or with clouds, and equally through all time illumined with a soft serenity and a pure light as though such were a home most agreeable for a blessed and immortal nature; and yet, in the meanwhile, affirm that the gods themselves are full of trouble and enmity and anger and other passions, which no way become or belong to even men that have any understanding. But this will, perhaps, seem a subject fitter for some other consideration, and that ought to be treated of in some other place.

The course of public affairs after his death produced a quick and speedy sense of the loss of Pericles. Those who, while he lived, resented his great authority, as that which eclipsed themselves, presently after his quitting the stage, making trial of other orators and demagogues, readily acknowledged that there never had been in nature such a disposition as his was, more moderate and reasonable in the height of that state he took upon him, or more grave and impressive in the mildness which he used. And that invidious arbitrary power, to which formerly they gave the name of monarchy and tyranny, did then appear to have been the chief bulwark of public safety; so great a corruption and such a flood of mischief and vice followed which he, by keeping weak and low, had withheld from notice, and had prevented from attaining incurable height through a licentious impunity.

✤

ALCIBIADES

Alcibiades, as it is supposed, was anciently descended from Eurysaces, the son of Ajax, by his father's side; and by his mother's side from Alcmaeon. Dinomache, his mother, was the daughter of Megacles. His father, Clinias, having fitted out a galley at his own expense, gained great honour in the sea-fight at Artemisium, and was afterwards slain in the battle of Coronea, fighting against the Boeotians. Pericles and Ariphon, the sons of Xanthippus, nearly related to him, became the guardians of Alcibiades. It has been said not untruly that the friendship which Socrates felt for him has much contributed to his fame; and certain it is, that, though we have no account from any writer concerning the mother of Nicias or Demosthenes, of Lamachus or Phormion, of Thrasybulus or Theramenes, notwithstanding these were all illustrious men of the same period, yet we know even the nurse of Alcibiades, that her country was Lacedaemon, and her name Amycla; and that Zopyrus was his teacher and attendant; the one being recorded by Antisthenes, and the other by Plato.

It is not, perhaps, material to say anything of the beauty of Alcibiades, only that it bloomed with him in all the ages of his life, in his infancy, in his youth, and in his manhood; and, in the peculiar character becoming to each of these periods, gave him, in every one of them, a grace and a charm. What Euripides says, that—

"Of all fair things the autumn, too, is fair,"

is by no means universally true. But it happened so with Alcibiades, amongst few others, by reason of his happy constitution and natural vigour of body. It is said that his lisping, when he spoke, became him well, and gave a grace and persuasiveness to his rapid speech. Aristophanes takes notice of it in the verses in which he jests at Theorus; "How like a *colax* he is," says Alcibiades, meaning a *corax;* on which it is remarked,—

"How very happily he lisped the truth."

Archippus also alludes to it in a passage where he ridicules the son of Alcibiades:—

"That people may believe him like his father,
He walks like one dissolved in luxury,
Lets his robe trail behind him on the ground,
Carelessly leans his head, and in his talk
Affects to lisp."

His conduct displayed many great inconsistencies and variations, not unnaturally, in accordance with the many and wonderful vicissitudes of his fortunes; but among the many strong passions of his real character, the one most prevailing of all was his ambition and desire of superiority, which appears in several anecdotes told of his sayings whilst he was a child. Once being hard pressed in wrestling, and fearing to be thrown, he got the hand of his antagonist to his mouth, and bit it with all his force; and when the other loosed his hold presently, and said, "You bite, Alcibiades, like a woman." "No," replied he, "like a lion." Another time as he played at dice in the street, being then but a child, a loaded cart came that way, when it was his turn to throw; at first he called to the driver to stop, because he was to throw in the way over which the cart was to pass; but the man giving him no attention and driving on, when the rest of the boys divided and gave way, Alcibiades threw himself on his face before the cart and, stretching himself out, bade the carter pass on now if he would; which so startled the man, that he put back his horses, while all that saw it were terrified, and, crying out, ran to assist Alcibiades. When he began to study, he obeyed all his other masters fairly well, but refused to learn to play upon the flute, as a sordid thing, and not becoming a free citizen; saying that to play on the lute or the harp does not in any way disfigure a man's body or face, but one is hardly to be known by the most intimate friends when playing on the flute. Besides, one who plays on the harp may speak or sing at the same time; but the use of the flute stops the mouth, intercepts the voice, and prevents all articulation. "Therefore," said he, "let the Theban youths pipe, who do not know how to speak, but we Athenians, as our ancestors have told us, have Minerva for our patroness, and Apollo for our protector, one of whom threw away the flute, and the other stripped the Flute-player of his skin." Thus, between raillery and good earnest, Alcibiades kept not only himself but other boys from learning, as it presently became the talk of the young boys, how Alcibiades despised playing on the flute, and ridiculed those who studied it. In consequence of which, it ceased to be reckoned amongst the liberal accomplishments, and became generally neglected.

It is stated in the invective which Antiphon wrote against Alcibiades, that once, when he was a boy, he ran away to the house of Democrates, one of those who made a favourite of him, and that Ariphon had determined to cause proclamation to be made for him, had not Pericles diverted him from it, by saying, that if he were dead, the proclaiming of him could only cause it to be discovered one day sooner, and if he were safe, it would be a reproach to him as long as he lived. Antiphon also says, that he killed one of his own servants with the blow of a staff in Sibyrtius's wrestling ground. But it is unreasonable to give credit to all that is objected by an enemy, who makes open profession of his design to defame him.

It was manifest that the many well-born persons who were continually seeking his company, and making their court to him, were attracted and captivated by his brilliant and extraordinary beauty only. But the affection which

Socrates entertained for him is a great evidence of the natural noble qualities and good disposition of the boy, which Socrates, indeed, detected both in and under his personal beauty; and, fearing that his wealth and station, and the great number both of strangers and Athenians who flattered and caressed him, might at last corrupt him, resolved, if possible, to interpose, and preserve so hopeful a plant from perishing in the flower, before its fruit came to perfection. For never did fortune surround and enclose a man with so many of those things which we vulgarly call goods, or so protect him from every weapon of philosophy, and fence him from every access of free and searching words, as she did Alcibiades; who, from the beginning, was exposed to the flatteries of those who sought merely his gratification, such as might well unnerve him, and indispose him to listen to any real adviser or instructor. Yet such was the happiness of his genius, that he discerned Socrates from the rest, and admitted him, whilst he drove away the wealthy and the noble who made court to him. And, in a little time, they grew intimate, and Alcibiades, listening now to language entirely free from every thought of unmanly fondness and silly displays of affection, finding himself with one who sought to lay open to him the deficiencies of his mind, and repress his vain and foolish arrogance—

"Dropped like the craven cock his conquered wing."

He esteemed these endeavours of Socrates as most truly a means which the gods made use of for the care and preservation of youth, and began to think meanly of himself and to admire him; to be pleased with his kindness, and to stand in awe of his virtue; and, unawares to himself, there became formed in his mind that reflex image and reciprocation of Love, or Anteros, that Plato talks of. It was a matter of general wonder, when people saw him joining Socrates in his meals and his exercises, living with him in the same tent, whilst he was reserved and rough to all others who made their addresses to him, and acted, indeed, with great insolence to some of them. As in particular to Anytus, the son of Anthemion, one who was very fond of him, and invited him to an entertainment which he had prepared for some strangers. Alcibiades refused the invitation; but, having drunk to excess at his own house with some of his companions, went thither with them to play some frolic; and, standing at the door of the room where the guests were enjoying themselves, and seeing the tables covered with gold and silver cups, he commanded his servants to take away the one-half of them, and carry them to his own house; and then, disdaining so much as to enter into the room himself, as soon as he had done this, went away. The company was indignant, and exclaimed at his rude and insulting conduct; Anytus, however, said, on the contrary, he had shown great consideration and tenderness in taking only a part when he might have taken all.

He behaved in the same manner to all others who courted him except only one stranger, who, as the story is told, having but a small estate, sold it all for about a hundred staters, which he presented to Alcibiades, and besought him to accept. Alcibiades, smiling and well pleased at the thing, invited him to supper, and, after a very kind entertainment, gave him his gold again, requiring him, moreover, not to fail to be present the next day, when the public revenue was offered a talent more than the existing rate; upon which the have excused himself, because the contract was so large, and would cost many talents; but Alcibiades, who had at that time a private pique against the existing farmers of the revenue, threatened to have him beaten if he refused. The next morning, the stranger, coming to the market-place, offered a talent more than the existing rate; upon which the farmers, enraged and consulting together, called upon him to name his sureties, concluding that he could find none. The poor man, being startled at the proposal, began to retire; but Alcibiades, standing at a distance, cried out to the magistrates, "Set my name down, he is a friend of mine; I will be security for him." When the other bidders heard this, they perceived that all their contrivance was defeated; for their way was, with the profits of the second year to pay the rent for the year preceding; so that, not seeing any other way to extricate themselves out of the difficulty, they began to entreat the stranger, and offered him a sum of money. Alcibiades would not suffer him to accept of less than a talent; but when that was paid down, he commanded him to relinquish the bargain, having by this device relieved his necessity.

Though Socrates had many and powerful rivals, yet the natural good qualities of Alcibiades gave his affection the mastery. His words overcame him so much, as to draw tears from his eyes, and to disturb his very soul. Yet sometimes he would abandon himself to flatterers, when they proposed to him varieties of pleasure, and would desert Socrates; who, then, would pursue him, as if he had been a fugitive slave. He despised every one else, and had no reverence or awe for any one but him. Cleanthes the philosopher, speaking of one to whom he was attached, says his only hold on him was by his ears, while his rivals had all the others offered them; and there is no question that Alcibiades was very easily caught by pleasure; and the expression used by Thucydides about the excesses of his habitual course of living gives occasion to believe so. But those who endeavoured to corrupt Alcibiades took advantage chiefly of his vanity and ambition, and thrust him on unseasonably to undertake great enterprises, persuading him, that as soon as he began to concern himself in public affairs, he would not only obscure the rest of the generals and statesmen, but outdo the authority and the reputation which Pericles himself had gained in Greece. But in the same manner as iron which is softened by the fire grows hard with the cold and all its parts are closed again, so, as often as Socrates observed Alcibiades to be misled by luxury or pride, he reduced and corrected him by his addresses, and made him humble and modest, by showing him in how many things he was deficient, and how very far from perfection in virtue.

When he was past his childhood, he went once to a grammar-school, and asked the master for one of Homer's books; and he making answer that he had nothing of Homer's, Alcibiades gave him a blow with his fist, and went away. Another schoolmaster telling him that he had Homer corrected

by himself; "How?" said Alcibiades, "and do you employ
your time in teaching children to read? You, who are able
to amend Homer, may well undertake to instruct men."
Being once desirous to speak with Pericles, he went to his
house and was told there that he was not at leisure, but
busied in considering how to give up his accounts to the
Athenians; Alcibiades, as he went away, said, it "were better
for him to consider how he might avoid giving up his accounts at all."

Whilst he was very young, he was a soldier in the expedition against Potidaea, where Socrates lodged in the same
tent with him, and stood next to him in battle. Once there
happened a sharp skirmish, in which they both behaved
with signal bravery; but Alcibiades receiving a wound, Socrates threw himself before him to defend him, and beyond
any question saved him and his arms from the enemy, and
so in all justice might have challenged the prize of valour.
But the generals appearing eager to adjudge the honour to
Alcibiades, because of his rank, Socrates, who desired to
increase his thirst after glory of a noble kind, was the first to
give evidence for him, and pressed them to crown him, and
to decree to him the complete suit of armour. Afterwards,
in the battle of Delium, when the Athenians were routed,
and Socrates with a few others was retreating on foot, Alcibiades, who was on horseback, observing it, would not pass
on, but stayed to shelter him from the danger, and brought
him safe off, though the enemy pressed hard upon them,
and cut off many. But this happened some time after.

He gave a box on the ear to Hipponicus, the father of
Callias, whose birth and wealth made him a person of great
influence and repute. And this he did unprovoked by any
passion or quarrel between them, but only because, in a
frolic, he had agreed with his companions to do it. People
were justly offended at this insolence when it became known
through the city; but early the next morning, Alcibiades
went to his house and knocked at the door, and being admitted to him, took off his outer garment, and presenting his
naked body, desired him to scourge and chastise him as he
pleased. Upon this Hipponicus forgot all his resentment, and

not only pardoned him, but soon after gave him his daughter Hipparete in marriage. Some say that it was not Hipponicus, but his son Callias, who gave Hipparete to Alcibiades, together with a portion of ten talents, and that after, when she had a child, Alcibiades forced him to give ten talents more, upon pretence that such was the agreement if she brought him any children. Afterwards, Callias, for fear of coming to his death by his means, declared, in a full assembly of the people, that, if he should happen to die without children, the state should inherit his house and all his goods. Hipparete was a virtuous and dutiful wife, but, at last, growing impatient of the outrages done to her by her husband's continual entertaining of courtesans, as well strangers as Athenians, she departed from him and retired to her brother's house. Alcibiades seemed not at all concerned at this, and lived on still in the same luxury; but the law requiring that she should deliver to the archon in person, and not by proxy, the instrument by which she claimed a divorce, when, in obedience to the law, she presented herself before him to perform this, Alcibiades came in, caught her up, and carried her home through the market-place, no one daring to oppose him nor to take her from him. She continued with him till her death, which happened not long after, when Alcibiades had gone to Ephesus. Nor is this violence to be thought so very enormous or unmanly. For the law, in making her who desires to be divorced appear in public, seems to design to give her husband an opportunity of treating with her, and endeavouring to retain her.

Alcibiades had a dog which cost him seventy minas, and was a very large one, and very handsome. His tail, which was his principal ornament, he caused to be cut off, and his acquaintances exclaiming at him for it, and telling him that all Athens was sorry for the dog, and cried out upon him for this action, he laughed, and said, "Just what I wanted has happened then. I wished the Athenians to talk about this, that they might not say something worse of me."

It is said that the first time he came into the assembly was upon occasion of a largess of money which he made to the

people. This was not done by design, but as he passed along
he heard a shout, and inquiring the cause, and having
learned that there was a donative making to the people, he
went in amongst them and gave money also. The multitude
thereupon applauding him, and shouting, he was so transported at it, that he forgot a quail which he had under his
robe, and the bird, being frightened with the noise, flew off;
upon which the people made louder acclamations than before, and many of them started up to pursue the bird; and
one Antiochus, a pilot, caught it and restored it to him, for
which he was ever after a favourite with Alcibiades.

He had great advantages for entering public life; his noble
birth, his riches, the personal courage he had shown in
divers battles, and the multitude of his friends and depend-
ents, threw open, so to say, folding-doors for his admittance. But he did not consent to let his power with the people rest on anything, rather than on his own gift of eloquence. That he was a master in the art of speaking, the
comic poets bear him witness; and the most eloquent of
public speakers, in his oration against Midias, allows that
Alcibiades, among other perfections, was a most accomplished orator. If, however, we give credit to Theophrastus,
who of all philosophers was the most curious inquirer, and
the greatest lover of history, we are to understand that Alcibiades had the highest capacity for inventing, for discerning
what was the right thing to be said for any purpose, and on
any occasion; but aiming not only at saying what was required, but also at saying it well, in respect, that is, of
words and phrases, when these did not readily occur, he
would often pause in the middle of his discourse for want of
the apt word, and would be silent and stop till he could
recollect himself, and had considered what to say.

His expenses in horses kept for the public games, and in
the number of his chariots, were matter of great observation; never did any one but he, either private person or king,
send seven chariots to the Olympic games. And to have carried away at once, the first, the second, and the fourth prize,
as Thucydides says, or the third, as Euripides relates it, out-

does far away every distinction that ever was known or
thought of in that kind. Euripides celebrates his success in
this manner:—

> "—But my song to you,
> Son of Clinias, is due.
> Victory is noble; how much more
> To do as never Greek before;
> To obtain in the great chariot race
> The first, the second, and third place;
> With easy step advanced to fame
> To bid the herald three times claim
> The olive for one victor's name."

The emulation displayed by the deputations of various states
in the presents which they made to him, rendered this success yet more illustrious. The Ephesians erected a tent for
him, adorned magnificently; the city of Chios furnished him
with provender for his horses and with great numbers of
beasts for sacrifice; and the Lesbians sent him wine and
other provisions for the many great entertainments which
he made. Yet in the midst of all this he escaped not without
censure, occasioned either by the ill-nature of his enemies
or by his own misconduct. For it is said, that one Diomedes,
an Athenian, a worthy man and a friend to Alcibiades, passionately desiring to obtain the victory at the Olympic
games, and having heard much of a chariot which belonged
to the state at Argos, where he knew that Alcibiades had
great power and many friends, prevailed with him to undertake to buy the chariot. Alcibiades did indeed buy it, but
then claimed it for his own, leaving Diomedes to rage at
him, and to call upon the gods and men to bear witness to
the injustice. It would seem there was a suit at law commenced upon this occasion, and there is yet extant an oration concerning the chariot, written by Isocrates in defence
of the son of Alcibiades. But the plaintiff in this action is
named Tisias, and not Diomedes.

As soon as he began to intermeddle in the government,
which was when he was very young, he quickly lessened the

credit of all who aspired to the confidence of the people except Phaeax, the son of Erasistratus, and Nicias, the son of
Niceratus, who alone could contest it with him. Nicias was
arrived at a mature age, and was esteemed their first general. Phaeax was but a rising statesman like Alcibiades; he
was descended from noble ancestors, but was his inferior,
as in many other things, so, principally, in eloquence. He
possessed rather the art of persuading in private conversation than of debate before the people, and was, as Eupolis
said of him—

"The best of talkers, and of speakers worst."

There is extant an oration written by Phaeax against Alcibiades, in which, amongst other things, it is said, that Alcibiades made daily use at his table of many gold and silver
vessels, which belonged to the commonwealth, as if they
had been his own.

There was a certain Hyperbolus, of the township of
Perithoedae, whom Thucydides also speaks of as a man of
bad character, a general butt for the mockery of all the
comic writers of the time, but quite unconcerned at the
worst things they could say, and, being careless of glory,
also insensible of shame; a temper which some people call
boldness and courage, whereas it is indeed impudence and
recklessness. He was liked by nobody, yet the people made
frequent use of him, when they had a mind to disgrace or
calumniate any persons in authority. At this time, the people, by his persuasions, were ready to proceed to pronounce
the sentence of ten years' banishment, called ostracism.
This they made use of to humiliate and drive out of the city
such citizens as outdid the rest in credit and power, indulging not so much perhaps their apprehensions as their jealousies in this way. And when, at this time, there was no
doubt but that the ostracism would fall upon one of those
three, Alcibiades contrived to form a coalition of parties,
and, communicating his project to Nicias, turned the sentence upon Hyperbolus himself. Others say, that it was not
with Nicias, but Phaeax, that he consulted, and by help of

his party procured the banishment of Hyperbolus, when he suspected nothing less. For, before that time, no mean or obscure person had ever fallen under the punishment, so that Plato, the comic poet, speaking of Hyperbolus, might well say—

> "The man deserved the fate; deny't who can?
> Yes, but the fate did not deserve the man;
> Not for the like of him and his slave-brands
> Did Athens put the sherd into our hands."

But we have given elsewhere a fuller statement of what is known to us of the matter.

Alcibiades was not less disturbed at the distinctions which Nicias gained amongst the enemies of Athens than at the honours which the Athenians themselves paid to him. For though Alcibiades was the proper appointed person to receive all Lacedaemonians when they came to Athens, and had taken particular care of those that were made prisoners at Pylos, yet, after they had obtained the peace and restitution of the captives, by the procurement chiefly of Nicias, they paid him very special attentions. And it was commonly said in Greece, that the war was begun by Pericles, and that Nicias made an end of it, and the peace was generally called the peace of Nicias. Alcibiades was extremely annoyed at this, and being full of envy, set himself to break the league. First, therefore, observing that the Argives, as well out of fear as hatred to the Lacedaemonians, sought for protection against them, he gave them a secret assurance of alliance with Athens. And communicating, as well in person as by letters, with the chief advisers of the people there, he encouraged them not to fear the Lacedaemonians, nor make concessions to them, but to wait a little, and keep their eyes on the Athenians, who, already, were all but sorry they had made peace, and would soon give it up. And afterwards, when the Lacedaemonians had made a league with the Boeotians, and had not delivered up Panactum entire, as they ought to have done by the treaty, but only after first destroying it, which gave great offence to the people of

Athens, Alcibiades laid hold of that opportunity to exasperate them more highly. He exclaimed fiercely against Nicias, and accused him of many things, which seemed probable enough: as that, when he was general, he made no attempt himself to capture their enemies that were shut up in the isle of Sphacteria, but, when they were afterwards made prisoners by others, he procured their release and sent them back to the Lacedaemonians, only to get favour with them; that he would not make use of his credit with them to prevent their entering into this confederacy with the Boeotians and Corinthians, and yet, on the other side, that he sought to stand in the way of those Greeks who were inclined to make an alliance and friendship with Athens, if the Lacedaemonians did not like it.

It happened, at the very time when Nicias was by these arts brought into disgrace with the people, that ambassadors arrived from Lacedaemon, who, at their first coming, said what seemed very satisfactory, declaring that they had full powers to arrange all matters in dispute upon fair and equal terms. The council received their propositions, and the people were to assemble on the morrow to give them audience. Alcibiades grew very apprehensive of this, and contrived to gain a secret conference with the ambassadors. When they were met, he said: "What is it you intend, you men of Sparta? Can you be ignorant that the council always act with moderation and respect towards ambassadors, but that the people are full of ambition and great designs? So that, if you let them know what full powers your commission gives you, they will urge and press you to unreasonable conditions. Quit, therefore, this indiscreet simplicity, if you expect to obtain equal terms from the Athenians, and would not have things extorted from you contrary to your inclinations, and begin to treat with the people upon some reasonable articles, not avowing yourselves plenipotentiaries; and I will be ready to assist you, out of good-will to the Lacedaemonians." When he had said thus, he gave them his oath for the performance of what he promised, and by this way drew them from Nicias to rely entirely upon himself, and left them full of admiration of the discernment and sagacity they had seen in him. The next day, when the people were assembled and the ambassadors introduced, Alcibiades, with great apparent courtesy, demanded of them, With what powers they were come? They made answer that they were not come as plenipotentiaries.

Instantly upon that, Alcibiades, with a loud voice, as though he had received and not done the wrong, began to call them dishonest prevaricators, and to urge that such men could not possibly come with a purpose to say or do anything that was sincere. The council was incensed, the people were in a rage, and Nicias, who knew nothing of the deceit and the imposture, was in the greatest confusion, equally surprised and ashamed at such a change in the men. So thus the Lacedaemonian ambassadors were utterly rejected, and Alcibiades was declared general, who presently united the Argives, the Eleans, and the people of Mantinea, into a confederacy with the Athenians.

No man commended the method by which Alcibiades effected all this, yet it was a great political feat thus to divide and shake almost all Peloponnesus, and to combine so many men in arms against the Lacedaemonians in one day before Mantinea; and, moreover, to remove the war and the danger so far from the frontier of the Athenians, that even success would profit the enemy but little, should they be conquerors, whereas, if they were defeated, Sparta itself was hardly safe.

After this battle at Mantinea, the select thousand of the army of the Argives attempted to overthrow the government of the people in Argos, and make themselves masters of the city; and the Lacedaemonians came to their aid and abolished the democracy. But the people took arms again, and gained the advantage, and Alcibiades came in to their aid and completed the victory, and persuaded them to build long walls, and by that means to join their city to the sea, and so to bring it wholly within reach of the Athenian power. To this purpose he procured them builders and masons from Athens, and displayed the greatest zeal for their service, and gained no less honour

and power to himself than to the commonwealth of
Athens. He also persuaded the people of Patrae to join
their city to the sea, by building long walls; and when some
one told them, by way of warning, that the Athenians
would swallow them up at last, Alcibiades made answer,
"Possibly it may be so, but it will be by little and little,
and beginning at the feet, whereas the Lacedaemonians
will begin at the head and devour you all at once." Nor
did he neglect either to advise the Athenians to look to
their interests by land, and often put the young men in
mind of the oath which they had made at Agraulos, to the
effect that they would account wheat and barley, and vines
and olives, to be the limits of Attica; by which they were
taught to claim a title to all land that was cultivated and
productive.

But with all these words and deeds, and with all this
sagacity and eloquence, he intermingled exorbitant luxury
and wantonness, in his eating and drinking and dissolute
living; wore long purple robes like a woman, which dragged
after him as he went through the market-place; caused the
planks of his galley to be cut away, that so he might lie
the softer, his bed not being placed on the boards, but
hanging upon girths. His shield, again, which was richly
gilded, had not the usual ensigns of the Athenians, but a
Cupid, holding a thunderbolt in his hand, was painted upon
it. The sight of all this made the people of good repute in
the city feel disgust and abhorrence, and apprehension also,
at his free living, and his contempt of law, as things monstrous in themselves, and indicating designs of usurpation.
Aristophanes has well expressed the people's feelings toward him—

"They love, and hate, and cannot do without him."

And still more strongly, under a figurative expression,—

"Best rear no lion in your state, 'tis true;
But treat him like a lion if you do."

The truth is, his liberalities, his public shows, and other munificence to the people, which were such as nothing could exceed, the glory of his ancestors, the force of his eloquence, the grace of his person, his strength of body, joined with his great courage and knowledge in military affairs, prevailed upon the Athenians to endure patiently his excesses, to indulge many things to him, and, according to their habit, to give the softest names to his faults, attributing them to youth and good nature. As, for example, he kept Agatharcus, the painter, a prisoner till he had painted his whole house, but then dismissed him with a reward. He publicly struck Taureas, who exhibited certain shows in opposition to him and contended with him for the prize. He selected for himself one of the captive Melian women, and had a son by her, whom he took care to educate. This the Athenians styled great humanity, and yet he was the principal cause of the slaughter of all the inhabitants of the isle of Melos who were of age to bear arms, having spoken in favour of that decree. When Aristophon, the painter, had drawn Nemea sitting and holding Alcibiades in her arms, the multitudes seemed pleased with the piece, and thronged to see it, but older people disliked and disrelished it, and looked on these things as enormities, and movements towards tyranny. So that it was not said amiss by Archestratus, that Greece could not support a second Alcibiades. Once, when Alcibiades succeeded well in an oration which he made, and the whole assembly attended upon him to do him honour, Timon the misanthrope did not pass slightly by him, nor avoid him, as did others, but purposely met him, and taking him by the hand, said, "Go on boldly, my son, and increase in credit with the people, for thou wilt one day bring them calamities enough." Some that were present laughed at the saying, and some reviled Timon; but there were others upon whom it made a deep impression; so various was the judgment which was made of him, and so irregular his own character.

The Athenians, even in the lifetime of Pericles, had already cast a longing eye upon Sicily; but did not attempt anything till after his death. Then, under pretence of aiding their confederates, they sent succours upon all occasions to those who were oppressed by the Syracusans, preparing the way for sending over a greater force. But Alcibiades was the person who inflamed this desire of theirs to the height, and prevailed with them no longer to proceed secretly, and by little and little, in their design, but to sail out with a great fleet, and undertake at once to make themselves masters of the island. He possessed the people with great hopes, and he himself entertained yet greater; and the conquest of Sicily, which was the utmost bound of their ambition, was but the mere outset of his expectation. Nicias endeavoured to divert the people from the expedition, by representing to them that the taking of Syracuse would be a work of great difficulty; but Alcibiades dreamed of nothing less than the conquest of Carthage and Libya, and by the accession of these conceiving himself at once made master of Italy and Peloponnesus, seemed to look upon Sicily as little more than a magazine for the war. The young men were soon elevated with these hopes, and listened gladly to those of riper years, who talked wonders of the countries they were going to; so that you might see great numbers sitting in the wrestling grounds and public places, drawing on the ground the figure of the island and the situation of Libya and Carthage. Socrates the philosopher and Meton the astrologer are said, however, never to have hoped for any good to the commonwealth from this war; the one, it is to be supposed, presaging what would ensue, by the intervention of his attendant Genius; and the other, either upon rational consideration of the project or by use of the art of divination, conceived fears for its issue, and, feigning madness, caught up a burning torch, and seemed as if he would have set his own house on fire. Others report, that he did not take upon him to act the madman, but secretly in the night set his house on fire, and the next morning besought the people, that for his comfort, after such a calamity, they would spare his son from the expedition. By which artifice he deceived his fellow-citizens, and obtained of them what he desired.

Together with Alcibiades, Nicias, much against his will, was appointed general; and he endeavoured to avoid the command, not the less on account of his colleague. But the Athenians thought the war would proceed more prosperously, if they did not send Alcibiades free from all restraint, but tempered his heat with the caution of Nicias. This they chose the rather to do, because Lamachus, the third general, though he was of mature years, yet in several battles had appeared no less hot and rash than Alcibiades himself. When they began to deliberate of the number of forces, and of the manner of making the necessary provisions, Nicias made another attempt to oppose the design, and to prevent the war; but Alcibiades contradicted him, and carried his point with the people. And one Demostratus, an orator, proposing to give the generals absolute power over the preparations and the whole management of the war, it was presently decreed so. When all things were fitted for the voyage, many unlucky omens appeared. At that very time the feast of Adonis happened in which the women were used to expose, in all parts of the city, images resembling dead men carried out to their burial, and to represent funeral solemnities by lamentations and mournful songs. The mutilation, however, of the images of Mercury, most of which, in one night, had their faces all disfigured, terrified many persons who were wont to despise most things of that nature. It was given out that it was done by the Corinthians, for the sake of the Syracusans, who were their colony, in hopes that the Athenians, by such prodigies, might be induced to delay or abandon the war. But the report gained no credit with the people, nor yet the opinion of those who would not believe that there was anything ominous in the matter, but that it was only an extravagant action, committed, in that sort of sport which runs into licence, by wild young men coming from a debauch. Alike enraged and terrified at the thing, looking upon it to proceed from a conspiracy of persons who designed some commotions in the state, the council, as well as the assembly of the people, which were held frequently in a few days' space, examined diligently everything that might administer ground for suspicion. During this examination, Androcles, one of the demagogues, produced certain slaves and strangers before them, who accused Alcibiades and some of his friends of defacing other images in the same manner, and of having profanely acted the sacred mysteries at a drunken meeting, where one Theodorus represented the herald, Polytion the torch-bearer, and Alcibiades the chief priest, while the rest of the party appeared as candidates for initiation, and received the title Initiates. These were the matters contained in the articles of information which Thessalus, the son of Cimon, exhibited against Alcibiades, for his impious mockery of the goddesses Ceres and Proserpine. The people were highly exasperated and incensed against Alcibiades upon this accusation, which being aggravated by Androcles, the most malicious of all his enemies, at first disturbed his friends exceedingly. But when they perceived that all the seamen designed for Sicily were for him, and the soldiers also, and when the Argive and Mantinean auxiliaries, a thousand men at arms, openly declared that they had undertaken this distant maritime expedition for the sake of Alcibiades, and that, if he was ill-used, they would all go home, they recovered their courage, and became eager to make use of the present opportunity for justifying him. At this his enemies were again discouraged, fearing lest the people should be more gentle to him in their sentence, because of the occasion they had for his service. Therefore, to obviate this, they contrived that some other orators, who did not appear to be enemies to Alcibiades, but really hated him no less than those who avowed it, should stand up in the assembly and say that it was a very absurd thing that one who was created general of such an army with absolute power, after his troops were assembled, and the confederates were come, should lose the opportunity, whilst the people were choosing his judges by lot, and appointing times for the hearing of the cause. And, therefore, let him set sail at once, good fortune attend him; and when the war should be at an end, he might then in person make his defence according to the laws.

Alcibiades perceived the malice of this postponement, and, appearing in the assembly, represented that it was monstrous for him to be sent with the command of so large an army, when he lay under such accusations and calumnies; that he deserved to die, if he could not clear himself of the crimes objected to him; but when he had so done, and had proved his innocence, he should then cheerfully apply himself to the war, as standing no longer in fear of false accusers. But he could not prevail with the people, who commanded him to sail immediately. So he departed, together with the other generals, having with them near 140 galleys, 5,100 men at arms, and about 1,300 archers, slingers, and light-armed men, and all the other provisions corresponding.

Arriving on the coast of Italy, he landed at Rhegium, and there stated his views of the manner in which they ought to conduct the war. He was opposed by Nicias; but Lamachus being of his opinion, they sailed for Sicily forthwith, and took Catana. This was all that was done while he was there, for he was soon after recalled by the Athenians to abide his trial. At first, as we before said, there were only some slight suspicions advanced against Alcibiades, and accusations by certain slaves and strangers. But afterwards, in his absence, his enemies attacked him more violently, and confounded together the breaking the images with the profanation of the mysteries, as though both had been committed in pursuance of the same conspiracy for changing the government. The people proceeded to imprison all that were accused, without distinction, and without hearing them, and repented now, considering the importance of the charge, that they had not immediately brought Alcibiades to his trial, and given judgment against him. Any of his friends or acquaintance who fell into the people's hands, whilst they were in this fury, did not fail to meet with very severe usage. Thucydides has omitted to name the informers, but others mention Dioclides and Teucer. Amongst whom is Phrynichus, the comic poet, in whom we find the following:—

"O dearest Hermes! only do take care,
  And mind you do not miss your footing there;
  Should you get hurt, occasion may arise
  For a new Dioclides to tell lies."

To which he makes Mercury return this answer:—

  "will so, for I feel no inclination
  To reward Teucer for more information."

The truth is, his accusers alleged nothing that was certain
or solid against him. One of them, being asked how he
knew the men who defaced the images, replying, that he
saw them by the light of the moon, made a palpable mis-
statement, for it was just new moon when the fact was
committed. This made all men of understanding cry out
upon the thing; but the people were as eager as ever to receive further accusations, nor was their first heat at all
abated, but they instantly seized and imprisoned every one
that was accused. Amongst those who were detained in
prison for their trials was Andocides the orator, whose descent the historian Hellanicus deduces from Ulysses. He was
always supposed to hate popular government, and to support oligarchy. The chief ground of his being suspected of defacing the images was because the great Mercury, which
stood near his house, and was an ancient monument of
the tribe Aegeïs, was almost the only statute of all the remarkable ones which remained entire. For this cause, it is
now called the Mercury of Andocides, all men giving it
that name, though the inscription is evidence to the contrary. It happened that Andocides, amongst the rest who
were prisoners upon the same account, contracted particular acquaintance and intimacy with one Timaeus, a person
inferior to him in repute, but of remarkable dexterity and
boldness. He persuaded Andocides to accuse him and some
few others of this crime, urging to him that, upon his confession, he would be, by the decree of the people, secure
of his pardon, whereas the event of judgment is uncertain

to all men, but to great persons, such as he was, most formidable. So that it was better for him, if he regarded himself, to save his life by falsity, than to suffer an infamous death, as really guilty of the crime. And if he had regard to the public good, it was commendable to sacrifice a few suspected men, by that means to rescue many excellent persons from the fury of the people. Andocides was prevailed upon, and accused himself and some others, and, by the terms of the decree, obtained his pardon, while all the persons named by him, except some few who had saved themselves by flight, suffered death. To gain the greater credit to his information, he accused his own servants amongst others. But notwithstanding this, the people's anger was not wholly appeased; and being now no longer diverted by the mutilators, they were at leisure to pour out their whole rage upon Alcibiades. And, in conclusion, they sent the galley named Salaminian to recall him. But they expressly commanded those that were sent to use no violence, nor seize upon his person, but address themselves to him in the mildest terms, requiring him to follow them to Athens in order to abide his trial, and clear himself before the people. For they feared mutiny and sedition in the army in an enemy's country, which indeed it would have been easy for Alcibiades to effect, if he had wished it. For the soldiers were dispirited upon his departure, expecting for the future tedious delays, and that the war would be drawn out into a lazy length by Nicias, when Alcibiades, who was the spur to action, was taken away. For though Lamachus was a soldier, and a man of courage, poverty deprived him of authority and respect in the army. Alcibiades, just upon his departure, prevented Messena from falling into the hands of the Athenians. There were some in that city who were upon the point of delivering it up, but he, knowing the persons, gave information to some friends of the Syracusans, and so defeated the whole contrivance. When he arrived at Thurii, he went on shore, and, concealing himself there, escaped those who searched after him. But to one who knew him, and asked him if he durst not trust his own native country, he made answer, "In everything else, yes; but in a matter that touches my life, I would not even my own mother, lest she might by mistake throw in the black ball instead of the white." When, afterwards, he was told that the assembly had pronounced judgment of death against him, all he said was, "I will make them feel that I am alive."

The information against him was conceived in this form:—

"Thessalus, the son of Cimon, of the township of Lacia, lays information that Alcibiades, the son of Clinias of the township of the Scambonidae, has committed a crime against the goddesses Ceres and Proserpine, by representing in derision the holy mysteries, and showing them to his companions in his own house. Where, being habited in such robes as are used by the chief priest when he shows the holy things, he named himself the chief priest, Polytion the torch-bearer, and Theodorus, of the township of Phegaea, the herald; and saluted the rest of his company as Initiates and Novices, all which was done contrary to the laws and institutions of the Eumolpidae, and the heralds and priests of the temple at Eleusis."

He was condemned as contumacious upon his not appearing, his property confiscated, and it was decreed that all priests and priestesses should solemnly curse him. But one of them, Theano, the daughter of Menon, of the township of Agraule, is said to have opposed that part of the decree, saying that her holy office obliged her to make prayers, but not execrations.

Alcibiades, lying under these heavy decrees and sentences, when first he fled from Thurii, passed over into Peloponnesus and remained some time at Argos. But being there in fear of his enemies, and seeing himself utterly hopeless of return to his native country, he sent to Sparta, desiring safe conduct, and assuring them that he would make them amends by his future services for all the mischief he had done them while he was their enemy. The Spartans giving him the security he desired, he went eagerly, was well received, and, at his very first coming, succeeded in inducing them, without any further caution or delay, to send aid

to the Syracusans; and so roused and excited them, that
they forthwith despatched Gylippus into Sicily to crush
the forces which the Athenians had in Sicily. A second
point was to renew the war upon the Athenians at home.
But the third thing, and the most important of all, was to
make them fortify Decelea, which above everything reduced
and wasted the resources of the Athenians.

The renown which he earned by these public services
was equalled by the admiration he attracted to his private
life; he captivated and won over everybody by his conformity to Spartan habits. People who saw him wearing
his hair close cut, bathing in cold water, eating coarse
meal, and dining on black broth, doubted, or rather could
not believe, that he ever had a cook in his house, or had
ever seen a perfumer, or had worn a mantle of Milesian
purple. For he had, as it was observed, this peculiar talent and artifice for gaining men's affections, that he could
at once comply with and really embrace and enter into
their habits and ways of life, and change faster than the
chameleon. One colour, indeed, they say the chameleon
cannot assume: it cannot itself appear white; but Alcibiades, whether with good men or with bad, could adapt
himself to his company, and equally wear the appearance
of virtue or vice. At Sparta, he was devoted to athletic
exercises, was frugal and reserved; in Ionia, luxurious, gay,
and indolent; in Thrace, always drinking; in Thessaly, ever
on horseback; and when he lived with Tisaphernes the
Persian satrap, he exceeded the Persians themselves in
magnificence and pomp. Not that his natural disposition
changed so easily, nor that his real character was so vari-
able, but, whether he was sensible that by pursuing his
own inclinations he might give offence to those with whom
he had occasion to converse, he transformed himself into
any shape, and adopted any fashion, that he observed to
be most agreeable to them. So that to have seen him at
Lacedaemon, a man, judging by the outward appearance,
would have said, " 'Tis not Achilles's son, but he himself;
the very man" that Lycurgus designed to form; while his
real feeling and acts would have rather provoked the ex-

clamation, " 'Tis the same woman still." For while king Agis was absent, and abroad with the army, he corrupted his wife Timaea, and had a child born by her. Nor did she even deny it, but when she was brought to bed of a son, called him in public Leotychides, but, amongst her confidants and attendants, would whisper that his name was Alcibiades, to such a degree was she transported by her passion for him. He, on the other side, would say, in his vain way, he had not done this thing out of mere wantonness of insult, nor to gratify a passion, but that his race might one day be kings over the Lacedaemonians.

There were many who told Agis that this was so, but time itself gave the greatest confirmation to the story. For Agis, alarmed by an earthquake, had quitted his wife, and for ten months after was never with her; Leotychides, therefore, being born after these ten months, he would not acknowledge him for his son; which was the reason that afterwards he was not admitted to the succession.

After the defeat which the Athenians received in Sicily, ambassadors were despatched to Sparta at once from Chios and Lesbos and Cyzicus, to signify their purpose of revolting from the Athenians. The Boeotians interposed in favour of the Lesbians, and Pharnabazus of the Cyzicenes, but the Lacedaemonians, at the persuasion of Alcibiades, chose to assist Chios before all others. He himself, also, went instantly to sea, procured the immediate revolt of almost all Ionia, and, co-operating with the Lacedaemonian generals, did great mischief to the Athenians. But Agis was his enemy, hating him for having dishonoured his wife, and also impatient of his glory, as almost every enterprise and every success was ascribed to Alcibiades. Others, also, of the most powerful and ambitious amongst the Spartans were possessed with jealousy of him, and at last prevailed with the magistrates in the city to send orders into Ionia that he should be killed. Alcibiades, however, had secret intelligence of this, and in apprehension of the result, while he communicated all affairs to the Lacedaemonians, yet took care not to put himself into their power. At last he retired to Tisaphernes, the King of Persia's satrap, for his security, and immediately became the first and most influential person about him. For this barbarian, not being himself sincere, but a lover of guile and wickedness, admired his address and wonderful subtlety. And, indeed, the charm of daily intercourse with him was more than any character could resist or any disposition escape. Even those who feared and envied him could not but take delight, and have a sort of kindness for him, when they saw him and were in his company. So that Tisaphernes, otherwise a cruel character, and, above all other Persians, a hater of the Greeks, was yet so won by the flatteries of Alcibiades, that he set himself even to exceed him in responding to them. The most beautiful of his parks, containing salubrious streams and meadows, where he had built pavilions, and places of retirement royally and exquisitely adorned, received by his direction the name of Alcibiades, and was always so called and so spoken of.

Thus Alcibiades, quitting the interests of the Spartans, whom he could no longer trust, because he stood in fear of Agis, endeavoured to do them ill offices, and render them odious to Tisaphernes, who by his means was hindered from assisting them vigorously, and from finally ruining the Athenians. For his advice was to furnish them but sparingly with money, and so wear them out, and consume them insensibly; when they had wasted their strength upon one another, they would both become ready to submit to the king. Tisaphernes readily pursued his counsel, and so openly expressed the liking and admiration which he had for him, that Alcibiades was looked up to by the Greeks of both parties, and the Athenians, now in their misfortunes, repented them of their severe sentence against him. And he, on the other side, began to be troubled for them, and to fear lest, if that commonwealth were utterly destroyed, he should fall into the hands of the Lacedaemonians, his enemies.

At that time the whole strength of the Athenians was in Samos. Their fleet maintained itself here, and issued from these headquarters to reduce such as had revolted, and protect the rest of their territories; in one way or other still contriving to be a match for their enemies at sea. What they stood in fear of was Tisaphernes and the Phoenician fleet of one hundred and fifty galleys, which was said to be already under sail; if those came, there remained then no hopes for the commonwealth of Athens. Understanding this, Alcibiades sent secretly to the chief men of the Athenians, who were then at Samos, giving them hopes that he would make Tisaphernes their friend; he was willing, he implied, to do some favour, not to the people, not in reliance upon them, but to the better citizens, if only, like brave men, they would make the attempt to put down the insolence of the people, and, by taking upon them the government, would endeavour to save the city from ruin. All of them gave a ready ear to the proposal made by Alcibiades, except only Phrynichus, of the township of Dirades, one of the generals, who suspected, as the truth was, that Alcibiades concerned not himself whether the government were in the people or the better citizens, but only sought by any means to make way for his return into his native country, and to that end inveighed against the people, thereby to gain the others, and to insinuate himself into their good opinion. But when Phrynichus found his counsel to be rejected and that he was himself become a declared enemy of Alcibiades, he gave secret intelligence to Astyochus, the enemy's admiral, cautioning him to beware of Alcibiades and to seize him as a double dealer, unaware that one traitor was making discoveries to another. For Astyochus, who was eager to gain the favour of Tisaphernes, observing the credit Alcibiades had with him, revealed to Alcibiades all that Phrynichus had said against him. Alcibiades at once despatched messengers to Samos, to accuse Phrynichus of the treachery. Upon this, all the commanders were enraged with Phrynichus, and set themselves against him; he, seeing no other way to extricate himself from the present danger, attempted to remedy one evil by a greater. He sent to Astyochus to reproach him for betraying him, and to make an offer to him at the same time to deliver into his hands both the army and the navy of the Athenians. This occasioned no damage to the Athenians, because Astyochus repeated his treachery and revealed also this proposal to Alcibiades. But this again was foreseen by Phrynichus, who, expecting a second accusation from Alcibiades to anticipate him, advertised the Athenians beforehand that the enemy was ready to sail in order to surprise them, and therefore advised them to fortify their camp, and be in a readiness to go aboard their ships. While the Athenians were intent upon doing these things, they received other letters from Alcibiades, admonishing them to beware of Phrynichus, as one who designed to betray their fleet to the enemy, to which they then gave no credit at all, conceiving that Alcibiades, who knew perfectly the counsels and preparations of the enemy, was merely making use of that knowledge, in order to impose upon them in this false accusation of Phrynichus. Yet, afterwards, when Phrynichus was stabbed with a dagger in the market-place by Hermon, one of the guards, the Athenians, entering into an examination of the cause, solemnly condemned Phrynichus of treason, and decreed crowns to Hermon and his associates. And now the friends of Alcibiades, carrying all before them at Samos, despatched Pisander to Athens, to attempt a change of government, and to encourage the aristocratical citizens to take upon themselves the government, and overthrow the democracy, representing to them, that upon these terms, Alcibiades would procure them the friendship and alliance of Tisaphernes.

This was the colour and pretence made use of by those who desired to change the government of Athens to an oligarchy. But as soon as they prevailed, and had got the administration of affairs into their hands, under the name of the Five Thousand (whereas, indeed, they were but four hundred), they slighted Alcibiades altogether, and prosecuted the war with less vigour; partly because they durst not yet trust the citizens, who secretly detested this change, and partly because they thought the Lacedaemonians who always befriended the government of the few, would be inclined to give them favourable terms.

The people in the city were terrified into submission, many of those who had dared openly to oppose the four hundred having been put to death. But those who were at Samos, indignant when they heard the news, were eager to set sail instantly for the Piraeus; sending for Alcibiades, they declared him general, requiring him to lead them on to put down the tyrants. He, however, in that juncture, did not, as it might have been thought a man would, on being suddenly exalted by the favour of a multitude, think himself under an obligation to gratify and submit to all the wishes of those who, from a fugitive and an exile, had created him general of so great an army, and given him the command of such a fleet. But, as became a great captain, he opposed himself to the precipitate resolutions which their rage led them to, and, by restraining them from the great error they were about to commit, unequivocally saved the commonwealth. For if they then sailed to Athens, all Ionia and the islands and the Hellespont would have fallen into the enemies' hands without opposition, while the Athenians, involved in civil war, would have been fighting with one another within the circuit of their own walls. It was Alcibiades, alone, or, at least, principally, who prevented all this mischief; for he not only used persuasion to the whole army, and showed them the danger, but applied himself to them, one by one, entreating some, and constraining others. He was much assisted, however, by Thrasybulus of Stiria, who having the loudest voice, as we are told, of all the Athenians, went along with him, and cried out to those who were ready to be gone. A second great service which Alcibiades did for them was, his undertaking that the Phoenician fleet, which the Lacedaemonians expected to be sent to them by the King of Persia, should either come in aid of the Athenians or otherwise should not come at all. He sailed off with all expedition in order to perform this, and the ships, which had already been seen as near as Aspendus, were not brought any further by Tisaphernes, who thus deceived the Lacedaemonians; and it was by both sides believed that they had been diverted by the procurement of Alcibiades. The

Lacedaemonians, in particular, accused him, that he had advised the Barbarian to stand still, and suffer the Greeks to waste and destroy one another, as it was evident that the accession of so great a force to either party would enable them to take away the entire dominion of the sea from the other side.

Soon after this, the four hundred usurpers were driven out, the friends of Alcibiades vigorously assisting those who were for the popular government. And now the people in the city not only desired, but commanded Alcibiades to return home from his exile. He, however, desired not to owe his return to the mere grace and commiseration of the people, and resolved to come back, not with empty hands, but with glory, and after some service done. To this end, he sailed from Samos with a few ships, and cruised on the sea of Cnidos, and about the isle of Cos, but receiving intelligence there that Mindarus, the Spartan admiral, had sailed with his whole army into the Hellespont, and that the Athenians had followed him, he hurried back to succour the Athenian commanders, and, by good fortune, arrived with eighteen galleys at a critical time. For both the fleets having engaged near Abydos, the fight between them had lasted till night, the one side having the advantage on one quarter, and the other on another. Upon his first appearance, both sides formed a false impression; the enemy was encouraged and the Athenians terrified. But Alcibiades suddenly raised the Athenian ensign in the admiral ship, and fell upon those galleys of the Peloponnesians which had the advantage and were in pursuit. He soon put these to flight, and followed them so close that he forced them on shore, and broke the ships in pieces, the sailors abandoning them and swimming away in spite of all the efforts of Pharnabazus, who had come down to their assistance by land and did what he could to protect them from the shore. In fine, the Athenians, having taken thirty of the enemy's ships, and recovered all their own, erected a trophy. After the gaining of so glorious a victory, his vanity made him eager to show himself to Tisaphernes, and, having furnished himself with gifts and presents, and an equipage suitable to his dignity, he set out to visit him. But the thing did not succeed as he had imagined, for Tisaphernes had been long suspected by the Lacedaemonians, and was afraid to fall into disgrace with his king upon that account, and therefore thought that Alcibiades arrived very opportunely, and immediately caused him to be seized, and sent away prisoner to Sardis; fancying, by this act of injustice, to clear himself from all former imputations.

But about thirty days after, Alcibiades escaped from his keeping, and having got a horse, fled to Clazomenae, where he procured Tisaphernes additional disgrace by professing he was a party to his escape. From there he sailed to the Athenian camp, and, being informed there that Mindarus and Pharnabazus were together at Cyzicus, he made a speech to the soldiers, telling them that sea-fighting, land-fighting, and, by the gods, fighting against fortified cities too, must be all one for them, as unless they conquered everywhere, there was no money for them. As soon as ever he got them on shipboard, he hastened to Proconnesus, and gave command to seize all the small vessels they met, and guard them safely in the interior of the fleet, that the enemy might have no notice of his coming; and a great storm of rain, accompanied with thunder and darkness, which happened at the same time, contributed much to the concealment of his enterprise. Indeed, it was not only undiscovered by the enemy, but the Athenians themselves were ignorant of it, for he commanded them suddenly on board, and set sail when they had abandoned all intention of it. As the darkness presently passed away, the Peloponnesian fleet was seen riding out at sea in front of the harbour of Cyzicus. Fearing, if they discovered the number of his ships, they might endeavour to save themselves by land, he commanded the rest of the captains to slacken, and follow him slowly, whilst he, advancing with forty ships, showed himself to the enemy, and provoked them to fight. The enemy, being deceived as to their numbers, despised them, and, supposing they were to contend with those only, made themselves ready and began the fight. But as soon as they were engaged, they perceived the other part of the fleet coming down upon them, at which they were so terrified that they fled immediately. Upon that, Alcibiades, breaking through the midst of them with twenty of his best ships, hastened to the shore, disembarked, and pursued those who abandoned their ships and fled to land, and made a great slaughter of them. Mindarus and Pharnabazus, coming to their succour, were utterly defeated. Mindarus was slain upon the place, fighting valiantly; Pharnabazus saved himself by flight. The Athenians slew great numbers of their enemies, won much spoil, and took all their ships. They also made themselves masters of Cyzicus which was deserted by Pharnabazus, and destroyed its Peloponnesian garrison, and thereby not only secured to themselves the Hellespont, but by force drove the Lacedaemonians from out of the rest of the sea. They intercepted some letters written to the ephors, which gave an account of this fatal overthrow, after their short laconic manner. "Our hopes are at an end. Mindarus is slain. The men starve. We know not what to do."

The soldiers who followed Alcibiades in this last fight were so exalted with their success, and felt that degree of pride, that, looking on themselves as invincible, they disdained to mix with the other soldiers, who had been often overcome. For it happened not long before, Thrasyllus had received a defeat near Ephesus, and, upon that occasion, the Ephesians erected their brazen trophy to the disgrace of the Athenians. The soldiers of Alcibiades reproached those who were under the command of Thrasyllus with this misfortune, at the same time magnifying themselves and their own commander, and it went so far that they would not exercise with them, nor lodge in the same quarters. But soon after, Pharnabazus, with a great force of horse and foot, falling upon the soldiers of Thrasyllus, as they were laying waste the territory of Abydos, Alcibiades came to their aid, routed Pharnabazus, and together with Thrasyllus pursued him till it was night; and in this action the troops united, and returned together to the camp, rejoicing and congratulating one another. The

next day he erected a trophy, and then proceeded to lay
waste with fire and sword the whole province which was
under Pharnabazus, where none ventured to resist; and he
took divers priests and priestesses, but released them without ransom. He prepared next to attack the Chalcedonians,
who had revolted from the Athenians, and had received a
Lacedaemonian governor and garrison. But having intelligence that they had removed their corn and cattle out of
the fields, and were conveying it all to the Bithynians, who
were their friends, he drew down his army to the frontier
of the Bithynians, and then sent a herald to charge them
with this proceeding. The Bithynians, terrified at his approach, delivered up to him the booty, and entered into alliance with him.

Afterwards he proceeded to the siege of Chalcedon, and
enclosed it with a wall from sea to sea. Pharnabazus advanced with his forces to raise the siege, and Hippocrates,
the governor of the town, at the same time, gathering together all the strength he had, made a sally upon the
Athenians. Alcibiades divided his army so as to engage
both at once, and not only forced Pharnabazus to a dishonourable flight, but defeated Hippocrates, and killed
him and a number of the soldiers with him. After this he
sailed into the Hellespont, in order to raise supplies of
money, and took the city of Selymbria, in which action,
through his precipitation, he exposed himself to great danger. For some within the town had undertaken to betray
it into his hands, and, by agreement, were to give him a
signal by a lighted torch about midnight. But one of the
conspirators beginning to repent himself of the design,
the rest, for fear of being discovered, were driven to give
the signal before the appointed hour. Alcibiades, as soon
as he saw the torch lifted up in the air, though his army
was not in readiness to march, ran instantly towards the
walls, taking with him about thirty men only, and commanding the rest of the army to follow him with all possible speed. When he came hither, he found the gate
opened for him and entered with his thirty men, and about
twenty more light-armed men, who were come up to them.

They were no sooner in the city, but he perceived the
Selymbrians all armed, coming down upon him; so that
there was no hope of escaping if he stayed to receive
them; and, on the other hand, having been always successful till that day, wherever he commanded, he could
not endure to be defeated and fly. So, requiring silence
by sound of a trumpet, he commanded one of his men to
make proclamation that the Selymbrians should not take
arms against the Athenians. This cooled such of the inhabitants as were fiercest for the fight, for they supposed that
all their enemies were within the walls, and it raised the
hopes of others who were disposed to an accommodation.
Whilst they were parleying, and propositions making on
one side and the other, Alcibiades's whole army came up
to the town. And now, conjecturing rightly that the Selymbrians were well inclined to peace, and fearing lest the
city might be sacked by the Thracians, who came in great
numbers to his army to serve as volunteers, out of kindness for him, he commanded them all to retreat without
the walls. And upon the submission of the Selymbrians,
he saved them from being pillaged, only taking of them a
sum of money, and, after placing an Athenian garrison in
the town, departed.

During this action, the Athenian captains who besieged
Chalcedon concluded a treaty with Pharnabazus upon
these articles: That he should give them a sum of money;
that the Chalcedonians should return to the subjection of
Athens, and that the Athenians should make no inroad
into the province whereof Pharnabazus was governor; and
Pharnabazus was also to provide safe conducts for the
Athenian ambassadors to the King of Persia. Afterwards,
when Alcibiades returned thither, Pharnabazus required
that he also should be sworn to the treaty; but he refused
it, unless Pharnabazus would swear at the same time.
When the treaty was sworn to on both sides, Alcibiades
went against the Byzantines, who had revolted from the
Athenians, and drew a line of circumvallation about the
city. But Anaxilaus and Lycurgus, together with some others, having undertaken to betray the city to him upon his

engagement to preserve the lives and property of the inhabitants, he caused a report to be spread abroad, as if by reason of some unexpected movement in Ionia, he should be obliged to raise the siege. And, accordingly, that day he made a show to depart with his whole fleet; but returned the same night, and went ashore with all his men at arms, and, silently and undiscovered, marched up to the walls. At the same time, his ships rowed into the harbour with all possible violence, coming on with much fury, and with great shouts and outcries. The Byzantines, thus surprised and astonished, while they all hurried to the defence of their port and shipping, gave opportunity to those who favoured the Athenians securely to receive Alcibiades into the city. Yet the enterprise was not accomplished without fighting, for the Peloponnesians, Boeotians, and Megarians, not only repulsed those who came out of the ships, and forced them on board again, but, hearing that the Athenians were entered on the other side, drew up in order, and went to meet them. Alcibiades, however, gained the victory after some sharp fighting, in which he himself had the command of the right wing, and Theramenes of the left, and took about three hundred, who survived of the enemy, prisoners of war. After the battle, not one of the Byzantines was slain, or driven out of the city, according to the terms upon which the city was put into his hands, that they should receive no prejudice in life or property. And thus Anaxilaus, being afterwards accused at Lacedaemon for this treason, neither disowned nor professed to be ashamed of the action; for he urged that he was not a Lacedaemonian, but a Byzantine, and saw not Sparta, but Byzantium, in extreme danger; the city so blockaded that it was not possible to bring in any new provisions, and the Peloponnesians and Boeotians, who were in garrison, devouring the old stores, whilst the Byzantines, with their wives and children, were starving, that he had not, therefore, betrayed his country to enemies, but had delivered it from the calamities of war, and had but followed the example of the most worthy Lacedaemonians, who esteemed nothing to be honourable and just,

but what was profitable for their country. The Lacedaemonians, upon hearing his defence, respected it, and discharged all that were accused.

And now Alcibiades began to desire to see his native
country again, or rather to show his fellow-citizens a person who had gained so many victories for them. He set sail
for Athens, the ships that accompanied him being adorned
with great numbers of shields and other spoils, and tow-
ing after them many galleys taken from the enemy, and
the ensigns and ornaments of many others which he had
sunk and destroyed; all of them together amounting to two
hundred. Little credit, perhaps, can be given to what Duris
the Samian, who professed to be descended from Alcibiades, adds, that Chrysogonus, who had gained a victory
at the Pythian games, played upon his flute for the galleys,
whilst the oars kept time with the music; and that Callip-
pides, the tragedian, attired in his buskins, his purple robes,
and other ornaments used in the theatre, gave the word
to the rowers, and that the admiral galley entered into the
port with a purple sail. Neither Theopompus, nor Ephorus,
nor Xenophon, mention them. Nor, indeed, is it credible,
that one who returned from so long an exile, and such
variety of misfortunes, should come home to his countrymen in the style of revellers breaking up from a drinking-
party. On the contrary, he ventured the harbour full of
fear, nor would he venture to go on shore, till, standing
on the deck, he saw Euryptolemus, his cousin, and others
of his friends and acquaintance, who were ready to receive
him, and invited him to land. As soon as he was landed,
the multitude who came out to meet him scarcely seemed
so much as to see any of the other captains, but came in
throngs about Alcibiades, and saluted him with loud acclamations, and still followed him; those who could press
near him crowned him with garlands, and they who could
not come up so close yet stayed to behold him afar off,
and the old men pointed him out, and showed him to the
young ones. Nevertheless, this public joy was mixed with
some tears, and the present happiness was alloyed by the
remembrance of the miseries they had endured. They made

reflections, that they could not have so unfortunately miscarried in Sicily, or been defeated in any of their other expectations, if they had left the management of their affairs formerly, and the command of their forces, to Alcibiades, since, upon his undertaking the administration, when they were in a manner driven from the sea, and could scarce defend the suburbs of their city by land, and, at the same time, were miserably distracted with intestine factions, he had raised them up from this low and deplorable condition, and had not only restored them to their ancient dominion of the sea, but had also made them everywhere victorious over their enemies on land.

There had been a decree for recalling him from his banishment already passed by the people, at the instance of Critias, the son of Callaeschrus, as appears by his elegies, in which he puts Alcibiades in mind of this service:—

"From my proposal did that edict come,
   Which from your tedious exile brought you home.
   The public vote at first was moved by me,
   And my voice put the seal to the decree."

The people being summoned to an assembly, Alcibiades came in amongst them, and first bewailed and lamented his own sufferings, and, in gentle terms complaining of the usage he had received, imputed all to his hard fortune, and some ill-genius that attended him: then he spoke at large of their prospects, and exhorted them to courage and good hope. The people crowned him with crowns of gold, and created him general, both at land and sea, with absolute power. They also made a decree that his estate should be restored to him, and that the Eumolpidae and the holy herald should absolve him from the curses which they had solemnly pronounced against him by sentence of the people. Which when all the rest obeyed, Theodorus, the high priest, excused himself, "For," said he, 'if he is innocent, I never cursed him."

But notwithstanding the affairs of Alcibiades went so prosperously, and so much to his glory, yet many were still somewhat disturbed, and looked upon the time of his arrival to be ominous. For on the day that he came into the port, the feast of the goddess Minerva, which they call the Plynteria, was kept. It is the twenty-first day of Thargelion, when the Praxiergidae solemnise their secret rites, taking all the ornaments from off her image, and keeping the part of the temple where it stands close covered. Hence the Athenians esteem this day most inauspicious, and never undertake anything of importance upon it; and, therefore, they imagined that the goddess did not receive Alcibiades graciously and propitiously, thus hiding her face and rejecting him. Yet, notwithstanding, everything succeeded according to his wish. When the one hundred galleys, that were to return with him, were fitted out and ready to sail, an honourable zeal detained him till the celebration of the mysteries was over. For ever since Decelea had been occupied, as the enemy commanded the roads leading from Athens to Eleusis, the procession, being conducted by sea, had not been performed with any proper solemnity; they were forced to omit the sacrifices and dances and other holy ceremonies, which had usually been performed in the way, when they led forth Iacchus. Alcibiades, therefore, judged it would be a glorious action, which would do honour to the gods and gain him esteem with men, if he restored the ancient splendour to these rites, escorting the procession again by land, and protecting it with his army in the face of the enemy. For either, if Agis stood still and did not oppose, it would very much diminish and obscure his reputation, or, in the other alternative, Alcibiades would engage in a holy war, in the cause of the gods, and in defence of the most sacred and solemn ceremonies; and this in the sight of his country, where he should have all his fellow-citizens witness of his valour. As soon as he had resolved upon this design, and had communicated it to the Eumolpidae and heralds, he placed sentinels on the tops of the hills, and at the break of day sent forth his scouts. And then taking with him the priests and Initiates and the Initiators, and encompassing them with his soldiers, he conducted them with great order and profound silence; an august and venerable procession, wherein all who did not envy him said he performed at once the office of a high priest and of a general. The enemy did not dare to attempt anything against them, and thus he brought them back in safety to the city. Upon which, as he was exalted in his own thought, so the opinion which the people had of his conduct was raised that degree, that they looked upon their armies as irresistible and invincible while he commanded them; and he so won, indeed, upon the lower and meaner sort of people, that they passionately desired to have him "tyrant" over them, and some of them did not scruple to tell him so, and to advise him to put himself out of the reach of envy, by abolishing the laws and ordinances of the people, and suppressing the idle talkers that were ruining the state, that so he might act and take upon him the management of affairs, without standing in fear of being called to an account.

How far his own inclinations led him to usurp sovereign power is uncertain, but the most considerable persons in the city were so much afraid of it, that they hastened him on shipboard as speedily as they could, appointing the colleagues whom he chose, and allowing him all other things as he desired. Thereupon he set sail with a fleet of one hundred ships, and, arriving at Andros, he there fought with and defeated as well the inhabitants as the Lacedaemonians who assisted them. He did not, however, take the city; which gave the first occasion to his enemies for all their accusations against him. Certainly, if ever man was ruined by his own glory, it was Alcibiades. For his continual success had produced such an idea of his courage and conduct, that if he failed in anything he undertook, it was imputed to his neglect, and no one would believe it was through want of power. For they thought nothing was too hard for him, if he went about it in good earnest. They fancied, every day, that they should hear news of the reduction of Chios, and of the rest of Ionia, and grew impatient that things were not effected as fast and as rapidly as they could wish for them. They never considered how extremely money was wanting, and that,

having to carry on war with an enemy who had supplies
of all things from a great king, he was often forced to quit
his armament in order to procure money and provisions
for the subsistence of his soldiers. This it was which gave
occasion for the last accusation which was made against
him. For Lysander, being sent from Lacedaemon with a
commission to be admiral of their fleet, and being furnished by Cyrus with a great sum of money, gave every
sailor four obols a day, whereas before they had but three.
Alcibiades could hardly allow his men three obols, and
therefore was constrained to go into Caria to furnish himself with money. He left the care of the fleet, in his absence, to Antiochus, an experienced seaman, but rash and
inconsiderate, who had express orders from Alcibiades not
to engage, though the enemy provoked him. But he
slighted and disregarded these directions to that degree,
that, having made ready his own galley and another, he
stood for Ephesus, where the enemy lay, and, as he sailed
before the heads of their galleys, used every provocation
possible, both in words and deeds. Lysander at first
manned out a few ships, and pursued him. But all the
Athenian ships coming in to his assistance, Lysander, also,
brought up his whole fleet, which gained an entire victory.
He slew Antiochus himself, took many men and ships, and
erected a trophy.

As soon as Alcibiades heard this news, he returned to
Samos, and loosing from hence with his whole fleet, came
and offered battle to Lysander. But Lysander, content with
the victory he had gained, would not stir. Amongst others
in the army who hated Alcibiades, Thrasybulus, the son
of Thrason, was his particular enemy, and went purposely
to Athens to accuse him, and to exasperate his enemies
in the city against him. Addressing the people, he represented that Alcibiades had ruined their affairs and lost
their ships by mere self-conceited neglect of his duties,
committing the government of the army, in his absence, to
men who gained his favour by drinking and scurrilous talking, whilst he wandered up and down at pleasure to raise
money, giving himself up to every sort of luxury and ex-

cess amongst the courtesans of Abydos and Ionia at a time when the enemy's navy were on the watch close at hand. It was also objected to him, that he had fortified a castle near Bisanthe in Thrace, for a safe retreat for himself, as one that either could not, or would not, live in his own country. The Athenians gave credit to these informations, and showed the resentment and displeasure which they had conceived against him by choosing other generals.

As soon as Alcibiades heard of this, he immediately forsook the army, afraid of what might follow; and, collecting a body of mercenary soldiers, made war upon his own account against those Thracians who called themselves free, and acknowledged no king. By this means he amassed to himself a considerable treasure, and, at the same time, secured the bordering Greeks from the incursions of the barbarians.

Tydeus, Menander, and Adimantus, the new-made generals, were at that time posted at Aegospotami, with all the ships which the Athenians had left. From whence they were used to go out to sea every morning, and offer battle to Lysander, who lay near Lampsacus; and when they had done so, returning back again, lay, all the rest of the day, carelessly and without order, in contempt of the enemy. Alcibiades, who was not far off, did not think so slightly of their danger, nor neglect to let them know it, but, mounting his horse, came to the generals, and represented to them that they had chosen a very inconvenient station, where there was no safe harbour, and where they were distant from any town; so that they were constrained to send for their necessary provisions as far as Sestos. He also pointed out to them their carelessness in suffering the soldiers, when they went ashore, to disperse and wander up and down at their pleasure, while the enemy's fleet, under the command of one general, and strictly obedient to discipline, lay so very near them. He advised them to remove the fleet to Sestos. But the admirals not only disregarded what he said, but Tydeus, with insulting expressions, commanded him to be gone, saying, that now not he, but others, had the command of the forces. Alcibiades, suspecting something of treachery in them, departed, and told his friends, who accompanied him out of the camp, that if the generals had not used him with such insupportable contempt, he would within a few days have forced the Lacedaemonians, however unwilling, either to have fought the Athenians at sea or to have deserted their ships. Some looked upon this as a piece of ostentation only; others said, the thing was probable, for that he might have brought down by land great numbers of the Thracian cavalry and archers, to assault and disorder them in their camp. The event, however, soon made it evident how rightly he had judged of the errors which the Athenians committed. For Lysander fell upon them on a sudden, when they least suspected it, with such fury that Conon alone, with eight galleys, escaped him; all the rest, which were about two hundred, he took and carried away, together with three thousand prisoners, whom he put to death. And within a short time after, he took Athens itself, burnt all the ships which he found there, and demolished their long walls.

After this, Alcibiades, standing in dread of the Lacedaemonians, who were now masters both at sea and land, retired into Bithynia. He sent thither great treasure before him, took much with him, but left much more in the castle where he had before resided. But he lost great part of his wealth in Bithynia, being robbed by some Thracians who lived in those parts, and thereupon determined to go to the court of Artaxerxes, not doubting but that the king, if he would make trial of his abilities, would find him not inferior to Themistocles, besides that he was recommended by a more honourable cause. For he went not, as Themistocles did, to offer his service against his fellow-citizens, but against their enemies, and to implore the king's aid for the defence of his country. He concluded that Pharnabazus would most readily procure him a safe conduct, and therefore went into Phrygia to him, and continued to dwell there some time, paying him great respect, and being honourably treated by him. The Athenians, in the meantime, were miserably afflicted at their loss of empire; but when they were deprived of liberty also, and Lysander set up thirty despotic rulers in the city, in their ruin now they began to turn to those thoughts which, while safety was yet possible, they would not entertain; they acknowledged and bewailed their former errors and follies, and judged this second ill-usage of Alcibiades to be all the more inexcusable. For he was rejected without any fault committed by himself, and only because they were incensed against his subordinate for having shamefully lost a few ships, they much more shamefully deprived the commonwealth of its most valiant and accomplished general. Yet in this sad state of affairs they had still some faint hopes left them, nor would they utterly despair of the Athenian commonwealth while Alcibiades was safe. For they persuaded themselves that if before, when he was an exile, he could not content himself to live idly and at ease, much less now, if he could find any favourable opportunity, would he endure the insolence of the Lacedaemonians, and the outrages of the Thirty. Nor was it an absurd thing in the people to entertain such imaginations, when the Thirty themselves were so very solicitous to be informed and to get intelligence of all his actions and designs. In fine, Critias represented to Lysander that the Lacedaemonians could never securely enjoy the dominion of Greece till the Athenian democracy was absolutely destroyed; and, though now the people of Athens seemed quietly and patiently to submit to so small a number of governors, yet so long as Alcibiades lived, the knowledge of this fact would never suffer them to acquiesce in their present circumstances.

Yet Lysander would not be prevailed upon by these representations, till at last he received secret orders from the magistrates of Lacedaemon, expressly requiring him to get Alcibiades despatched: whether it was that they feared his energy and boldness in enterprising what was hazardous, or that it was done to gratify King Agis. Upon receipt of this order, Lysander sent away a messenger to Pharnabazus, desiring him to put it in execution. Pharnabazus committed the affair to Magaeus, his brother, and to his uncle Susamithres. Alcibiades resided at that time in a small village in Phrygia, together with Timandra, a mistress of his. As he slept, he had this dream: he had thought himself attired in his mistress's habit, and that she, holding him in her arms, dressed his head and painted his face as if he had been a woman; others say, he dreamed that he saw Magaeus cut off his head and burn his body; at any rate, it was but a little while before his death that he had these visions. Those who were sent to assassinate him had not courage enough to enter the house, but surrounded it first, and set it on fire. Alcibiades, as soon as he perceived it, getting together great quantities of clothes and furniture, threw them upon the fire to choke it, and, having wrapped his cloak about his left arm, and holding his naked sword in his right, he cast himself into the middle of the fire, and escaped securely through it before his clothes were burnt. The barbarians, as soon as they saw him, retreated and none of them durst stay to wait for him, or to engage with him, but, standing at a distance, they slew him with their darts and arrows. When he was dead the barbarians departed, and Timandra took up his dead body, and, covering and wrapping it up in her own robes, she buried it as decently and as honourably as her circumstances would allow. It is said, that the famous Lais, who was called the Corinthian, though she was a native of Hyccara, a small town in Sicily, from whence she was brought a captive, was the daughter of this Timandra. There are some who agree with this account of Alcibiades's death in all points, except that they impute the cause of it neither to Pharnabazus, nor Lysander, nor the Lacedaemonians; but they say he was keeping with him a young lady of a noble house, whom he had debauched, and that her brothers, not being able to endure the indignity, set fire by night to the house where he was living, and, as he endeavoured to save himself from the flames, slew him with their darts, in the manner just related.

TIMOLEON

It was for the sake of others that I first commenced writing biographies; but I find myself proceeding and attaching myself to it for my own; the virtues of these great men serving me as a sort of looking-glass, in which I may see how to adjust and adorn my own life. Indeed, it can be compared to nothing but daily living and associating together; we receive, as it were, in our inquiry, and entertain each successive guest, view—

"Their stature and their qualities,"

and select from their actions all that is noblest and worthiest to know,

"Ah, and what greater pleasure can one have?"

or what more effective means to one's moral improvement? Democritus tells us we ought to pray that of the phantasms appearing in the circumambient air, such may present themselves to us as are propitious, and that we may rather meet with those that are agreeable to our natures and are good than the evil and unfortunate; which is simply introducing into philosophy a doctrine untrue in itself, and leading to endless superstitions. My method, on the contrary, is, by the study of history, and by the familiarity acquired in writing, to habituate my memory to receive and retain images of the best and worthiest characters. I thus am enabled to free myself from any ignoble, base, or vicious impressions, contracted from the contagion of ill company that I may be unavoidably engaged in; by the remedy of turning my thoughts in a happy and calm temper to view these noble examples. Of this kind is that of Timoleon the Corinthian, to write whose life is my present business.

The affairs of the Syracusans, before Timoleon was sent into Sicily, were in this posture; after Dion had driven out Dionysius the tyrant, he was slain by treachery, and those that had assisted him in delivering Syracuse were divided among themselves; and thus the city by a continual change of governors, and a train of mischiefs that succeeded each other, became almost abandoned; while of the rest of Sicily, part was now utterly depopulated and desolate through long continuance of war, and most of the cities that had been left standing were in the hands of barbarians and soldiers out of employment, that were ready to embrace every turn of government. Such being the state of things, Dionysius takes the opportunity, and in the tenth year of his banishment, by the help of some mercenary troops he had got together, forces out Nysaeus, then master of Syracuse, recovers all afresh, and is again settled in his dominion; and as at first he had been strangely deprived of the greatest and most absolute power that ever was by a very small party, so now, in a yet stranger manner, when in exile and of mean condition, he became the sovereign of those who had ejected him. All therefore that remained in Syracuse had to serve under a tyrant, who at the best was of an ungentle nature, and exasperated now to a degree of savageness by the late misfortunes and calamities he had suffered. The better and more distinguished citizens, having timely retired thence to Hicetes, ruler of the Leontines, put themselves under his protection, and chose him for their general in the war; not that he was much preferable to any open and avowed tyrant, but they had no other sanctuary at present, and it gave them some ground of confidence that he was of a Syracusan family, and had forces able to encounter those of Dionysius.

In the meantime the Carthaginians appeared before Sicily with a great navy, watching when and where they might make a descent upon the island; and terror at this fleet

made the Sicilians incline to send an embassy into Greece
to demand succours from the Corinthians, whom they confided in rather than others, not only upon the account of
their near kindred, and the great benefits they had often
received by trusting them, but because Corinth had ever
shown herself attached to freedom and averse from tyranny and had engaged in many noble wars, not for empire or aggrandisement, but for the sole liberty of the
Greeks. But Hicetes, who made it the business of his command not so much to deliver the Syracusans from other
tyrants, as to enslave them to himself, had already entered
into some secret conferences with those of Carthage, while
in public he commended the design of his Syracusan cli-
ents, and despatched ambassadors from himself, together
with theirs, into Peloponnesus; not that he really desired
any relief to come from there, but in case the Corinthians,
as was likely enough, on account of the troubles of Greece
and occupation at home, should refuse their assistance, hoping then he should be able with less difficulty to dispose
and incline things for the Carthaginian interest, and so
make use of these foreign pretenders, as instruments and
auxiliaries for himself, either against the Syracusans or
Dionysius, as occasion served. This was discovered a while
after.

The ambassadors being arrived, and their request known,
the Corinthians, who had always a great concern for all
their colonies and plantations, but especially for Syracuse,
since by good fortune there was nothing to molest them in
their own country, where they were enjoying peace and
leisure at that time, readily and with one accord passed
a vote for their assistance. And when they were deliberating about the choice of a captain for the expedition, and
the magistrates were urging the claims of various aspirants
for reputation, one of the crowd stood up and named
Timoleon, son of Timodemus, who had long absented himself from public business, and had neither any thoughts
of, nor the least pretensions to, an employment of that
nature. Some god or other, it might rather seem, had put
it in the man's heart to mention him; such favour and

good-will on the part of Fortune seemed at once to be shown in his election, and to accompany all his following actions, as though it were on purpose to commend his worth, and add grace and ornament to his personal virtues. As regards his parentage, both Timodemus his father, and his mother Demariste, were of high rank in the city; and as for himself, he was noted for his love of his country, and his gentleness of temper, except in his extreme hatred to tyrants and wicked men. His natural abilities for war were so happily tempered, that while a rare prudence might be seen in all the enterprises of his younger years, an equal courage showed itself in the last exploits of his declining age. He had an elder brother, whose name was Timophanes, who was every way unlike him, being indiscreet and rash, and infected by the suggestions of some friends and foreign soldiers, whom he kept always about him, with a passion for absolute power. He seemed to have a certain force and vehemence in all military service, and even to delight in dangers, and thus he took much with the people, and was advanced to the highest charges, as a vigorous and effective warrior; in the obtaining of which offices and promotions, Timoleon much assisted him, helping to conceal or at least to extenuate his errors, embellishing by his praise whatever was commendable in him, and setting off his good qualities to the best advantage.

It happened once in the battle fought by the Corinthians against the forces of Argos and Cleonae, that Timoleon served among the infantry, when Timophanes, commanding their cavalry, was brought into extreme danger; as his horse being wounded fell forward and threw him headlong amidst the enemies, while part of his companions dispersed at once in a panic, and the small number that remained, bearing up against a great multitude, had much ado to maintain any resistance. As soon, therefore, as Timoleon was aware of the accident, he ran hastily in to his brother's rescue, and covering the fallen Timophanes with his buckler, after having received abundance of darts, and several strokes by the sword upon his body and his

armour, he at length with much difficulty obliged the enemies to retire, and brought off his brother alive and safe.
But when the Corinthians, for fear of losing their city a
second time, as they had once before, by admitting their
allies, made a decree to maintain four hundred mercenaries for its security, and gave Timophanes the command
over them, he, abandoning all regard to honour and equity,
at once proceeded to put into execution his plans for
making himself absolute, and bringing the place under
his own power; and having cut off many principal citizens, uncondemned and without trial, who were most likely
to hinder his designs, he declared himself tyrant of Corinth;
a procedure that infinitely afflicted Timoleon, to whom the
wickedness of such a brother appeared to be his own reproach and calamity. He undertook to persuade him by
reasoning, that desisting from that wild and unhappy ambition, he would bethink himself how he should make the
Corinthians some amends, and find out an expedient to
remedy and correct the evils he had done them. When his
single admonition was rejected and contemned by him, he
makes a second attempt, taking with him Aeschylus his
kinsman, brother to the wife of Timophanes, and a certain
diviner, that was his friend, whom Theopompus in his history calls Satyrus, but Ephorus and Timaeus mention in
theirs by the name of Orthagoras. After a few days, then,
he returns to his brother with this company, all three of
them surrounding and earnestly importuning him upon
the same subject, that now at length he would listen to
reason, and be of another mind. But when Timophanes began first to laugh at the men's simplicity, and presently
broke out into rage and indignation against them, Timoleon stepped aside from him and stood weeping with his
face covered, while the other two, drawing out their
swords, despatched him in a moment.

On the rumour of this act being soon scattered about,
the better and more generous of the Corinthians highly
applauded Timoleon for the hatred of wrong and the greatness of soul that had made him, though of a gentle disposition and full of love and kindness for his family,

think the obligations to his country stronger than the ties
of consanguinity, and prefer that which is good and just
before gain and interest and his own particular advantage.
For the same brother, who with so much bravery had been
saved by him when he fought valiantly in the cause of
of Corinth, he had now as nobly sacrificed for enslaving
her afterwards by a base usurpation. But then, on the
other side, those that knew not how to live in a democracy, and had been used to make their humble court to
the men of power, though they openly professed to rejoice
at the death of the tyrant, nevertheless, secretly reviling
Timoleon, as one that had committed an impious and abom-
inable act, drove him into melancholy and dejection. And
when he came to understand how heavily his mother took
it, and that she likewise uttered the saddest complaints and
most terrible imprecations against him, he went to satisfy
and comfort her as to what had happened; and finding
that she would not endure so much as to look upon him,
but caused her doors to be shut, that he might have no
admission into her presence, with grief at this he grew
so disordered in his mind and so disconsolate, that he
determined to put an end to his perplexity with his life,
by abstaining from all manner of sustenance. But through
the care and diligence of his friends, who were very instant with him, and added force to their entreaties, he
came to resolve and promise at last, that he would endure
living, provided it might be in solitude, and remote from
company; so that, quitting all civil transactions and commerce with the world for a long while after his first retirement, he never came into Corinth, but wandered up
and down the fields, full of anxious and tormenting
thoughts, and spent his time in desert places, at the farthest
distance from society and human intercourse. So true it
is that the minds of men are easily shaken and carried off
from their own sentiments through the casual commendation or reproof of others, unless the judgments that we
make, and the purposes we conceive, be confirmed by
reason and philosophy, and thus obtain strength and steadiness. An action must not only be just and laudable in its

own nature, but it must proceed likewise from motives
and a lasting principle, that so we may fully and constantly
approve the thing, and be perfectly satisfied in what we
do; for otherwise, after having put our resolution into practice, we shall out of pure weakness come to be troubled
at the performance, when the grace and godliness, which
rendered it before so amiable and pleasing to us, begin to
decay and wear out of our fancy; like greedy people, who,
seizing on the more delicious morsels of any dish with a
keen appetite, are presently disgusted when they grow
full, and find themselves oppressed and uneasy now by
what they before so greedily desired. For a succeeding dislike spoils the best of actions, and repentance makes that
which was never so well done become base and faulty;
whereas the choice that is founded upon knowledge and
wise reasoning does not change by disappointment, or suffer us to repent, though it happen perchance to be less
prosperous in the issue. And thus, Phocion, of Athens,
having always vigorously opposed the measures of Leosthenes, when success appeared to attend them, and he
saw his countrymen rejoicing and offering sacrifice in honour of their victory, "I should have been as glad," said he
to them, "that I myself had been the author of what Leosthenes has achieved for you, as I am that I gave you my
own counsel against it." A more vehement reply is recorded to have been made by Aristides the Locrian, one of
Plato's companions, to Dionysius the elder, who demanded
one of his daughters in marriage: "I had rather," said he
to him, "see the virgin in her grave than in the palace of a
tyrant." And when Dionysius, enraged at the affront, made
his sons be put to death a while after, and then again in-
sultingly asked, whether he were still in the same mind as
to the disposal of his daughters, his answer was, "I cannot
but grieve at the cruelty of your deeds, but am not sorry
for the freedom of my own words." Such expressions as
these may belong perhaps to a more sublime and accomplished virtue.

The grief, however, of Timoleon at what had been done,
whether it arose from commiseration of his brother's fate

or the reverence he bore his mother, so shattered and broke his spirits, that for the space of almost twenty years he had not offered to concern himself in any honourable or public action. When, therefore, he was pitched upon for a general, and, joyfully accepted as such by the suffrages of the people, Teleclides, who was at that time the most powerful and distinguished man in Corinth, began to exhort him that he would act now like a man of worth and gallantry: "For," said he, "if you do bravely in this service we shall believe that you delivered us from a tyrant; but if otherwise that you killed your brother." While he was yet preparing to set sail, and enlisting soldiers to embark with him, there came letters to the Corinthians from Hicetes, plainly disclosing his revolt and treachery. For his ambassadors had no sooner gone for Corinth, but he openly joined the Carthaginians, negotiating that they might assist him to throw out Dionysius, and become master of Syracuse in his room. And fearing he might be disappointed of his aim if troops and a commander should come from Corinth before this were effected, he sent a letter of advice thither, in all haste, to prevent their setting out, telling them they need not be at any cost and trouble upon his account, or run the hazard of a Sicilian voyage, especially since the Carthaginians, alliance with whom against Dionysius the slowness of their motions had compelled him to embrace, would dispute their passage, and lay in wait to attack them with a numerous fleet. This letter being publicly read, if any had been cold and indifferent before as to the expedition in hand, the indignation they now conceived against Hicetes so exasperated and inflamed them all that they willingly contributed to supply Timoleon, and endeavoured with one accord to hasten his departure.

When the vessels were equipped, and his soldiers every way provided for, the female priest of Proserpina had a dream or vision wherein she and her mother Ceres appeared to them in a travelling garb, and were heard to say that they were going to sail with Timoleon into Sicily; whereupon the Corinthians, having built a sacred galley, devoted it to them, and called it the galley of the goddesses. Timoleon went in person to Delphi, where he sacrificed to Apollo, and, descending into the place of prophecy, was surprised with the following marvellous occurrence. A riband, with crowns and figures of victory embroidered upon it, slipped off from among the gifts that were there consecrated and hung up in the temple, and fell directly down upon his head; so that Apollo seemed already to crown him with success, and send him thence to conquer and triumph. He put to sea only with seven ships of Corinth, two of Corcyra, and a tenth which was furnished by the Leucadians; and when he was now entered into the deep by night, and carried with a prosperous gale, the heaven seemed all on a sudden to break open, and a bright spreading flame to issue forth from it, and hover over the ship he was in; and, having formed itself into a torch, not unlike those that are used in the mysteries, it began to steer the same course, and run along in their company, guiding them by its light to that quarter of Italy where they designed to go ashore. The soothsayers affirmed that this apparition agreed with the dream of the holy woman, since the goddesses were now visibly joining in the expedition, and sending this light from heaven before them: Sicily being thought sacred to Proserpina, as poets feign that the rape was committed there, and that the island was given her in dowry when she married Pluto.

These early demonstrations of divine favour greatly encouraged his whole army; so that making all the speed they were able, by a voyage across the open sea, they were soon passing along the coast of Italy. But the tidings that came from Sicily much perplexed Timoleon, and disheartened his soldiers. For Hicetes, having already beaten Dionysius out of the field, and reduced most of the quarters of Syracuse itself, now hemmed him in and besieged him in the citadel and what is called the Island, whither he was fled for his last refuge; while the Carthaginians, by agreement, were to make it their business to hinder Timoleon from landing in any port of Sicily; so that he and his party being driven back, they might with ease and at their own leisure divide the island among themselves. In pursuance of which design the Carthaginians sent away twenty of their galleys to Rhegium, having aboard them certain ambassadors from Hicetes to Timoleon, who carried instructions suitable to these proceedings, specious amusements, and plausible stories, to colour and conceal dishonest purposes. They had order to propose and demand that Timoleon himself, if he liked the offer, should come and advise with Hicetes and partake of all his conquests, but that he might send back his ships and forces to Corinth, since the war was in a manner finished, and the Carthaginians had blocked up the passage, determined to oppose them if they should try to force their way towards the shore. When, therefore, the Corinthians met with these envoys at Rhegium, and received their message, and saw the Phoenician vessels riding at anchor in the bay, they became keenly sensible of the abuse that was put upon them, and felt a general indignation against Hicetes, and great apprehensions for the Siceliots, whom they now plainly perceived to be as it were a prize and recompense to Hicetes on one side for his perfidy, and to the Carthaginians on the other for the sovereign power they secured to him. For it seemed utterly impossible to force and overbear the Carthaginian ships that lay before them and were double their number, as also to vanquish the victorious troops which Hicetes had with him in Syracuse, to take the lead of which very troops they had undertaken their voyage.

The case being thus, Timoleon, after some conference with the envoys of Hicetes and the Carthaginian captains, told them he should readily submit to their proposals (to what purpose would it be to refuse compliance?): he was desirous only, before his return to Corinth, that what had passed between them in private might be solemnly declared before the people of Rhegium, a Greek city, and a common friend to the parties; this, he said, would very much conduce to his own security and discharge, and they likewise would more strictly observe articles of agreement, on behalf of the Syracusans, which they had obliged themselves to in the presence of so many witnesses. The design of all which was only to divert their attention, while he got an opportunity of slipping away from their fleet; a contrivance that all the principal Rhegians were privy and assisting to, who had a great desire that the affairs of Sicily should fall into Corinthian hands, and dreaded the consequences of having barbarian neighbours. An assembly was therefore called, and the gates shut, that the citizens might have no liberty to turn to other business; and a succession of speakers came forward, addressing the people at great length, to the same effect, without bringing the subject to any conclusion, making way each for another and purposely spinning out the time, till the Corinthian galleys should get clear of the haven; the Carthaginian commanders being detained there without any suspicion, as also Timoleon still remained present, and gave signs as if he were just preparing to make an oration. But upon secret notice that the rest of the galleys were already gone off, and that his alone remained waiting for him, by the help and concealment of those Rhegians that were about the hustings and favoured his departure, he made shift to slip away through the crowd, and running down to the port, set sail with all speed; and having reached his other vessels, they came all safe to Tauromenium in Sicily, whither they had been formerly invited, and where they were now kindly received by Andromachus, then ruler of the city. This man was father of Timaeus the historian, and incomparably the best of all those that bore sway in Sicily at that time, governing his citizens according to law and justice and openly professing an aversion and enmity to all tyrants; upon which account he gave Timoleon leave to muster up his troops there, and to make that city the seat of war, persuading the inhabitants to join their arms with the Corinthian forces, and assist them in the design of delivering Sicily.

But the Carthaginians who were left in Rhegium perceiving, when the assembly was dissolved, that Timoleon had given them the go-by, were not a little vexed to see themselves out-witted, much to the amusement of the Rhe-

gians, who could not but smile to find Phoenicians complain of being cheated. However, they despatched a messenger aboard one of their galleys to Tauromenium, who,
after much blustering in the insolent barbaric way, and
many menaces to Andromachus if he did not forthwith
send the Corinthians off, stretched out his hand with the
inside upward, and then turning it down again, threatened
he would handle their city even so, and turn it topsy-turvy
in as little time, and with as much ease. Andromachus,
laughing at the man's confidence, made no other reply,
but, imitating his gesture, bid him hasten his own departure, unless he had a mind to see that kind of dexterity
practised first upon the galley which brought him hither.

Hicetes, informed that Timoleon had made good his
passage, was in great fear of what might follow, and sent
to desire the Carthaginians that a large number of galleys might be ordered to attend and secure the coast.
And now it was that the Syracusans began wholly to despair of safety, seeing the Carthaginians possessed of their
haven, Hicetes master of the town, and Dionysius supreme
in the citadel; while Timoleon had as yet but a slender
hold of Sicily, as it were by the fringe or border of it, in
the small city of the Tauromenians, with a feeble hope and a
poor company; having but a thousand soldiers at the most,
and no more provisions, either of corn or money, than
were just necessary for the maintenance and the pay of
that inconsiderable number. Nor did the other towns of
Sicily confide in him, overpowered as they were with violence and outrage, and embittered against all that should
offer to lead armies by the treacherous conduct chiefly of
Callipus, an Athenian, and Pharax, a Lacedaemonian captain, both of whom, after giving out that the design of
their coming was to introduce liberty and to depose tyrants, so tyrannised themselves, that the reign of former
oppressors seemed to be a golden age in comparison, and
the Sicilians began to consider those more happy who
had expired in servitude, than any that had lived to see
such a dismal freedom.

Looking, therefore, for no better usage from the Corin-

thian general, but imagining that it was only the same old
course of things once more, specious pretences and false
professions to allure them by fair hopes and kind promises into the obedience of a new master, they all, with one
accord, unless it were the people of Adranum, suspected
the exhortations, and rejected the overtures that were
made them in his name. These were inhabitants of a small
city, consecrated to Adranus, a certain god that was in
high veneration throughout Sicily, and, as it happened,
they were then at variance among themselves, insomuch
that one party called in Hicetes and the Carthaginians to
assist them, while the other sent proposals to Timoleon. It
so fell out that these auxiliaries, striving which should be
soonest, both arrived at Adranum about the same time;
Hicetes bringing with him at least five thousand men,
while all the force Timoleon could make did not exceed
twelve hundred. With these he marched out of Tauromenium, which was about three hundred and forty furlongs distant from that city. The first day he moved but
slowly, and took up his quarters betimes after a short journey; but the day following he quickened his pace, and,
having passed through much difficult ground, towards
evening received advice that Hicetes was just approaching
Adranum, and pitching his camp before it; upon which
intelligence, his captains and other officers caused the vanguard to halt, that the army being refreshed, and having
reposed a while, might engage the enemy with better
heart. But Timoleon, coming up in haste, desired them
not to stop for that reason, but rather use all possible diligence to surprise the enemy, whom probably they would
now find in disorder, as having lately ended their march
and being taken up at present in erecting tents and preparing supper; which he had no sooner said, but laying
hold of his buckler and putting himself in the front, he
led them on as it were to certain victory. The braveness
of such a leader made them all follow him with like courage and assurance. They were now within less than thirty
furlongs of Adranum, which they quickly traversed, and
immediately fell in upon the enemy, who were seized with

confusion, and began to retire at their first approaches; one consequence of which was that, amidst so little opposition, and so early and general a flight, there were not many more than three hundred slain, and about twice the number made prisoners. Their camp and baggage, however, was all taken. The fortune of this onset soon induced the Adranitans to unlock their gates, and to embrace the interest of Timoleon, to whom they recounted, with a mixture of affright and admiration, how, at the very minute of the encounter, the doors of their temple flew open of their own accord, that the javelin also, which their god held in his hand, was observed to tremble at the point, and that drops of sweat had been seen running down his face; prodigies that not only presaged the victory then obtained, but were an omen, it seemed, of all his future exploits, to which this first happy action gave the occasion.

For now the neighbouring cities and potentates sent deputies, one upon another, to seek his friendship and make offer of their service. Among the rest Mamercus, the tyrant of Catana, an experienced warrior, and a wealthy prince, made proposals of alliance with him, and what was of greater importance still, Dionysius himself, being now grown desperate, and well-nigh forced to surrender, despising Hicetes who had been thus shamefully baffled, and admiring the valour of Timoleon, found means to advertise him and his Corinthians that he should be content to deliver up himself and the citadel into their hands. Timoleon, gladly embracing this unlooked-for advantage, sends away Euclides and Telemachus, two Corinthian captains, with four hundred men, for the seizure and custody of the castle, with directions to enter not all at once, or in open view, that being impracticable so long as the enemy kept guard, but by stealth, and in small companies. And so they took possession of the fortress and the palace of Dionysius, with all the stores and ammunition he had prepared and laid up to maintain the war. They found a good number of horses, every variety of engines, a multitude of darts, and weapons to arm seventy thousand men (a magazine that had been formed from ancient time), besides two thousand soldiers that were then with him, whom he gave up with the rest for Timoleon's service. Dionysius himself, putting his treasure aboard, and taking a few friends, sailed away unobserved by Hicetes, and being brought to the camp of Timoleon, there first appeared in the humble dress of a private person, and was shortly after sent to Corinth with a single ship and a small sum of money. Born and educated in the most splendid court and the most absolute monarchy that ever was, which he held and kept up for the space of ten years succeeding his father's death, he had, after Dion's expedition, spent twelve other years in a continual agitation of wars and contests, and great variety of fortune, during which time all the mischiefs he had committed in his former reign were more than repaid by the ills he himself then suffered, since he lived to see the deaths of his sons in the prime and vigour of their age, and the rape of his daughters in the flower of their virginity, and the wicked abuse of his sister and his wife, who, after being first exposed to all the lawless insults of the soldiery, was then murdered with her children, and cast into the sea.

Upon the news of his landing at Corinth, there was hardly a man in Greece who had not the curiosity to come and view the late formidable tyrant, and say some words to him; part, rejoicing at his disasters, were led thither out of mere spite and hatred, that they might have the pleasure of trampling, as it were, on the ruins of his broken fortune; but others, letting their attention and their sympathy turn rather to the changes and revolutions of his life, could not but see in them a proof of the strength and potency with which divine and unseen causes operate amidst the weakness of human and visible things. For neither art nor nature did in that age produce anything comparable to this work and wonder of fortune which showed the very same man, that was not long before supreme monarch of Sicily, loitering about perhaps in the fish-market, or sitting in a perfumer's shop drinking the diluted wine of taverns, or squabbling in the street with common women, or pretending to instruct the sing-

ing women of the theatre, and seriously disputing with
them about the measure and harmony of pieces of music
that were performed there. Such behaviour on his part
was variously criticised. He was thought by many to act
thus out of pure compliance with his own natural indolent
and vicious inclinations; while finer judges were of the
opinion, that in all this he was playing a politic part, with
a design to be contemned among them, and that the Corinthians might not feel any apprehension or suspicion of his
being uneasy under his reverse of fortune, or solicitous
to retrieve it; to avoid which danger, he purposely and
against his true nature affected an appearance of folly and
want of spirit in his private life and amusements.

However it be, there are sayings and repartees of his left
still upon record, which seem to show that he not ignobly
accommodated himself to his present circumstances; as
may appear in part from the ingenuousness of the avowal
he made on coming to Leucadia, which, as well as Syracuse, was a Corinthian colony, where he told the inhabitants that he found himself not unlike boys who had been
in fault, who can talk cheerfully with their brothers, but
are ashamed to see their father; so likewise he, he said,
could gladly reside with them in that island, whereas he
felt a certain awe upon his mind which made him averse
to the sight of Corinth, that was a common mother to
them both. The thing is further evident from the reply
he once made to a stranger in Corinth, who deriding him
in a rude and scornful manner about the conferences he
used to have with philosophers, whose company had been
one of his pleasures while yet a monarch, and demanding,
in fine, what he was the better now for all those wise and
learned discourses of Plato, "Do you think," said he, "I
have made no profit of his philosophy when you see me
bear my change of fortune as I do?" And when Aristoxenus
the musician, and several others, desired to know how
Plato offended him, and what had been the ground of his
displeasure with him, he made answer that, of the many
evils attaching to the condition of sovereignty, the one
greatest infelicity was that none of those who were ac-

counted friends would venture to speak freely, or tell the plain truth; and that by means of such he had been deprived of Plato's kindness. At another time, when one of those pleasant companions that are desirous to pass for wits, in mockery to Dionysius, as if he were still the tyrant, shook out the folds of his cloak, as he was entering into a room where he was, to show there were no concealed weapons about him, Dionysius, by way of retort, observed, that he would prefer he would do so on leaving the room, as a security that he was carrying nothing off with him. And when Philip of Macedon, at a drinking party, began to speak in banter about the verses and tragedies which his father, Dionysius the elder, had left behind him, and pretended to wonder how he could get any time from his other business to compose such elaborate and ingenious pieces, he replied, very much to the purpose, "It was at those leisurable hours, which such as you and I, and those we call happy men, bestow upon our cups." Plato had not the opportunity to see Dionysius at Corinth, being already dead before he came thither; but Diogenes of Sinope, at their first meeting in the street there, saluted him with the ambiguous expression, "O Dionysius, how little you deserve your present life!" Upon which Dionysius stopped and replied, "I thank you, Diogenes, for your condolence." "Condole with you!" replied Diogenes; "do you not suppose that, on the contrary, I am indignant that such a slave as you, who, if you had your due, should have been let alone to grow old and die in the state of tyranny, as your father did before you, should now enjoy the ease of private persons, and be here to sport and frolic in our society?" So that when I compare those sad stories of Philistus, touching the daughters of Leptines, where he makes pitiful moan on their behalf, as fallen from all the blessings and advantages of powerful greatness to the miseries of an humble life, they seem to me like the lamentations of a woman who has lost her box of ointment, her purple dresses, and her golden trinkets. Such anecdotes will not, I conceive, be thought either foreign to my purpose of writing Lives, or unprofitable in themselves, by such readers as are not in too much haste, or busied and taken up with other concerns.

But if the misfortune of Dionysius appears strange and extraordinary, we shall have no less reason to wonder at the good fortune of Timoleon, who, within fifty days after his landing in Sicily, both recovered the citadel of Syracuse and sent Dionysius an exile into Peloponnesus. This lucky beginning so animated the Corinthians, that they ordered him a supply of two thousand foot and two hundred horse, who, reaching Thurii, intended to cross over thence into Sicily; but finding the whole sea beset with Carthaginian ships, which made their passage impracticable, they were constrained to stop there, and watch their opportunity: which time, however, was employed in a noble action. For the Thurians, going out to war against their Bruttian enemies, left their city in charge with these Corinthian strangers who defended it as carefully as if it had been their own country, and faithfully resigned it up again.

Hicetes, in the interim, continued still to besiege the castle of Syracuse, and hindered all provisions from coming in by sea to relieve the Corinthians that were in it. He had engaged also, and despatched towards Adranum, two unknown foreigners to assassinate Timoleon, who at no time kept any standing guard about his person, and was then altogether secure, diverting himself, without any apprehension, among the citizens of the place, it being a festival in honour of their gods. The two men that were sent, having casually heard that Timoleon was about to sacrifice, came directly into the temple with poniards under their cloaks, and pressing in among the crowd, by little and little got up close to the altar; but, as they were just looking for a sign from each other to begin the attempt, a third person struck one of them over the head with a sword, upon whose sudden fall, neither he that gave the blow, nor the partisan of him that received it, kept their stations any longer; but the one, making way with his bloody sword, put no stop to his flight, till he gained the top of a certain lofty precipice, while the other, laying hold of the altar, besought Timoleon to spare his life, and he would reveal to him the whole conspiracy. His pardon being granted, he confessed that both himself and his dead companion were sent thither purposely to slay him. While this discovery was made, he that killed the other conspirator had been fetched down from his sanctuary of the rock, loudly and often protesting, as he came along, that there was no injustice in the fact, as he had only taken righteous vengeance for his father's blood, whom this man had murdered before in the city of Leontini; the truth of which was attested by several there present, who could not choose but wonder too at the strange dexterity of fortune's operations, the facility with which she makes one event the spring and motion to something wholly different, uniting every scattered accident and loose particular and remote action, and interweaving them together to serve her purpose; so that things that in themselves seem to have no connection or interdependence whatsoever, become in her hands, so to say, the end and the beginning of each other. The Corinthians, satisfied as to the innocence of this seasonable feat, honoured and rewarded the author with a present of ten pounds in their money, since he had, as it were, lent the use of his just resentment to the tutelar genius that seemed to be protecting Timoleon, and had not pre-expended this anger, so long ago conceived, but had reserved and deferred, under fortune's guidance, for his preservation, the revenge of a private quarrel.

But this fortunate escape had effects and consequences beyond the present, as it inspired the highest hopes and future expectations of Timoleon, making people reverence and protect him as a sacred person sent by heaven to revenge and redeem Sicily. Hicetes, having missed his aim in this enterprise, and perceiving, also, that many went off and sided with Timoleon, began to chide himself for his foolish modesty, that, when so considerable a force of the Carthaginians lay ready to be commanded by him, he had employed them hitherto by degrees and in small numbers, introducing their reinforcements by stealth and clandestinely, as if he had been ashamed of the action. There-

fore, now laying aside his former nicety, he calls in Mago,
their admiral, with his whole navy, who presently set sail,
and seized upon the port with a formidable fleet of at least
a hundred and fifty vessels, landing there sixty thousand
foot, which were all lodged within the city of Syracuse;
so that, in all men's opinion, the time anciently talked of
and long expected, wherein Sicily should be subjugated
by barbarians, was now come to its fatal period. For in
all their preceding wars and many desperate conflicts with
Sicily, the Carthaginians had never been able, before this,
to take Syracuse; whereas Hicetes now receiving them and
putting them into their hands, you might see it become
now as it were a camp of barbarians. By this means,
the Corinthian soldiers that kept the castle found themselves brought into great danger and hardship; as, besides
that their provision grew scarce, and they began to be in
want, because the havens were strictly guarded and blocked
up, the enemy exercised them still with skirmishes and
combats about their walls, and they were not only obliged
to be continually in arms, but to divide and prepare themselves for assaults and encounters of every kind, and to
repel every variety of the means of offence employed by a
besieging army.

Timoleon made shift to relieve them in these straits, sending corn from Catana by small fishing-boats and little
skiffs, which commonly gained a passage through the
Carthaginian galleys in times of storm, stealing up when
the blockading ships were driven apart and dispersed by
the stress of weather; which Mago and Hicetes observing,
they agreed to fall upon Catana, from whence these supplies were brought in to the besieged, and accordingly put
off from Syracuse, taking with them the best soldiers in
their whole army. Upon this Neon the Corinthian, who
was captain of those that kept the citadel, taking notice
that the enemies who stayed there behind were very negli-
gent and careless in keeping guard, made a sudden sally
upon them as they lay scattered, and, killing some and putting others to flight, he took and possessed himself of that
quarter which they call Acradina, and was thought to be the

strongest and most impregnable part of Syracuse, a city made up and compacted, as it were, of several towns put together. Having thus stored himself with corn and money, he did not abandon the place, nor retire again into the castle, but fortifying the precincts of Acradina, and joining it by works to the citadel, he undertook the defence of both. Mago and Hicetes were now come near to Catana, when a horseman, despatched from Syracuse, brought them tidings that Acradina was taken; upon which they returned, in all haste, with great disorder and confusion, having neither been able to reduce the city they went against, nor to preserve that they were masters of.

These successes, indeed, were such as might leave foresight and courage a pretence still of disputing it with fortune, which contributed most to the result. But the next following event can scarcely be ascribed to anything but pure felicity. The Corinthian soldiers who stayed at Thurii, partly for fear of the Carthaginian galleys which lay in wait for them under the command of Hanno, and partly because of tempestuous weather which had lasted for many days, and rendered the sea dangerous, took a resolution to march by land over the Bruttian territories, and what with persuasion and force together, made good their passage through those barbarians to the city of Rhegium, the sea being still rough and raging as before. But Hanno, not expecting the Corinthians would venture out, and supposing it would be useless to wait there any longer, bethought himself, as he imagined, of a most ingenious and clever strategem apt to delude and ensnare the enemy; in pursuance of which he commanded the seamen to crown themselves with garlands, and adorning his galleys with bucklers both of the Greek and Carthaginian make, he sailed away for Syracuse in this triumphant equipage, and using all his oars as he passed under the castle with much shouting and laughter, cried out, on purpose to dishearten the besieged, that he was come from vanquishing and taking the Corinthian succours, which he fell upon at sea as they were passing over into Sicily. While he was thus trifling and playing his tricks before Syracuse, the Corin-

thians, now come as far as Rhegium, observing the coast
clear, and that the wind was laid, as it were by miracle, to
afford them in all appearance a quiet and smooth passage,
went immediately aboard on such little barks and fishing-
boats as were then at hand, and got over to Sicily with
such complete safety and in such an extraordinary calm,
that they drew their horses by the reins, swimming along
by them as the vessels went across.

When they were all landed, Timoleon came to receive
them, and by their means at once obtained possession of
Messena, from whence he marched in good order to Syracuse, trusting more to his late prosperous achievements
than to his present strength, as the whole army he had then
with him did not exceed the number of four thousand:
Mago, however, was troubled and fearful at the first notice
of his coming, and grew more apprehensive and jealous
still upon the following occasion. The marshes about Syracuse, that receive a great deal of fresh water, as well from
springs as from lakes and rivers discharging themselves
into the sea, breed abundance of eels, which may be always
taken there in great quantities by any that will fish for
them. The mercenary soldiers that served on both sides
were wont to follow the sport together at their vacant
hours, and upon any cessation of arms; who being all
Greeks, and having no cause of private enmity to each
other, as they would venture bravely in fight, so in times
of truce used to meet and converse amicably together.
And at this present time, while engaged about this common
business of fishing, they fell into talk together; and some
expressing their admiration of the neighbouring sea, and
others telling how much they were taken with the convenience and commodiousnes of the buildings and public
works, one of the Corinthian party took occasion to demand of the others: "And is it possible that you who are
Grecians born should be so forward to reduce a city of
this greatness, and enjoying so many rare advantages, into
the state of barbarism; and lend your assistance to plant
Carthaginans, that are the worst and bloodiest of men, so
much the nearer to us? whereas you should rather wish

there were many more Sicilies to lie between them and Greece. Have you so little sense as to believe, that they come hither with an army, from the Pillars of Hercules and the Atlantic Sea, to hazard themselves for the establishment of Hicetes? who, if he had had the consideration which becomes a general, would never have thrown out his ancestors and founders to bring in the enemies of his country in the room of them, when he might have enjoyed all suitable honour and command, with consent of Timoleon and the rest of Corinth." The Greeks that were in pay with Hicetes, noising these discourses about their camp, gave Mago some ground to suspect, as indeed he had long sought for a pretence to be gone, that there was treachery contrived against him; so that, although Hicetes entreated him to tarry, and made it appear how much stronger they were than the enemy, yet, conceiving they came far more short of Timoleon in respect of courage and fortune than they surpassed him in number, he presently went aboard and set sail for Africa, letting Sicily escape out of his hands with dishonour to himself, and for such uncertain causes, that no human reason could give an account of his departure.

The day after he went away, Timoleon came up before the city in array for a battle. But when he and his company heard of this sudden flight, and saw the docks all empty, they could not forbear laughing at the cowardice of Mago, and in mockery caused proclamation to be made through the city that a reward would be given to any one who could bring them tidings whither the Carthaginian fleet had conveyed itself from them. However, Hicetes resolving to fight it out alone, and not quitting his hold of the city, but sticking close to the quarters he was in possession of, places that were well fortified and not easy to be attacked, Timoleon divided his forces into three parts, and fell himself upon the side where the river Anapas ran, which was most strong and difficult of access; and he commanded those that were led by Isias, a Corinthian captain, to make their assault from the post of Acradina, while Dinarchus and Demaretus, that brought him the last supply from

Corinth, were, with a third division, to attempt the quarter called Epipolae. A considerable impression being made from every side at once, the soldiers of Hicetes were beaten off and put to flight; and this—that the city came to be taken by storm, and fall suddenly into their hands, upon the defeat and rout of the enemy—we must in all justice ascribe to the valour of the assailants and the wise conduct of their general; but that not so much as a man of the Corinthians was either slain or wounded in the action, this the good fortune of Timoleon seems to challenge for her own work, as though, in a sort of rivalry with his own personal exertions, she made it her aim to exceed and obscure his actions by her favours, that those who heard him commended for his noble deeds might rather admire the happiness than the merit of them. For the fame of what was done not only passed through all Sicily, and filled Italy with wonder, but even Greece itself, after a few days, came to ring with the greatness of his exploit; insomuch that those of Corinth, who had as yet no certainty that their auxiliaries were landed on the island, had tidings brought them at the same time that they were safe and were conquerors. In so prosperous a course did affairs run, and such was the speed and celerity of execution with which fortune, as with a new ornament, set off the native lustres of the performance.

Timoleon, being master of the citadel, avoided the error which Dion had been guilty of. He spared not the place for the beauty and sumptuousness of its fabric, and, keeping clear of those suspicions which occasioned first the unpopularity and afterwards the fall of Dion, made a public crier give notice that all the Syracusans who were willing to have a hand in the work should bring pick-axes and mattocks, and other instruments, and help him to demolish the fortifications of the tyrants. When they all came up with one accord, looking upon that order and that day as the surest foundation of their liberty, they not only pulled down the castle, but overturned the palaces and monuments adjoining, and whatever else might preserve any memory of former tyrants. Having soon levelled and cleared the place, he there presently erected courts for administration of justice, ratifying the citizens by this means, and building popular government on the fall and ruin of tyranny. But since he had recovered a city destitute of inhabitants, some of them dead in civil wars and insurrections, and others being fled to escape tyrants, so that through solitude and want of people the great market-place of Syracuse was overgrown with such quantity of rank herbage that it became a pasture for their horses, the grooms lying along in the grass as they fed by them; while also other towns, very few excepted, were become full of stags and wild boars, so that those who had nothing else to do went frequently a-hunting, and found game in the suburbs and about the walls; and not one of those who possessed themselves of castles, or made garrisons in the country, could be persuaded to quit their present abode, or would accept an invitation to return back into the city, so much did they all dread and abhor the very name of assemblies and forms of government and public speaking, that had produced the greater part of those usurpers who had successively assumed a dominion over them—Timoleon, therefore, with the Syracusans that remained, considering this vast desolation, and how little hope there was to have it otherwise supplied, thought good to write to the Corinthians, requesting that they would send a colony out of Greece to repeople Syracuse. For else the land about it would lie unimproved; and besides this, they expected to be involved in a greater war from Africa, having news brought them that Mago had killed himself, and that the Carthaginians, out of rage for his ill-conduct in the late expedition, had caused his body to be nailed upon a cross, and that they were raising a mighty force, with design to make their descent upon Sicily the next summer.

These letters from Timoleon being delivered at Corinth, and the ambassadors of Syracuse beseeching them at the same time that they would take upon them the care of their poor city, and once again become the founders of it, the Corinthians were not tempted by any feeling of cupidity to lay hold of the advantage. Nor did they seize and appropriate the city to themselves, but going about first to the games that are kept as sacred in Greece, and to the most numerously attended religious assemblages, they made publication by heralds, that the Corinthians, having destroyed the usurpation at Syracuse and driven out the tyrant, did thereby invite the Syracusan exiles, and any other Siceliots, to return and inhabit the city, with full enjoyment of freedom under their own laws, the land being divided among them in just and equal proportions. And after this, sending messengers into Asia and the several islands where they understood that most of the scattered fugitives were then residing, they bade them all repair to Corinth, engaging that the Corinthians would afford them vessels and commanders, and a safe convoy, at their own charges, to Syracuse. Such generous proposals, being thus spread about, gained them the just and honourable recompense of general praise and benediction, for delivering the country from oppressors, and saving it from barbarians, and restoring it at length to the rightful owners of the place. These, when they were assembled at Corinth, and found how insufficient their company was, besought the Corinthians that they might have a supplement of other persons, as well out of their city as the rest of Greece, to go with them as joint colonists; and so raising themselves to the number of ten thousand, they sailed together to Syracuse. By this time great multitudes, also, from Italy and Sicily had flocked in to Timoleon, so that, as Athanis reports, their entire body amounted now to sixty thousand men. Among these he divided the whole territory, and sold the houses for a thousand talents; by which method he both left it in the power of the old Syracusans to redeem their own, and made it a means also for raising a stock for the community, which had been so much impoverished of late and was so unable to defray other expenses, and especially those of a war, that they exposed their very statues to sale, a regular process being observed, and sentence of auction passed upon each of them by majority of votes, as if they had been so many criminals taking their trial; in the course of which it is said that while condemnation was pronounced upon all other statues, that of the an-

cient usurper Gelo was exempted, out of admiration and
honour and for the sake of the victory he gained over the
Carthaginian forces at the river Himera.

Syracuse being thus happily revived, and replenished
again by the general concourse of inhabitants from all parts,
Timoleon was desirous now to rescue other cities from the
like bondage, and wholly and once for all to extirpate arbitrary government out of Sicily. And for this purpose, marching in to the territories of those that used it, he compelled
Hicetes first to renounce the Carthaginian interest, and, de-
molishing the fortresses which were held by him, to live
henceforth among the Leontinians as a private person. Leptines, also, the tyrant of Apollonia and divers other little
towns, after some resistance made, seeing the danger he
was in of being taken by force, surrendered himself; upon
which Timoleon spared his life, and sent him away to Corinth, counting it a glorious thing that the mother city should
expose to the view of other Greeks these Sicilian tyrants,
living now in an exiled and a low condition. After this he
returned to Syracuse, that he might have leisure to attend
to the establishment of the new constitution, and assist
Cephalus and Dionysius, who were sent from Corinth to
make laws, in determining the most important points of it.
In the meanwhile, desirous that his hired soldiers should not
want action, but might rather enrich themselves by some
plunder from the enemy, he despatched Dinarchus and
Demaretus with a portion of them into the part of the island belonging to the Carthaginians, where they obliged
several cities to revolt from the barbarians, and not only
lived in great abundance themselves, but raised money from
their spoil to carry on the war.

Meantime, the Carthaginians landed at the promontory
of Lilybaeum, bringing with them an army of seventy thousand men on board two hundred galleys, besides a thousand
other vessels laden with engines of battery, chariots, corn,
and other military stores, as if they did not intend to manage the war by piecemeal and in parts as heretofore, but to
drive the Greeks altogether and at once out of all Sicily.
And indeed it was a force sufficient to overpower the Sice-

liots, even though they had been at perfect union among
themselves, and had never been enfeebled by intestine quarrels. Hearing that part of their subject territory was suffering devastation, they forthwith made toward the Corinthians
with great fury, having Asdrubal and Hamilcar for their
generals; the report of whose numbers and strength coming
suddenly to Syracuse, the citizens were so terrified, that
hardly three thousand, among so many myriads of them,
had the courage to take up arms and join Timoleon. The
foreigners, serving for pay, were not above four thousand
in all, and about a thousand of these grew faint-hearted by
the way, and forsook Timoleon in his march towards the
enemy, looking on him as frantic and distracted, destitute of
the sense which might have been been expected from his
time of life, thus to venture out against an army of seventy
thousand men, with no more than five thousand foot and a
thousand horse; and, when he should have kept those forces
to defend the city, choosing rather to remove them eight
days' journey from Syracuse, so that if they were beaten
from the field, they would have no retreat, nor any burial
if they fell upon it. Timoleon, however, reckoned it some
kind of advantage, that these had thus discovered themselves before the battle, and encouraging the rest, led them
with all speed to the river Crimesus, where it was told him
the Carthaginians were drawn together.

As he was marching up an ascent, from the top of which
they expected to have a view of the army and of the
strength of the enemy, there met him by chance a train of
mules loaded with parsley; which his soldiers conceived to
be an ominous occurrence or ill-boding token, because this
is the herb with which we not unfrequently adorn the sepul-
chres of the dead; and there is a proverb derived from the
custom, used of one who is dangerously sick, that he has
need of nothing but parsley. So to ease their minds, and free
them from any superstitious thoughts or forebodings of evil,
Timoleon halted, and concluded an address suitable to the
occasion, by saying, that a garland of triumph was here
luckily brought them, and had fallen into their hands of its
own accord, as an anticipation of victory: the same with

which the Corinthians crown the victors in the Isthmian
games, accounting chaplets of parsley the sacred wreath
proper to their country; parsley being at that time still the
emblem of victory at the Isthmian, as it is now at the Ne-
mean sports; and it is not so very long ago that the pine
first began to be used in its place.

Timoleon, therefore, having thus bespoke his soldiers,
took part of the parsley, and with it made himself a chaplet first, his captains and their companies all following the
example of their leader. The soothsayers then, observing
also two eagles on the wing towards them, one of which
bore a snake struck through with her talons, and the other,
as she flew, uttered a loud cry indicating boldness and assurance, at once showed them to the soldiers, who with one
consent fell to supplicate the gods, and call them in to their
assistance. It was now about the beginning of summer, and
conclusion of the month called Thargelion, not far
from the solstice; and the river sending up a thick mist, all
the adjacent plain was at first darkened with the fog, so that
for a while they could discern nothing from the enemy's
camp; only a confused buzz and undistinguished mixture of
voices came up to the hill from the distant motions and
clamours of so vast a multitude. When the Corinthians had
mounted, and stood on the top, and had laid down their
bucklers to take breath and repose themselves, the sun coming round and drawing up the vapours from below, the gross
foggy air that was now gathered and condensed above
formed in a cloud upon the mountains; and, all the under
places being clear and open, the river Crimesus appeared to
them again, and they could descry the enemies passing over
it, first with their formidable four-horse chariots of war,
and then ten thousand footmen bearing white shields,
whom they guessed to be all Carthaginians, from the splendour of their arms, and the slowness and order of their
march. And when now the troops of various other nations,
flowing in behind them, began to throng for passage in a
tumultuous and unruly manner, Timoleon, perceiving that
the river gave them opportunity to single off whatever
number of their enemies they had a mind to engage at once,

and bidding his soldiers observe how their forces were divided into two separate bodies by the intervention of the stream, some being already over, and others still to ford it, gave Demaretus command to fall in upon the Carthaginians with his horse, and disturb their ranks before they should be drawn up into form of battle; and coming down into the plain himself forming his right and left wing of other Sicilians, intermingling only a few strangers in each, he placed the natives of Syracuse in the middle, with the stoutest mercenaries he had about his own person; and waiting a little to observe the action of his horse, when they saw they were not only hindered from grappling with the Carthaginians by the armed chariots that ran to and fro before the army, but forced continually to wheel about to escape having their ranks broken, and so to repeat their charges anew, he took his buckler in his hand, and crying out to the foot that they should follow him with courage and confidence, he seemed to speak with a more than human accent, and a voice stronger than ordinary; whether it were that he naturally raised it so high in the vehemence and ardour with his mind to assault the enemy, or else, as many then thought, some god or other spoke with him. When his soldiers quickly gave an echo to it, and besought him to lead them on without any further delay, he made a sign to the horse, that they should draw off from the front where the chariots were, and pass sidewards to attack their enemies in the flank; then, making his vanguard firm by joining man to man and buckler to buckler, he caused the trumpet to sound, and so bore in upon the Carthaginians.

They, for their part, stoutly received and sustained his first onset; and having their bodies armed with breastplates of iron, and helmets of brass on their heads, besides great bucklers to cover and secure them, they could easily repel the charge of the Greek spears. But when the business came to a decision by the sword, where mastery depends no less upon art than strength, all on a sudden from the mountain-tops violent peals of thunder and vivid flashes of lightning broke out; following upon which the darkness, that had been hovering about the higher grounds and the crests of the hills, descending to the place of battle and bringing a tempest of rain and of wind and hail along with it, was driven upon the Greeks behind, and fell only at their backs, but discharged itself in the very faces of the barbarians, the rain beating on them, and the lightning dazzling them without cessation; annoyances that in many ways distressed at any rate the inexperienced, who had not been used to such hardships, and, in particular, the claps of thunder, and the noise of the rain and hail beating on their arms, kept them from hearing the commands of their officers. Besides which, the very mud also was a great hindrance to the Carthaginians, who were not lightly equipped, but as I said before, loaded with heavy armour; and then their shirts underneath getting drenched, the foldings about the bosom filled with water, grew unwieldy and cumbersome to them as they fought, and made it easy for the Greeks to throw them down, and, when they were once down, impossible for them, under that weight, to disengage themselves and rise again with weapons in their hands. The river Crimesus, too, swollen partly by the rain, and partly by the stoppage of its course with the numbers that were passing through, overflowed its banks; and the level ground by the side of it, being so situated as to have a number of small ravines and hollows of the hillside descending upon it, was now filled with rivulets and currents that had no certain channel, in which the Carthaginians stumbled and rolled about, and found themselves in great difficulty. So that, in fine, the storm bearing still upon them, and the Greeks having cut in pieces four hundred men of their first ranks, the whole body of their army began to fly. Great numbers were overtaken in the plain, and put to the sword there; and many of them, as they were making their way back through the river, falling foul upon others that were yet coming over, were borne away and overwhelmed by the waters; but the major part, attempting to get up the hill so as to make their escape, were intercepted and destroyed by the light-armed troops. It is said that, of ten thousand who lay dead after the fight, three thousand, at least, were Carthaginian citizens; a heavy loss and great grief to their countrymen; those that fell being men inferior to none among them as to birth, wealth, or reputation. Nor do their records mention that so many native Carthaginians were ever cut off before in any one battle; as they usually employed Africans, Spaniards, and Numidians in their wars, so that if they chanced to be defeated, it was still at the cost and damage of other nations.

The Greeks easily discovered of what condition and account the slain were by the richness of their spoils; for when they came to collect the booty, there was little reckoning made either of brass or iron, so abundant were better metals, and so common were silver and gold. Passing over the river they became masters of their camp and carriages. As for captives, a great many of them were stolen away and sold privately by the soldiers but about five thousand were brought in and delivered up for the benefit of the public; two hundred of their chariots of war were also taken. The tent of Timoleon then presented a most glorious and magnificent appearance, being heaped up and hung round with every variety of spoils and military ornaments, among which there were a thousand breastplates of rare workmanship and beauty, and bucklers to the number of ten thousand. The victors being but few to strip so many that were vanquished, and having such valuable booty to occupy them, it was the third day after the fight before they could erect and finish the trophy of their conquest. Timoleon sent tidings of his victory to Corinth, with the best and goodliest arms he had taken as a proof of it; that he thus might render his country an object of emulation to the whole world, when, of all the cities of Greece, men should there alone behold the chief temples adorned, not with Grecian spoils, nor offerings obtained by the bloodshed and plunder of their own countrymen and kindred, and attended, therefore, with sad and unhappy remembrances, but with such as had been stripped from barbarians and enemies to their nation, with the noblest titles inscribed upon them, titles telling of the justice as well as fortitude of the conquerors; namely, that the people of Corinth, and Timoleon their general, having redeemed the Greeks of Sicily from Carthaginian bondage, made oblation of these to the gods, in grateful acknowledgment of their favour.

Having done this, he left his hired soldiers in the enemy's country to drive and carry away all they could throughout the subject-territory of Carthage, and so marched with the rest of his army to Syracuse, where he issued an edict for banishing the thousand mercenaries who had basely deserted him before the battle, and obliged them to quit the city before sunset. They, sailing into Italy, lost their lives there by the hands of the Bruttians, in spite of a public assurance of safety previously given them; thus receiving, from the divine power, a just reward of their own treachery. Mamercus, however, the tyrant of Catana, and Hicetes, after all, either envying Timoleon the glory of his exploits, or fearing him as one that would keep no agreement, or having any peace with tyrants, made a league with the Carthaginians, and pressed them much to send a new army and commander into Sicily, unless they would be content to hazard all and to be wholly ejected out of that island.

Not long after, Timoleon, marching up to the city of the Leontines, took Hicetes alive, and his son Eupolemus, and Euthymus, the commander of his horse, who were bound and brought to him by their own soldiers. Hicetes and the stripling his son were then executed as tyrants and traitors; and Euthymus, though a brave man, and one of singular courage, could obtain no mercy, because he was charged with contemptuous language in disparagement of the Corinthians when they first sent their forces into Sicily; it is said that he told the Leontini in a speech that the news did not sound terrible, nor was any great danger to be feared because of—

"Corinthian women coming out of doors."

So true it is that men are usually more stung and galled by reproachful words than hostile actions: and they bear an affront with less patience than an injury; to do harm and mischief by deeds is counted pardonable from the enemies, as

nothing less can be expected in a state of war; whereas viru-
lent and contumelious words appear to be the expression of
needless hatred, and to proceed from an excess of rancour.

After this, he moved towards Catana against Mamercus,
who gave him battle near the river Abolus, and was overthrown and put to flight, losing above two thousand men, a
considerable part of whom were the Phoenician troops sent
by Gisco to his assistance. After this defeat the Carthaginians sued for peace; which was granted on the conditions
that they should confine themselves to the country within
the river Lycus, that those of the inhabitants who wished
to remove to the Syracusan territories should be allowed to
depart with their whole families and fortunes, and, lastly,
that Carthage should renounce all engagements to the tyrants. Mamercus, now forsaken and despairing of success,
took ship for Italy with the design of bringing in the Lu-
canians against Timoleon and the people of Syracuse;
but the men in his galleys turning back and landing
again and delivering up Catana to Timoleon, thus obliged
him to fly for his own safety to Messena, where Hippo
was tyrant. Timoleon, however, coming up against them,
and besieging the city both by sea and land, Hippo,
fearful of the event, endeavoured to slip away in a vessel; which the people of Messena surprised as it was
putting off, and seizing on his person, and bringing all
their children from school into the theatre, to witness
the glorious spectacle of a tyrant punished, they first publicly scourged and then put him to death. Mamercus made
surrender of himself to Timoleon, with the proviso that he
should be tried at Syracuse and Timoleon should take no
part in his accusation. Thither he was brought accordingly,
and presenting himself to plead before the people, he es-
sayed to pronounce an oration he had long before composed in his own defence; but finding himself interrupted
by noise and clamours, and observing from their aspect and
demeanour that the assembly was inexorable, he threw off
his upper garment, and running across the theatre as hard
as he could, dashed his head against one of the stones under
the seats with intention to have killed himself; but he had

not the fortune to perish as he designed, but was taken up alive, and suffered the death of a robber.

Thus did Timoleon cut the nerves of tyranny and put a period to the wars; and, whereas, at his first entering upon Sicily, the island was as it were become wild again, and was hateful to the very natives on account of the evils and miseries they suffered there, he so civilised and restored it, and rendered it so desirable to all men, that even strangers now came by sea to inhabit those towns and places which their own citizens had formerly forsaken and left desolate. Agrigentum and Gela, two famous cities that had been ruined and laid waste by the Carthaginians after the Attic war, were then peopled again, the one by Megellus and Pheristus from Elea, the other by Gorgus, from the island of Ceos, partly with new settlers, partly with the old inhabitants whom they collected again from various parts; to all of whom Timoleon not only afforded a secure and peaceful abode after so obstinate a war, but was further so zealous in assisting and providing for them that he was honoured among them as their founder. Similar feelings also possessed to such a degree all the rest of the Sicilians that there was no proposal for peace, nor reformation of laws, nor assignation of land, nor reconstruction of government, which they could think well of, unless he lent his aid as a chief architect, to finish and adorn the work, and superadd some touches from his own hand, which might render it pleasing both to God and man.

Although Greece had in his time produced several persons of extraordinary worth, and much renowned for their achievements, such as Timotheus and Agesilaus and Pelopidas and (Timoleon's chief model) Epaminondas, yet the lustre of their best actions was obscured by a degree of violence and labour, insomuch that some of them were matter of blame and of repentance; whereas there is not any one act of Timoleon's, setting aside the necessity he was placed under in reference to his brother, to which, as Timaeus observes, we may not fitly apply that exclamation of Sophocles—

> "O gods! what Venus, or what grace divine,
>   Did here with human workmanship combine?"

For as the poetry of Antimachus, and the painting of Dionysius, the artists of Colophon, though full of force and vigour, yet appeared to be strained and elaborate in comparison with the pictures of Nicomachus and the verses of Homer, which, besides their general strength and beauty, have the peculiar charm of seeming to have been executed with perfect ease and readiness; so the expeditions and acts of Epaminondas or Agesilaus, that were full of toil and effort, when compared with the easy and natural as well as noble and glorious achievements of Timoleon, compel our fair and unbiased judgment to pronounce the latter not indeed the effect of fortune, but the success of fortunate merit. Though he himself indeed ascribed that success to the sole favour of fortune; and both in the letters which he wrote to his friends at Corinth, and in the speeches he made to the people of Syracuse, he would say, that he was thankful unto God, who, designing to save Sicily, was pleased to honour him with the name and title of the deliverance he vouchsafed it. And having built a chapel in his house, he there sacrificed to Good Hap, as a deity that had favoured him, and devoted the house itself to the Sacred Genius; it being a house which the Syracusans had selected for him, as a special reward and monument of his brave exploits, granting him together with it the most agreeable and beautiful piece of land in the whole country, where he kept his residence for the most part, and enjoyed a private life with his wife and children, who came to him from Corinth. For he returned thither no more, unwilling to be concerned in the broils and tumults of Greece, or to expose himself to public envy (the fatal mischief which great commanders continually run into, from the insatiable appetite for honours and authority); but wisely chose to spend the remainder of his days in Sicily, and there partake of the blessings he himself had procured, the greatest of which was to behold so many cities flourish, and so many thousands of people live happy through his means.

As, however, not only, as Simonides says, on "every lark must grow a crest," but also in every democracy there must spring up a false accuser, so was it at Syracuse: two of their popular spokesmen, Laphystius and Demaenetus by name, fell to slander Timoleon. The former of whom requiring him to put in sureties that he would answer to an indictment that would be brought against him, Timoleon would not suffer the citizens, who were incensed at this demand, to oppose it or hinder the proceeding, since he of his own accord had been, he said, at all that trouble, and run so many dangerous risks for this very end and purpose, that every one who wished to try matters by law should freely have recourse to it. And when Demaenetus, in a full audience of the people, laid several things to his charge which had been done while he was general, he made no reply to him, but only said he was much indebted to the gods for granting the request he had so often made them, namely, that he might live to see the Syracusans enjoy that liberty of speech which they now seemed to be masters of.

Timoleon, therefore, having by confession of all done the greatest and the noblest things of any Greek of his age, and alone distinguished himself in those actions to which their orators and philosophers, in their harangues and panegyrics at their solemn national assemblies, used to exhort and incite the Greeks, and being withdrawn beforehand by happy fortune, unspotted and without blood, from the calamities of civil war, in which ancient Greece was soon after involved; having also given full proof, as of his sage conduct and manly courage to the barbarians and tyrants, so of his justice and gentleness to the Greeks, and his friends in general; having raised, too, the greater part of those trophies he won in battle without any tears shed or any mourning worn by the citizens either of Syracuse or Corinth, and within less than eight years' space delivered Sicily from its inveterate grievances and intestine distempers, and given it up free to the native inhabitants, began, as he was now growing old, to find his eyes fail, and awhile after became perfectly blind. Not that he had done anything himself which might occasion this defect, or was deprived of his sight by any outrage of fortune; it seems rather to have been some inbred and hereditary weakness that was founded in natural causes, which by length of time came to discover itself. For it is said, that several of his kindred and family were subject to the like gradual decay, and lost all use of their eyes, as he did, in their declining years. Athanis the historian tells us that even during the war against Hippo and Mamercus, while he was in his camp at Mylae, there appeared a white speck within his eye, from whence all could foresee the deprivation that was coming on him; this, however, did not hinder him then from continuing the siege, and prosecuting the war, till he got both the tyrants into his power; but upon his coming back to Syracuse, he presently resigned the authority of sole commander, and besought the citizens to excuse him from any further service, since things were already brought to so fair an issue. Nor is it so much to be wondered that he himself should bear the misfortune without any marks of trouble; but the respect and gratitude which the Syracusans showed him when he was entirely blind may justly deserve our admiration. They used to go themselves to visit him in troops and brought all the strangers that travelled through their country to his house and manor, that they also might have the pleasure to see their noble benefactor; making it the great matter of their joy and exultation, that when, after so many brave and happy exploits, he might have returned with triumph into Greece, he should disregard all the glorious preparations that were there made to receive him, and choose rather to stay here and end his days among them. Of the various things decreed and done in honour of Timoleon, I consider one most signal testimony to have been the vote which they passed, that, whenever they should be at war with any foreign nation, they should make use of none but a Corinthian general. The method, also, of their proceeding in council was a noble demonstration of the same deference for his person. For, determining matters of less consequence themselves, they always called him to advise in the more difficult cases, and such as were of greater moment. He was, on these occasions, carried through the market-place in a litter, and brought in, sitting, into the theatre, where the people with one voice saluted him by his name; and then, after returning the courtesy, and pausing for a time, till the noise of their gratulations and blessings began to cease, he heard the business in debate, and delivered his opinion. This being confirmed by a general suffrage, his servants went back with the litter through the midst of the assembly, the people waiting on him out with acclamations and applauses, and then returning to consider other public matters, which they could despatch in his absence. Being thus cherished in his old age, with all the respect and tenderness due to a common father, he was seized with a very slight indisposition, which, however, was sufficient, with the aid of time, to put a period to his life. There was an allotment then of certain days given, within the space of which the Syracusans were to provide whatever should be necessary for his burial, and all the neighbouring country people and strangers were to make their appearance in a body; so that the funeral pomp was set out with great splendour and magnificence in all other respects, and the bier, decked with ornaments and trophies, was borne by a select body of young men over that ground where the palace and castle of Dionysius stood before they were demolished by Timoleon. There attended on the solemnity several thousands of men and women, all crowned with flowers, and arrayed in fresh and clean attire, which made it look like the procession of a public festival; while the language of all, and their tears mingling with their praise and benediction of the dead Timoleon, manifestly showed that it was not any superficial honour, or commanded homage, which they paid him, but the testimony of a just sorrow for his death, and the expression of true affection. The bier at length being placed upon the pile of wood that was kindled to consume his corpse, Demetrius, one of their loudest criers, proceeded to read a proclamation to the following purpose: "The people of Syracuse have made a special decree to inter Timoleon, the son of Timodemus, the Corinthian, at the common expense of two hundred minas, and to honour his memory for ever, by the establishment of annual prizes to be competed for in music, and horse-races, and all sorts of bodily exercise; and this, because he suppressed the tyrants, overthrew the barbarians, replenished the principal cities, that were desolate, with new inhabitants, and then restored the Sicilian Greeks to the privilege of living by their own laws." Besides this, they made a tomb for him in the market-place, which they afterwards built round with colonnades, and attached to it places of exercise for the young men, and gave it the name of the Timoleonteum. And keeping to that form and order of civil policy and observing those laws and constitutions which he left them, they lived themselves a long time in great prosperity.

✤

ALEXANDER

It being my purpose to write the lives of Alexander the king, and of Caesar, by whom Pompey was destroyed, the multitude of their great actions affords so large a field that I were to blame if I should not by way of apology forewarn my reader that I have chosen rather to epitomise the most celebrated parts of their story, than to insist at large on every particular circumstance of it. It must be borne in mind that my design is not to write histories, but lives. And the most glorious exploits do not always furnish us with the clearest discoveries of virtue or vice in men; sometimes a matter of less moment, an expression or a jest, informs us better of their characters and inclinations, than the most famous sieges, the greatest armaments, or the bloodiest battles whatsoever. Therefore, as portrait-painters are more exact in the lines and features of the face, in which the character is seen, than in the other parts of the body, so I must be allowed to give my more particular attention to the marks and indications of the souls of men, and while I endeavour by these to portray their lives, may be free to leave more weighty matters and great battles to be treated of by others.

It is agreed on by all hands, that on the father's side, Alexander descended from Hercules by Caranus, and from Aeacus by Neoptolemus on the mother's side. His father Philip, being in Samothrace, when he was quite young, fell in love there with Olympias, in company with whom he was initiated in the religious ceremonies of the country, and her father and mother being both dead, soon after, with the consent of her brother, Arymbas, he married her. The night before the consummation of their marriage, she dreamed that a thunderbolt fell upon her body, which kindled a great fire, whose divided flames dispersed themselves all about, and then were extinguished. And Philip, some time after he was married, dreamt that he sealed up his wife's body with a seal, whose impression, as he fancied, was the figure of a lion. Some of the diviners interpreted this as a warning to Philip to look narrowly to his wife; but Aristander of Telmessus, considering how unusual it was to seal up anything that was empty, assured him the meaning of his dream was that the queen was with child of a boy, who would one day prove as stout and courageous as a lion. Once, moreover, a serpent was found lying by Olympias as she slept, which more than anything else, it is said, abated Philip's passion for her; and whether he feared her as an enchantress, or thought she had commerce with some god, and so looked on himself as excluded, he was ever after less fond of her conversation. Others say, that the women of this country having always been extremely addicted to the enthusiastic Orphic rites, and the wild worship of Bacchus (upon which account they were called Clodones, and Mimallones), imitated in many things the practices of the Edonian and Thracian women about Mount Haemus, from whom the word *threskeuein* seems to have been derived, as a special term for superfluous and over-curious forms of adoration; and that Olympias, zealously affecting these fanatical and enthusiastic inspirations, to perform them with more barbaric dread, was wont in the dances proper to these ceremonies to have great tame serpents about her, which sometimes creeping out of the ivy in the mystic fans, sometimes winding themselves about the sacred spears, and the women's chaplets, made a spectacle which men could not look upon without terror.

Philip, after this vision, sent Chaeron of Megalopolis to consult the oracle of Apollo at Delphi, by which he was commanded to perform sacrifice, and henceforth pay particular honour, above all other gods, to Ammon; and was told he should one day lose that eye with which he presumed to peep through that chink of the door, when he saw the god, under the form of a serpent, in the company of his wife. Eratosthenes says that Olympias, when she attended Alexander on his way to the army in his first expedition, told him the secret of his birth, and bade him behave himself with courage suitable to his divine extraction. Others again affirm that she wholly disclaimed any pretensions of the kind, and was wont to say, "When will Alexander leave off slandering me to Juno?"

Alexander was born the sixth of Hecatombaeon, which month the Macedonians call Lous, the same day that the temple of Diana at Ephesus was burnt; which Hegesias of Magnesia makes the occasion of a conceit, frigid enough to have stopped the conflagration. The temple, he says, took fire and was burnt while its mistress was absent, assisting at the birth of Alexander. And all the Eastern soothsayers who happened to be then at Ephesus, looking upon the ruin of this temple to be the forerunner of some other calamity, ran about the town, beating their faces, and crying that this day had brought forth something that would prove fatal and destructive to all Asia.

Just after Philip had taken Potidaea, he received these three messages at one time, that Parmenio had overthrown the Illyrians in a great battle, that his race-horse had won the course at the Olympic games, and that his wife had given birth to Alexander; with which being naturally well pleased, as an addition to his satisfaction, he was assured by the diviners that a son, whose birth was accompanied with three such successes, could not fail of being invincible.

The statues that gave the best representation of Alexander's person were those of Lysippus (by whom alone he would suffer his image to be made), those peculiarities which many of his successors afterwards and his friends used to affect to imitate, the inclination of his head a little on one side towards his left shoulder, and his melting eye, having been expressed by this artist with great exactness. But Apelles, who drew him with thunderbolts in his hand, made his complexion browner and darker than it was naturally; for he was fair and of a light colour, passing into ruddiness in his face and upon his breast. Aristoxenus in his

Memoirs tells us that a most agreeable odour exhaled from
his skin, and that his breath and body all over was so fragrant as to perfume the clothes which he wore next him;
the cause of which might probably be the hot and adust
temperament of his body. For sweet smells, Theophrastus
conceives, are produced by the concoction of moist humours by heat, which is the reason that those parts of the
world which are driest and most burnt up afford spices of
the best kind and in the greatest quantity; for the heat of
the sun exhausts all the superfluous moisture which lies in
the surface of bodies, ready to generate putrefaction. And
this hot constitution, it may be, rendered Alexander so addicted to drinking, and so choleric. His temperance, as to
the pleasures of the body, was apparent in him in his very
childhood, as he was with much difficulty incited to them,
and always used them with great moderation; though in
other things he was extremely vehement, and in his love of
glory, and the pursuit of it, he showed a solidity of high
spirit and magnanimity far above his age. For he neither
sought nor valued it upon every occasion, as his father
Philip did (who affected to show his eloquence almost to a
degree of pedantry, and took care to have the victories of
his racing chariots at the Olympic games engraven on his
coin), but when he was asked by some about him, whether
he would run a race in the Olympic games, as he was very
swift-footed, he answered, he would, if he might have kings
to run with him. Indeed, he seems in general to have looked
with indifference, if not with dislike, upon the professed
athletes. He often appointed prizes, for which not only
tragedians and musicians, pipers and harpers, but rhapso-
dists also, strove to outvie one another; and delighted in all
manner of hunting and cudgel-playing, but never gave any
encouragement to contests either of boxing or of the pan-
cratium.

While he was yet very young, he entertained the ambassadors from the King of Persia, in the absence of his father,
and entering much into conversations with them, gained so
much upon them by his affability, and the questions he
asked them, which were far from being childish or trifling

(for he inquired of them the length of the ways, the nature of the road into inner Asia, the character of their king, how he carried himself to his enemies, and what forces he was able to bring into the field), that they were struck with admiration of him, and looked upon the ability so much famed of Philip to be nothing in comparison with the forwardness and high purpose that appeared thus early in his son. Whenever he heard Philip had taken any town of importance, or won any signal victory, instead of rejoicing at it altogether, he would tell his companions that his father would anticipate everything, and leave him and them no opportunities of performing great and illustrious actions. For being more bent upon action and glory than either upon pleasure or riches, he esteemed all that he should receive from his father as a diminution and prevention of his own future achievements; and would have chosen rather to succeed to a kingdom involved in troubles and wars, which would have afforded him frequent exercise of his courage, and a large field of honour, than to one already flourishing and settled, where his inheritance would be an inactive life, and the mere enjoyment of wealth and luxury.

The care of his education, as it might be presumed, was committed to a great many attendants, preceptors, and teachers, over the whole of whom Leonidas, a near kinsman of Olympias, a man of an austere temper, presided, who did not indeed himself decline the name of what in reality is a noble and honourable office, but in general his dignity, and his near relationship, obtained him from other people the title of Alexander's fosterfather and governor. But he who took upon him the actual place and style of his pedagogue was Lysimachus the Acarnanian, who, though he had nothing specially to recommend him, but his lucky fancy of calling himself Phoenix, Alexander Achilles, and Philip Peleus, was therefore well enough esteemed, and ranked in the next degree after Leonidas.

Philonicus the Thessalian brought the horse Bucephalus to Philip, offering to sell him for thirteen talents; but when they went into the field to try him, they found him so very vicious and unmanageable, that he reared up when they

endeavoured to mount him, and would not so much as endure the voice of any of Philip's attendants. Upon which,
as they were leading him away as wholly useless and untractable, Alexander, who stood by, said, "What an excellent horse do they lose for want of address and boldness
to manage him!" Philip at first took no notice of what he
said; but when he heard him repeat the same thing several
times, and saw he was much vexed to see the horse sent
away, "Do you reproach," said he to him, "those who are
older than yourself, as if you knew more, and were better
able to manage him than they?" "I could manage this
horse," replied he, "better than others do." "And if you do
not," said Philip, "what will you forfeit for your rashness?"
"I will pay," answered Alexander, "the whole price of the
horse." At this the whole company fell a-laughing; and as
soon as the wager was settled amongst them, he immediately ran to the horse, and taking hold of the bridle, turned
him directly towards the sun, having, it seems, observed
that he was disturbed at and afraid of the motion of his
own shadow; then letting him go forward a little, still keeping the reins in his hands, and stroking him gently when he
found him begin to grow eager and fiery, he let fall his upper garment softly, and with one nimble leap securely
mounted him, and when he was seated, by little and little
drew in the bridle, and curbed him without either striking
or spurring him. Presently, when he found him free from
all rebelliousness, and only impatient for the course, he let
him go at full speed, inciting him now with a commanding
voice, and urging him also with his heel. Philip and his
friends looked on at first in silence and anxiety for the result, till seeing him turn at the end of his career, and
come back rejoicing and triumphing for what he had performed, they all burst out into acclamations of applause;
and his father shedding tears, it is said, for joy, kissed him
as he came down from his horse, and in his transport said,
"O my son, look thee out a kingdom equal to and worthy
of thyself, for Macedonia is too little for thee."

After this, considering him to be of a temper easy to be
led to his duty by reason, but by no means to be compelled,

he always endeavoured to persuade rather than to command or force him to anything; and now looking upon the instruction and tuition of his youth to be of greater difficulty and importance than to be wholly trusted to the ordinary masters in music and poetry, and the common school subjects, and to require, as Sophocles says—

"The bridle and the rudder too,"

he sent for Aristotle, the most learned and most celebrated philosopher of his time, and rewarded him with a munificence proportionable to and becoming the care he took to instruct his son. For he repeopled his native city Stagira, which he had caused to be demolished a little before, and restored all the citizens, who were in exile or slavery, to their habitations. As a place for the pursuit of their studies and exercise, he assigned the temple of the Nymphs, near Mieza, where, to this very day, they show you Aristotle's stone seats, and the shady walks which he was wont to frequent. It would appear that Alexander received from him not only his doctrines of Morals and of Politics, but also something of those more abstruse and profound theories which these philosophers, by the very names they gave them, professed to reserve for oral communication to the initiated, and did not allow many to become acquainted with. For when he was in Asia, and heard Aristotle had published some treatises of that kind, he wrote to him, using very plain language to him in behalf of philosophy, the following letter. "Alexander to Aristotle, greeting. You have not done well to publish your books of oral doctrine; for what is there now that we excel others in, if those things which we have been particularly instructed in be laid open to all? For my part, I assure you, I had rather excel others in the knowledge of what is excellent, than in the extent of my power and dominion. Farewell." And Aristotle, soothing this passion for pre-eminence, speaks, in his excuse for himself, of these doctrines as in fact both published and not published: as indeed, to say the truth, his books on metaphysics are written in a style which makes them useless for ordinary teaching, and instructive only, in the way of memoranda, for those who have been already conversant in that sort of learning.

Doubtless also it was to Aristotle that he owed the inclination he had, not to the theory only, but likewise to the practice of the art of medicine. For when any of his friends were sick, he would often prescribe them their course of diet, and medicines proper to their disease, as we may find in his epistles. He was naturally a great lover of all kinds of learning and reading; and Onesicritus informs us that he constantly laid Homer's Iliads, according to the copy corrected by Aristotle, called the casket copy, with his dagger under his pillow, declaring that he esteemed it a perfect portable treasure of all military virtue and knowledge. When he was in the upper Asia, being destitute of other books, he ordered Harpalus to send him some; who furnished him with Philistus's History, a great many of the plays of Euripides, Sophocles, and Aeschylus, and some dithyrambic odes, composed by Telestes and Philoxenus. For a while he loved and cherished Aristotle no less, as he was wont to say himself, than if he had been his father, giving this reason for it, that as he had received life from the one, so the other had taught him to live well. But afterwards, upon some mistrust of him, yet not so great as to make him do him any hurt, his familiarity and friendly kindness to him abated so much of its former force and affectionateness, as to make it evident he was alienated from him. However, his violent thirst after and passion for learning, which were once implanted, still grew up with him, and never decayed; as appears by his veneration of Anaxarchus, by the present of fifty talents which he sent to Xenocrates, and his particular care and esteem of Dandamis and Calanus.

While Philip went on his expedition against the Byzantines, he left Alexander, then sixteen years old, his lieutenant in Macedonia, committing the charge of his seal to him; who, not to sit idle, reduced the rebellious Maedi, and having taken their chief town by storm, drove out the barbarous inhabitants, and planting a colony of several nations in their room, called the place after his own name, Alexandropolis. At the battle of Chaeronea, which his father fought against the Grecians, he is said to have been the first man that charged the Thebans' sacred band. And even in my remembrance, there stood an old oak near the river Cephisus, which people called Alexander's oak, because his tent was pitched under it. And not far off are to be seen the graves of the Macedonians who fell in that battle. This early bravery made Philip so fond of him, that nothing pleased him more than to hear his subjects call himself their general and Alexander their king.

But the disorders of his family, chiefly caused by his new marriages and attachments (the troubles that began in the women's chambers spreading, so to say, to the whole kingdom), raised various complaints and differences between them, which the violence of Olympias, a woman of a jealous and implacable temper, made wider, by exasperating Alexander against his father. Among the rest, this accident contributed most to their falling out. At the wedding of Cleopatra, whom Philip fell in love with and married, she being much too young for him, her uncle Attalus in his drink desired the Macedonians would implore the gods to give them a lawful successor to the kingdom by his niece. This so irritated Alexander, that throwing one of the cups at his head, "You villain," said he, "what, am I then a bastard?" Then Philip, taking Attalus's part, rose up and would have run his son through; but by good fortune for them both, either his over-hasty rage, or the wine he had drunk, made his foot slip, so that he fell down on the floor. At which Alexander reproachfully insulted over him: "See there," said he, "the man who makes preparations to pass out of Europe into Asia, overturned in passing from one seat to another." After this debauch, he and his mother Olympias withdrew from Philip's company, and when he had placed her in Epirus, he himself retired into Illyria.

About this time, Demaratus the Corinthian, an old friend of the family, who had the freedom to say anything among them without offence, coming to visit Philip, after the first compliments and embraces were over, Philip asked him whether the Grecians were at amity with one another. "It ill becomes you," replied Demaratus, "to be so solicitous about Greece, when you have involved your own house in so many dissensions and calamities." He was so convinced by this seasonable reproach, that he immediately sent for his son home, and by Demaratus's mediation prevailed with him to return. But this reconciliation lasted not long; for when Pixodorus, viceroy of Caria, sent Aristocritus to treat for a match between his eldest daughter and Philip's son, Arrhidaeus, hoping by this alliance to secure his assistance upon occasion, Alexander's mother, and some who pretended to be his friends, presently filled his head with tales and calumnies, as if Philip, by a splendid marriage and important alliance, were preparing the way for settling the kingdom upon Arrhidaeus. In alarm at this, he despatched Thessalus, the tragic actor, into Caria, to dispose Pixodorus to slight Arrhidaeus, both illegitimate and a fool, and rather to accept of himself for his son-in-law. This proposition was much more agreeable to Pixodorus than the former. But Philip, as soon as he was made acquainted with this transaction, went to his son's apartment, taking with him Philotas, the son of Parmenio, one of Alexander's intimate friends and companions, and there reproved him severely, and reproached him bitterly, that he should be so degenerate, and unworthy of the power he was to leave him, as to desire the alliance of a mean Carian, who was at best but the slave of a barbarous prince. Nor did this satisfy his resentment, for he wrote to the Corinthians to send Thessalus to him in chains, and banished Harpalus, Nearchus, Erigyius, and Ptolemy, his son's friends and favourites, whom Alexander afterwards recalled and raised to great honour and preferment.

Not long after this, Pausanias, having had an outrage done to him at the instance of Attalus and Cleopatra, when he found he could get no reparation for his disgrace at Philip's hands, watched his opportunity and murdered him. The guilt of which fact was laid for the most part upon Olympias, who was said to have encouraged and exasperated the enraged youth to revenge; and some sort of suspicion attached even to Alexander himself, who, it was said, when Pausanias came and complained to him of the injury he had received, repeated the verse out of Euripides's Medea—

"On husband, and on father, and on bride."

However, he took care to find out and punish the accomplices of the conspiracy severely, and was very angry with Olympias for treating Cleopatra inhumanly in his absence.

Alexander was but twenty years old when his father was murdered, and succeeded to a kingdom, beset on all sides with great dangers and rancorous enemies. For not only the barbarous nations that bordered on Macedonia were impatient of being governed by any but their own native princes, but Philip likewise, though he had been victorious over the Grecians, yet, as the time had not been sufficient for him to complete his conquest and accustom them to his sway, had simply left all things in a general disorder and confusion. It seemed to the Macedonians a very critical time; and some would have persuaded Alexander to give up all thought of retaining the Grecians in subjection by force of arms, and rather to apply himself to win back by gentle means the allegiance of the tribes who were designing revolt, and try the effect of indulgence in arresting the first motions towards revolution. But he rejected this counsel as weak and timorous, and looked upon it to be more prudence to secure himself by resolution and magnanimity, than, by seeming to truckle to any, to encourage all to trample on him. In pursuit of this opinion, he reduced the barbarians to tranquillity, and put an end to all fear of war from them, by a rapid expedition into their country as far as the river Danube, where he gave Syrmus, King of the Tribalians, an entire overthrow. And hearing the Thebans were in revolt, and the Athenians in correspondence with them, he immediately marched through the pass of Thermopylae, saying that to Demosthenes, who had called him a child while he was in Illyria and in the country of the Triballians, and a youth when he was in Thessaly, he would appear a man before the walls of Athens.

When he came to Thebes, to show how willing he was to accept of their repentance for what was past, he only demanded of them Phoenix and Prothytes, the authors of the rebellion, and proclaimed a general pardon to those who would come over to him. But when the Thebans merely retorted by demanding Philotas and Antipater to be delivered into their hands, and by a proclamation on their part invited all who would assert the liberty of Greece to come over to them, he presently applied himself to make them feel the last extremities of war. The Thebans indeed defended themselves with a zeal and courage beyond their strength, being much outnumbered by their enemies. But when the Macedonian garrison sallied out upon them from the citadel, they were so hemmed in on all sides that the greater part of them fell in the battle; the city itself being taken by storm, was sacked and razed. Alexander's hope being that so severe an example might terrify the rest of Greece into obedience, and also in order to gratify the hostility of his confederates, the Phocians and Plataeans. So that, except the priests, and some few who had heretofore been the friends and connections of the Macedonians, the family of the poet Pindar, and those who were known to have opposed the public vote for the war, all the rest, to the number of thirty thousand, were publicly sold for slaves; and it is computed that upwards of six thousand were put to the sword.

Among the other calamities that befell the city, it happened that some Thracian soldiers, having broken into the house of a matron of high character and repute, named Timoclea, their captain, after he had used violence with her, to satisfy his avarice as well as lust, asked her, if she knew of any money concealed; to which she readily answered she did, and bade him follow her into a garden, where she showed him a well, into which, she told him, upon the taking of the city, she had thrown what she had of most value. The greedy Thracian presently stooping down to view the place where he thought the treasure lay, she came behind him and pushed him into the well, and then flung great stones in upon him, till she had killed him. After which, when the soldiers led her away bound to Alexander, her very mien and gait showed her to be a woman of dignity, and of a mind no less elevated, not betraying the least sign of fear or astonishment. And when the king asked her who she was, "I am," said she, "the sister of Theagenes, who fought the battle of Chaeronea with your father Philip, and fell there in command for the liberty of Greece." Alexander was so surprised, both at what she had done and what she said, that he could not choose but give her and her children their freedom to go whither they pleased.

After this he received the Athenians into favour, although they had shown themselves so much concerned at the calamity of Thebes that out of sorrow they omitted the celebration of the Mysteries, and entertained those who escaped with all possible humanity. Whether it were, like the lion, that his passion was now satisfied, or that, after an example of extreme cruelty, he had a mind to appear merciful, it happened well for the Athenians; for he not only forgave them all past offences, but bade them look to their affairs with vigilance, remembering that if he should miscarry, they were likely to be the arbiters of Greece. Certain it is, too, that in aftertime he often repented of his severity to the Thebans, and his remorse had such influence on his temper as to make him ever after less rigorous to all others. He imputed also the murder of Clitus, which he committed in his wine, and the unwillingness of the Macedonians to follow him against the Indians, by which his enterprise and glory was left imperfect, to the wrath and vengeance of Bacchus, the protector of Thebes. And it was observed that whatsoever any Theban, who had the good fortune to survive this victory, asked of him, he was sure to grant without the least difficulty.

Soon after, the Grecians, being assembled at the Isthmus, declared their resolution of joining with Alexander in the war against the Persians, and proclaimed him their general. While he stayed here, many public ministers and philosophers came from all parts to visit him and congratulated him on his election, but contrary to his expectation, Diogenes of Sinope, who then was living at Corinth, thought so little of him, that instead of coming to compliment him, he never so much as stirred out of the suburb called the Cranium, where Alexander found him lying alone in the sun. When he saw so much company near him, he raised himself a little, and vouchsafed to look upon Alexander; and when he kindly asked him whether he wanted anything, "Yes," said he, "I would have you stand from between me and the sun." Alexander was so struck at this answer, and surprised at the greatness of the man, who had taken so little notice of him, that as he went away he told his followers, who were laughing at the moroseness of the philosopher, that if he were not Alexander, he would choose to be Diogenes.

Then he went to Delphi, to consult Apollo concerning the success of the war he had undertaken, and happening to come on one of the forbidden days, when it was esteemed improper to give any answer from the oracle, he sent messengers to desire the priestess to do her office; and when she refused, on the plea of a law to the contrary, he went up himself, and began to draw her by force into the temple, until tired and overcome with his importunity, "My son," said she, "thou art invincible." Alexander taking hold of what she spoke, declared he had received such an answer as he wished for, and that it was needless to consult the god any further. Among other prodigies that attended the departure of his army, the image of Orpheus at Libethra, made of cypress-wood, was seen to sweat in great abundance, to the discouragement of many. But Aristander told him that, far from presaging any ill to him, it signified he should perform acts so important and glorious as would make the poets and musicians of future ages labour and sweat to describe and celebrate them.

His army, by their computation who make the smallest amount, consisted of thirty thousand foot and four thousand horse; and those who make the most of it, speak but of forty-three thousand foot and three thousand horse. Aristobulus says, he had not a fund of above seventy talents for their pay, nor had he more than thirty days' provision, if we may believe Duris; Onesicritus tells us he was two hundred talents in debt. However narrow and disproportionable the beginnings of so vast an undertaking might seem to be, yet he would not embark his army until he had informed himself particularly what means his friends had to enable them to follow him, and supplied what they wanted, by giving good farms to some, a village to one, and the revenue of some hamlet or harbour-town to another. So that at last he had portioned out or engaged almost all the royal property; which giving Perdiccas an occasion to ask him what he would leave himself, he replied, his hopes. "Your soldiers," replied Perdiccas, "will be your partners in those," and refused to accept of the estate he had assigned him. Some others of his friends did the like, but to those who willingly received or desired assistance of him, he liberally granted it, as far as his patrimony in Macedonia would reach, the most part of which was spent in these donations.

With such vigorous resolutions, and his mind thus disposed, he passed the Hellespont, and at Troy sacrificed to Minerva, and honoured the memory of the heroes who were buried there, with solemn libations; especially Achilles, whose gravestone he anointed, and with his friends, as the ancient custom is, ran naked about his sepulchre, and crowned it with garlands, declaring how happy he esteemed him, in having while he lived so faithful a friend, and when he was dead, so famous a poet to proclaim his actions. While he was viewing the rest of the antiquities and curiosities of the place, being told he might see Paris's harp, if he pleased, he said he thought it not worth looking on, but he should be glad to see that of Achilles, to which he used to sing the glories and great actions of brave men.

In the meantime, Darius's captains, having collected large forces, were encamped on the further bank of the river Granicus, and it was necessary to fight, as it were, in the gate of Asia for an entrance into it. The depth of the river, with the unevenness and difficult ascent of the opposite bank, which was to be gained by main force, was apprehended by most, and some pronounced it an improper time to engage, because it was unusual for the kings of Macedonia to march with their forces in the month called Daesius. But Alexander broke through these scruples, telling them they should call it a second Artemisius. And when Parmenio advised him not to attempt anything that day, because it was late, he told him that he should disgrace the Hellespont should he fear the Granicus. And so, without more saying, he immediately took the river with thirteen troops of horse, and advanced against whole showers of darts thrown from the steep opposite side, which was covered with armed multitudes of the enemy's horse and foot, notwithstanding the disadvantage of the ground and the rapidity of the stream; so that the action seemed to have more frenzy and desperation in it, than prudent conduct. However, he persisted obstinately to gain the passage, and at last with much ado making his way up the banks, which were extremely muddy and slippery, he had instantly to join in a mere confused hand-to-hand combat with the enemy, before he could draw up his men, who were still passing over, into any order. For the enemy pressed upon him with loud and warlike outcries; and charging horse against horse, with their lances, after they had broken and spent these, they fell to it with their swords. And Alexander, being easily known by his buckler, and a large plume of white feathers on each side of his helmet, was attacked on all sides, yet escaped wounding, though his cuirass was pierced by a javelin in one of the joinings. And Rhoesaces and Spithridates, two Persian commanders, falling upon him at once, he avoided one of them, and struck at Rhoesaces, who had a good cuirass on, with such force that, his spear breaking in his hand, he was glad to betake himself to his dagger. While they were thus engaged, Spithridates came up on one side of him, and raising himself upon his horse, gave him such a blow with his battle-axe on the helmet that he cut off the crest of it, with one of his plumes, and the helmet was only just so far strong enough to save him, that the edge of the weapon touched the hair of his head. But as he was about to repeat his stroke, Clitus, called the black Clitus, prevented him, by running him through the body with his spear. At the same time Alexander despatched Rhoesaces with his sword. While the horse were thus dangerously engaged, the Macedonian phalanx passed the river, and the foot on each side advanced to fight. But the enemy hardly sustaining the first onset, soon gave ground and fled, all but the mercenary Greeks, who, making a stand upon a rising ground, desired quarter, which Alexander, guided rather by passion than judgment, refused to grant, and charging them himself first, had his horse (not Bucephalus, but another) killed under him. And this obstinacy of his to cut off these experienced desperate men cost him the lives of more of his own soldiers than all the battle before, besides those who were wounded. The Persians lost in this battle twenty thousand foot and two thousand five hundred horse. On Alexander's side, Aristobulus says there were not wanting above four-and-thirty, of whom nine were foot-soldiers; and in memory of them he caused so many statues of brass, of Lysippus's making, to be erected. And that the Grecians might participate in the honour of his victory he sent a portion of the spoils home to them, particularly to the Athenians three hundred bucklers, and upon all the rest he ordered this inscription to be set: "Alexander the son of Philip, and the Grecians, except the Lacedaemonians, won these from the barbarians who inhabit Asia." All the plate and purple garments, and other things of the same kind that he took from the Persians, except a very small quantity which he reserved for himself, he sent as a present to his mother.

This battle presently made a great change of affairs to Alexander's advantage. For Sardis itself, the chief seat of the barbarian's power in the maritime provinces, and many other considerable places, were surrendered to him; only Halicarnassus and Miletus stood out, which he took by force, together with the territory about them. After which he was a little unsettled in his opinion how to proceed. Sometimes he thought it best to find out Darius as soon as he could, and put all to the hazard of a battle; another while he looked upon it as a more prudent course to make

an entire reduction of the sea-coast, and not to seek the
enemy till he had first exercised his power here and made
himself secure of the resources of these provinces. While
he was thus deliberating what to do, it happened that a
spring of water near the city of Xanthus in Lycia, of its
own accord, swelled over its banks, and threw up a copper
plate, upon the margin of which was engraven in ancient
characters, that the time would come when the Persian
empire should be destroyed by the Grecians. Encouraged
by this accident, he proceeded to reduce the maritime parts
of Cilicia and Phoenicia, and passed his army along the sea-
coasts of Pamphylia with such expedition that many historians have described and extolled it with that height of admiration, as if it were no less than a miracle, and an extraordinary effect of divine favour, that the waves which usually
come rolling in violently from the main, and hardly ever
leave so much as a narrow beach under the steep, broken
cliffs at any time uncovered, should on a sudden retire to
afford him passage. Menander, in one of his comedies, alludes to this marvel when he says—

> "Was Alexander ever favoured more?
> Each man I wish for meets me at my door,
> And should I ask for passage through the sea,
> The sea I doubt not would retire for me."

But Alexander himself in his epistles mentions nothing
unusual in this at all, but says he went from Phaselis, and
passed through what they call the Ladders. At Phaselis he
stayed some time, and finding the statue of Theodectes,
who was a native of this town and was now dead, erected
in the market-place, after he had supped, having drunk
pretty plentifully, he went and danced about it, and
crowned it with garlands, honouring not ungracefully, in
his sport, the memory of a philosopher whose conversation
he had formerly enjoyed when he was Aristotle's scholar.

Then he subdued the Pisidians who made head against
him, and conquered the Phrygians, at whose chief city,
Gordium, which is said to be the seat of the ancient Midas,

he saw the famous chariot fastened with cords made of the rind of the cornel-tree, which whosoever should untie, the inhabitants had a tradition, that for him was reserved the empire of the world. Most authors tell the story that Alexander finding himself unable to untie the knot, the ends of which were secretly twisted round and folded up within it, cut it asunder with his sword. But Aristobulus tells us it was easy for him to undo it, by only pulling the pin out of the pole, to which the yoke was tied, and afterwards drawing off the yoke itself from below. From hence he advanced in to Paphlagonia and Cappadocia, both which countries he soon reduced to obedience, and then hearing of the death of Memnon, the best commander Darius had upon the sea-coasts, who, if he had lived, might, it was supposed, have put many impediments and difficulties in the way of the progress of his arms, he was the rather encouraged to carry the war into the upper provinces of Asia.

Darius was by this time upon his march from Susa, very confident, not only in the number of his men, which amounted to six hundred thousand, but likewise in a dream, which the Persian soothsayers interpreted rather in flattery to him than according to the natural probability. He dreamed that he saw the Macedonian phalanx all on fire, and Alexander waiting on him, clad in the same dress which he himself had been used to wear when he was courier to the late king; after which, going into the temple of Belus, he vanished out of his sight. The dream would appear to have supernaturally signified to him the illustrious actions the Macedonians were to perform, and that as he, from a courier's place, had risen to the throne, so Alexander should come to be master of Asia, and not long surviving his conquests, conclude his life with glory. Darius's confidence increased the more, because Alexander spent so much time in Cilicia, which he imputed to his cowardice. But it was sickness that detained him there, which some say he contracted from his fatigues, others from bathing in the river Cydnus, whose waters were exceedingly cold. However it happened, none of his physicians would venture to give him any remedies, they thought his case so desperate, and

were so afraid of the suspicions and ill-will of the Macedonians if they should fail in the cure; till Philip, the Acarnanian, seeing how critical his case was, but relying on his
own well-known friendship for him, resolved to try the last
efforts of his art, and rather hazard his own credit and life
than suffer him to perish for want of physic, which he confidently administered to him, encouraging him to take it
boldly, if he desired a speedy recovery, in order to prosecute the war. At this very time, Parmenio wrote to Alexander from the camp, bidding him have a care of Philip,
as one who was bribed by Darius to kill him, with great
sums of money, and a promise of his daughter in marriage.
When he had perused the letter, he put it under his pillow,
without showing it so much as to any of his most intimate
friends, and when Philip came in with the potion, he took
it with great cheerfulness and assurance, giving him meantime the letter to read. This was a spectacle well worth being present at, to see Alexander take the draught and Philip
read the letter at the same time, and then turn and look
upon one another, but with different sentiments; for Alexander's looks were cheerful and open, to show his kindness
to and confidence in his physician, while the other was full
of surprise and alarm at the accusation, appealing to the
gods to witness his innocence, sometimes lifting up his hands
to heaven, and then throwing himself down by the bedside,
and beseeching Alexander to lay aside all fear, and follow
his directions without apprehension. For the medicine at
first worked so strongly as to drive, so to say, the vital
forces into the interior; he lost his speech, and falling into
a swoon, had scarce any sense or pulse left. However, in
no long time, by Philip's means, his health and strength
returned, and he showed himself in public to the Macedonians, who were in continual fear and dejection until they saw
him abroad again.

There was at this time in Darius's army a Macedonian
refugee, named Amyntas, one who was pretty well acquainted with Alexander's character. This man, when he
saw Darius intended to fall upon the enemy in the passes
and defiles, advised him earnestly to keep where he was,

in the open and extensive plains, it being the advantage of a numerous army to have field-room enough when it engaged with a lesser force. Darius, instead of taking his counsel, told him he was afraid the enemy would endeavour to run away, and so Alexander would escape out of his hands. "That fear," replied Amyntas, "is needless, for assure yourself that far from avoiding you, he will make all the speed he can to meet you, and is now most likely on his march toward you." But Amyntas's counsel was to no purpose, for Darius immediately decamping, marched into Cilicia at the same time that Alexander advanced into Syria to meet him; and missing one another in the night, they both turned back again. Alexander, greatly pleased with the event, made all the haste he could to fight in the defiles, and Darius to recover his former ground, and draw his army out of so disadvantageous a place. For now he began to perceive his error in engaging himself too far in a country in which the sea, the mountains, and the river Pinarus running through the midst of it, would necessitate him to divide his forces, render his horse almost unserviceable, and only cover and support the weakness of the enemy. Fortune was not kinder to Alexander in the choice of the ground, than he was careful to improve it to his advantage. For being much inferior in numbers, so far from allowing himself to be outflanked, he stretched his right wing much further out than the left wing of his enemies, and fighting there himself in the very foremost ranks, put the barbarians to flight. In this battle he was wounded in the thigh, Chares says, by Darius, with whom he fought hand to hand. But in the account which he gave Antipater of the battle, though indeed he owns he was wounded in the thigh with a sword, though not dangerously, yet he takes no notice who it was that wounded him.

Nothing was wanting to complete this victory, in which he overthrew above an hundred and ten thousand of his enemies, but the taking the person of Darius, who escaped very narrowly by flight. However, having taken his chariot and his bow, he returned from pursuing him, and found his own men busy in pillaging the barbarians' camp, which (though to disburden themselves they had left most of their baggage at Damascus) was exceedingly rich. But Darius's tent, which was full of splendid furniture and quantities of gold and silver, they reserved for Alexander himself, who, after he had put off his arms, went to bathe himself saying, "Let us now cleanse ourselves from the toils of war in the bath of Darius." "Not so," replied one of his followers, "but in Alexander's rather; for the property of the conquered is and should be called the conqueror's." Here, when he beheld the bathing vessels, the water-pots, the pans, and the ointment boxes, all of gold curiously wrought, and smelt the fragrant odours with which the whole place was exquisitely perfumed, and from thence passed into a pavilion of great size and height, where the couches and tables and preparations for an entertainment were perfectly magnificent, he turned to those about him and said, "This, it seems, is royalty."

But as he was going to supper, word was brought him that Darius's mother and wife and two unmarried daughters, being taken among the rest of the prisoners, upon the sight of his chariot and bow, were all in mourning and sorrow, imagining him to be dead. After a little pause, more lively affected with their affliction than with his own success, he sent Leonnatus to them, to let them know Darius was not dead, and that they need not fear any harm from Alexander, who made war upon him only for dominion; they should themselves be provided with everything they had been used to receive from Darius. This kind message could not but be very welcome to the captive ladies, especially being made good by actions no less humane and generous. For he gave them leave to bury whom they pleased of the Persians, and to make use for this purpose of what garments and furniture they thought fit out of the booty. He diminished nothing of their equipage, or of the attentions and respect formerly paid them, and allowed larger pensions for their maintenance than they had before. But the noblest and most royal part of their usage was, that he treated these illustrious prisoners according to their virtue and character, not suffering them to hear, or receive, or so much as to apprehend anything that was unbecoming. So that they seemed rather lodged in some temple, or some holy virgin chambers, where they enjoyed their privacy sacred and un-interrupted, than in the camp of an enemy. Nevertheless Darius's wife was accounted the most beautiful princess then living, as her husband the tallest and handsomest man of his time, and the daughters were not unworthy of their parents. But Alexander, esteeming it more kingly to govern himself than to conquer his enemies, sought no intimacy with any one of them, nor indeed with any other women be-fore marriage, except Barsine, Memnon's widow, who was taken prisoner at Damascus. She had been instructed in the Grecian learning, was of a gentle temper, and by her father, Artabazus, royally descended, with good qualities, added to the solicitations and encouragement of Parmenio, as Aris-tobulus tells us, made him the more willing to attach himself to so agreeable and illustrious a woman. Of the rest of the female captives, though remarkably handsome and well pro-portioned, he took no further notice than to say jestingly that Persian women were terrible eyesores. And he himself, retaliating, as it were, by the display of the beauty of his own temperance and self-control, bade them be removed, as he would have done so many lifeless images. When Phi-loxenus, his lieutenant on the sea-coast, wrote to him to know if he would buy two young boys of great beauty, whom one Theodorus, a Tarentine, had to sell, he was so offended that he often expostulated with his friends what baseness Philoxenus had ever observed in him that he should presume to make him such a reproachful offer. And he im-mediately wrote him a very sharp letter, telling him Theo-dorus and his merchandise might go with his good-will to destruction. Nor was he less severe to Hagnon, who sent him word he would buy a Corinthian youth named Croby-lus, as a present for him. And hearing that Damon and Timotheus, two of Parmenio's Macedonian soldiers, had abused the wives of some strangers who were in his pay, he wrote to Parmenio, charging him strictly, if he found them guilty, to put them to death, as wild beasts that were only made for the mischief of mankind. In the same letter

he added, that he had not so much as seen or desired to
see the wife of Darius, no, nor suffered anybody to speak
of her beauty before him. He was wont to say that sleep and
the act of generation chiefly made him sensible that he was
mortal; as much as to say, that weariness and pleasure proceed both from the same frailty and imbecility of human
nature.

In his diet, also, he was most temperate, as appears,
omitting many other circumstances, by what he said to Ada,
whom he adopted, with the title of mother, and afterwards
created Queen of Caria. For when she, out of kindness, sent
him every day many curious dishes and sweetmeats, and
would have furnished him with some cooks and pastry-men,
who were thought to have great skill, he told her he wanted
none of them, his preceptor, Leonidas, having already given
him the best, which were a night march to prepare for
breakfast, and a moderate breakfast to create an appetite
for supper. Leonidas also, he added, used to open and
search the furniture of his chamber and his wardrobe, to
see if his mother had left him anything that was delicate or
superfluous. He was much less addicted to wine than was
generally believed; that which gave people occasion to
think so of him was, that when he had nothing else to do,
he loved to sit long and talk, rather than drink, and over
every cup hold a long conversation. For when his affairs
called upon him, he would not be detained, as other generals often were, either by wine, or sleep, nuptial solemnities,
spectacles, or any other diversion whatsoever; a convincing
argument of which is, that in the short time he lived, he
accomplished so many and so great actions. When he was
free from employment, after he was up, and had sacrificed
to the gods, he used to sit down to breakfast, and then
spend the rest of the day in hunting, or writing memoirs,
giving decisions on some military questions, or reading. In
marches that required no great haste, he would practise
shooting as he went along, or to mount a chariot and alight
from it in full speed. Sometimes, for sport's sake, as his
journals tell us, he would hunt foxes and go fowling. When
he came in for the evening, after he had bathed and was

anointed, he would call for his bakers and chief cooks, to know if they had his dinner ready. He never cared to dine till it was pretty late and beginning to be dark, and was wonderfully circumspect at meals that every one who sat with him should be served alike and with proper attention; and his love of talking, as was said before, made him delight to sit long at his wine. And then, though otherwise no prince's conversation was ever so agreeable, he would fall into a temper of ostentation and soldierly boasting, which gave his flatterers a great advantage to ride him, and made his better friends very uneasy. For though they thought it too base to strive who should flatter him most, yet they found it hazardous not to do it; so that between the shame and the danger, they were in a great strait how to behave themselves. After such an entertainment, he was wont to bathe, and then perhaps he would sleep till noon, and sometimes all day long. He was so very temperate in his eating, that when any rare fish or fruits were sent him, he would distribute them among his friends, and often reserve nothing for himself. His table, however, was always magnificent, the expense of it still increasing with his good fortune, till it amounted to ten thousand drachmas a day, to which sum he limited it, and beyond this he would suffer none to lay out in any entertainment where he himself was the guest.

After the battle of Issus, he sent to Damascus to seize upon the money and baggage, the wives and children, of the Persians, of which spoil the Thessalian horsemen had the greatest share; for he had taken particular notice of their gallantry in the fight, and sent them thither on purpose to make their reward suitable to their courage. Not but that the rest of the army had so considerable a part of the booty as was sufficient to enrich them all. This first gave the Macedonians such a taste of the Persian wealth and women and barbaric splendour of living, that they were ready to pursue and follow upon it with all the eagerness of hounds upon a scent. But Alexander, before he proceeded any further, thought it necessary to assure himself of the sea-coast. Those who governed in Cyprus put that island into his possession, and Phoenicia, Tyre only excepted, was surrendered to him. During the siege of this city, which, with mounds of earth cast up, and battering engines, and two hundred galleys by sea, was carried on for seven months together, he dreamt that he saw Hercules upon the walls, reaching out his hands, and calling to him. And many of the Tyrians in their sleep fancied that Apollo told them he was displeased with their actions, and was about to leave them and go over to Alexander. Upon which, as if the god had been a deserting soldier, they seized him, so to say, in the act, tied down the statue with ropes, and nailed it to the pedestal, reproaching him that he was a favourer of Alexander. Another time Alexander dreamed he saw a satyr mocking him at a distance, and when he endeavoured to catch him, he still escaped from him, till at last with much perseverance, and running about after him, he got him into his power. The soothsayers, making two words of *Satyrus,* assured him that Tyre should be his own. The inhabitants at this time show a spring of water, near which they say Alexander slept when he fancied the satyr appeared to him.

While the body of the army lay before Tyre, he made an excursion against the Arabians who inhabit the Mount Antilibanus, in which he hazarded his life extremely to bring off his master Lysimachus, who would needs go along with him, declaring he was neither older nor inferior in courage to Phoenix, Achilles's guardian. For when, quitting their horses, they began to march up the hills on foot, the rest of the soldiers outwent them a great deal, so that night drawing on, and the enemy near, Alexander was fain to stay behind so long, to encourage and help up the lagging and tired old man, that before he was aware he was left behind, a great way from his soldiers, with a slender attendance, and forced to pass an extremely cold night in the dark, and in a very inconvenient place; till seeing a great many scattered fires of the enemy at some distance, and trusting to his agility of body, and as he was always wont by undergoing toils and labours himself to cheer and support the Macedonians in any distress, he ran straight to one of the nearest fires, and with his dagger despatching two of the barbarians that sat by it, snatched up a lighted brand, and returned with it to his own men. They immediately made a great fire, which so alarmed the enemy that most of them fled, and those that assaulted them were soon routed, and thus they rested securely the remainder of the night. Thus Chares writes.

But to return to the siege, it had this issue. Alexander, that he might refresh his army, harassed with many former encounters, had led only a small party towards the walls, rather to keep the enemy busy than with any prospect of much advantage. It happened at this time that Aristander, the soothsayer, after he had sacrificed, upon view of the entrails, affirmed confidently to those who stood by that the city should be certainly taken that very month, upon which there was a laugh and some mockery among the soldiers, as this was the last day of it. The king, seeing him in perplexity, and always anxious to support the credit of the predictions, gave order that they should not count it as the thirtieth, but as the twenty-third of the month, and ordering the trumpets to sound, attacked the walls more seriously than he at first intended. The sharpness of the assault so inflamed the rest of his forces who were left in the camp, that they could not hold from advancing to second it, which they performed with so much vigour that the Tyrians retired, and the town was carried that very day. The next place he sat down before was Gaza, one of the largest cities of Syria, when this accident befell him. A large bird flying over him let a clod of earth fall upon his shoulder, and then settling upon one of the battering engines, was suddenly entangled and caught in the nets, composed of sinews, which protected the ropes with which the machine was managed. This fell out exactly according to Aristander's prediction, which was, that Alexander should be wounded and the city reduced.

From hence he sent great part of the spoils to Olympias, Cleopatra, and the rest of his friends, not omitting his preceptor Leonidas, on whom he bestowed five hundred talents' weight of frankincense and an hundred of myrrh, in

remembrance of the hopes he had once expressed of him
when he was but a child. For Leonidas, it seems, standing
by him one day while he was sacrificing, and seeing him
take both his hands full of incense to throw into the fire,
told him it became him to be more sparing in his offerings,
and not to be so profuse till he was master of the countries
which those sweet gums and spices come from. So Alexander now wrote to him, saying, "We have sent you abundance of myrrh and frankincense, that for the future you
may not be stingy to the gods." Among the treasures and
other booty that was taken from Darius, there was a very
precious casket, which being brought to Alexander for a
great rarity, he asked those about him what they thought fittest to be laid up in it; and when they had delivered their
various opinions, he told them he should keep Homer's
Iliad in it. This is attested by many credible authors, and if
what those of Alexandria tell us, relying upon the authority
of Heraclides, be true, Homer was neither an idle nor an
unprofitable companion to him in his expedition. For when
he was master of Egypt, designing to settle a colony of
Grecians there, he resolved to build a large and populous
city, and give it his own name. In order to which, after he
had measured and staked out the ground with the advice of
the best architects, he chanced one night in his sleep to see
a wonderful vision; a grey-headed old man, of a venerable
aspect, appeared to stand by him, and pronounce these
verses:—

"An island lies, where loud the billows roar,
Pharos they call it, on the Egyptian shore."

Alexander upon this immediately rose up and went to
Pharos, which, at that time, was an island lying a little
above the Canobic mouth of the river Nile, though it has
now been joined to the mainland by a mole. As soon as he
saw the commodious situation of the place, it being a long
neck of land, stretching like an isthmus between large la-
goons and shallow waters on one side and the sea on the
other, the latter at the end of it making a spacious harbour,

he said, Homer, besides his other excellences, was a very
good architect, and ordered the plan of a city to be drawn
out answerable to the place. To do which, for want of
chalk, the soil being black, they laid out their lines with
flour, taking in a pretty large compass of ground in a semi-
circular figure, and drawing into the inside of the circumference equal straight lines from each end, thus giving it
something of the form of a cloak or cape; while he was
pleasing himself with his design, on a sudden an infinite
number of great birds of several kinds, rising like a black
cloud out of the river and the lake, devoured every morsel
of the flour that had been used in setting out the lines; at
which omen even Alexander himself was troubled, till the
augurs restored his confidence again by telling him it was a
sign the city he was about to build would not only abound
in all things within itself, but also be the nurse and feeder
of many nations. He commanded the workmen to proceed,
while he went to visit the temple of Ammon.

This was a long and painful, and, in two respects, a dangerous journey; first, if they should lose their provision of
water, as for several days none could be obtained; and,
secondly, if a violent south wind should rise upon them,
while they were travelling through the wide extent of deep
sands, as it is said to have done when Cambyses led his
army that way, blowing the sand together in heaps, and
raising, as it were, the whole desert like a sea upon them,
till fifty thousand were swallowed up and destroyed by it.
All these difficulties were weighed and represented to him;
but Alexander was not easily to be diverted from anything
he was bent upon. For fortune having hitherto seconded
him in his designs, made him resolute and firm in his opinions, and the boldness of his temper raised a sort of passion
in him for surmounting difficulties; as if it were not enough
to be always victorious in the field, unless places and sea-
sons and nature herself submitted to him. In this journey,
the relief and assistance the gods afforded him in his distresses were more remarkable, and obtained greater belief
than the oracles he received afterwards, which, however,
were valued and credited the more on account of those oc-

currences. For first, plentiful rains that fell preserved them
from any fear of perishing by drought, and, allaying the
extreme dryness of the sand, which now became moist and
firm to travel on, cleared and purified the air. Besides this,
when they were out of their way, and were wandering up
and down, because the marks which were wont to direct the
guides were disordered and lost, they were set right again
by some ravens, which flew before them when on their
march, and waited for them when they lingered and fell
behind; and the greatest miracle, as Callisthenes tells us,
was that if any of the company went astray in the night,
they never ceased croaking and making a noise till by that
means they had brought them into the right way again.
Having passed through the wilderness, they came to the
place where the high priest, at the first salutation, bade Alexander welcome from his father Ammon. And being asked
by him whether any of his father's murderers had escaped
punishment, he charged him to speak with more respect,
since his was not a mortal father. Then Alexander, changing his expression, desired to know of him if any of those
who murdered Philip were yet unpunished, and further concerning dominion, whether the empire of the world was reserved for him? This, the god answered, he should obtain,
and that Philip's death was fully revenged, which gave him
so much satisfaction that he made splendid offerings to
Jupiter, and gave the priests very rich presents. This is what
most authors write concerning the oracles. But Alexander,
in a letter to his mother, tells her there were some secret
answers, which at his return he would communicate to her
only. Others say that the priest, desirous as a piece of courtesy to address him in Greek, "O Paidion," by a slip in pronunciation ended with the s instead of the n, and said "O
Paidos," which mistake Alexander was well enough pleased
with, and it went for current that the oracle had called him
so.

Among the sayings of one Psammon, a philosopher,
whom he heard in Egypt, he most approved of this, that all
men are governed by God, because in everything, that which
is chief and commands is divine. But what he pronounced

himself upon this subject was even more like a philosopher, for he said, God was the common father of us all, but more particularly of the best of us. To the barbarians he carried himself very haughtily, as if he were fully persuaded of his divine birth and parentage; but to the Grecians more moderately, and with less affectation of divinity, except it were once in writing to the Athenians about Samos, when he tells them that he should not himself have bestowed upon them that free and glorious city; "You received it," he says, "from the bounty of him who at that time was called my lord and father," meaning Philip. However, afterwards being wounded with an arrow, and feeling much pain, he turned to those about him, and told them, "This, my friends, is real flowing blood, not Ichor—

"Such as immortal gods are wont to shed."

And another time, when it thundered so much that everybody was afraid, and Anaxarchus, the sophist, asked him if he who was Jupiter's son could do anything like this, "Nay," said Alexander, laughing, "I have no desire to be formidable to my friends, as you would have me, who despised my table for being furnished with fish, and not with the heads of governors of provinces." For in fact it is related as true, that Anaxarchus, seeing a present of small fishes, which the king sent to Hephaestion, had used this expression, in a sort of irony, and disparagement of those who undergo vast labours and encounter great hazards in pursuit of magnificent objects which after all bring them little more pleasure or enjoyment than what others have. From what I have said upon this subject, it is apparent that Alexander in himself was not foolishly affected, or had the vanity to think himself really a god, but merely used his claims to divinity as a means of maintaining among other people the sense of his superiority.

At his return out of Egypt into Phoenicia, he sacrificed and made solemn processions, to which were added shows of lyric dances and tragedies, remarkable not merely for the splendour of the equipage and decorations, but for the

competition among those who exhibited them. For the
kings of Cyprus were here the exhibitors, just in the same
manner as at Athens those who are chosen by lot out of the
tribes. And, indeed, they showed the greatest emulation to
outvie each other; especially Nicocreon, King of Salamis,
and Pasicrates of Soli, who furnished the chorus, and defrayed the expenses of the two most celebrated actors,
Athenodorus and Thessalus, the former performing for
Pasicrates, and the latter for Nicocreon. Thessalus was
most favoured by Alexander, though it did not appear till
Athenodorus was declared victor by the plurality of votes.
For then at his going away, he said the judges deserved to
be commended for what they had done, but that he would
willingly have lost part of his kingdom rather than to have
seen Thessalus overcome. However, when he understood
Athenodorus was fined by the Athenians for being absent at
the festivals of Bacchus, though he refused his request that
he would write a letter in his behalf, he gave him a sufficient
sum to satisfy the penalty. Another time, when Lycon of
Scarphia happened to act with great applause in the theatre,
and in a verse which he introduced into the comic part
which he was acting, begged for a present of ten talents, he
laughed and gave him the money.

Darius wrote him a letter, and sent friends to intercede
with him, requesting him to accept as a ransom of his captives the sum of a thousand talents, and offering him in exchange for his amity and alliance all the countries on this
side the river Euphrates, together with one of his daughters
in marriage. These propositions he communicated to his
friends, and when Parmenio told him that, for his part, if
he were Alexander, he should readily embrace them, "So
would I," said Alexander, "if I were Parmenio." Accordingly, his answer to Darius was, that if he would come and
yield himself up into his power he would treat him with
all possible kindness; if not, he was resolved immediately
to go himself and seek him. But the death of Darius's wife
in childbirth made him soon after regret one part of this
answer, and he showed evident marks of grief at being thus
deprived of a further opportunity of exercising his clem-

ency and good nature, which he manifested, however, as far as he could, by giving her a most sumptuous funeral.

Among the eunuchs who waited in the queen's chamber, and were taken prisoners with the women, there was one Tireus, who, getting out of the camp, fled away on horseback to Darius, to inform him of his wife's death. He, when he heard it, beating his head, and bursting into tears and lamentations, said, "Alas! how great is the calamity of the Persians! Was it not enough that their king's consort and sister was a prisoner in her lifetime, but she must, now she is dead, also be but meanly and obscurely buried?" "O king," replied the eunuch, "as to her funeral rites, or any respect or honour that should have been shown in them, you have not the least reason to accuse the ill fortune of your country; for to my knowledge neither your queen Statira when alive, nor your mother, nor children, wanted anything of their former happy condition, unless it were the light of your countenance, which I doubt not but the lord Oromasdes will yet restore to its former glory. And after her decease, I assure you, she had not only all due funeral ornaments, but was honoured also with the tears of your very enemies; for Alexander is as gentle after victory as he is terrible in the field." At the hearing of these words, such was the grief and emotion of Darius's mind, that they carried him into extravagant suspicions; and taking Tireus aside into a more private part of his tent, "Unless thou likewise," said he to him, "hast deserted me, together with the good fortune of Persia, and art become a Macedonian in thy heart; if thou yet ownest me for thy master Darius, tell me, I charge thee, by the veneration thou payest the light of Mithras, and this right hand of thy king, do I not lament the least of Statira's misfortunes in her captivity and death? Have I not suffered something more injurious and deplorable in her lifetime? And had I not been miserable with less dishonour if I had met with a more severe and inhuman enemy? For how is it possible a young man as he is should treat the wife of his opponent with so much distinction, were it not from some motive that does me disgrace?" Whilst he was yet speaking, Tireus threw himself at his feet, and besought him neither to wrong Alexander so much, nor his dead wife and sister, as to give utterance to any such thoughts, which deprived him of the greatest consolation left him in his adversity, the belief that he was overcome by a man whose virtues raised him above human nature; that he ought to look upon Alexander with love and admiration, who had given no less proofs of his continence towards the Persian women, than of his valour among the men. The eunuch confirmed all he said with solemn and dreadful oaths, and was further enlarging upon Alexander's moderation and magnanimity on other occasions, when Darius, breaking away from him into the other division of the tent, where his friends and courtiers were, lifted up his hands to heaven and uttered this prayer, "Ye gods," said he, "of my family, and of my kingdom, if it be possible, I beseech you to restore the declining affairs of Persia, that I may leave them in as flourishing a condition as I found them, and have it in my power to make a grateful return to Alexander for the kindness which in my adversity he has shown to those who are dearest to me. But if, indeed, the fatal time be come, which is to give a period to the Persian monarchy, if our ruin be a debt that must be paid to the divine jealousy and the vicissitude of things, then I beseech you grant that no other man but Alexander may sit upon the throne of Cyrus." Such is the narrative given by the greater number of the historians.

But to return to Alexander. After he had reduced all Asia on this side the Euphrates, he advanced towards Darius, who was coming down against him with a million of men. In his march a very ridiculous passage happened. The servants who followed the camp for sport's sake divided themselves into two parties, and named the commander of one of them Alexander, and the other Darius. At first they only pelted one another with clods of earth, but presently took to their fists, and at last, heated with contention, they fought in good earnest with stones and clubs, so that they had much ado to part them; till Alexander, upon hearing of it, ordered the two captains to decide the quarrel by single combat, and armed him who bore his name himself, while Philotas did the same to him who represented Darius. The whole army were spectators of this encounter, willing from the event of it to derive an omen of their own future success. After they had fought stoutly a pretty long while, at last he who was called Alexander had the better, and for a reward of his prowess had twelve villages given him, with leave to wear the Persian dress. So we are told by Eratosthenes.

But the great battle of all that was fought with Darius was not, as most writers tell us, at Arbela, but at Gaugamela, which, in their language, signifies the camel's house, forasmuch as one of their ancient kings having escaped the pursuit of his enemies on a swift camel, in gratitude to his beast, settled him at this place, with an allowance of certain villages and rents for his maintenance. It came to pass that in the month Boëdromion, about the beginning of the feast of Mysteries at Athens, there was an eclipse of the moon, the eleventh night after which, the two armies being now in view of one another, Darius kept his men in arms, and by torchlight took a general review of them. But Alexander, while his soldiers slept, spent the night before his tent with his diviner, Aristander, performing certain mysterious ceremonies, and sacrificing to the god Fear. In the meanwhile the oldest of his commanders, and chiefly Parmenio, when they beheld all the plain between Niphates and the Gordyaean mountains shining with the lights and fires which were made by the barbarians, and heard the uncertain and confused sounds of voices out of their camp, like the distant roaring of a vast ocean, were so amazed at the thoughts of such a multitude, that after some conference among themselves, they concluded it an enterprise too difficult and hazardous for them to engage so numerous an enemy in the day, and therefore meeting the king as he came from sacrificing, besought him to attack Darius by night, that the darkness might conceal the danger of the ensuing battle. To this he gave them the celebrated answer, "I will not steal a victory," which though some at the time thought a boyish and inconsiderate speech, as if he played with danger, others, however, regarded as an evidence that he confided in his present condition, and acted on a true judgment of the future, not wishing to leave Darius, in case he were worsted, the pretext of trying his fortune again, which he might suppose himself to have, if he could impute his overthrow to the disadvantage of the night, as he did before to the mountains, the narrow passages, and the sea. For while he had such numerous forces and large dominions still remaining, it was not any want of men or arms that could induce him to give up the war, but only the loss of all courage and hope upon the conviction of an undeniable and manifest defeat.

After they were gone from him with this answer, he laid himself down in his tent and slept the rest of the night more soundly than was usual with him, to the astonishment of the commanders, who came to him early in the morning, and were fain themselves to give order that the soldiers should breakfast. But at last, time not giving them leave to wait any longer, Parmenio went to his bedside, and called him twice or thrice by his name, till he waked him, and then asked him how it was possible, when he was to fight the most important battle of all, he could sleep as soundly as if he were already victorious. "And are we not so, indeed," replied Alexander, smiling, "since we are at last relieved from the trouble of wandering in pursuit of Darius through a wide and wasted country, hoping in vain that he would fight us?" And not only before the battle, but in the height of the danger, he showed himself great, and manifested the self-possession of a just foresight and confidence. For the battle for some time fluctuated and was dubious. The left wing, where Parmenio commanded, was so impetuously charged by the Bactrian horse that it was disordered and forced to give ground, at the same time that Mazaeus had sent a detachment round about to fall upon those who guarded the baggage, which so disturbed Parmenio that he sent messengers to acquaint Alexander that the camp and baggage would be all lost unless he immediately relieved the rear by a considerable reinforcement drawn out of the front. This message being brought him just as he was giving the signal to those about him for the onset, he bade

them tell Parmenio that he must have surely lost the use
of his reason, and had forgotten, in his alarm, that soldiers, if victorious, became masters of their enemies' baggage; and if defeated, instead of taking care of their wealth
or their slaves, have nothing more to do but to fight gallantly and die with honour. When he had said this, he put
on his helmet, having the rest of his arms on before he
came out of his tent, which were a coat of the Sicilian make,
girt close about him, and over that a breast-piece of thickly
quilted linen, which was taken among other booty at the
battle of Issus. The helmet, which was made by Theophilus,
though of iron, was so well wrought and polished that it
was as bright as the most refined silver. To this was fitted
a gorget of the same metal, set with precious stones. His
sword, which was the weapon he most used in fight, was
given him by the King of the Citieans, and was of an admirable temper and lightness. The belt which he also wore
in all engagements was of much richer workmanship than
the rest of his armour. It was a work of the ancient Helicon,
and had been presented to him by the Rhodians, as a mark
of their respect to him. So long as he was engaged in drawing up his men, or riding about to give orders or directions,
or to view them, he spared Bucephalus, who was now growing old, and made use of another horse; but when he was
actually to fight, he sent for him again, and as soon as he
was mounted, commenced the attack.

He made the longest address that day to the Thessalians
and other Greeks, who answered him with loud shouts, desiring him to lead them on against the barbarians, upon
which he shifted his javelin into his left hand, and with his
right lifted up towards heaven, besought the gods, as Callisthenes tells us, that if he was of a truth the son of Jupiter, they would be pleased to assist and strengthen the Grecians. At the same time the augur Aristander, who had a
white mantle about him, and a crown of gold on his head,
rode by and showed them an eagle that soared just over
Alexander, and directed his flight towards the enemy; which
so animated the beholders, that after mutual encourage-
ments and exhortations, the horse charged at full speed, and

were followed in a mass by the whole phalanx of the foot.
But before they could well come to blows with the first
ranks, the barbarians shrunk back, and were hotly pursued
by Alexander, who drove those that fled before him into
the middle of the battle, where Darius himself was in
person, whom he saw from a distance over the foremost
ranks, conspicuous in the midst of his life-guard, a tall and
fine-looking man, drawn in a lofty chariot, defended by an
abundance of the best horse, who stood close in order about
it ready to receive the enemy. But Alexander's approach
was so terrible, forcing those who gave back upon those
who yet maintained their ground, that he beat down and
dispersed them almost all. Only a few of the bravest and
valiantest opposed the pursuit, who were slain in their king's
presence, falling in heaps upon one another, and in the
very pangs of death striving to catch hold of the horses.
Darius now seeing all was lost, that those who were placed
in front to defend him were broken and beat back upon
him, that he could not turn or disengage his chariot without great difficulty, the wheels being clogged and entangled
among the dead bodies, which lay in such heaps as not
only stopped, but almost covered the horses, and made
them rear and grow so unruly that the frightened chariot-
eer could govern them no longer, in this extremity was
glad to quit his chariot and his arms, and mounting, it is
said, upon a mare that had been taken from her foal, betook himself to flight. But he had not escaped so either, if
Parmenio had not sent fresh messengers to Alexander, to
desire him to return and assist him against a considerable
body of the enemy which yet stood together, and would not
give ground. For, indeed, Parmenio is on all hands accused
of having been sluggish and unserviceable in this battle,
whether age had impaired his courage, or that, as Callisthenes says, he secretly disliked and envied Alexander's
growing greatness. Alexander, though he was not a little
vexed to be so recalled and hindered from pursuing his victory, yet concealed the true reason from his men, and causing a retreat to be sounded, as if it were too late to continue
the execution any longer, marched back towards the place

of danger, and by the way met the news of the enemy's total overthrow and flight.

This battle being thus over, seemed to put a period to the Persian empire; and Alexander, who was now proclaimed King of Asia, returned thanks to the gods in magnificent sacrifices, and rewarded his friends and followers with great sums of money, and places, and governments of provinces. Eager to gain honour with the Grecians, he wrote to them that he would have all tyrannies abolished, that they might live free according to their own laws, and specially to the Plataeans, that their city should be rebuilt, because their ancestors had permitted their countrymen of old to make their territory the seat of the war when they fought with the barbarians for their common liberty. He sent also part of the spoils into Italy, to the Crotoniats, to honour the zeal and courage of their citizen Phayllus, the wrestler, who, in the Median war, when the other Grecian colonies in Italy disowned Greece, that he might have a share in the danger, joined the fleet at Salamis, with a vessel set forth at his own charge. So affectionate was Alexander to all kind of virtue, and so desirous to preserve the memory of laudable actions.

From hence he marched through the province of Babylon, which immediately submitted to him, and in Ecbatana was much surprised at the sight of the place where fire issues in a continuous stream, like a spring of water, out of a cleft in the earth, and the stream of naphtha, which, not far from this spot, flows out so abundantly as to form a sort of lake. This naphtha, in other respects resembling bitumen, is so subject to take fire, that before it touches the flame it will kindle at the very light that surrounds it, and often inflame the intermediate air also. The barbarians, to show the power and nature of it, sprinkled the street that led to the king's lodgings with little drops of it, and when it was almost night, stood at the further end with torches, which being applied to the moistened places, the first at once taking fire, instantly, as quick as a man could think of it, it caught from one end to another, in such a manner that the whole street was one continued flame. Among those

who used to wait on the king and find occasion to amuse
him when he anointed and washed himself, there was one
Athenophanes, an Athenian, who desired him to make an
experiment of the naphtha upon Stephanus, who stood by
in the bathing place, a youth with a ridiculously ugly face,
whose talent was singing well, "For," said he, "if it take
hold of him and is not put out, it must undeniably be allowed to be the most invincible strength." The youth, as it
happened, readily consented to undergo the trial, and as
soon as he was anointed and rubbed with it, his whole body
broke out into such a flame, and was so seized by the fire,
that Alexander was in the greatest perplexity and alarm for
him, and not without reason; for nothing could have prevented his being consumed by it, if by good chance there
had not been people at hand with a great many vessels of
water for the service of the bath, with all which they had
much ado to extinguish the fire; and his body was so burned
all over that he was not cured of it for a good while after.
Thus it is not without some plausibility that they endeavour
to reconcile the fable to truth, who say this was the drug
in the tragedies with which Medea anointed the crown and
veil which she gave to Creon's daughter. For neither the
things themselves, nor the fire, could kindle of its own accord, but being prepared for it by the naphtha, they imper-
ceptibly attracted and caught a flame which happened to be
brought near them. For the rays and emanations of fire at
a distance have no other effect upon some bodies than bare
light and heat, but in others, where they meet with airy
dryness, and also sufficient rich moisture, they collect themselves and soon kindle and create a transformation. The
manner, however, of the production of naphtha admits of
a diversity of opinion . . . or whether this liquid substance
that feeds the flame does not rather proceed from a soil that
is unctuous and productive of fire, as that of the province
of Babylon is, where the ground is so very hot that oftentimes the grains of barley leap up and are thrown out, as
if the violent inflammation had made the earth throb; and
in the extreme heats the inhabitants are wont to sleep upon
skins filled with water. Harpalus, who was left governor of

this country, and was desirous to adorn the palace gardens and walks with Grecian plants, succeeded in raising all but ivy, which the earth would not bear, but constantly killed. For being a plant that loves a cold soil, the temper of this hot and fiery earth was improper for it. But such digressions as these the impatient reader will be more willing to pardon if they are kept within a moderate compass.

At the taking of Susa, Alexander found in the palace forty thousand talents in money ready coined, besides an unspeakable quantity of other furniture and treasure; amongst which was five thousand talents' worth of Hermionian purple, that had been laid up there an hundred and ninety years, and yet kept its colour as fresh and lively as at first. The reason of which, they say, is that in dyeing the purple they made use of honey, and of white oil in the white tincture, both which after the like space of time preserve the clearness and brightness of their lustre. Dinon also relates that the Persian kings had water fetched from the Nile and the Danube, which they laid up in their treasuries as a sort of testimony of the greatness of their power and universal empire.

The entrance into Persia was through a most difficult country, and was guarded by the noblest of the Persians, Darius himself having escaped further. Alexander, however, chanced to find a guide in exact correspondence with what the Pythia had foretold when he was a child, that a lycus should conduct him into Persia. For by such an one, whose father was a Lycian, and his mother a Persian, and who spoke both languages, he was now led into the country, by a way something about, yet without fetching any considerable compass. Here a great many of the prisoners were put to the sword, of which himself gives this account, that he commanded them to be killed in the belief that it would be for his advantage. Nor was the money found here less, he says, than at Susa, besides other movables and treasure, as much as ten thousand pair of mules and five thousand camels could well carry away. Amongst other things he happened to observe a large statue of Xerxes thrown carelessly down to the ground in the confusion made by the multitude of soldiers pressing into the palace. He stood still, and accosting it as if it had been alive, "Shall we," said he, "neglectfully pass thee by, now thou art prostrate on the ground because thou once invadedst Greece, or shall we erect thee again in consideration of the greatness of thy mind and thy other virtues?" But at last, after he had paused some time, and silently considered with himself, we went on without taking any further notice of it. In this place he took up his winter quarters, and stayed four months to refresh his soldiers. It is related that the first time he sat on the royal throne of Persia under the canopy of gold, Demaratus the Corinthian, who was much attached to him and had been one of his father's friends, wept, in an old man's manner, and deplored the misfortune of those Greeks whom death had deprived of the satisfaction of seeing Alexander seated on the throne of Darius.

From hence designing to march against Darius, before he set out he diverted himself with his officers at an entertainment of drinking and other pastimes, and indulged so far as to let every one's mistress sit by and drink with them. The most celebrated of them was Thais, an Athenian, mistress of Ptolemy, who was afterwards King of Egypt. She, partly as a sort of well-turned compliment to Alexander, partly out of sport, as the drinking went on, at last was carried so far as to utter a saying, not misbecoming her native country's character, though somewhat too lofty for her own condition. She said it was indeed some recompense for the toils she had undergone in following the camp all over Asia, that she was that day treated in, and could insult over, the stately palace of the Persian monarchs. But, she added, it would please her much better if, while the king looked on, she might in sport, with her own hands, set fire to the court of that Xerxes who reduced the city of Athens to ashes, that it might be recorded to posterity that the women who followed Alexander had taken a severer revenge on the Persians for the sufferings and affronts of Greece, than all the famed commanders had been able to do by sea or land. What she said was received with such universal liking and murmurs of applause, and so seconded by the encouragement and eagerness of the company, that the king himself, persuaded to be of the party, started from his seat, and with a chaplet of flowers on his head and a lighted torch in his hand, led them the way, while they went after him in a riotous manner, dancing and making loud cries about the place; which when the rest of the Macedonians perceived, they also in great delight ran thither with torches; for they hoped the burning and destruction of the royal palace was an argument that he looked homeward, and had no design to reside among the barbarians. Thus some writers give their account of this action, while others say it was done deliberately; however, all agree that he soon repented of it, and gave order to put out the fire.

Alexander was naturally most munificent, and grew more so as his fortune increased, accompanying what he gave with that courtesy and freedom which, to speak truth, is necessary to make a benefit really obliging. I will give a few instances of this kind. Ariston, the captain of the Paeonians, having killed an enemy, brought his head to show him, and told him that in his country such a present was recompensed with a cup of gold. "With an empty one," said Alexander, smiling, "but I drink to you in this, which I give you full of wine." Another time, as one of the common soldiers was driving a mule laden with some of the king's treasure, the beast grew tired, and the soldier took it upon his own back, and began to march with it, till Alexander seeing the man so overcharged asked what was the matter; and when he was informed, just as he was ready to lay down his burden for weariness, "Do not faint now," said he to him, "but finish the journey, and carry what you have there to your own tent for yourself." He was always more displeased with those who would not accept of what he gave than with those who begged of him. And therefore he wrote to Phocion, that he would not own him for his friend any longer if he refused his presents. He had never given anything to Serapion, one of the youths that played at ball with him, because he did not ask of him, till one day, it coming to Serapion's turn to play, he still threw

the ball to others, and when the king asked him why he did
not direct it to him, "Because you do not ask for it," said
he; which answer pleased him so that he was very liberal
to him afterwards. One Proteas, a pleasant, jesting, drinking fellow, having incurred his displeasure, got his friends
to intercede for him, and begged his pardon himself with
tears, which at last prevailed, and Alexander declared he
was friends with him. "I cannot believe it," said Proteas,
"unless you first give me some pledge of it." The king
understood his meaning, and presently ordered five talents
to be given him. How magnificent he was in enriching his
friends, and those who attended on his person, appears by
a letter which Olympias wrote to him, where she tells him
he should reward and honour those about him in a more
moderate way. "For now," said she, "you make them all
equal to kings, you give them power and opportunity of
making many friends of their own, and in the meantime
you leave yourself destitute." She often wrote to him to
this purpose, and he never communicated her letters to
anybody, unless it were one which he opened when Hephaestion was by, whom he permitted, as his custom was, to
read it along with him; but then as soon as he had done,
he took off his ring, and set the seal upon Hephaestion's
lips. Mazaeus, who was the most considerable man in Darius's court, had a son who was already governor of a province. Alexander bestowed another upon him that was better; he, however, modestly refused, and told him, instead
of one Darius, he went the way to make many Alexanders.
To Parmenio he gave Bagoas's house, in which he found a
wardrobe of apparel worth more than a thousand talents.
He wrote to Antipater, commanding him to keep a life-
guard about him for the security of his person against con-
spiracies. To his mother he sent many presents, but would
never suffer her to meddle with matters of state or war,
not indulging her busy temper, and when she fell out with
him on this account, he bore her ill-humour very patiently.
Nay more, when he read a long letter from Antipater full
of accusations against her, "Antipater," he said, "does not

know that one tear of a mother effaces a thousand such letters as these.".

But when he perceived his favourites grow so luxurious and extravagant in their way of living and expenses that Hagnon, the Teian, wore silver nails in his shoes, that Leonnatus employed several camels only to bring him powder out of Egypt to use when he wrestled, and that Philotas had hunting nets a hundred furlongs in length, that more used precious ointment than plain oil when they went to bathe, and that they carried about servants everywhere with them to rub them and wait upon them in their chambers, he reproved them in gentle and reasonable terms, telling them he wondered that they who had been engaged in so many single battles did not know by experience, that those who labour sleep more sweetly and soundly than those who are laboured for, and could fail to see by comparing the Persians' manner of living with their own that it was the most abject and slavish condition to be voluptuous, but the most noble and royal to undergo pain and labour. He argued with them further, how it was possible for any one who pretended to be a soldier, either to look well after his horse, or to keep his armour bright and in good order, who thought it much to let his hands be serviceable to what was nearest to him, his own body. "Are you still to learn," said he, "that the end and perfection of our victories is to avoid the vices and infirmities of those whom we subdue?" And to strengthen his precepts by example, he applied himself now more vigorously than ever to hunting and warlike expeditions, embracing all opportunities of hardship and danger, insomuch that a Lacedaemonian, who was there on an embassy to him, and chanced to be by when he encountered with and mastered a huge lion, told him he had fought gallantly with the beast, which of the two should be king. Craterus caused a representation to be made of this adventure, consisting of the lion and the dogs, of the king engaged with the lion, and himself coming in to his assistance, all expressed in figures of brass, some of which were by Lysippus, and the rest by Leochares; and had it dedicated in the temple of Apollo at Delphi. Alexander exposed his person to danger in this manner, with the object both of inuring himself and inciting others to the performance of brave and virtuous actions.

But his followers, who were grown rich, and consequently proud, longed to indulge themselves in pleasure and idleness, and were weary of marches and expeditions, and at last went on so far as to censure and speak ill of him. All which at first he bore very patiently, saying it became a king well to do good to others, and be evil spoken of. Meantime, on the smallest occasions that called for a show of kindness to his friends, there was every indication on his part of tenderness and respect. Hearing Peucestes was bitten by a bear, he wrote to him that he took it unkindly he should send others notice of it and not make him acquainted with it; "But now," said he, "since it is so, let me know how you do, and whether any of your companions forsook you when you were in danger, that I may punish them." He sent Hephaestion, who was absent about some business, word how, while they were fighting for their diversion with an ichneumon, Craterus was by chance run through both thighs with Perdiccas's javelin. And upon Peucestes's recovery from a fit of sickness, he sent a letter of thanks to his physician Alexippus. When Craterus was ill, he saw a vision in his sleep, after which he offered sacrifices for his health, and bade him do so likewise. He wrote also to Pausanias, the physician, who was about to purge Craterus with hellebore, partly out of an anxious concern for him, and partly to give him a caution how he used that medicine. He was so tender of his friends' reputation that he imprisoned Ephialtes and Cissus, who brought him the first news of Harpalus's flight and withdrawal from his service, as if they had falsely accused him. When he sent the old and infirm soldiers home, Eurylochus, a citizen of Aegae, got his name enrolled among the sick, though he ailed nothing, which being discovered, he confessed he was in love with a young woman named Telesippa, and wanted to go along with her to the sea-side. Alexander inquired to whom the woman belonged, and being told she was a free courtesan, "I will assist you," said he to Eurylochus, "in your armour if your mistress be to be gained either by presents or persuasions; but we must use no other means, because she is free-born."

It is surprising to consider upon what slight occasions he would write letters to serve his friends. As when he wrote one in which he gave order to search for a youth that belonged to Seleucus, who was run away into Cilicia; and in another thanked and commended Peucestes for apprehending Nicon, a servant of Craterus; and in one to Megabyzus, concerning a slave that had taken sanctuary in a temple, gave direction that he should not meddle with him while he was there, but if he could entice him out by fair means, then he gave him leave to seize him. It is reported of him that when he first sat in judgment upon capital causes he would lay his hand upon one of his ears while the accuser spoke, to keep it free and unprejudiced in behalf of the party accused. But afterwards such a multitude of accusations were brought before him, and so many proved true, that he lost his tenderness of heart, and gave credit to those also that were false; and especially when anybody spoke ill of him, he would be transported out of his reason, and show himself cruel and inexorable, valuing his glory and reputation beyond his life or kingdom.

He now, as we said, set forth to seek Darius, expecting he should be put to the hazard of another battle, but heard he was taken and secured by Bessus, upon which news he sent home the Thessalians, and gave them a largess of two thousand talents over and above the pay that was due to them. This long and painful pursuit of Darius—for in eleven days he marched thirty-three hundred furlongs— harassed his soldiers so that most of them were ready to give it up, chiefly for want of water. While they were in this distress, it happened that some Macedonians who had fetched water in skins upon their mules from a river they had found out came about noon to the place where Alexander was, and seeing him almost choked with thirst, presently filled an helmet and offered it him. He asked them to whom they were carrying the water; they told him to their children, adding, that if his life were but saved, it was no matter for them, they should be able well enough to repair that loss, though they all perished. Then he took the helmet into his hands, and looking round about, when he saw all those who were near him stretching their heads out and looking earnestly after the drink, he returned it again with thanks without tasting a drop of it. "For," said he, "if I alone drink, the rest will be out of heart." The soldiers no sooner took notice of his temperance and magnanimity upon this occasion, but they one and all cried out to him to lead them forward boldly, and began whipping on their horses. For whilst they had such a king they said they defied both weariness and thirst, and looked upon themselves to be little less than immortal. But though they were all equally cheerful and willing, yet not above threescore horse were able, it is said, to keep up, and to fall in with Alexander upon the enemy's camp, where they rode over abundance of gold and silver that lay scattered about, and passing by a great many chariots full of women that wandered here and there for want of drivers, they endeavoured to overtake the first of those that fled, in hopes to meet with Darius among them. And at last, after much trouble, they found him lying in a chariot, wounded all over with darts, just at the point of death. However, he desired they would give him some drink, and when he had drunk a little cold water, he told Polystratus, who gave it him, that it had become the last extremity of his ill fortune to receive benefits and not be able to return them. "But Alexander," said he, "whose kindness to my mother, my wife, and my children I hope the gods will recompense, will doubtless thank you for your humanity to me. Tell him, therefore, in token of my acknowledgment, I give him this right hand," with which words he took hold of Polystratus's hand and died. When Alexander came up to them, he showed manifest tokens of sorrow, and taking off his own cloak, threw it upon the body to cover it. And some time afterwards, when Bessus was taken, he ordered him to be torn in pieces in this manner. They fastened him to a couple of trees which were bound down so as to meet, and then being let loose, with a great force returned to their places, each of them carrying that part of the body along with it that was tied to it. Darius's body was laid in state, and sent to his mother with pomp suitable to his quality. His brother Exathres, Alexander received into the number of his intimate friends.

And now with the flower of his army he marched into Hyrcania, where he saw a large bay of an open sea, apparently not much less than the Euxine, with water, however, sweeter than that of other seas, but could learn nothing of certainty concerning it, further than that in all probability it seemed to him to be an arm issuing from the lake of Maeotis. However, the naturalists were better informed of the truth, and had given an account of it many years before Alexander's expedition; that of four gulfs which out of the main sea enter into the continent, this, known indifferently as the Caspian and as the Hyrcanian Sea, is the most northern. Here the barbarians, unexpectedly meeting with those who led Bucephalus, took them prisoners, and carried the horse away with them, at which Alexander was so much vexed that he sent an herald to let them know he would put them all to the sword, men, women, and children, without mercy, if they did not restore him. But on their doing so, and at the same time surrendering their cities into his hands, he not only treated them kindly, but also paid a ransom for his horse to those who took him.

From hence he marched into Parthia, where not having much to do, he first put on the barbaric dress, perhaps with the view of making the work of civilising them the easier, as nothing gains more upon men than a conformity to their fashions and customs. Or it may have been as a first trial, whether the Macedonians might be brought to *adore* as the Persians did their kings, by accustoming them by little and little to bear with the alteration of his rule and course of life in other things. However, he followed not the Median fashion, which was altogether foreign and uncouth, and adopted neither the trousers nor the sleeved vest, nor the tiara for the head, but taking a middle way between the Persian mode and the Macedonian, so contrived his habit that

it was not so flaunting as the one, and yet more pompous
and magnificent than the other. At first he wore this habit
only when he conversed with the barbarians, or within
doors, among his intimate friends and companions, but afterwards he appeared in it abroad, when he rode out, and at
public audiences, a sight which the Macedonians beheld
with grief; but they so respected his other virtues and good
qualities that they felt it reasonable in some things to
gratify his fancies and his passion of glory, in pursuit of
which he hazarded himself so far, that, besides his other
adventures, he had but lately been wounded in the leg by
an arrow, which had so shattered the shank-bone that
splinters were taken out. And on another occasion he received a violent blow with a stone upon the nape of the
neck, which dimmed his sight for a good while afterwards.
And yet all this could not hinder him from exposing himself freely to any dangers, insomuch that he passed the river
Orexartes, which he took to be the Tanais, and putting the
Scythians to flight, followed them above a hundred furlongs, though suffering all the time from a diarrhoea.

Here many affirm that the Amazon came to give him a
visit. So Clitarchus, Polyclitus, Onesicritus, Antigenes, and
Ister tell us. But Aristobulus and Chares, who held the
office of reporter of requests, Ptolemy and Anticlides, Phi-
lon the Theban, Philip of Theangela, Hecataeus the
Eretrian, Philip the Chalcidian, and Duris the Samian, say it
is wholly a fiction. And truly Alexander himself seems to
confirm the latter statement, for in a letter in which he
gives Antipater an account of all that happened, he tells
him that the King of Scythia offered him his daughter in
marriage, but makes no mention at all of the Amazon. And
many years after, when Onesicritus read this story in his
fourth book to Lysimachus, who then reigned, the king
laughed quietly and asked, "Where could I have been at
that time?"

But it signifies little to Alexander whether this be credited
or no. Certain it is, that apprehending the Macedonians
would be weary of pursuing the war, he left the greater part
of them in their quarters; and having with him in Hyrcania

the choice of his men only, amounting to twenty thousand foot and three thousand horse, he spoke to them to this effect: That hitherto the barbarians had seen them no otherwise than as it were in a dream, and if they should think of returning when they had only alarmed Asia, and not conquered it, their enemies would set upon them as upon so many women. However he told them he would keep none of them with him against their will, they might go if they pleased; he should merely enter his protest, that when on his way to make the Macedonians the masters of the world, he was left alone with a few friends and volunteers. This is almost word for word, as he wrote in a letter to Antipater, where he adds, that when he had thus spoken to them, they all cried out, they would go along with him whithersoever it was his pleasure to lead them. After succeeding with these, it was no hard matter for him to bring over the multitude, which easily followed the example of their betters. Now, also, he more and more accommodated himself in his way of living to that of the natives, and tried to bring them also as near as he could to the Macedonian customs, wisely considering that whilst he was engaged in an expedition which would carry him far from thence, it would be wiser to depend upon the good-will which might arise from intermixture and association as a means of maintaining tranquillity, than upon force and compulsion. In order to do this, he chose out thirty thousand boys, whom he put under masters to teach them the Greek tongue, and to train them up to arms in the Macedonian discipline. As for his marriage with Roxana, whose youthfulness and beauty had charmed him at a drinking entertainment, where he first happened to see her taking part in a dance, it was, indeed a love affair, yet it seemed at the same time to be conducive to the object he had in hand. For it gratified the conquered people to see him choose a wife from among themselves, and it made them feel the most lively affection for him, to find that in the only passion which he, the most temperate of men, was overcome by, he yet forbore till he could obtain her in a lawful and honourable way.

Noticing also that among his chief friends and favourites,

Hephaestion most approved all that he did, and complied
with and imitated him in his change of habits, while Craterus continued strict in the observation of the customs and
fashions of his own country, he made it his practice to employ the first in all transactions with the Persians, and the
latter when he had to do with the Greeks or Macedonians.
And in general he showed more affection for Hephaestion,
and more respect for Craterus; Hephaestion, as he used to
say, being Alexander's, and Craterus the king's friend. And
so these two friends always bore in secret a grudge to each
other, and at times quarrelled openly, so much so that once
in India they drew upon one another, and were proceeding
in good earnest, with their friends on each side to second
them, when Alexander rode up and publicly reproved Hephaestion, calling him fool and madman, not to be sensible
that without his favour he was nothing. He rebuked Craterus also in private, severely, and then causing them both
to come into his presence, he reconciled them, at the same
time swearing by Ammon and the rest of the gods, that he
loved them two above all other men, but if ever he perceived them fall out again he would be sure to put both of
them to death, or at least the aggressor. After which they
neither ever did or said anything, so much as in jest, to
offend one another.

There was scarcely any one who had greater repute
among the Macedonians than Philotas, the son of Parmenio. For besides that he was valiant and able to endure
any fatigue of war, he was also next to Alexander himself
the most munificent, and the greatest lover of his friends,
one of whom asking him for some money, he commanded
his steward to give it him; and when he told him he had not
wherewith, "Have you not any plate, then," said he, "or
any clothes of mine to sell?" But he carried his arrogance
and his pride of wealth and his habits of display and luxury
to a degree of assumption unbecoming a private man; and
affecting all the loftiness without succeeding in showing any
of the grace or gentleness of true greatness, by this mis-
taken and spurious majesty, he gained so much envy and
ill-will, that Parmenio would sometimes tell him, "My son,

to be not quite so great would be better." For he had long
before been complained of, and accused to Alexander. Particularly when Darius was defeated in Cilicia, and an immense booty was taken at Damascus, among the rest of the
prisoners who were brought into the camp, there was one
Antigone of Pydna, a very handsome woman, who fell to
Philotas's share. The young man one day in his cups, in the
vaunting, outspoken, soldier's manner, declared to his mistress, that all the great actions were performed by him and
his father, the glory and benefit of which, he said, together
with the title of king, the boy Alexander reaped and enjoyed by their means. She could not hold, but discovered
what he had said to one of her acquaintance, and he, as is
usual in such cases, to another, till at last the story came to
the ears of Craterus, who brought the woman secretly to
the king. When Alexander had heard what she had to say,
he commanded her to continue her intrigue with Philotas,
and give him an account from time to time of all that
should fall from him to this purpose. He, thus unwittingly
caught in a snare, to gratify sometimes a fit of anger, sometimes a love of vainglory, let himself utter numerous foolish, indiscreet speeches against the king in Antigone's hearing, of which, though Alexander was informed and convinced by strong evidence, yet he would take no notice of
it at present, whether it was that he confided in Parmenio's
affection and loyalty, or that he apprehended their authority
and interest in the army. But about this time, one Limnus,
a Macedonian of Chalastra, conspired against Alexander's
life, and communicated his design to a youth whom he was
fond of, named Nicomachus, inviting him to be of the
party. But he not relishing the thing, revealed it to his
brother Balinus, who immediately addressed himself to Philotas, requiring him to introduce them both to Alexander,
to whom they had something of great moment to impart
which very nearly concerned him. But he, for what reason
is uncertain, went not with them, professing that the king
was engaged with affairs of more importance. And when
they had urged him a second time, and were still slighted
by him, they applied themselves to another, by whose means

being admitted into Alexander's presence, they first told
about Limnus's conspiracy, and by the way let Philotas's
negligence appear who had twice disregarded their application to him. Alexander was greatly incensed, and on finding
that Limnus had defended himself, and had been killed by
the soldier who was sent to seize him, he was still more discomposed, thinking he had thus lost the means of detecting
the plot. As soon as his displeasure against Philotas began
to appear, presently all his old enemies showed themselves,
and said openly, the king was too easily imposed on, to
imagine that one so inconsiderable as Limnus, a Chalas-
trian, should of his own head undertake such an enterprise;
that in all likelihood he was but subservient to the design,
an instrument that was moved by some greater spring; that
those ought to be more strictly examined about the matter
whose interest it was so much to conceal it. When they had
once gained the king's ear for insinuations of this sort, they
went on to show a thousand grounds of suspicion against
Philotas, till at last they prevailed to have him seized and
put to the torture, which was done in the presence of the
principal officers, Alexander himself being placed behind
some tapestry to understand what passed. Where, when he
heard in what a miserable tone, and with what abject sub-
missions Philotas applied himself to Hephaestion, he broke
out, it is said, in this manner: "Are you so mean-spirited
and effeminate, Philotas, and yet can engage in so desperate a design?" After his death, he presently sent into
Media, and put also Parmenio, his father, to death, who had
done brave service under Philip, and was the only man of
his older friends and counsellors who had encouraged Alexander to invade Asia. Of three sons whom he had had in
the army, he had already lost two, and now was himself put
to death with the third. These actions rendered Alexander
an object of terror to many of his friends, and chiefly to
Antipater, who, to strengthen himself, sent messengers privately to treat for an alliance with the Aetolians, who stood
in fear of Alexander, because they had destroyed the town
of the Oeniadae; on being informed of which, Alexander
had said the children of the Oeniadae need not revenge their

father's quarrel, for he would himself take care to punish the Aetolians.

Not long after this happened the deplorable end of Clitus, which, to those who barely hear the matter, may seem more inhuman than that of Philotas; but if we consider the story with its circumstance of time, and weigh the cause, we shall find it to have occurred rather through a sort of mischance of the king's, whose anger and over-drinking offered an occasion to the evil genius of Clitus. The king had a present of Grecian fruit brought him from the sea-coast, which was so fresh and beautiful that he was surprised at it, and called Clitus to him to see it, and to give him a share of it. Clitus was then sacrificing, but he immediately left off and came, followed by three sheep, on whom the drink-offering had been already poured preparatory to sacrificing them. Alexander, being informed of this, told his diviners, Aristander and Cleomantis the Lacedaemonian, and asked them what it meant; on whose assuring him it was an ill omen, he commanded them in all haste to offer sacrifices for Clitus's safety, forasmuch as three days before he himself had seen a strange vision in his sleep, of Clitus all in mourning, sitting by Parmenio's sons who were dead. Clitus, however, stayed not to finish his devotions, but came straight to supper with the king, who had sacrificed to Castor and Pollux. And when they had drunk pretty hard, some of the company fell a-singing the verses of one Pranichus, or as others say of Pierion, which were made upon those captains who had been lately worsted by the barbarians, on purpose to disgrace and turn them to ridicule. This gave offence to the older men who were there, and they upbraided both the author and the singer of the verses, though Alexander and the younger men about him were much amused to hear them, and encouraged them to go on, till at last Clitus, who had drunk too much, and was besides of a forward and wilful temper, was so nettled that he could hold no longer, saying it was not well done to expose the Macedonians before the barbarians and their enemies, since though it was their unhappiness to be overcome, yet they were much better men than those who laughed at them. And when Alexander remarked, that Clitus was pleading his own cause, giving cowardice the name of misfortune, Clitus started up: "This cowardice, as you are pleased to term it," said he to him, "saved the life of a son of the gods, when in flight from Spithridates's sword; it is by the expense of Macedonian blood, and by these wounds, that you are now raised to such a height as to be able to disown your father Philip, and call yourself the son of Ammon." "Thou base fellow," said Alexander, who was now thoroughly exasperated, "dost thou think to utter these things everywhere of me, and stir up the Macedonians to sedition, and not be punished for it?" "We are sufficiently punished already," answered Clitus, "if this be the recompense of our toils, and we must esteem theirs a happy lot who have not lived to see their countrymen scourged with Median rods and forced to sue to the Persians to have access to their king." While he talked thus at random, and those near Alexander got up from their seats and began to revile him in turn, the elder men did what they could to compose the disorder. Alexander, in the meantime turning about to Xenodochus, the Pardian, and Artemius, the Colophonian, asked him if they were not of opinion that the Greeks, in comparison with the Macedonians, behaved themselves like so many demigods among wild beasts. But Clitus for all this would not give over, desiring Alexander to speak out if he had anything more to say, or else why did he invite men who were freeborn and accustomed to speak their minds openly without restraint to sup with him. He had better live and converse with barbarians and slaves who would not scruple to bow the knee to his Persian girdle and his white tunic. Which words so provoked Alexander that, not able to suppress his anger any longer, he threw one of the apples that lay upon the table at him, and hit him, and then looked about for his sword. But Aristophanes, one of his life-guard, had hid that out of the way, and others came about him and besought him, but in vain; for, breaking from them, he called out aloud to his guards in the Macedonian language, which was a certain sign of some great disturbance in him, and commanded a trumpeter to sound, giving him a blow with his clenched fist for not instantly obeying him; though afterwards the same man was commended for disobeying an order which would have put the whole army into tumult and confusion. Clitus still refusing to yield, was with much trouble forced by his friends out of the room. But he came in again immediately at another door, very irreverently and confidently singing the verses out of Euripides's Andromache,—

"In Greece, alas! how ill things ordered are!"

Upon this, at last, Alexander, snatching a spear from one of the soldiers, met Clitus as he was coming forward and was putting by the curtain that hung before the door, and ran him through the body. He fell at once with a cry and a groan. Upon which the king's anger immediately vanishing, he came perfectly to himself, and when he saw his friends about him all in a profound silence, he pulled the spear out of the dead body, and would have thrust it into his own throat, if the guards had not held his hands, and by main force carried him away into his chamber, where all that night and the next day he wept bitterly, till being quite spent with lamenting and exclaiming, he lay as it were speechless, only fetching deep sighs. His friends apprehending some harm from his silence, broke into the room, but he took no notice of what any of them said, till Aristander putting him in mind of the vision he had seen concerning Clitus, and the prodigy that followed, as if all had come to pass by an unavoidable fatality, he then seemed to moderate his grief. They now brought Callisthenes, the philosopher, who was the near friend of Aristotle, and Anaxarchus of Abdera, to him. Callisthenes used moral language, and gentle and soothing means, hoping to find access for words of reason, and get a hold upon the passion. But Anaxarchus, who had always taken a course of his own in philosophy, and had a name for despising and slighting his contemporaries, as soon as he came in, cried aloud, "Is this the Alexander whom the whole world looks to, lying here weeping like a slave, for fear of the censure and reproach of men, to whom he himself ought to be a law and measure of equity, if he would use the right his conquests have given him as supreme lord and governor of all, and not be the victim of a vain and idle opinion? Do not you know," said he, "that Jupiter is represented to have Justice and Law on each hand of him, to signify that all the actions of a conqueror are lawful and just?" With these and the like speeches, Anaxarchus indeed allayed the king's grief, but withal corrupted his character, rendering him more audacious and lawless than he had been. Nor did he fail these means to insinuate himself into his favour, and to make Callisthenes's company, which at all times, because of his austerity, was not very acceptable, more uneasy and disagreeable to him.

It happened that these two philosophers met at an entertainment where conversation turned on the subject of climate and the temperature of the air. Callisthenes joined with their opinion, who held that those countries were colder, and the winter sharper there than in Greece. Anaxarchus would by no means allow this, but argued against it with some heat. "Surely," said Callisthenes, "you cannot but admit this country to be colder than Greece, for there you used to have but one threadbare cloak to keep out the coldest winter, and here you have three good warm mantles one over another." This piece of raillery irritated Anaxarchus and the other pretenders to learning, and the crowd of flatterers in general could not endure to see Callisthenes so much admired and followed by the youth, and no less esteemed by the older men for his orderly life and his gravity and for being contented with his condition; and confirming what he had professed about the object he had in his journey to Alexander, that it was only to get his countrymen recalled from banishment, and to rebuild and repeople his native town. Besides the envy which his great reputation raised, he also, by his own deportment, gave those who wished him ill opportunity to do him mischief. For when he was invited to public entertainments, he would most times refuse to come, or if he were present at any, he put a constraint upon the company by his austerity

and silence, which seemed to intimate his disapproval of
what he saw. So that Alexander himself said in application
to him,—

> "That vain pretence to wisdom I detest,
> Where a man's blind to his own interest."

Being with many more invited to sup with the king, he was
called upon when the cup came to him, to make an oration
extempore in praise of the Macedonians; and he did it with
such a flow of eloquence, that all who heard it rose from
their seats to clap and applaud him, and threw their garland upon him; only Alexander told him out of Euripides,—

> "I wonder not that you have spoke so well,
> 'Tis easy on good subjects to excel."

"Therefore," said he, "if you will show the force of your
eloquence, tell my Macedonians their faults, and dispraise
them, that by hearing their errors they may learn to be better for the future." Callisthenes presently obeyed him, re-
tracting all he had said before, and, inveighing against the
Macedonians with great freedom, added, that Philip thrived
and grew powerful, chiefly by the discord of the Grecians,
applying this verse to him,—

> "In civil strife e'en villains rise to fame;"

which so offended the Macedonians, that he was odious to
them ever after. And Alexander said, that instead of his eloquence, he had only made his ill-will appear in what he had
spoken. Hermippus assures us that one Stroebus, a servant
whom Callisthenes kept to read to him, gave this account of
these passages afterwards to Aristotle; and that when he
perceived the king grow more and more averse to him, two
or three times, as he was going away, he repeated the
verses,—

"Death seiz'd at last on great Patroclus too,
    Though he in virtue far exceeded you."

Not without reason, therefore, did Aristotle give this character of Callisthenes, that he was, indeed, a powerful speaker, but had no judgment. He acted certainly a true philosopher's part in positively refusing, as he did, to pay adoration; and by speaking out openly against that which the best and gravest of the Macedonians only repined at in secret, he delivered the Grecians and Alexander himself from a great disgrace, when the practice was given up. But he ruined himself by it, because he went too roughly to work, as if he would have forced the king to that which he should have effected by reason and persuasion. Chares of Mitylene writes, that at a banquet Alexander, after he had drunk, reached the cup to one of his friends, who, on receiving it, rose up towards the domestic altar, and when he had drunk, first adored and then kissed Alexander, and afterwards laid himself down at the table with the rest. Which they all did one after another, till it came to Callisthenes's turn, who took the cup and drank, while the king, who was engaged in conversation with Hephaestion, was not observing, and then came and offered to kiss him. But Demetrius, surnamed Phidon, interposed, saying, "Sir, by no means let him kiss you, for he only of us all has refused to adore you;" upon which the king declined it, and all the concern Callisthenes showed was, that he said aloud, "Then I go away with a kiss less than the rest." The displeasure he incurred by this action procured credit for Hephaestion's declaration that he had broken his word to him in not paying the king the same veneration that others did, as he had faithfully promised to do. And to finish his disgrace, a number of such men as Lysimachus and Hagnon now came in with their asseverations that the sophist went about everywhere boasting of his resistance to arbitrary power, and that the young men all ran after him, and honoured him as the only man among so many thousands who had the courage to preserve his liberty. Therefore when Hermolaus's conspiracy came to be discovered, the charges which his enemies brought against him were the more easily believed, particularly that when the young man asked him what he should do to be the most illustrious person on earth, he told him the readiest way was to kill him who was already so, and that to incite him to commit the deed, he bade him not be awed by the golden couch, but remember Alexander was a man equally infirm and vulnerable as another. However, none of Hermolaus's accomplices, in the utmost extremity, made any mention of Callisthenes's being engaged in the design. Nay, Alexander himself, in the letters which he wrote soon after to Craterus, Attalus, and Alcetas, tells them that the young men who were put to the torture declared they had entered into the conspiracy of themselves, without any others being privy to or guilty of it. But yet afterwards, in a letter to Antipater, he accuses Callisthenes. "The young men," he says, "were stoned to death by the Macedonians, but for the sophist" (meaning Callisthenes), "I will take care to punish him with them too who sent him to me, and who harbour those in their cities who conspire against my life," an unequivocal declaration against Aristotle, in whose house Callisthenes, for his relationship's sake, being his niece Hero's son, had been educated. His death is variously related. Some say he was hanged by Alexander's orders; others, that he died of sickness in prison; but Chares writes he was kept in chains seven months after he was apprehended, on purpose that he might be proceeded against in full council, when Aristotle should be present; and that growing very fat, and contracting a disease of vermin, he there died, about the time that Alexander was wounded in India, in the country of the Malli Oxydracae, all which came to pass afterwards.

For to go on in order, Demaratus of Corinth, now quite an old man, had made a great effort, about this time, to pay Alexander a visit; and when he had seen him, said he pitied the misfortune of those Grecians, who were so unhappy as to die before they had beheld Alexander seated on the throne of Darius. But he did not long enjoy the benefit of the king's kindness for him, any otherwise than that soon after falling sick and dying, he had a magnificent funeral, and the army raised him a monument of earth fourscore cubits high, and of a vast circumference. His ashes were conveyed in a very rich chariot, drawn by four horses, to the seaside.

Alexander, now intent upon his expedition into India, took notice that his soldiers were so charged with booty that it hindered their marching. Therefore, at break of day, as soon as the baggage waggons were laden, first he set fire to his own, and to those of his friends, and then commanded those to be burnt which belonged to the rest of the army. An act which in the deliberation of it had seemed more dangerous and difficult than it proved in the execution, with which few were dissatisfied; for most of the soldiers, as if they had been inspired, uttering loud outcries and warlike shoutings, supplied one another with what was absolutely necessary, and burnt and destroyed all that was superfluous, the sight of which redoubled Alexander's zeal and eagerness for his design. And, indeed, he was now grown very severe and inexorable in punishing those who committed any fault. For he put Menander, one of his friends, to death for deserting a fortress where he had placed him in garrison, and shot Orsodates, one of the barbarians who revolted from him, with his own hand.

At this time a sheep happened to yean a lamb, with the perfect shape and colour of a tiara upon the head, and testicles on each side; which portent Alexander regarded with such dislike, that he immediately caused his Babylonian priests, whom he usually carried about with him for such purposes, to purify him, and told his friends he was not so much concerned for his own sake as for theirs, out of an apprehension that after his death the divine power might suffer his empire to fall into the hands of some degenerate, impotent person. But this fear was soon removed by a wonderful thing that happened not long after, and was thought to presage better. For Proxenus, a Macedonian, who was the chief of those who looked to the king's furniture, as he was breaking up the ground near the river Oxus, to set up the royal pavilion, discovered a spring of a fat oily liquor, which, after the top was taken off, ran pure, clear oil, with-

out any difference either of taste or smell, having exactly
the same smoothness and brightness, and that, too, in a
country where no olives grew. The water, indeed, of the
river Oxus, is said to be the smoothest to the feeling of all
waters, and to leave a gloss on the skins of those who bathe
themselves in it. Whatever might be the cause, certain it is
that Alexander was wonderfully pleased with it, as appears
by his letters to Antipater, where he speaks of it as one of
the most remarkable presages that God had ever favoured
him with. The diviners told him it signified his expedition
would be glorious in the event, but very painful and attended with many difficulties; for oil, they said, was bestowed on mankind by God as a refreshment of their labours.

Nor did they judge amiss, for he exposed himself to
many hazards in the battles which he fought, and received
very severe wounds, but the greatest loss in his army was
occasioned through the unwholesomeness of the air and
the want of necessary provisions. But he still applied himself to overcome fortune and whatever opposed him, by
resolution and virtue, and thought nothing impossible to
true intrepidity, and on the other hand nothing secure or
strong for cowardice. It is told of him that when he besieged Sisimithres, who held an inaccessible, impregnable
rock against him, and his soldiers began to despair of taking it, he asked Oxyartes whether Sisimithres was a man of
courage, who assuring him he was the greatest coward alive,
"Then you tell me," said he, "that the place may easily be
taken, since what is in command of it is weak." And in a
little time he so terrified Sisimithres that he took it without
any difficulty. At an attack which he made upon such another precipitous place with some of his Macedonian soldiers, he called to one whose name was Alexander, and told
him he at any rate must fight bravely if it were but for his
name's sake. The youth fought gallantly and was killed in
the action, at which he was sensibly afflicted. Another time,
seeing his men march slowly and unwillingly to the siege of
the place called Nysa, because of a deep river between them
and the town, he advanced before them, and standing upon

the bank, "What a miserable man," said he, "am I, that I
have not learned to swim!" and then was hardly dissuaded
from endeavouring to pass it upon his shield. Here, after the
assault was over, the ambassadors who from several towns
which he had blocked up came to submit to him and make
their peace, were surprised to find him still in his armour,
without any one in waiting or attendance upon him, and
when at last some one brought him a cushion, he made the
eldest of them, named Acuphis, take it and sit down upon
it. The old man, marvelling at his magnanimity and courtesy, asked him what his countrymen should do to merit
his friendship. "I would have them," said Alexander,
"choose you to govern them, and send one hundred of the
most worthy men among them to remain with me as hostages." Acuphis laughed and answered, "I shall govern
them with more ease, sir, if I send you so many of the
worst, rather than the best of my subjects."

The extent of King Taxiles's dominions in India was
thought to be as large as Egypt, abounding in good pas-
tures, and producing beautiful fruits. The king himself had
the reputation of a wise man, and at his first interview with
Alexander he spoke to him in these terms: "To what purpose," said he, "should we make war upon one another, if
the design of your coming into these parts be not to rob us
of our water or our necessary food, which are the only
things that wise men are indispensably obliged to fight for?
As for other riches and possessions, as they are accounted
in the eye of the world, if I am better provided of them than
you, I am ready to let you share with me; but if fortune
has been more liberal to you than me, I have no ob-
jection to be obliged to you." This discourse pleased
Alexander so much that, embracing him, "Do you think,"
said he to him, "your kind words and courteous behaviour will bring you off in this interview without a
contest? No, you shall not escape so. I shall contend and
do battle with you so far, that how obliging soever you are,
you shall not have the better of me." Then receiving some
presents from him, he returned him others of greater value,
and to complete his bounty gave him in money ready coined

one thousand talents; at which his old friends were much displeased, but it gained him the hearts of many of the barbarians. But the best soldiers of the Indians now entering into the pay of several of the cities, undertook to defend them, and did it so bravely, that they put Alexander to a great deal of trouble, till at last, after a capitulation, upon the surrender of the place, he fell upon them as they were marching away, and put them all to the sword. This one breach of his word remains as a blemish upon his achievements in war, which he otherwise had performed throughout with that justice and honour that became a king. Nor was he less incommoded by the Indian philosophers, who inveighed against those princes who joined his party, and solicited the free nations to oppose him. He took several of these also and caused them to be hanged.

Alexander, in his own letters, has given us an account of his war with Porus. He says the two armies were separated by the river Hydaspes, on whose opposite bank Porus continually kept his elephants in order of battle, with their heads towards their enemies, to guard the passage; that he, on the other hand, made every day a great noise and clamour in his camp, to dissipate the apprehensions of the barbarians; that one stormy dark night he passed the river, at a distance from the place where the enemy lay, into a little island, with part of his foot and the best of his horse. Here there fell a most violent storm of rain, accompanied with lightning and whirlwinds, and seeing some of his men burnt and dying with the lightning, he nevertheless quitted the island and made over to the other side. The Hydaspes, he says, now after the storm, was so swollen and grown so rapid as to have made a breach in the bank, and a part of the river was now pouring in here, so that when he came across it was with difficulty he got a footing on the land, which was slippery and unsteady, and exposed to the force of the currents on both sides. This is the occasion when he is related to have said, "O ye Athenians, will ye believe what dangers I incur to merit your praise?" This, however, is Onesicritus's story. Alexander says, here the men left their boats, and passed the breach in their armour, up to the breast in water, and that then he advanced with his horse about twenty furlongs before his foot, concluding that if the enemy charged him with their cavalry he should be too strong for them; if with their foot, his own would come up in time enough to his assistance. Nor did he judge amiss; for being charged by a thousand horse and sixty armed chariots, which advanced before their main body, he took all the chariots, and killed four hundred horse upon the place. Porus, by this time, guessing that Alexander himself had crossed over, came on with his whole army, except a party which he left behind, to hold the rest of the Macedonians in play, if they should attempt to pass the river. But he, apprehending the multitude of the enemy, and to avoid the shock of their elephants, dividing his forces, attacked their left wing himself, and commanded Coenus to fall upon the right, which was performed with good success. For by this means both wings being broken, the enemies fell back in their retreat upon the centre, and crowded in upon their elephants. There rallying, they fought a hand-to-hand battle, and it was the eighth hour of the day before they were entirely defeated. This description the conqueror himself has left us in his own epistles.

Almost all the historians agree in relating that Porus was four cubits and a span high, and that when he was upon his elephant, which was of the largest size, his stature and bulk were so answerable, that he appeared to be proportionately mounted, as a horseman on his horse. This elephant, during the whole battle, gave many singular proofs of sagacity and of particular care of the king, whom as long as he was strong and in a condition to fight, he defended with great courage, repelling those who set upon him; and as soon as he perceived him overpowered with his numerous wounds and the multitude of darts that were thrown at him, to prevent his falling off, he softly knelt down and began to draw out the darts with his proboscis. When Porus was taken prisoner, and Alexander asked him how he expected to be used, he answered, "As a king." For that expression, he said, when the same question was put to him a second time, comprehended everything. And Alexander, accordingly, not only suffered him to govern his own kingdom as satrap under himself, but gave him also the additional territory of various independent tribes whom he subdued, a district which, it is said, contained fifteen several nations, and five thousand considerable towns, besides abundance of villages. To another government, three times as large as this, he appointed Philip, one of his friends.

Some little time after the battle with Porus, Bucephalus died, as most of the authorities state, under cure of his wounds, or, as Onesicritus says, of fatigue and age, being thirty years old. Alexander was no less concerned at his death than if he had lost an old companion or an intimate friend, and built a city, which he named Bucephalia, in memory of him, on the bank of the river Hydaspes. He also, we are told, built another city, and called it after the name of a favourite dog, Peritas, which he had brought up himself. So Sotion assures us he was informed by Potamon of Lesbos.

But this last combat with Porus took off the edge of the Macedonians' courage, and stayed their further progress into India. For having found it hard enough to defeat an enemy who brought but twenty thousand foot and two thousand horse into the field, they thought they had reason to oppose Alexander's design of leading them on to pass the Ganges, too, which they were told was thirty-two furlongs broad and a hundred fathoms deep, and the banks on the further side covered with multitudes of enemies. For they were told the kings of the Gandaritans and Praesians expected them there with eighty thousand horse, two hundred thousand foot, eight thousand armed chariots, and six thousand fighting elephants. Nor was this a mere vain report, spread to discourage them. For Androcottus, who not long after reigned in those parts, made a present of five hundred elephants at once to Seleucus, and with an army of six hundred thousand men subdued all India. Alexander at first was so grieved and enraged at his men's reluctancy that he shut himself up in his tent and threw himself upon the ground, declaring, if they would not pass the Ganges, he owed them no thanks for anything they had hitherto done, and that to retreat now was plainly to confess himself vanquished. But at last the reasonable persuasions of his friends and the cries and lamentations of his soldiers, who in a suppliant manner crowded about the entrance of his tent, prevailed with him to think of returning. Yet he could not refrain from leaving behind him various deceptive memorials of his expedition, to impose upon aftertimes, and to exaggerate his glory with posterity, such as arms larger than were really worn, and mangers for horses, with bits and bridles above the usual size, which he set up, and distributed in several places. He erected altars, also, to the gods, which the kings of the Praesians even in our time do honour to when they pass the river, and offer sacrifice upon them after the Grecian manner. Androcottus, then a boy, saw Alexander there, and is said often afterwards to have been heard to say, that he missed but little of making himself master of those countries; their king, who then reigned, was so hated and despised for the viciousness of his life and the meanness of his extraction.

Alexander was now eager to see the ocean. To which purpose he caused a great many tow-boats and rafts to be built, in which he fell gently down the rivers at his leisure, yet so that his navigation was neither unprofitable nor inactive. For by several descents upon the bank, he made himself master of the fortified towns, and consequently of the country on both sides. But at a siege of a town of the Mallians, who have the repute of being the bravest people of India, he ran in great danger of his life. For having beaten off the defendants with showers of arrows, he was the first man that mounted the wall by a scaling-ladder, which, as soon as he was up, broke and left him almost alone, exposed to the darts which the barbarians threw at him in great numbers from below. In this distress, turning himself as well as he could, he leaped down in the midst of his enemies, and had the good fortune to light upon his feet. The brightness and clattering of his armour when he came to the ground made the barbarians think they saw rays of light, or some bright phantom playing before his body, which frightened them so at first that they ran away and dispersed. Till seeing him seconded but by two of his guards, they fell upon him hand to hand, and some, while he bravely defended himself, tried to wound him through his armour with their swords and spears. And one who stood further off drew a bow with such strength that the arrow, finding its way through his cuirass, stuck in his ribs under the breast. This stroke was so violent that it made him give back, and set one knee to the ground, upon which the man ran up with his drawn scimitar, thinking to despatch him, and had done it, if Peucestes and Limnaeus had not interposed, who were both wounded, Limnaeus mortally, but Peucestes stood his ground, while Alexander killed the barbarians. But this did not free him from danger; for, besides many other wounds, at last he received so weighty a stroke of a club upon his neck that he was forced to lean his body against the wall, still, however, facing the enemy. At this extremity, the Macedonians made their way in and gathered round him. They took him up, just as he was fainting away, having lost all sense of what was done near him, and conveyed him to his tent, upon which it was presently reported all over the camp that he was dead. But when they had with great difficulty and pains sawed off the shaft of the arrow, which was of wood, and so with much trouble got off his cuirass, they came to cut the head of it, which was three fingers broad and four long, and stuck fast in the bone. During the operation he was taken with almost mortal swoonings, but when it was out he came to himself again. Yet though all danger was past, he continued very weak, and confined himself a great while to a regular diet and the method of his cure, till one day hearing the Macedonians clamouring outside in their eagerness to see him, he took his cloak and went out. And having sacrificed to the gods, without more delay he went on board again, and as he coasted along subdued a great deal of the country on both sides, and several considerable cities.

In this voyage he took ten of the Indian philosophers prisoners who had been most active in persuading Sabbas to revolt, and had caused the Macedonians a great deal

of trouble. These men, called Gymnosophists, were reputed
to be extremely ready and succinct in their answers, which
he made trial of, by putting difficult questions to them, letting them know that those whose answers were not pertinent
should be put to death, of which he made the eldest of them
judge. The first being asked which he thought the most
numerous, the dead or the living, answered, "The living because those who are dead are not at all." Of the second, he
desired to know whether the earth or the sea produced the
largest beasts; who told him, "The earth, for the sea is but
a part of it." His question to the third was, Which is the
cunningest of beasts? "That," said he, "which men have not
yet found out." He bade the fourth tell him what argument
he used to Sabbas to persuade him to revolt. "No other,"
said he, "than that he should either live or die nobly." Of
the fifth he asked, Which was the eldest, night or day? The
philosopher replied, "Day was eldest, by one day at least."
But perceiving Alexander not well satisfied with that account, he added, that he ought not to wonder if strange
questions had as strange answers made to them. Then he
went on and inquired of the next, what a man should do to
be exceedingly beloved. "He must be very powerful," said
he, "without making himself too much feared." The answer
of the seventh to his question, how a man might become a
god, was, "By doing that which was impossible for men to
do." The eighth told him, "Life is stronger than death, because it supports so many miseries." And the last being
asked, how long he thought it decent for a man to live,
said, "Till death appeared more desirable than life." Then
Alexander turned to him whom he had made judge, and
commanded him to give sentence. "All that I can determine," said he, "is, that they have every one answered
worse than another." "Nay," said the king, "then you shall
die first, for giving such a sentence." "Not so, O king," replied the gymnosophist, "unless you said falsely that he
should die first who made the worst answer." In conclusion he gave them presents and dismissed them.

But to those who were in greatest reputation among them,
and lived a private quiet life, he sent Onesicritus, one of

Diogenes the Cynic's disciples, desiring them to come to him. Calanus, it is said, very arrogantly and roughly commanded him to strip himself and hear what he said naked, otherwise he would not speak a word to him, though he came from Jupiter himself. But Dandamis received him with more civility, and hearing him discourse of Socrates, Pythagoras, and Diogenes, told him he thought them men of great parts and to have erred in nothing so much as in having too great respect for the laws and customs of their country. Others say Dandamis only asked him the reason why Alexander undertook so long a journey to come into those parts. Taxiles, however, persuaded Calanus to wait upon Alexander. His proper name was Sphines, but because he was wont to say *Cale*, which in the Indian tongue is a form of salutation to those he met with anywhere, the Greeks called him Calanus. He is said to have shown Alexander an instructive emblem of government, which was this. He threw a dry shrivelled hide upon the ground, and trod upon the edges of it. The skin when it was pressed in one place still rose up in another, wheresoever he trod round about it, till he set his foot in the middle, which made all the parts lie even and quiet. The meaning of this similitude being that he ought to reside most in the middle of his empire, and not spend too much time on the borders of it.

His voyage down the rivers took up seven months' time, and when he came to the sea, he sailed to an island which he himself called Scillustis, others Psiltucis, where going ashore, he sacrificed, and made what observations he could as to the nature of the sea and the sea-coast. Then having besought the gods that no other man might ever go beyond the bounds of this expedition, he ordered his fleet, of which he made Nearchus admiral and Onesicritus pilot, to sail round about, keeping the Indian shore on the right hand, and returned himself by land through the country of the Orites, where he was reduced to great straits for want of provisions, and lost a vast number of his men, so that of an army of one hundred and twenty thousand foot and fifteen thousand horse, he scarcely brought back above a fourth part out of India, they were so diminished by disease,

ill diet, and the scorching heats, but most by famine. For
their march was through an uncultivated country whose inhabitants fared hardly, possessing only a few sheep, and
those of a wretched kind, whose flesh was rank and unsa-
voury, by their continual feeding upon sea-fish.

After sixty days' march he came into Gedrosia, where he
found great plenty of all things, which the neighbouring
kings and governors of provinces, hearing of his approach,
had taken care to provide. When he had here refreshed his
army, he continued his march through Carmania, feasting
all the way for seven days together. He with his most intimate friends banqueted and revelled night and day upon
a platform erected on a lofty, conspicuous scaffold, which
was slowly drawn by eight horses. This was followed by a
great many chariots, some covered with purple and embroidered canopies, and some with green boughs, which
were continually supplied afresh, and in them the rest of
his friends and commanders drinking, and crowned with
garlands of flowers. Here was now no target or helmet or
spear to be seen; instead of armour, the soldiers handled
nothing but cups and goblets and Thericlean drinking vessels, which, along the whole way, they dipped into large
bowls and jars, and drank healths to one another, some
seating themselves to it, others as they went along. All
places resounded with music of pipes and flutes, with harp-
ing and singing, and women dancing as in the rites of Bacchus. For this disorderly, wandering march, besides the
drinking part of it, was accompanied with all the sportive-
ness and insolence of bacchanals, as much as if the god himself had been there to countenance and lead the procession.
As soon as he came to the royal palace of Gedrosia, he
again refreshed and feasted his army; and one day after he
had drunk pretty hard, it is said, he went to see a prize of
dancing contended for, in which his favourite Bagoas, having gained the victory, crossed the theatre in his dancing
habit, and sat down close by him, which so pleased the
Macedonians that they made loud acclamations for him to
kiss Bagoas, and never stopped clapping their hands and

shouting till Alexander put his arms round him and kissed him.

Here his admiral, Nearchus, came to him, and delighted him so with the narrative of his voyage, that he resolved himself to sail out of the mouth of the Euphrates with a great fleet, with which he designed to go round by Arabia and Africa, and so by Hercules's Pillars into the Mediterranean; in order for which, he directed all sorts of vessels to be built at Thapsacus, and made great provisions everywhere of seamen and pilots. But the tidings of the difficulties he had gone through in his Indian expedition, the danger of his person among the Mallians, the reported loss of a considerable part of his forces, and a general doubt as to his own safety, had begun to give occasion for revolt among many of the conquered nations, and for acts of great injustice, avarice, and insolence on the part of the satraps and commanders in the provinces, so that there seemed to be an universal fluctuation and disposition to change. Even at home, Olympias and Cleopatra had raised a faction against Antipater, and divided his government between them, Olympias seizing upon Epirus, and Cleopatra upon Macedonia. When Alexander was told of it, he said his mother had made the best choice, for the Macedonians would never endure to be ruled by a woman. Upon this he despatched Nearchus again to his fleet, to carry the war into the maritime provinces, and as he marched that way himself he punished those commanders who had behaved ill, particularly Oxyartes, one of the sons of Abuletes, whom he killed with his own hand, thrusting him through the body with his spear. And when Abuletes, instead of the necessary provisions which he ought to have furnished, brought him three thousand talents in coined money, he ordered it to be thrown to his horses, and when they would not touch it, "What good," he said, "will this provision do us?" and sent him away to prison.

While he came into Persia, he distributed money among the women, as their own kings had been wont to do, who as often as they came thither gave every one of them a piece of gold; on account of which custom, some of them, it is said, had come but seldom, and Ochus was so sordidly covetous that, to avoid this expense, he never visited his native country once in all his reign. Then finding Cyrus's sepulchre opened and rifled, he put Polymachus, who did it, to death, though he was a man of some distinction, a born Macedonian of Pella. And after he had read the inscription, he caused it to be cut again below the old one in Greek characters; the words being these: "O man, whosoever thou art, and from whencesoever thou comest (for I know thou wilt come), I am Cyrus, the founder of the Persian empire; do not grudge me this little earth which covers my body." The reading of this sensibly touched Alexander, filling him with the thought of the uncertainty and mutability of human affairs. At the same time Calanus, having been a little while troubled with a disease in the bowels, requested that he might have a funeral pile erected, to which he came on horseback, and, after he had said some prayers and sprinkled himself and cut off some of his hair to throw into the fire, before he ascended it, he embraced and took leave of the Macedonians who stood by, desiring them to pass that day in mirth and good-fellowship with their king, whom in a little time, he said, he doubted not to see again at Babylon. Having said this, he lay down, and covering up his face, he stirred not when the fire came near him, but continued still in the same posture as at first, and so sacrificed himself, as it was the ancient custom of the philosophers in those countries to do. The same thing was done long after by another Indian who came with Caesar to Athens, where they still show you, "the Indian's monument." At his return from the funeral pile, Alexander invited a great many of his friends and principal officers to supper, and proposed a drinking match, in which the victor should receive a crown. Promachus drank twelve quarts of wine, and won the prize, which was a talent from them all; but he survived his victory but three days, and was followed, as Chares says, by forty-one more, who died of the same debauch, some extremely cold weather having set in shortly after.

At Susa, he married Darius's daughter Statira, and celebrated also the nuptials of his friends, bestowing the noblest of the Persian ladies upon the worthiest of them, at the same time making it an entertainment in honour of the other Macedonians whose marriages had already taken place. At this magnificent festival, it is reported, there were no less than nine thousand guests, to each of whom he gave a golden cup for the libations. Not to mention other instances of his wonderful magnificence, he paid the debts of his army, which amounted to nine thousand eight hundred and seventy talents. But Antigenes, who had lost one of his eyes, though he owed nothing, got his name set down in the list of those who were in debt, and bringing one who pretended to be his creditor, and to have supplied him from the bank, received the money. But when the cheat was found out, the king was so incensed at it, that he banished him from court, and took away his command, though he was an excellent soldier and a man of great courage. For when he was but a youth, and served under Philip at the siege of Perinthus, where he was wounded in the eye by an arrow shot out of an engine, he would neither let the arrow be taken out nor be persuaded to quit the field till he had bravely repulsed the enemy and forced them to retire into the town. Accordingly he was not able to support such a disgrace with any patience, and it was plain that grief and despair would have made him kill himself, but the king fearing it, not only pardoned him, but let him also enjoy the benefit of his deceit.

The thirty thousand boys whom he left behind him to be taught and disciplined were so improved at his return, both in strength and beauty, and performed their exercises with such dexterity and wonderful agility, that he was extremely pleased with them, which grieved the Macedonians, and made them fear he would have the less value for them. And when he proceeded to send down the infirm and maimed soldiers to the sea, they said they were unjustly and infamously dealt with, after they were worn out in his service upon all occasions, now to be turned away with disgrace and sent home into their country among their friends and relations in a worse condition than when they came out; therefore they desired him to dismiss them one and all, and to account his Macedonians useless, now he was so well furnished with a set of dancing boys, with whom, if he pleased, he might go on and conquer the world. These speeches so incensed Alexander that, after he had given them a great deal of reproachful language in his passion, he drove them away, and committed the watch to Persians, out of whom he chose his guards and attendants. When the Macedonians saw him escorted by these men, and themselves excluded and shamefully disgraced, their high spirits fell, and conferring with one another, they found that jealousy and rage had almost distracted them. But at last coming to themselves again, they went without their arms, with only their under garments on, crying and weeping to offer themselves at his tent, and desired him to deal with them as their baseness and ingratitude deserved. However, this would not prevail; for though his anger was already something mollified, yet he would not admit them into his presence, nor would they stir from thence, but continued two days and nights before his tent, bewailing themselves, and imploring him as their lord to have compassion on them. But the third day he came out to them, and seeing them very humble and penitent, he wept himself a great while, after a gentle reproof spoke kindly to them, and dismissed those who were unserviceable with magnificent rewards, and with his recommendation to Antipater, that when they came home, at all public shows and in the theatres, they should sit on the best and foremost seats, crowned with chaplets of flowers. He ordered, also, that the children of those who had lost their lives in his service should have their father's pay continued to them.

When he came to Ecbatana in Media, and had despatched his most urgent affairs, he began to divert himself again with spectacles and public entertainments, to carry on which he had a supply of three thousand actors and artists, newly arrived out of Greece. But they were soon interrupted by Hephaestion's falling sick of a fever, in which, being a young man and a soldier, too, he could not confine

himself to so exact a diet as was necessary; for whilst his
physician, Glaucus, was gone to the theatre, he ate a fowl
for his dinner, and drank a large draught of wine, upon
which he became very ill, and shortly after died. At this
misfortune, Alexander was so beyond all reason transported
that, to express his sorrow, he immediately ordered the
manes and tails of all his horses and mules to be cut, and
threw down the battlements of the neighbouring cities. The
poor physician he crucified, and forbade playing on the
flute or any other musical instrument in the camp a great
while, till directions came from the oracle of Ammon, and
enjoined him to honour Hephaestion, and sacrifice to him
as a hero. Then seeking to alleviate his grief in war, he set
out, as it were, to a hunt and chase of men, for he fell upon
the Cossaeans, and put the whole nation to the sword. This
was called a sacrifice to Hephaestion's ghost. In his sepulchre and monument and the adorning of them he intended
to bestow ten thousand talents; and designing that the excellence of the workmanship and the singularity of the design
might outdo the expense, his wishes turned, above all other
artists, to Stasicrates, because he always promised something very bold, unusual, and magnificent in his projects.
Once when they had met before, he had told him that, of
all the mountains he knew, that of Athos in Thrace was the
most capable of being adapted to represent the shape and
lineaments of a man; that if he pleased to command him, he
would make it the noblest and most durable statue in the
world, which in its left hand should hold a city of ten thousand inhabitants, and out of its right should pour a copious
river into the sea. Though Alexander declined this proposal,
yet now he spent a great deal of time with workmen to invent and contrive others even more extravagant and sumptuous.

As he was upon his way to Babylon Nearchus, who had
sailed back out of the ocean up the mouth of the river Euphrates, came to tell him he had met with some Chaldaean
diviners, who had warned him against Alexander's going
thither. Alexander, however, took no thought of it, and
went on, and when he came near the walls of the place, he

saw a great many crows fighting with one another, some of
whom fell down just by him. After this, being privately informed that Apollodorus, the governor of Babylon, had
sacrificed, to know what would become of him, he sent for
Pythagoras, the soothsayer, and on his admitting the thing,
asked him in what condition he found the victim; and when
he told him the liver was defective in its lobe, "A great
presage indeed!" said Alexander. However, he offered Pythagoras no injury, but was sorry that he had neglected
Nearchus's advice, and stayed for the most part outside the
town, removing his tent from place to place, and sailing up
and down the Euphrates. Besides this, he was disturbed by
many other prodigies. A tame ass fell upon the biggest and
handsomest lion that he kept, and killed him by a kick. And
one day after he had undressed himself to be anointed, and
was playing at ball, just as they were going to bring his
clothes again, the young men who played with him perceived a man clad in the king's robes with a diadem upon
his head, sitting silently upon his throne. They asked him
who he was, to which he gave no answer a good while, till
at last, coming to himself, he told them his name was
Dionysius, that he was of Messenia, that for some crime of
which he was accused he was brought thither from the seaside, and had been kept long in prison, that Serapis appeared to him, had freed him from his chains, conducted
him to that place, and commanded him to put on the king's
robe and diadem, and to sit where they found him, and to
say nothing. Alexander, when he heard this, by the direction
of his soothsayers, put the fellow to death, but he lost his
spirits, and grew diffident of the protection and assistance
of the gods, and suspicious of his friends. His greatest apprehension was of Antipater and his sons, one of whom,
Iolaus, was his chief cupbearer; and Cassander, who had
lately arrived, and had been bred up in Greek manners, the
first time he saw some of the barbarians adore the king
could not forbear laughing at it aloud, which so incensed
Alexander that he took him by the hair with both hands
and dashed his head against the wall. Another time, Cassander would have said something in defence of Antipater to

those who accused him, but Alexander interrupting him, said, "What is it you say? Do you think people, if they had received no injury, would come such a journey only to calumniate your father?" To which when Cassander replied, that their coming so far from the evidence was a great proof of the falseness of their charges, Alexander smiled, and said those were some of Aristotle's sophisms, which would serve equally on both sides; and added, that both he and his father should be severely punished, if they were found guilty of the least injustice towards those who complained. All which made such a deep impression of terror in Cassander's mind that, long after, when he was King of Macedonia and master of Greece, as he was walking up and down at Delphi, and looking at the statues, at the sight of that of Alexander he was suddenly struck with alarm, and shook all over, his eyes rolled, his head grew dizzy, and it was long before he recovered himself.

When once Alexander had given way to fears of supernatural influence, his mind grew so disturbed and so easily alarmed that, if the least unusual or extraordinary thing happened, he thought it a prodigy or a presage, and his court was thronged with diviners and priests whose business was to sacrifice and purify and foretell the future. So miserable a thing is incredulity and contempt of divine power on the one hand, and so miserable, also, superstition on the other, which like water, where the level has been lowered, flowing in and never stopping, fills the mind with slavish fears and follies, as now in Alexander's case. But upon some answers which were brought him from the oracle concerning Hephaestion, he laid aside his sorrow, and fell again to sacrificing and drinking; and having given Nearchus a splendid entertainment, after he had bathed, as was his custom, just as he was going to bed, at Medius's request he went to supper with him. Here he drank all the next day, and was attacked with a fever, which seized him, not as some write, after he had drunk of the bowl of Hercules, nor was he taken with any sudden pain in his back, as if he had been struck with a lance, for these are the inventions of some authors who thought it their duty to make the

last scene of so great an action as tragical and moving as
they could. Aristobulus tells us, that in the rage of his fever
and a violent thirst, he took a draught of wine, upon which
he fell into delirium, and died on the thirtieth day of the
month Daesius.

But the journals give the following record. On the eight-
eenth day of the month he slept in the bathing-room on account of his fever. The next day he bathed and removed
into his chamber, and spent his time in playing at dice with
Medius. In the evening he bathed and sacrificed, and ate
freely, and had the fever on him through the night. On the
twentieth, after the usual sacrifices and bathing, he lay in
the bathing-room and heard Nearchus's narrative of his
voyage, and the observations he had made in the great sea.
The twenty-first he passed in the same manner, his fever
still increasing, and suffered much during the night. The
next day the fever was very violent, and he had himself removed and his bed set by the great bath, and discoursed
with his principal officers about finding fit men to fill up
the vacant places in the army. On the twenty-fourth he was
much worse, and was carried out of his bed to assist at the
sacrifices, and gave order that the general officers should
wait within the court, whilst the inferior officers kept watch
without doors. On the twenty-fifth he was removed to his
palace on the other side the river, where he slept a little,
but his fever did not abate, and when the generals came
into his chamber, he was speechless and continued so the
following day. The Macedonians, therefore, supposing he
was dead, came with great clamours to the gates, and men-
aced his friends so that they were forced to admit them,
and let them all pass through unarmed by his bedside. The
same day Python and Seleucus were despatched to the temple of Serapis to inquire if they should bring Alexander
thither, and were answered by the god that they should
not remove him. On the twenty-eighth, in the evening, he
died. This account is most of it word for word as it is written in the diary.

At the time, nobody had any suspicion of his being poi-
soned, but upon some information given six years after, they

say Olympias put many to death, and scattered the ashes of Iolaus, then dead, as if he had given it him. But those who affirm that Aristotle counselled Antipater to do it, and that by his means the poison was brought, adduced one Hagnothemis as their authority, who, they say, heard King Antigonus speak of it, and tell us that the poison was water, deadly cold as ice, distilled from a rock in the district of Nonacris, which they gathered like a thin dew, and kept in an ass's hoof; for it was so very cold and penetrating that no other vessel would hold it. However, most are of opinion that all this is a mere made-up story, no slight evidence of which is, that during the dissensions among the commanders, which lasted several days, the body continued clear and fresh, without any sign of such taint or corruption, though it lay neglected in a close sultry place.

Roxana, who was now with child, and upon that account much honoured by the Macedonians, being jealous of Statira, sent for her by a counterfeit letter, as if Alexander had been still alive; and when she had her in her power, killed her and her sister, and threw their bodies into a well, which they filled up with earth, not without the privity and assistance of Perdiccas, who in the time immediately following the king's death, under cover of the name of Arrhidaeus, whom he carried about him as a sort of guard to his person, exercised the chief authority. Arrhidaeus, who was Philip's son by an obscure woman of the name of Philinna, was himself of weak intellect, not that he had been originally deficient either in body or mind, on the contrary, in his childhood, he had showed a happy and promising character enough. But a diseased habit of body, caused by drugs which Olympias gave him, had ruined, not only his health, but his understanding.

DEMOSTHENES

Whoever it was, Sosius, that wrote the poem in honour of
Alcibiades, upon his winning the chariot-race at the Olympian Games, whether it were Euripides, as is most commonly thought, or some other person, he tells us that to a
man's being happy it is in the first place requisite he should
be born in "some famous city." But for him that would attain to true happiness, which for the most part is placed in
the qualities and disposition of the mind, it is, in my opinion, of no other disadvantage to be of a mean, obscure
country, than to be born of a small or plain-looking woman.
For it were ridiculous to think that Iulis, a little part of
Ceos, which itself is no great island, and Aegina, which an
Athenian once said ought to be removed, like a small eye-
sore, from the port of Piraeus, should breed good actors
and poets, and yet should never be able to produce a just,
temperate, wise, and high-minded man. Other arts, whose
end it is to acquire riches or honour, are likely enough to
wither and decay in poor and undistinguished towns; but
virtue, like a strong and durable plant, may take root and
thrive in any place where it can lay hold of an ingenuous
nature, and a mind that is industrious. I, for my part, shall
desire that for any deficiency of mine in right judgment or
action, I myself may be, as in fairness, held accountable,
and shall not attribute it to the obscurity of my birthplace.

But if any man undertake to write a history that has to
be collected from materials gathered by observation and
the reading of works not easy to be got in all places, nor
written always in his own language, but many of them
foreign and dispersed in other hands, for him, undoubtedly,

it is in the first place and above all things most necessary to reside in some city of good note, addicted to liberal arts, and populous; where he may have plenty of all sorts of books, and upon inquiry may hear and inform himself of such particulars as, having escaped the pens of writers, are more faithfully preserved in the memories of men, lest his work be deficient in many things, even those which it can least dispense with.

But for me, I live in a little town, where I am willing to continue, lest it should grow less; and having had no leisure, while I was in Rome and other parts of Italy, to exercise myself in the Roman language, on account of public business and of those who came to be instructed by me in philosophy, it was very late, and in the decline of my age, before I applied myself to the reading of Latin authors. Upon which that which happened to me may seem strange, though it be true; for it was not so much by the knowledge of words that I came to the understanding of things, as by my experience of things I was enabled to follow the meaning of words. But to appreciate the graceful and ready pronunciation of the Roman tongue, to understand the various figures and connection of words, and such other ornaments, in which the beauty of speaking consists, is, I doubt not, an admirable and delightful accomplishment; but it requires a degree of practice and study which is not easy, and will better suit those who have more leisure, and time enough yet before them for the occupation.

And so in this fifth book of my Parallel Lives, in giving an account of Demosthenes and Cicero, my comparison of their natural dispositions and their characters will be formed upon their actions and their lives as statesmen, and I shall not pretend to criticise their orations one against the other, to show which of the two was the more charming or the more powerful speaker. For there, as Ion says—

"We are but like a fish upon dry land;"

a proverb which Caecilius perhaps forgot, when he employed his always adventurous talents in so ambitious an attempt as a comparison of Demosthenes and Cicero; and, possibly, if it were a thing obvious and easy for every man to *know himself*, the precept had not passed for an oracle.

The divine power seems originally to have designed Demosthenes and Cicero upon the same plan, giving them many similarities in their natural characters, as their passion for distinction and their love of liberty in civil life, and their want of courage in dangers and war, and at the same time also to have added many accidental resemblances. I think there can hardly be found two other orators, who, from small and obscure beginnings, became so great and mighty; who both contested with kings and tyrants; both lost their daughters, were driven out of their country, and returned with honour; who, flying from thence again, were both seized upon by their enemies, and at last ended their lives with the liberty of their countrymen. So that if we were to suppose there had been a trial of skill between nature and fortune, as there is sometimes between artists, it would be hard to judge whether that succeeded best in making them alike in their dispositions and manners, or this in the coincidences of their lives. We will speak of the eldest first.

Demosthenes, the father of Demosthenes, was a citizen of good rank and quality, as Theopompus informs us, surnamed the Sword-maker, because he had a large workhouse, and kept servants skilful in that art at work. But of that which Aeschines the orator said of his mother, that she was descended of one Gylon, who fled his country upon an accusation of treason, and of a barbarian woman, I can affirm nothing, whether he spoke true, or slandered and maligned her. This is certain, that Demosthenes, being as yet but seven years old, was left by his father in affluent circumstances, the whole value of his estate being little short of fifteen talents, and that he was wronged by his guardians, part of his fortune being embezzled by them, and the rest neglected; insomuch that even his teachers were defrauded of their salaries. This was the reason that he did not obtain the liberal education that he should have had; besides that, on account of weakness and delicate health, his mother

would not let him exert himself, and his teachers forbore
to urge him. He was meagre and sickly from the first, and
hence had his nickname of Batalus given him, it is said, by
the boys, in derision of his appearance; Batalus being, as some tell us, a certain enervated flute-player, in
ridicule of whom Antiphanes wrote a play. Others speak
of Batalus as a writer of wanton verses and drinking
songs. And it would seem that some part of the body,
not decent to be named, was at that time called *batalus*
by the Athenians. But the name of Argas, which also
they say was a nickname of Demosthenes, was given
him for his behaviour, as being savage and spiteful,
argas being one of the poetical words for a snake; or for
his disagreeable way of speaking, Argas being the name of
a poet who composed very harshly and disagreeably. So
much, as Plato says, for such matters.

The first occasion of his eager inclination to oratory,
they say, was this. Callistratus, the orator, being to plead
in open court for Oropus, the expectation of the issue of
that cause was very great, as well for the ability of the
orator, who was then at the height of his reputation, as
also for the fame of the action itself. Therefore, Demosthenes, having heard the tutors and school-masters agree-
ing among themselves to be present at this trial, with much
importunity persuades his tutor to take him along with him
to the hearing; who, having some acquaintance with the
doorkeepers, procured a place where the boy might sit unseen, and hear what was said. Callistratus having got the
day, and being much admired, the boy began to look upon
his glory with a kind of emulation, observing how he was
courted on all hands, and attended on his way by the multitude; but his wonder was more than all excited by the power
of his eloquence, which seemed able to subdue and win
over anything. From this time, therefore, bidding farewell
to other sorts of learning and study, he now began to exercise himself, and to take pains in declaiming, as one that
meant to be himself also an orator. He made use of Isaeus
as his guide to the art of speaking, though Isocrates at that
time was giving lessons; whether, as some say, because he

was an orphan, and was not able to pay Isocrates his appointed fee of ten minae, or because he preferred Isaeus's
speaking, as being more businesslike and effective in actual
use. Hermippus says that he met with certain memoirs without any author's name, in which it was written that Demosthenes was a scholar to Plato, and learnt much of his eloquence from him; and he also mentions Ctesibius, as re-
porting from Callias of Syracuse and some others, that Demosthenes secretly obtained a knowledge of the systems of
Isocrates and Alcidamas, and mastered them thoroughly.

As soon, therefore, as he was grown up to man's estate,
he began to go to law with his guardians, and to write orations against them; who, in the meantime, had recourse to
various subterfuges and pleas for new trials, and Demosthenes, though he was thus, as Thucydides says, taught his
business in dangers, and by his own exertions was successful in his suit, was yet unable for all this to recover so
much as a small fraction of his patrimony. He only attained some degree of confidence in speaking, and some
competent experience in it. And having got a taste of the
honour and power which are acquired by pleadings, he now
ventured to come forth, and to undertake public business.
And, as it is said of Laomedon, the Orchomenian, that, by
advice of his physician, he used to run long distances to
keep off some disease of his spleen, and by that means having, through labour and exercise, framed the habit of his
body, he betook himself to the great garland games, and became one of the best runners at the long race; so it happened to Demosthenes, who, first venturing upon oratory
for the recovery of his own private property, by this acquired ability in speaking, and at length, in public business,
as it were in the great games, came to have the pre-eminence of all competitors in the assembly. But when he first
addressed himself to the people, he met with great discour-
agements, and was derided for his strange and uncouth
style, which was cumbered with long sentences and tor-
tured with formal arguments to a most harsh and disagreeable excess. Besides, he had, it seems, a weakness in his
voice, a perplexed and indistinct utterance and a shortness

of breath, which, by breaking and disjointing his sentences, much obscured the sense and meaning of what he spoke. So that in the end being quite disheartened, he forsook the assembly; and as he was walking carelessly and sauntering about the Piraeus, Eunomus, the Thriasian, then a very old man, seeing him, upbraided him, saying that his diction was very much like that of Pericles, and that he was wanting to himself through cowardice and meanness of spirit, neither bearing up with courage against popular outcry, nor fitting his body for action, but suffering it to languish through mere sloth and negligence.

Another time, when the assembly had refused to hear him, and he was going home with his head muffled up, taking it very heavily, they relate that Satyrus, the actor, followed him, and being his familiar acquaintance, entered into conversation with him. To whom, when Demosthenes bemoaned himself, that having been the most industrious of all the pleaders, and having almost spent the whole strength and vigour of his body in that employment, he could not yet find any acceptance with the people, that drunken sots, mariners, and illiterate fellows were heard, and had the hustings for their own, while he himself was despised, "You say true, Demosthenes," replied Satyrus, "but I will quickly remedy the cause of all this, if you will repeat to me some passage out of Euripides or Sophocles." Which when Demosthenes had pronounced, Satyrus presently taking it up after him, gave the same passage, in his rendering of it, such a new form, by accompanying it with the proper mien and gesture, that to Demosthenes it seemed quite another thing. By this, being convinced how much grace and ornament language acquires from action, he began to esteem it a small matter, and as good as nothing for a man to exercise himself in declaiming, if he neglected enunciation and delivery. Hereupon he built himself a place to study in under ground (which was still remaining in our time), and hither he would come constantly every day to form his action and to exercise his voice; and here he would continue, oftentimes without intermission, two or three months together, shaving one half of his head, that so for shame he might not go abroad, though he desired it ever so much.

Nor was this all, but he also made his conversation with people abroad, his common speech, and his business, subservient to his studies, taking from hence occasions and arguments as matter to work upon. For as soon as he was parted from his company, down he would go at once into his study, and run over everything in order that had passed, and the reasons that might be alleged for and against it. Any speeches, also, that he was present at, he would go over again with himself, and reduce into periods; and whatever others spoke to him, or he to them, he would correct, transform, and vary several ways. Hence it was that he was looked upon as a person of no great natural genius, but one who owed all the power and ability he had in speaking to labour and industry. Of the truth of which it was thought to be no small sign that he was very rarely heard to speak upon the occasion, but though he were by name frequently called upon by the people, as he sat in the assembly, yet he would not rise unless he had previously considered the subject, and came prepared for it. So that many of the popular pleaders used to make it a jest against him; and Pytheas once, scoffing at him, said that his arguments smelt of the lamp. To which Demosthenes gave the sharp answer, "It is true, indeed, Pytheas, that your lamp and mine are not conscious of the same things." To others, however, he would not much deny it, but would admit frankly enough, that he neither entirely wrote his speeches beforehand, nor yet spoke wholly extempore. And he would affirm that it was the more truly popular act to use premeditation, such preparation being a kind of respect to the people; whereas, to slight and take no care how what is said is likely to be received by the audience, shows something of an oligarchical temper, and is the course of one that intends force rather than persuasion. Of his want of courage and assurance to speak offhand, they make it also another argument that, when he was at a loss and discomposed, Demades would often rise up on the sudden to support him, but he was never observed to do the same for Demades.

Whence then, may some say, was it, that Aeschines speaks of him as a person so much to be wondered at for his boldness in speaking? Or, how could it be, when Python, the Byzantine, with so much confidence and such a torrent of words inveighed against the Athenians, that Demosthenes alone stood up to oppose him? Or when Lamarchus, the Myrinaean, had written a panegyric upon King Philip and Alexander, in which he uttered many things in reproach of the Thebans and Olynthians, and at the Olympic Games recited it publicly, how was it that he, rising up, and recounting historically and demonstratively what benefits and advantages all Greece had received from the Thebans and Chalcidians, and, on the contrary, what mischiefs the flatterers of the Macedonians had brought upon it, so turned the minds of all that were present that the sophist, in alarm at the outcry against him, secretly made his way out of the assembly? But Demosthenes, it should seem, regarded other points in the character of Pericles to be unsuited to him; but his reserve and his sustained manner, and his forbearing to speak on the sudden, or upon every occasion, as being the things to which principally he owed his greatness, these he followed, and endeavoured to imitate, neither wholly neglecting the glory which present occasion offered, nor yet willing too often to expose his faculty to the mercy of chance. For, in fact, the orations which were spoken by him had much more of boldness and confidence in them than those that he wrote, if we may believe Eratosthenes, Demetrius the Phalerian, and the comedians. Eratosthenes says that often in his speaking he would be transported into a kind of ecstasy, and Demetrius, that he uttered the famous metrical adjuration to the people—

"By the earth, the springs, the rivers, and the streams,"

as a man inspired and beside himself. One of the comedians calls him a *rhopoperperethras*, and another scoffs at him for his use of antithesis:—

"And what he took, took back; a phrase to please,
  The very fancy of Demosthenes."

Unless, indeed, this also is meant by Antiphanes for a jest
upon the speech on Halonesus, in which Demosthenes advised the Athenians not to *take* at Philip's hands, but to *take
back*.

All, however, used to consider Demades, in the mere use
of his natural gifts, an orator impossible to surpass, and
that in what he spoke on the sudden, he excelled all the
study and preparation of Demosthenes. And Ariston, the
Chian, has recorded a judgment which Theophrastus passed
upon the orators; for being asked what kind of orator he accounted Demosthenes, he answered, "Worthy of the city of
Athens;" and then what he thought of Demades, he answered, "Above it." And the same philosopher reports
that Polyeuctus, the Sphettian, one of the Athenian politi-
cians about that time, was wont to say that Demosthenes
was the greatest orator, but Phocion the ablest, as he expressed the most sense in the fewest words. And, indeed,
it is related that Demosthenes himself, as often as Phocion
stood up to plead against him, would say to his acquaintance, "Here comes the knife to my speech." Yet it does
not appear whether he had this feeling for his powers of
speaking, or for his life and character, and meant to say
that one word or nod from a man who was really trusted
would go further than a thousand lengthy periods from others.

Demetrius, the Phalerian, tells us that he was informed
by Demosthenes himself, now grown old, that the ways he
made use of to remedy his natural bodily infirmities and
defects were such as these; his inarticulate and stammering
pronunciation he overcame and rendered more distinct by
speaking with pebbles in his mouth; his voice he disciplined
by declaiming and reciting speeches or verses when he was
out of breath, while running or going up steep places; and
that in his house he had a large looking-glass, before which
he would stand and go through his exercises. It is told that
some one once came to request his assistance as a pleader,

and related how he had been assaulted and beaten. "Certainly," said Demosthenes, "nothing of the kind can have happened to you." Upon which the other, raising his voice, exclaimed loudly, "What, Demosthenes, nothing has been done to me?" "Ah," replied Demosthenes, "now I hear the voice of one that has been injured and beaten." Of so great consequence towards the gaining of belief did he esteem the tone and action of the speaker. The action which he used himself was wonderfully pleasing to the common people, but by well-educated people, as, for example, by Demetrius, the Phalerian, it was looked upon as mean, humiliating, and unmanly. And Hermippus says of Aesion, that, being asked his opinion concerning the ancient orators, and those of his own time, he answered that it was admirable to see with what composure and in what high style they addressed themselves to the people; but that the orations of Demosthenes, when they are read, certainly appear to be superior in point of construction, and more effective. His written speeches, beyond all question, are characterised by austere tone and by their severity. In his extempore retorts and rejoinders, he allowed himself the use of jest and mockery. When Demades said, "Demosthenes teach me! So might the sow teach Minerva!" he replied, "Was it this Minerva, that was lately found playing the harlot in Collytus?" When a thief, who had the nickname of the Brazen, was attempting to upbraid him for sitting up late, and writing by candle-light, "I know very well," said he, "that you had rather have all lights out; and wonder not, O ye men of Athens, at the many robberies which are committed, since we have thieves of brass and walls of clay." But on these points, though we have much more to mention, we will add nothing at present. We will proceed to take an estimate of his character from his actions and his life as a statesman.

His first entering into public business was much about the time of the Phocian war, as himself affirms, and may be collected from his Philippic orations. For of these, some were made after that action was over, and the earliest of them refer to its concluding events. It is certain that he engaged in the accusation of Midias when he was but two-and-thirty years old, having as yet no interest or reputation as a politician. And this it was, I consider, that induced him to withdraw the action, and accept a sum of money as a compromise. For of himself—

"He was no easy or good-natured man,"

but of a determined disposition, and resolute to see himself righted; however, finding it a hard matter and above his strength to deal with Midias, a man so well secured on all sides with money, eloquence, and friends, he yielded to the entreaties of those who interceded for him. But had he seen any hopes or possibility of prevailing, I cannot believe that three thousand drachmas could have taken off the edge of his revenge. The object which he chose for himself in the commonwealth was noble and just, the defence of the Grecians against Philip; and in this he behaved himself so worthily that he soon grew famous, and excited attention everywhere for his eloquence and courage in speaking. He was admired through all Greece, the King of Persia courted him, and by Philip himself he was more esteemed than all the other orators. His very enemies were forced to confess that they had to do with a man of mark; for such a character even Aeschines and Hyperides give him, where they accuse and speak against him.

So that I cannot imagine what ground Theopompus had to say that Demosthenes was of a fickle, unsettled disposition, and could not long continue firm either to the same men or the same affairs; whereas the contrary is most apparent, for the same party and post in politics which he held from the beginning, to these he kept constant to the end; and was so far from leaving them while he lived that he chose rather to forsake his life than his purpose. He was never heard to apologise for shifting sides like Demades, who would say he often spoke against himself, but never against the city; nor as Melanopus, who, being generally against Callistratus, but being often bribed off with money, was wont to tell the people, "The man indeed is my enemy, but we must submit for the good of our country;"

nor again as Nicodemus, the Messenian, who having first appeared on Cassander's side, and afterwards taken part with Demetrius, said the two things were not in themselves contrary, it being always most advisable to obey the conqueror. We have nothing of this kind to say against Demosthenes, as one who would turn aside or prevaricate, either in word or deed. There could not have been less variation in his public acts if they had all been played, so to say, from first to last, from the same score. Panaetius, the philosopher, said that most of his orations are so written as if they were to prove this one conclusion, that what is honest and virtuous is for itself only to be chosen; as that of the Crown, that against Aristocrates, that for the Immunities, and the Philippics; in all which he persuades his fellow-citizens to pursue not that which seems most pleasant, easy, or profitable; but declares, over and over again, that they ought in the first place to prefer that which is just and honourable before their own safety and preservation. So that if he had kept his hands clean, if his courage for the wars had been answerable to the generosity of his principles, and the dignity of his orations, he might deservedly have his name placed, not in the number of such orators as Moerocles, Polyeuctus, and Hyperides, but in the highest rank with Cimon, Thucydides, and Pericles.

Certainly amongst those who were contemporary with him, Phocion, though he appeared on the less commendable side in the commonwealth, and was counted as one of the Macedonian party, nevertheless, by his courage and his honesty, procured himself a name not inferior to these of Ephialtes, Aristides, and Cimon. But Demosthenes, being neither fit to be relied on for courage in arms, as Demetrius says, nor on all sides inaccessible to bribery (for how invincible soever he was against the gifts of Philip and the Macedonians, yet elsewhere he lay open to assault, and was overpowered by the gold which came down from Susa and Ecbatana), was therefore esteemed better able to recommend than to imitate the virtues of past times. And yet (excepting only Phocion), even in his life and manners, he far surpassed the other orators of his time. None of them addressed the people so boldly; he attacked the faults, and opposed himself to the unreasonable desires of the multitude, as may be seen in his orations. Theopompus writes, that the Athenians having by name selected Demosthenes, and called upon him to accuse a certain person, he refused to do it; upon which the assembly being all in an uproar, he rose up and said, "Your counsellor, whether you will or no, O ye men of Athens, you shall always have me; but a sycophant or false accuser, though you would have me, I shall never be." And his conduct in the case of Antiphon was perfectly aristocratical; whom, after he had been acquitted in the assembly, he took and brought before the court of Areopagus, and, setting at naught the displeasure of the people, convicted him there of having promised Philip to burn the arsenal; whereupon the man was condemned by that court, and suffered for it. He accused, also, Theoris, the priestess, amongst other misdemeanours, of having instructed and taught the slaves to deceive and cheat their masters, for which the sentence of death was passed upon her, and she was executed.

The oration which Apollodorus made use of, and by it carried the cause against Timotheus, the general, in an action of debt, it is said was written for him by Demosthenes; as also those against Phormion and Stephanus, in which latter case he was thought to have acted dishonourably, for the speech which Phormion used against Apollodorus was also of his making; he, as it were, having simply furnished two adversaries out of the same shop with weapons to wound one another. Of his orations addressed to the public assemblies, that against Androtion, and those against Timocrates and Aristocrates, were written for others, before he had come forward himself as a politician. They were composed, it seems, when he was but seven or eight and twenty years old. That against Aristogiton, and that for the Immunities, he spoke himself, at the request, as he says, of Ctesippus, the son of Chabrias, but, as some say, out of courtship to the young man's mother. Though, in fact, he did not marry her, for his wife was a woman of Samos, as Demetrius, the Magnesian, writes, in his book on Persons of the same Name. It is not certain whether his oration against Aeschines, for Misconduct as Ambassador, was ever spoken; although Idomeneus says that Aeschines wanted only thirty voices to condemn him. But this seems not to be correct, at least so far as may be conjectured from both their orations concerning the Crown; for in these, neither of them speaks clearly or directly of it, as a cause that ever came to trial. But let others decide this controversy.

It was evident, even in time of peace, what course Demosthenes would steer in the commonwealth; for whatever was done by the Macedonian, he criticised and found fault with, and upon all occasions was stirring up the people of Athens, and inflaming them against him. Therefore, in the court of Philip, no man was so much talked of, or of so great account as he; and when he came thither, one of the ten ambassadors who were sent into Macedonia, though all had audience given them, yet his speech was answered with most care and exactness. But in other respects, Philip entertained him not so honourably as the rest, neither did he show him the same kindness and civility with which he applied himself to the party of Aeschines and Philocrates. So that, when the others commended Philip for his able speaking, his beautiful person, nay, and also for his good companionship in drinking, Demosthenes could not refrain from cavilling at these praises; the first, he said, was a quality which might well enough become a rhetorician, the second a woman, and the last was only the property of a sponge; no one of them was the proper commendation of a prince.

But when things came at last to war, Philip on the one side being not able to live in peace, and the Athenians, on the other side, being stirred up by Demosthenes, the first action he put them upon was the reducing of Euboea, which, by the treachery of the tyrants, was brought under subjection to Philip. And on his proposition, the decree was voted, and they crossed over thither and chased the Macedonians out of the island. The next was the relief of the Byzantines and Perinthians, whom the Macedonians at that time were attacking. He persuaded the people to lay aside their enmity against these cities, to forget the offences committed by them in the Confederate War, and to send them such succours as eventually saved and secured them. Not long after, he undertook an embassy through the states of Greece, which he solicited and so far incensed against Philip that, a few only excepted, he brought them all into a general league. So that, besides the forces composed of the citizens themselves, there was an army consisting of fifteen thousand foot and two thousand horse, and the money to pay these strangers was levied and brought in with great cheerfulness. On which occasion it was, says Theophrastus, on the allies requesting that their contributions for the war might be ascertained and stated, Crobylus, the orator, made use of the saying, "War can't be fed at so much a day." Now was all Greece up in arms, and in great expectation what would be the event. The Euboeans, the Achaeans, the Corinthians, the Megarians, the Leucadians, and Corcyraeans, their people and their cities, were all joined together in a league. But the hardest task was yet behind, left for Demosthenes, to draw the Thebans into this confederacy with the rest. Their country bordered next upon Attica, they had great forces for the war, and at that time they were accounted the best soldiers of all Greece, but it was no easy matter to make them break with Philip, who, by many good offices, had so lately obliged them in the Phocian war; especially considering how the subjects of dispute and variance between the two cities were continually renewed and exasperated by petty quarrels, arising out of the proximity of their frontiers.

But after Philip, being now grown high and puffed up with his good success at Amphissa, on a sudden surprised Elatea and possessed himself of Phocis, and the Athenians were in a great consternation, none durst venture to rise up to speak, no one knew what to say, all were at a loss, and the whole assembly in silence and perplexity, in this extremity of affairs Demosthenes was the only man who appeared, his counsel to them being alliance with the Thebans. And having in other ways encouraged the people, and, as his manner was, raised their spirits up with hopes, he, with some others, was sent ambassador to Thebes. To oppose him, as Marsyas says, Philip also sent thither his envoys, Amyntas and Clearchus, two Macedonians, besides Daochus, a Thessalian, and Thrasydaeus. Now the Thebans, in their consultations, were well enough aware what suited best with their own interest, but every one had before his eyes the terrors of war, and their losses in the Phocian troubles were still recent: but such was the force and power of the orator, fanning up, as Theopompus says, their courage, and firing their emulation, that, casting away every thought of prudence, fear, or obligation, in a sort of divine possession, they chose the path of honour, to which his words invited them. And this success, thus accomplished by an orator, was thought to be so glorious and of such consequence, that Philip immediately sent heralds to treat and petition for a peace: all Greece was aroused, and up in arms to help. And the commanders-in-chief, not only of Attica, but of Boeotia, applied themselves to Demosthenes, and observed his directions. He managed all the assemblies of the Thebans, no less than those of the Athenians; he was beloved both by the one and by the other, and exercised the same supreme authority with both; and that not by unfair means, or without just cause, as Theopompus professes, but indeed it was no more than was due to his merit.

But there was, it would seem, some divinely ordered fortune, commissioned, in the revolution of things, to put a period at this time to the liberty of Greece, which opposed and thwarted all their actions, and by many signs foretold what should happen. Such were the sad predictions uttered by the Pythian priestess, and this old oracle cited out of the Sibyl's verses:—

"The battle on Thermodon that shall be
    Safe at a distance I desire to see,
Far, like an eagle, watching in the air,
    Conquered shall weep, and conqueror perish there."

This Thermodon, they say, is a little rivulet here in our country in Chaeronea, running into the Cephisus. But we know of none that is so called at the present time; and can only conjecture that the streamlet which is now called Haemon, and runs by the Temple of Hercules, where the Grecians were encamped, might perhaps in those days be called Thermodon, and after the fight, being filled with blood and dead bodies, upon this occasion, as we guess, might change its old name for that which it now bears. Yet Duris says that this Thermodon was no river, but that some of the soldiers, as they were pitching their tents and digging trenches about them, found a small stone statue, which, by the inscription, appeared to be the figure of Thermodon, carrying a wounded Amazon in his arms; and that there was another oracle current about it, as follows:—

> "The battle on Thermodon that shall be,
>   Fail not, black raven, to attend and see;
>   The flesh of men shall there abound for thee."

In fine, it is not easy to determine what is the truth. But of Demosthenes it is said that he had such great confidence in the Grecian forces, and was so excited by the sight of the courage and resolution of so many brave men ready to engage the enemy, that he would by no means endure they should give any heed to oracles, or hearken to prophecies, but gave out that he suspected even the prophetess herself, as if she had been tampered with to speak in favour of Philip. The Thebans he put in mind of Epaminondas, the Athenians of Pericles, who always took their own measures and governed their actions by reason, looking upon things of this kind as mere pretexts for cowardice. Thus far, therefore, Demosthenes acquitted himself like a brave man. But in the fight he did nothing honourable, nor was his performance answerable to his speeches. For he fled, deserting his place disgracefully, and throwing away his arms, not ashamed, as Pytheas observed, to belie the inscription written on his shield, in letters of gold, "With good fortune."

In the meantime Philip, in the first moment of victory, was so transported with joy, that he grew extravagant, and going out after he had drunk largely to visit the dead bodies, he chanted the first words of the decree that had been passed on the motion of Demosthenes—

"The motion of Demosthenes, Demosthenes's son,"

dividing it metrically into feet, and marking the beats.

But when he came to himself, and had well considered the danger he was lately under, he could not forbear from shuddering at the wonderful ability and power of an orator who had made him hazard his life and empire on the issue of a few brief hours. The fame of it also reached even to the court of Persia, and the king sent letters to his lieutenants commanding them to supply Demosthenes with money, and to pay every attention to him, as the only man of all the Grecians who was able to give Philip occupation and find employment for his forces near home, in the troubles of Greece. This afterwards came to the knowledge of Alexander, by certain letters of Demosthenes which he found at Sardis, and by other papers of the Persian officers, stating the large sums which had been given him.

At this time, however, upon the ill-success which now happened to the Grecians, those of the contrary faction in the commonwealth fell foul upon Demosthenes and took the opportunity to frame several informations and indictments against him. But the people not only acquitted him of these accusations, but continued towards him their former respect, and still invited him, as a man that meant well, to take a part in public affairs. Insomuch that when the bones of those who had been slain at Chaeronea were brought home to be solemnly interred, Demosthenes was the man they chose to make the funeral oration. They did not show, under the misfortunes which befell them, a base or ignoble mind, as Theopompus writes in his exaggerated style, but on the contrary, by the honour and respect paid to their counsellor, they made it appear that they were noway dissatisfied with the counsels he had given them.

The speech, therefore, was spoken by Demosthenes. But the subsequent decrees he would not allow to be passed in his own name, but made use of those of his friends, one after another, looking upon his own as unfortunate and inauspicious; till at length he took courage again after the death of Philip, who did not long outlive his victory at Chaeronea. And this, it seems, was that which was foretold in the last verse of the oracle—

"Conquered shall weep, and conqueror perish there."

Demosthenes had secret intelligence of the death of Philip, and laying hold of this opportunity to prepossess the people with courage and better hopes for the future, he came into the assembly with a cheerful countenance, pretending to have had a dream that presaged some great good fortune for Athens; and, not long after, arrived the messengers who brought the news of Philip's death. No sooner had the people received it, but immediately they offered sacrifice to the gods, and decreed that Pausanias should be presented with a crown. Demosthenes appeared publicly in a rich dress, with a chaplet on his head, though it were but the seventh day since the death of his daughter, as is said by Aeschines, who upbraids him upon this account, and rails at him as one void of natural affection towards his children. Whereas, indeed, he rather betrays himself to be of a poor, low spirit, and effeminate mind, if he really means to make wailings and lamentation the only signs of a gentle and affectionate nature, and to condemn those who bear such accidents with more temper and less passion. For my own part, I cannot say that the behaviour of the Athenians on this occasion was wise or honourable, to crown themselves with garlands and to sacrifice to the gods for the death of a prince who, in the midst of his success and victories, when they were a conquered people, had used them with so much clemency and humanity. For besides provoking fortune, it was a base thing, and unworthy in itself, to make him a citizen of Athens, and pay him honours while he lived, and yet as soon as he fell by another's hand, to set no bounds to their jollity, to insult over him dead, and to sing triumphant songs of victory, as if by their own valour they had vanquished him. I must at the same time commend the behaviour of Demosthenes, who, leaving tears and lamentations and domestic sorrows to the women, made it his business to attend to the interests of the commonwealth. And I think it the duty of him who would be accounted to have a soul truly valiant, and fit for government, that, standing always firm to the common good, and letting private griefs and troubles find their compensation in public blessings, he should maintain the dignity of his character and station, much more than actors who represent the persons of kings and tyrants, who, we see, when they either laugh or weep on the stage, follow, not their own private inclinations, but the course consistent with the subject and with their position. And if, moreover, when our neighbour is in misfortune, it is not our duty to forbear offering any consolation, but rather to say whatever may tend to cheer him, and to invite his attention to any agreeable objects, just as we tell people who are troubled with sore eyes to withdraw their sight from bright and offensive colours to green, and those of a softer mixture, from whence can a man seek, in his own case, better arguments of consolation for afflictions in his family, than from the prosperity of his country, by making public and domestic chances count, so to say, together, and the better fortune of the state obscure and conceal the less happy circumstances of the individual. I have been induced to say so much, because I have known many readers melted by Aeschines's language into a soft and unmanly tenderness.

But now to turn to my narrative. The cities of Greece were inspirited once more by the efforts of Demosthenes to form a league together. The Thebans, whom he had provided with arms, set upon their garrison, and slew many of them; the Athenians made preparations to join their forces with them; Demosthenes ruled supreme in the popular assembly, and wrote letters to the Persian officers who commanded under the king in Asia, inciting them to make war upon the Macedonian, calling him child and simpleton. But as soon as Alexander had settled matters in his own country, and came in person with his army into Boeotia, down fell the courage of the Athenians, and Demosthenes was hushed; the Thebans, deserted by them, fought by themselves, and lost their city. After which, the people of Athens, all in distress and great perplexity, resolved to send ambassadors to Alexander, and amongst others, made choice of Demosthenes for one: but his heart failing him for fear of the king's anger, he returned back from Cithaeron, and left the embassy. In the meantime, Alexander sent to Athens, requiring ten of their orators to be delivered up to him, as Idomeneus and Duris have reported, but as the most and best historians say, he demanded these eight only,—Demosthenes, Polyeuctus, Ephialtes, Lycurgus, Moerocles, Demon, Callisthenes, and Charidemus. It was upon this occasion that Demosthenes related to them the fable in which the sheep are said to deliver up their dogs to the wolves; himself and those who with him contended for the people's safety being, in his comparison, the dogs that defended the flock, and Alexander "the Macedonian arch-wolf." He further told them, "As we see corn-masters sell their whole stock by a few grains of wheat which they carry about with them in a dish, as a sample of the rest, so you by delivering up us, who are but a few, do at the same time unawares surrender up yourselves all together with us;" so we find it related in the history of Aristobulus, the Cassandrian. The Athenians were deliberating, and at a loss what to do, when Demades, having agreed with the persons whom Alexander had demanded, for five talents, undertook to go ambassador, and to intercede with the king for them; and, whether it was that he relied on his friendship and kindness, or that he hoped to find him satiated, as a lion glutted with slaughter, he certainly went, and prevailed with him both to pardon the men, and to be reconciled to the city.

So he and his friends, when Alexander went away, were great men, and Demosthenes was quite put aside. Yet when Agis, the Spartan, made his insurrection, he also for a short time attempted a movement in his favour; but he

soon shrunk back again, as the Athenians would not take
any part in it, and, Agis being slain, the Lacedaemonians
were vanquished. During this time it was that the indictment against Ctesiphon, concerning the crown, was brought
to trial. The action was commenced a little before the battle in Chaeronea, when Chaerondas was archon, but it was
not proceeded with till about ten years after, Aristophon
being then archon. Never was any public cause more celebrated than this, alike for the fame of the orators, and for
the generous courage of the judges, who, though at that
time the accusers of Demosthenes were in the height of
power, and supported by all the favour of the Macedonians,
yet would not give judgment against him, but acquitted him
so honourably, that Aeschines did not obtain the fifth part
of their suffrages on his side, so that, immediately after, he
left the city, and spent the rest of his life in teaching rhetoric about the island of Rhodes, and upon the continent in
Ionia.

It was not long after that Harpalus fled from Alexander,
and came to Athens out of Asia; knowing himself guilty of
many misdeeds into which his love of luxury had led him,
and fearing the king, who was now grown terrible even to
his best friends. Yet this man had no sooner addressed himself to the people, and delivered up his goods, his ships,
and himself to their disposal, but the other orators of the
town had their eyes quickly fixed upon his money, and
came in to his assistance, persuading the Athenians to receive and protect their suppliant. Demosthenes at first gave
advice to chase him out of the country, and to beware lest
they involved their city in a war upon an unnecessary and
unjust occasion. But some few days after, as they were
taking an account of the treasure, Harpalus, perceiving how
much he was pleased with a cup of Persian manufacture,
and how curiously he surveyed the sculpture and fashion
of it, desired him to poise it in his hand, and consider the
weight of the gold. Demosthenes, being amazed to feel how
heavy it was, asked him what weight it *came to*. "To you,"
said Harpalus, smiling, "it shall *come with* twenty talents."
And presently after, when night drew on, he sent him the

cup with so many talents. Harpalus, it seems, was a person of singular skill to discern a man's covetousness by the air of his countenance, and the look and movements of his eyes. For Demosthenes could not resist the temptation, but admitting the present, like an armed garrison, into the citadel of his house, he surrendered himself up to the interest of Harpalus. The next day, he came into the assembly with his neck swathed about with wool and rollers, and when they called on him to rise up and speak, he made signs as if he had lost his voice. But the wits, turning the matter to ridicule, said that certainly the orator had been seized that night with no other than a silver quinsy. And soon after, the people, becoming aware of the bribery, grew angry, and would not suffer him to speak, or make any apology for himself, but ran him down with noise; and one man stood up, and cried out, "What, ye men of Athens, will you not hear the cup-bearer?" So at length they banished Harpalus out of the city; and fearing lest they should be called to account for the treasure which the orators had purloined, they made a strict inquiry, going from house to house; only Callicles, the son of Arrhenidas, who was newly married, they would not suffer to be searched, out of respects, as Theopompus writes, to the bride, who was within.

Demosthenes resisted the inquisition, and proposed a decree to refer the business to the court of Areopagus, and to punish those whom that court should find guilty. But being himself one of the first whom the court condemned, when he came to the bar, he was fined fifty talents, and committed to prison; where, out of shame of the crime for which he was condemned, and through the weakness of his body, growing incapable of supporting the confinement, he made his escape, by the carelessness of some and by the contrivance of others of the citizens. We are told, at least, that he had not fled far from the city when, finding that he was pursued by some of those who had been his adversaries, he endeavoured to hide himself. But when they called him by his name, and coming up nearer to him, desired he would accept from them some money which they had brought from home as a provision for his journey, and to that purpose only had followed him, when they entreated him to take courage, and to bear up against his misfortune, he burst out into much greater lamentation, saying, "But how is it possible to support myself under so heavy an affliction, since I leave a city in which I have such enemies, as in any other it is not easy to find friends." He did not show much fortitude in his banishment, spending his time for the most part in Aegina and Troezen, and, with tears in his eyes, looking towards the country of Attica. And there remain upon record some sayings of his, little resembling those sentiments of generosity and bravery which he used to express when he had the management of the commonwealth. For, as he was departing out of the city, it is reported, he lifted up his hands towards the Acropolis, and said, "O Lady Minerva, how is it that thou takest delight in three such fierce untractable beasts, the owl, the snake, and the people?" The young men that came to visit and converse with him, he deterred from meddling with state affairs, telling them, that if at first two ways had been proposed to him, the one leading to the speaker's stand and the assembly, the other going direct to destruction, and he could have foreseen the many evils which attend those who deal in public business, such as fears, envies, calumnies, and contentions, he would certainly have taken that which led straight on to his death.

But now happened the death of Alexander, while Demosthenes was in this banishment which we have been speaking of. And the Grecians were once again up in arms, encouraged by the brave attempts of Leosthenes, who was then drawing a circumvallation about Antipater, whom he held close besieged in Lamia. Pytheas, therefore, the orator, and Callimedon, called the Crab, fled from Athens, and taking sides with Antipater, went about with his friends and ambassadors to keep the Grecians from revolting and taking part with the Athenians. But, on the other side, Demosthenes, associating himself with the ambassadors that came from Athens, used his utmost endeavours and gave them his best assistance in persuading the cities to fall unanimously upon the Macedonians, and to drive them out of

Greece. Phylarchus says that in Arcadia there happened a
rencounter between Pytheas and Demosthenes, which came
at last to downright railing, while the one pleaded for the
Macedonians, and the other for the Grecians. Pytheas said,
that as we always suppose there is some disease in the family to which they bring asses' milk, so wherever there
comes an embassy from Athens that city must needs be in-
disposed. And Demosthenes answered him, retorting the
comparison: "Asses' milk is brought to restore health and
the Athenians come for the safety and recovery of the
sick." With this conduct the people of Athens were so well
pleased that they decreed the recall of Demosthenes from
banishment. The decree was brought in by Demon the
Paeanian, cousin to Demosthenes. So they sent him a ship
to Aegina, and he landed at the port of Piraeus, where he
was met and joyfully received by all the citizens, not so
much as an archon or a priest staying behind. And Demetrius, the Magnesian, says that he lifted up his hands
towards heaven, and blessed this day of his happy return,
as far more honourable than that of Alcibiades; since he
was recalled by his countrymen, not through any force or
constraint put upon them, but by their own good-will and
free inclinations. There remained only his pecuniary fine,
which, according to law, could not be remitted by the
people. But they found out a way to elude the law. It was a
custom with them to allow a certain quantity of silver to
those who were to furnish and adorn the altar for the sacrifice of Jupiter Soter. This office, for that turn, they bestowed on Demosthenes, and for the performance of it ordered him fifty talents, the very sum in which he was condemned.

Yet it was no long time that he enjoyed his country after
his return, the attempts of the Greeks being soon all utterly
defeated. For the battle of Cranon happened in Metagit-
nion, in Boëdromion the garrison entered into Munychia,
and in the Pyanepsion following died Demosthenes after
this manner.

Upon the report that Antipater and Craterus were coming to Athens, Demosthenes with his party took their op-

portunity to escape privily out of the city; but sentence of
death was, upon the motion of Demades, passed upon
them by the people. They dispersed themselves, flying some
to one place, some to another; and Antipater sent about his
soldiers into all quarters to apprehend them. Archias was
their captain, and was thence called the exile-hunter. He
was a Thurian born, and is reported to have been an actor
of tragedies, and they say that Polus, of Aegina, the best
actor of his time, was his scholar; but Hermippus reckons
Archias among the disciples of Lacritus, the orator, and
Demetrius says he spent some time with Anaximenes. This
Archias finding Hyperides the orator, Aritonicus of Marathon, and Himeraeus, the brother of Demetrius the Phalerian, in Aegina, took them by force out of the temple
of Aecus, whither they were fled for safety, and sent them
to Antipater, then at Cleonae, where they were all put to
death; and Hyperides, they say, had his tongue cut out.

Demosthenes, he heard, had taken sanctuary at the temple of Neptune in Calauria and, crossing over thither in
some light vessels, as soon as he had landed himself, and
the Thracian spearmen that came with him, he endeavoured
to persuade Demosthenes to accompany him to Antipater,
as if he should meet with no hard usage from him. But
Demosthenes, in his sleep the night before, had a strange
dream. It seemed to him that he was acting a tragedy, and
contended with Archias for the victory; and though he acquitted himself well, and gave good satisfaction to the spectators, yet for want of better furniture and provision for
the stage, he lost the day. And so, while Archias was dis-
coursing to him with many expressions of kindness, he sat
still in the same posture, and looking up steadfastly upon
him, "O Archias," said he, "I am as little affected by your
promises now as I used formerly to be by your acting."
Archias at this beginning to grow angry and to threaten
him, "Now," said Demosthenes, "you speak like the genu-
ine Macedonian oracle; before you were but acting a part.
Therefore forbear only a little, while I write a word or two
home to my family." Having thus spoken, he withdrew into
the temple and taking a scroll as if he meant to write, he

put the reed into his mouth, and biting it as he was wont
to do when he was thoughtful or writing, he held it there
some time. Then he bowed down his head and covered it.
The soldiers that stood at the door, supposing all this to
proceed from want of courage and fear of death, in derision called him effeminate, and faint-hearted, and coward. And Archias drawing near, desired him to rise up,
and repeating the same kind of thing he had spoken before,
he once more promised to make his peace with Antipater.
But Demosthenes, perceiving that now the poison had
pierced, and seized his vitals, uncovered his head, and fixing his eyes upon Archias, "Now," said he, "as soon as you
please, you may commence the part of Creon in the tragedy, and cast out this body of mine unburied. But, O
gracious Neptune, I, for my part while I am yet alive will
rise up and depart out of this sacred place; though Antipater and the Macedonians have not left so much as thy
temple unpolluted." After he had thus spoken and desired
to be held up, because already he began to tremble and
stagger, as he was going forward, and passing by the altar,
he fell down, and with a groan gave up the ghost.

Ariston says that he took the poison out of a reed, as we
have shown before. But Pappus, a certain historian whose
history was recovered by Hermippus, says, that as he fell
near the altar, there was found in his scroll this beginning
only of a letter, and nothing more, "Demosthenes to Antipater." And that when his sudden death was much wondered at, the Thracians who guarded the doors reported
that he took the poison into his hand out of a rag, and put
it in his mouth, and that they imagined it had been gold
which he swallowed, but the maid that served him, being
examined by the followers of Archias, affirmed that he had
worn it in a bracelet for a long time, as an amulet. And
Eratosthenes also says that he kept the poison in a hollow
ring, and that that ring was the bracelet which he wore
about his arm. There are various other statements made by
the many authors who had related the story, but there is
no need to enter into their discrepancies; yet I must not
omit what is said by Demochares the relation of Demos-

thenes, who is of opinion it was not by the help of poison that he met with so sudden and so easy a death, but that by the singular favour and providence of the gods he was thus rescued from the cruelty of the Macedonians. He died on the sixteenth of Pyanepsion, the most sad and solemn day of the Thesmophoria, which the women observe by fasting in the temple of the goddess.

Soon after his death, the people of Athens bestowed on him such honours as he had deserved. They erected his statue of brass; they decreed that the eldest of his family should be maintained in the Prytaneum; and on the base of his statue was engraven the famous inscription—

"Had you for Greece been strong, as wise you were,
The Macedonian had not conquered her."

For it is simply ridiculous to say, as some have related, that Demosthenes made these verses himself in Calauria, as he was about to take the poison.

A little before he went to Athens, the following incident was said to have happened. A soldier, being summoned to appear before his superior officer, and answer to an accusation brought against him, put that little gold which he had into the hands of Demosthenes's statue. The fingers of this statue were folded one within another, and near it grew a small plane-tree, from which many leaves, either accidentally blown thither by the wind, or placed so on purpose by the man himself, falling together and lying round about the gold, concealed it for a long time. In the end, the soldier returned and found his treasure entire, and the fame of this incident was spread abroad. And many ingenious persons of the city competed with each other, on this occasion, to vindicate the integrity of Demosthenes in several epigrams which they made on the subject.

As for Demades, he did not long enjoy the new honours he now came in for, divine vengeance for the death of Demosthenes pursuing him into Macedonia, where he was justly put to death by those whom he had basely flattered. They were weary of him before, but at this time the guilt he lay under was manifest and undeniable. For some of his letters were intercepted, in which he had encouraged Perdiccas to fall upon Macedonia, and to save the Grecians, who, he said, hung only by an old rotten thread, meaning Antipater. Of this he was accused by Dinarchus, the Corinthian, and Cassander was so enraged, that he first slew his son in his bosom, and then gave orders to execute him; who might now at last, by his own extreme misfortunes, learn the lesson that traitors who made sale of their country sell themselves first; a truth which Demosthenes had often foretold him, and he would never believe. Thus, Sosius, you have the life of Demosthenes from such accounts as we have either read or heard concerning him.

INDEX OF NAMES

THE LAUREL CLASSICAL DRAMA SERIES

Edited, with introductions, by Robert W. Corrigan